AF479277

Muslims and Citizens

Muslims and Citizens

Islam, Politics, and the French Revolution

Ian Coller

Yale

UNIVERSITY PRESS

NEW HAVEN AND LONDON

Published with assistance from the Annie Burr Lewis Fund.

Yale University Press books may be purchased in quantity for educational, business, or promotional use. For information, please e-mail sales.press@yale.edu (U.S. office) or sales@yaleup.co.uk (U.K. office).

Set in Fournier MT type by IDS Infotech, Ltd.
Printed in the United States of America.

Library of Congress Control Number: 2019939489
ISBN 978-0-300-24336-9 (hardcover : alk. paper)

A catalogue record for this book is available from the British Library.

This paper meets the requirements of ANSI/NISO Z39.48-1992 (Permanence of Paper).

10 9 8 7 6 5 4 3 2 1

Contents

Preface

In 2011, a wave of revolutions began in Tunisia and grew in force until it toppled dictatorships in Tunis, Cairo, and Tripoli; shook regimes in Bahrain, Yemen, Morocco, and Iran; and sent shock waves across Africa, Asia, Europe, and the Americas. Some commentators rushed to dub this the "Arab 1789"—as though it had taken the Arab world more than two centuries to catch up with the West. When I visited Tunis in May 2011, it was clear that this was not a delayed sequel but a seizing of historical agency in its own right—a revolution that set its own precedent, and was at the same time part of a larger seismic wave. Instead of seeing Tunisia through the lens of 1789, I saw—and felt—the experience of the French Revolution anew through the sense of universal possibility that knew no frontier of category or nation. I wanted to ask a different question about 1789, seeing it not as a matrix for thinking about later revolutions but rather as a simultaneous historical experience. It is a self-evident proposition that Muslims were part of the world of the French Revolution. Yet that simultaneity has proven almost impossible for many historians to imagine: the "Muslim world," they insist, existed in a different temporality altogether.

Three decades ago, some historians came to the conclusion that the French Revolution was over—*terminé*—with the collapse of communism and the Soviet Union, which curiously coincided with the celebration of the bicentenary of 1789. In reality all that was "over" was an interpretation that had tied itself to this particular world-historical outcome. The waning of the classical paradigm liberated studies of the French Revolution to explore a multiplicity of other dimensions of this rich, varied, and fascinating moment. The shift in interpretation has not reduced the significance of 1789: on the contrary, it has opened up a wider field for understanding the ways in which the French Revolution shaped our shared modern world. This book sets out to contribute to a rethinking of the Revolution for the modern age, with a belief that its principles still have much to offer: it is not a scientific anatomy, but a living reflection.

In writing this book I was fortunate to receive a generous grant from the Australian Research Council to complete much of the research; the library staff at the University of California, Irvine, and La Trobe University provided me with invaluable support. The earliest period in the gestation of the book was spent at the European University Institute in Florence, where I benefited from stimulating conversations in a glorious setting, and my ideas were further extended in a visiting appointment at the University of Paris 8 in 2012. I am deeply grateful to my colleagues at La Trobe University for their support and collegiality. Since arriving at UCI, I have been fortunate to gain a wonderful range of friends and colleagues in French, European, and world history who have pushed me to think further and refine my arguments. Initial sketches of some of the arguments made here were published in edited collections, and I would like to thank Lynn Hunt, Suzanne Desan, William Nelson, Alan Forrest, Matthias Middell, Patricia Lorcin, Todd Shepard, Glenda Sluga, Tim Rowse, John Harvey, Konstantina Zanou, and Maurizio Isabella for all they have offered me in critical feedback and enrichment. As always, I owe a huge debt to Peter McPhee, an extraordinarily generous mentor and model, and I have benefited immensely from the critical advice of Tim Tackett, a towering authority on the French Revolution. I was fortunate to benefit from the brilliance of the late Chris Bayly, a sorely missed mentor and friend. I owe thanks and love to many friends and family: my brothers, Ross and Matt; my sister, Jen, and her children, Leo and Lara; and my father, Bruce, a constant support. I dedicate this book to the memory of my mother, Mair, an endless inspiration and an incalculable loss.

Introduction

When the French arrived on the shores of Egypt in July 1798, they carried with them a brochure printed in Arabic headed by a laurel-wreathed vignette of Marianne carrying the familiar symbols of a pike topped by a liberty cap, and the fasces of the French Republic bound around an axe. Beneath this official stamp ran a long string of Arabic text: "In the name of Allah, the most gracious, the most merciful, there is no God but God, he has no son, and no associate in his kingdom." This statement of faith—a compilation of the *basmala*, the *shahada*, and the renunciation of *shirk*, idolatry—was made in the name of the republic. The document went further, declaring, "Tell your people that the French are also sincere Muslims" (qūlū li-ummatikum ʿan al-farānsawiyya hum aydhan muslimīn khālisīn).

What led these revolutionary Frenchmen to assert that they were Muslims? In his final years Napoléon Bonaparte explained it as a ruse to win local support. Could Bonaparte or any other Frenchman really have imagined that Egyptian Muslims would believe it? My answer is yes. Over the course of the preceding decade, the French had come in some sense to believe it themselves, or at least to imagine it was a plausible assertion. For reasons that emerged from 1789 and the events that followed, the revolutionaries of the 1790s came to conceive that Muslims would indeed welcome their arrival. Egypt, they believed, could serve as the bridge for the onward march of the French Revolution into Africa and Asia. The proclamation proudly cited the Revolution's destructive assault on the Roman Catholic Church as proof that the French had abandoned doctrines incompatible with Islam. Some Frenchmen did indeed convert—notably General Jacques-Abdullah

Menou—although the bulk remained attached to the strange hybrids of atheism, deism, and Catholic ritual that emerged after the collapse of the church in France. When Egyptian Muslims rose up against the occupation in 1799, the French rapidly identified Islam with the detested forces of refractory Catholicism. They defiled copies of the Koran and entered the great mosque of Al-Azhar on horseback. This was only the last stage in the incorporation of Islam into the political culture of the Revolution.

This book tells the story of how the vision of an essential compatibility with Islam emerged in the revolutionary imagination and came to be so dominant that 50,000 French troops were ultimately lured across the Mediterranean by its global promise. This idea was not cut from whole cloth in 1798. Its threads stretched back to 1789 and even earlier, and were intimately woven into the revolutionary transformation from the outset. Nor was it simply the result of orientalist imaginings about Muslims in distant lands. Revolutionary visions of Islam arose from a very concrete set of circumstances that drew Muslims—both real and imagined—into the whirlwind of politicization. The rapid transformations of the revolutionary age set people in motion along hitherto unimaginable paths: among them were Muslims who came into direct contact with transforming conceptions of religion, rights, and citizenship and left their own marks on the French Revolution. These trajectories are important in tracing the larger sweep of this book. They can help set aside the misconception that we are dealing here merely with a Western imaginary, with an "orientalism" of the French Revolution. As it is hardly possible to consider Muslims' responses to the Revolution through their own recorded words, which only rarely addressed revolutionary events or ideas directly, we must instead consider their itineraries as in themselves indices of response and participation.

In 1789, as the first events of the French Revolution unfolded, an Ottoman Muslim named Ishak Bey was living near Versailles, on a mission entrusted to him by the Ottoman heir apparent, Shahzade Selim. Ishak moved in the circles of the liberal aristocracy, with intimate connections to the extended family of the Marquis de Lafayette. His mission was intended to avert a potential disaster for the Ottoman Empire, which had tumbled precipitately into war with Russia and Austria: Louis XVI, chary of any further international involvement after the American imbroglio, turned a deaf ear to Ottoman requests. Like the previous year's visit of Muslim ambassadors requesting support for Tipu Sultan's resistance to British expansion in India, Ishak's presence was a lightning rod intensifying public consciousness of the monarchy's failure to accomplish its primary task of maintaining French prestige in the global order. These Muslims drew much attention in the intensely politicized climate of the pre-Revolution and were liberally ventriloquized in plays and pamphlets. But Ishak's case was different. He was not just an envoy but a foreign patriot attracted by the great transformations taking place in France; and like many others he found himself deeply troubled by the events of October, which set in train the collapse of the monarchy. Leaving France, he returned to Istanbul, where he helped put in place Selim's *nizam-i-jedid* reforms of the Ottoman system. In one of those ironies of which the revolutionary era is full, in 1801 he would be the Ottoman signatory of the treaty of French withdrawal from Egypt.

In the middle of 1794, at the height of the period that has become known as the Terror, an Indian Muslim arrived in Paris. Ahmed Khan, a Gujarati from the city of Bharuch, had spent more than a year in France, after his brother fell dangerously ill in Lyon. The brothers lived through the Jacobin ascendancy, the reaction and overthrow of the municipal government, and the ultimate crushing of the federalist insurgency by the revolutionary army. At a moment in which resentment and revenge cut so deep, these two Muslims were not treated with suspicion: they were afforded all the hospitality that a city shocked by war could provide, even halal meat when it could be obtained. After his brother at last succumbed to his illness, Ahmed traveled to Paris, where his case was presented to the Committee of Public Safety. Maximilien Robespierre was among those who signed a decree offering Ahmed assistance and requesting he extend his stay in France; there are signs that this influence was mutual. On his own volition, it seems, Ahmed undertook the first Persian translation of the Declaration of the Rights of Man and Citizen of 1793—a document that would soon become invalid with the coup of Thermidor.

Five years later, reacting to the unprovoked French aggression in Egypt, the Ottoman sultan declared a jihad against the French Republic. Early in 1799, the Directory issued orders for the surveillance of Muslims and the arrest of North Africans. The commissioner of Seine-et-Marne replied to inform the minister of police that he had located a Muslim living in one of the cantons of his department: in this case, the commissioner added, "he has made the declaration necessary to enjoy the rights of a French citizen, after the law prescribed by the constitution."[1] This man, a former prisoner of war named Fertali, had adopted a French forename and was living peaceably without fanfare in a rural part of Brie. His presence might never have come to light without the events happening far away on the other side of the Mediterranean. This otherwise unremarkable character is thus by chance the first attested Muslim citizen of the French Republic, a product of the great shifts of the revolutionary age.

Over the past half century, the French Revolution's cast of characters has been slowly changing. No longer a procession of white, middle-class Frenchmen, a handful of liberal aristocrats, and a rambunctious mass of peasants and proletarians, the Revolution that comes into view is a more diverse phenomenon. Women, Jews, enslaved and free people of color, foreigners, and other once-forgotten groups have moved from the footnotes into the foreground. No longer just window dressing to the "real" history of the Revolution, they now share the spotlight as actors, shapers, and interlocutors of a revolutionary transformation whose contours thereby emerge differently. In the process, we have come to see the French Revolution as a more plural experience, recognizing the significance of debates and struggles that once seemed inessential. The France of revolutionary historiography has exploded outward from the narrow corridors of the National Assembly to consider provincial towns and villages, market stalls and churches, enclaves and colonies, Atlantic and European spaces. The trans-Mediterranean dimensions of the Revolution, by contrast, have remained largely unexplored, on the presumption that Muslims were ignorant of, uninterested in, or incompatible with the revolutionary transformation by virtue of their religion.

While the "Muslim question" has rarely been posed in the many thousands of works published about the Revolution, during the course of the Revolution itself it was posed frequently by revolutionaries and counterrevolutionaries alike, in the context of debates about liberty, equality, citizenship, rights, religion, diplomacy, subsistence, and above all fraternity. These debates may seem fanciful or tangential today, if we view the Revolution as primarily an internal, French phenomenon, or even one defined by the limits of Europe or the Atlantic. That is not how revolutionaries viewed it. For them, the Revolution was a watershed in human history, a transformation with a universal vocation. This was not a simple proposition: revolutionaries disagreed, sometimes violently, on the meanings and consequences of universality, and this applied equally to thinking about Muslims and the nature of their potential participation. Some believed that strategic alliances with Muslim rulers were the best hope for stabilizing the Revolution, even as they anathematized the "kings and tyrants" of Europe. Others hoped to draw Muslims into a broader front of revolution that would sweep away their "despots" and give rise to sympathetic sister regimes or even, more radically, a single, universal republic. They disagreed, too, on the role and meaning of Islam as a religious system: Was it a more "rational" deistic belief compatible with republican ideals, an erroneous superstition to be wiped away by the triumph of reason, or a fanatical faith more hostile to revolutionary ideas than Christianity?

A simple quantitative analysis of references to Muslims will not give us a credible picture of the meanings of these discussions. In fact, on most counts, the middle years of the Revolution saw a drop in published references to Muslims, after an early peak in the years 1789–1790.[2] This data is supported by the work of Marie-Louise Dufrenoy, who offered a catalog of orientalist works published from 1700 to 1800. The number in the period from 1791 to 1797 is the lowest in the century, with only one or two orientalist publications each year in contrast to the 14 that appeared in each of 1787 and 1788, and the 19 published in 1789. As Carla Hesse indicates, book publishing as a whole dropped sharply in this period, after a massive increase from 1784 to 1789.[3] This does not mean that Muslims disappeared from the discursive landscape: they can be found consistently in other places. For example, an analysis of 100 pamphlets on the 1790 Civil Constitution of the Clergy shows references to Muslims in more than 25 percent of cases.[4] Similarly, a limited search of the *Archives parlementaires* shows an analogous development, with nine direct references to Muslims in 1789, 18 in 1790, 30 in 1791, 32 in 1792, and 32 in 1793.[5] References in newspapers and pamphlets are more difficult to quantify. I have located hundreds of individual examples across these years. What these figures do suggest is that while the publication of orientalist literature was in decline, references to Muslims in other domains were simultaneously increasing. The significance of these references, I would argue, lies precisely in the absence or muting of the conventional orientalist context. These were no longer simply exotic tropes. They were part of the systematic thinking-through of the consequences of the revolutionary transformation, by radicals and reactionaries alike. From late 1789 onward the "Muslim question" emerged successively in the scapegoating of revolutionary violence, in the struggles over religion and the state, and in the geopolitical question of global expansion.

In contrast, evidence of Muslims themselves and their responses to the Revolution—whether resident or traveling in France, or observing from a distance—remains scattered, fragmentary, and challenging to recover. The archives offer up only a few dozen names. Some, like Ahmed Khan, Ishak Bey, Hassan Ben Karaly, and Muhammad D'Ghies, were present for substantial periods in revolutionary France and participated in the shaping of the Revolution, whether as witnesses, local intermediaries, ideological allies, or carriers of ideas. Behind and around them were other, less visible Muslims: servants, workers, merchants, travelers. Their presence is brought to light only here and there through some mundane accident: a drunken altercation—like the one in which a cook accused a Muslim of being "a spy of Lafayette" in 1792— an imprudent love affair, a burglary. In the port city of Marseille, we can find traces of political action on behalf of a small community of "Turks and Algerians" petitioning for their right to make use of a terrain allocated for their use as a cemetery, and, in the early months of the Revolution, stepping in to help negotiate contentious issues between France and Algiers. The presence of even small numbers of Muslims in Marseille, and in other cities like Toulon and Paris, reveals emergent changes in how Muslims themselves considered European societies, and France in particular. Traditional religious requirements made extended residence even in a "tolerant" non-Muslim land difficult, and its permissibility was debated.[6] As this "invisible integration" became more visible, the new frameworks of toleration were shadowed by religious violence.[7] Muslims outside of France also played roles in interpreting and responding to the Revolution, and on occasion interfering directly in its politics, in ways that had long-term consequences for the relationship between France and the Muslim world.

The absence of any significant population of Muslims in France makes it all the more remarkable that they should have been invoked so often throughout the Revolution. The same can in some sense be said for Jews, the largest non-Christian minority in France but still less than half of 1 percent of the overall population. Jews, as Ronald Schechter has demonstrated, were a veritable obsession for eighteenth-century social reformers—and not always in a positive sense.[8] Borrowing the formula of Claude Lévi-Strauss, Schechter has argued that Jews were "good to think with": they opened up a variety of issues, from the universality of human nature to the limits of national inclusivity.[9] Jews did not remain passive in this "thinking": they solicited the intervention of philosophers, entered essay competitions, petitioned the authorities.[10] Where Schechter saw the Enlightenment and Revolution as ultimately imposing a Faustian bargain on Jews—the sacrifice of their particularity in exchange for inclusion in the nation—Maurice Samuels has argued that 1789 broke with this conception, recognizing a "right to difference" that insisted Jews must be part of the nation regardless of their particularity.[11] But the consequences of that "difference" were left unresolved by the Revolution, as Jacques Revel has argued.[12] Schechter and Samuels note that Muslims, too, were "rich in symbolic meaning," but they miss the larger ways in which discourses about Jews and Muslims were entangled from an early point.[13] If, like Jews, Muslims were "good to think with"—particularly about religious tolerance and universalism—that thinking was undertaken in a dynamic and often turbulent relationship with the largest and most powerful cultural arena on Europe's borders. Even small misunderstandings that arose between France and Muslim powers could have powerful effects on the subsistence and security of French people, endangering trade and shipping, and threatening the military and diplomatic balance. In revolutionary conditions, as all of Europe united to attack and blockade France, these relations became even more crucial. Debates over the place that Muslims might take as citizens in the new order were not merely rhetorical, although they were often entangled with other, unrelated political issues. It is for this reason that it is crucial to explore the nexus between the uses of Islam and the wider structures of revolutionary politics.

When Muslims did enter the political orbit of revolutionary politics, they were thus in some sense already anticipated, and that anticipation served in important ways to shape the French relationship to Islam over the centuries that followed. Within a decade, revolutionary France ruled (if only briefly) over millions of Muslims in Egypt; from 1830 onward, French empire in the Muslim world never ceased to expand, until by 1939 Algeria, Tunisia, Morocco, Syria, Lebanon, and most of West Africa had come under French control. That France should have become a major Muslim power in the nineteenth century, ruling over tens of millions of Muslims and ultimately dependent on their labor, resources, and military service, was, in both direct and indirect ways, connected to the Revolution and its relationships with the Muslim world. The attempt to shut down the revolutionary promise of the "Muslim citizen," limiting it to just a handful of those millions of subjects, and only through the renunciation of their religious identity, was one of the catastrophic failures that helped fracture the French imperial project. In order to move on from that failure, and those that have followed in the postcolonial era, we could do worse than to return to the very source of ideas about citizenship, rights, and the republic, with a new and more inclusive reading.

This book sets out to investigate the intersection of revolutionary responses to Islam with the lives and trajectories of Muslims themselves, in order to reconstitute the space of possibility for the Muslim citizen that was thereby created, along with the contradictions and paradoxes by which, from the first, it was characterized. It is not primarily a book about the Muslim world or Islam in the revolutionary age, a subject that deserves a larger and more comprehensive rethinking than I can undertake here.[14] It is very much a book about the French Revolution, one that seeks to dismantle the self-evidence of the "modern," "secular," and "French" dress in which this crucial world-historical moment has been clothed. It does not do so in order to negate these important and useful categories, but instead to open them up to a reconsideration of their limits and exclusions. In this sense, it responds to Lynn Hunt's call for an account of the French Revolution that would seek out connections between internal and external causes, effects, and processes, in order to situate it more fully in the global context.[15] That is not simply a reaction to a fashionable "global turn" in historiography that some critics have derided, but a shift that has emerged both from within the study of the Revolution itself and from the questions posed by the world in which we live.[16]

In recent decades, scholars of the Revolution have asked penetrating questions about the ways in which discursive structures shaped revolutionary action. Other historians have stressed the reverse: how the unfolding of revolutionary circumstances molded and changed the way revolutionaries thought, felt, and spoke about their world and the events that were transforming it. This book sets out with both of these winds at its back. In uncovering the contours of revolutionary discourse on Islam and Muslims, I am conscious of their internal regularities as well as their rapid transformation in the maelstrom of revolutionary events. I have sought to think dialectically about the relationship between ideas and events, across the often haphazard journeys of individuals who found themselves at a point of historical agency created—sometimes quite unexpectedly—by the revolutionary transformation taking place around them.

The reconstruction of this dialectic is not an easy process. As Michel-Rolph Trouillot has so cogently argued, archives are structured from the outset by constitutive silences. Silences enter the process of historical production in the creation and archiving of the historical sources themselves—first in what counts as worth recording, and what is considered insignificant; then once again in deciding which of these "facts" should be chosen to tell the story. In the historical narratives shaped from those sources, these gaps are reinforced and legitimated by relations of power that reserve historical agency for particular groups. We cannot therefore consider the archive as a complete and unmediated historical reality: we must take into account the processes that served to construct it, and the historical narratives to which it seems "naturally" to give rise. "To put it differently," Trouillot continues, "any historical narrative is a particular bundle of silences, the result of a unique process, and the operation required to deconstruct these silences will vary accordingly."[17]

It is easier to break a silence than to make the silence itself speak. Joan Scott aptly characterized those historians who insisted that their "understanding of the French Revolution is not changed by knowing that women participated in it."[18] Since then, scholarship has shown persuasively that a French Revolution with women is *not* the same revolution as one made by—and studied by—men alone.[19] Women did not meekly accept their exclusion: they formed political clubs, gave patriotic gifts, marched and protested, and even on occasion voted, despite their official status as "passive citizens."[20] Moreover, to think differently about women is also to think more consciously about men. Gender was both a question of actual juridical categories that determined access to political participation and a symbolic terrain that could be mined to great political effect. Lynn Hunt's seminal work showed how the pornographic attack on Marie Antoinette helped to undermine and "desacralize" the monarchy; Antoine de Baecque directed attention to the king's male body, to explore how symbolic crises around royal impotence contributed to the weakening of the monarchy.[21]

It is important, therefore, to consider the overwhelmingly masculine nature of the sources that compose the fragmentary record of Muslims in revolutionary France. Masculinity was not only a site for production of meaning but also a concrete peculiarity of the presence of the small Muslim minority in France. Unlike Jews or people of color, those Muslims who can be identified in early modern France were almost exclusively male.[22] Evidence of Muslim women—attested only in a few questionable cases associated with conversion—would alter fundamentally the understanding of this Muslim presence. Indeed, this masculine predominance continued for almost two centuries as a dimension of Muslim France, until the 1970s, when circular migration came to an end and family migration began. Recent contemporary historians have traced the phantasms to which this masculine sexualized threat gave rise in the period after decolonization.[23] There are reasons to trace this sexualization of Muslim men—and not only Arabs but also Turks and Africans—further back in French history. At the same time, Islam was at moments used, as it is today, as a projection in arguments over the rights of women. In 1793, when the Jacobin leader Amar accused women of being "more enslaved by aristocratic and religious prejudice than men" and "the first cause of the troubles that afflict the Republic," another member protested that "unless, like Muhammad, we make it a general rule that [women] are exclusively destined for our pleasure, . . . you cannot prevent them from assembling to discuss public affairs amongst themselves."[24] This entanglement of women, Islam, and anticlericalism has long haunted French politics: Muslim women would be the last of all categories to gain the vote, in 1958.

These anxieties intersected with troubles over race. The work of Sue Peabody and Pierre Boulle first opened up evidence of the policing of racial boundaries in early modern France, in the metropole as well as in the colonies.[25] This also reveals the contours of a population of color, coming from Africa, the Caribbean, the Indian Ocean colonies, or the subcontinent. Erick Noël has studied the lives of black people in eighteenth-century France, and has recognized among them many "Indians" from Pondicherry, Chandernagore, and other places, who were conflated with emancipated servants from Martinique and Saint-Domingue, and even on occasion deported to the Caribbean.[26] Most of these individuals were nominally Christian, even if names like Rama and Vishnu suggested a different birthright. Some were also of Muslim origin: young Senegalese "Moors" sold as slaves in France, and the famous Zamor, the Bengali servant of the Comtesse du Barry.[27] They were often dressed and named in ways that recalled the Muslim world. However, if they had been at some time Muslim, their removal at an early age deprived them of connection to their religious and cultural origins.[28]

Islam was also present in the colonies: some significant part of the enslaved population had certainly come from Muslim parts of Africa. In some cases Islam could serve to "whiten" the enslaved, when their civilizational attainments of literacy in Arabic and religious practice were recognized.[29] Several rebel leaders in Saint-Domingue, such as François Macandal, a feared Maroon leader in the early part of the century, and the Haitian religious leader Boukman have been associated in various ways with Islam.[30] The so-called Mahomet of Saint-Domingue, Romaine Rivière, a crossdressing (and possibly transgender) free black prophetess, wore a turban and had "some knowledge of Islam" according to a recent study.[31] In

Saint-Domingue in 1793, flags carried by slave rebels were reported to mix tricolor, fleur-de-lis, and Islamic inscriptions.[32]

This book seeks to consider Muslims, not as an "absolute" category, but as one that overlapped, intersected, and interacted with others, and was produced and shaped in new ways by the revolutionary context. It is the revolutionary politicization of this category that is of primary interest to me. This politicization could take place from above, in the ideas, debates, allusions, and performances that emerged from revolutionary discursive production, as well as from below, from Muslims themselves who entered into the spaces created for them by the revolutionary transformation, reshaping those abstract categories through their concrete presence. The evidence of that process is fragmentary and elusive, captured only at rare moments that I have sought to restore and reconnect with one another. The story that thereby emerges is not so much a correction of the historical record as an exploration of its multiplicity and diversity: a demonstration that in selecting certain historical lines of force, in organizing them into constitutive narratives, we necessarily exclude other elements that do not fit into our picture. The past remains an ocean whose depths we can never fully know, full of rich and strange possibilities.

The prologue of this book offers a snapshot of what Islam and Muslims meant for the France of the late ancien régime and observes the shifts that were already emerging as 1789 approached. Recent scholars have shown that geopolitical questions played a crucial and entangled role in the accelerating politicization of these months: chapter 1 examines the presence of Muslim envoys in France as an intentional political act from France's periphery that thrust concerns about France's global position—the very substance of royal authority—to the fore. Those concerns were reflected and refracted in the exploding pamphlet literature, images, and newspapers of the period leading up to the Estates General and in the "crisis of representation" that emerged after the Bastille fell in July 1789. That crisis is traced through the October Days in chapter 2: the march of women on Versailles unleashed a further revolutionary split over the fragmentation of monarchical sovereignty, accompanied by burgeoning anxieties around gender and the patriarchal stability of the ancien régime model. Chapter 3 follows the revolutionary attempt to stabilize these anxieties through a Declaration of Rights that would frame a new conception of the citizen—a category still riven by contradictions over religion, race, and gender. As the exclusions of the ancien régime were addressed, new questions emerged around the plurality of religions and their relation to the state. In June 1790, on the anniversary of the declaration of the National Assembly, the appearance of a deputation of foreigners led by the Prussian baron Jean-Baptiste (later Anacharsis) Cloots set off a remarkable chain of events that led to the abolition of noble titles in France. The visible presence of Muslims in this deputation played a key role in catalyzing the explosion of enthusiasm that followed: so much so that counterrevolutionary voices clamored to insist that these Muslims were impostors dressed in costumes from the opera. Chapter 4 investigates the wave of revolutionary universalism launched by this piece of revolutionary theater, and symbolized by the turban, even as that universalism was riven from within by contradictions over race and religion.

Chapter 5 traces the appearance of Muslims in debates over religious plurality and the clerical oath. As the new constitution at last came into force, revolutionary France was assailed by problems from within and without. The euphoria of success turned into fears of invasion and counterrevolution, and universality was increasingly expressed by the influential group of deputies known as the Girondins as a need to defend France by attacking the enemies of the Revolution. In this context, Muslims did not disappear from revolutionary concerns but were instead invoked repeatedly by counterrevolutionary writers, at first as threatening or ridiculous examples of the consequences of religious liberty, and then—as the religious tide began to turn against them—as precedents for their claims to freedom of religious conscience. In response, revolutionaries affirmed the new pluralism, suggesting that Muslims did indeed possess these rights, insofar as they did not disturb the civic order in the manner of "refractory" priests. With the final collapse of the monarchy and the declaration of the Republic in 1792, France was divided and besieged by hostile neighbors and insurgents from within: chapter 6 traces the growing interconnection with the Ottoman Empire, and in particular the North African powers, who rejected pressures to join the coalition against France and became increasingly critical partners in economic, military, and diplomatic terms. The dey of Algiers demonstrated particular support for the new French Republic, offering financial support that would never be repaid, and which would ultimately serve as a catalyst for the French invasion of Algeria four decades later.

Chapters 7 to 9 trace the period retrospectively labeled "the Terror," and the ways in which the struggle over religion, the internal and external politics of the Revolution, and the trajectories of Muslims themselves can shed a different light on this period. Chapter 7 explores the struggle over "dechristianization" and its ways of reconceiving Islam as a historical precedent for religious revolution, as a more rational deism better aligned with revolutionary principles, or as a fanatical superstition to be eliminated. This was not simply a conflict between religion and secularism, but a struggle over what should replace religion that divided even the radical party of revolutionaries. Yet as the example of Ahmed Khan explored in chapter 8 shows, Muslims themselves were greeted with hospitality by the Revolution. Indeed, despite the hostility of leading Jacobins to the expansion of revolutionary proselytism into allied states like the Ottoman Empire, the appearance of this Indian Muslim could set in train a project to translate the Declaration of the Rights of Man and Citizen into Persian. That project was encouraged by Maximilien Robespierre, even as he rejected the attempts by French subjects in the Muslim world to establish revolutionary societies. As Robespierre sought a cautious policy that would engage the Ottoman Empire in France's favor, his championing of a civic religious policy against the "atheists" became a focus for opposition. In the events of Thermidor that brought down the Committee of Public Safety and the Paris Commune, the script of Voltaire's satirical play was used to paint Robespierre as a new "Mahomet," suggesting that he was both an impostor and a fanatic with the preternatural power to make his followers believe his doctrine. The fall of Robespierre also saw the return of a "Girondin" universalism that sought to spread revolutionary ideas by force.

The use of religion to achieve political power was a theme that fascinated a young Corsican officer, Napoleone di Buonaparte, who became close to a Robespierre family; at the beginning of the Revolution, he explored this question in a short story about a Muslim prophet, drawn from his extensive reading on Islamic history. Chapter 10 explores this ongoing fascination with Islam, arguing that the impulsion that eventually took him to Egypt was formed in the context of his early experience of Corsican nationalism, radical disappointment, and revolutionary commitment to the new France that emerged after 1789. The belief that this invasion would be welcomed by Muslims—indeed, that they would somehow greet the French as fellow believers—was the product of a revolutionary politicization of Islam that was further overheated under the Directory. The catastrophic decision to invade Egypt effectively brought the Revolution to an end: Buonaparte brought back the taste for arbitrary rule he had established in Egypt to his rule over France and much of Europe.

The ultimate betrayal of Muslim support for the Revolution helped turn the tide against the new "French" ideas of liberty and equality in the

Muslim world; French colonial aggression would only further entrench the conception that such ideas were mere masks for European cupidity. Yet their traces never quite disappeared. On 10 Floréal Year 3 (29 April 1795) a letter written by Muhammad D'Ghies, a North African Muslim, was read aloud in the National Convention. D'Ghies swore a solemn oath to the ideals of the Revolution, in the name of the Prophet. "I love the justice that you love," he declared passionately. "I worship the principles of humanity that you consistently profess. Your good deeds have elevated my soul, and that alone makes us brothers in our hearts." He promised to accompany his words with deeds, helping to secure southern France against the threat of famine by dispatching shiploads of grain across the Mediterranean.[33] His son Hassuna D'Ghies would travel to Paris and London, where he worked with Jeremy Bentham on a constitutional plan for Tripoli.[34] In the twentieth century, the echoes of the French Revolution would be heard in the Young Turk Revolution of 1908 and even in the anticolonial struggles of revolutionaries like the Algerian Kateb Yacine, who wrote that he was imprisoned by the French "for having believed too much in the principles of 1789."[35]

The presence of Muslims in the French Revolution was amplified in the context of a symbolic and political shift that rendered old cultural forms obsolete and created a great hunger for new, "regenerated" ideas and symbols. Among the forms that came to fill this gap were shifting conceptions of Islam and the Muslim world. Revolutionaries, in their chiliastic fervor for the creation of a new world of universal humanity, of liberty, equality, and fraternity, were ready to think in new ways about Islam, to establish closer ties with the Muslim world, and to welcome Muslims into revolutionary participation. The rupture with the Muslim world that took place after the invasion of Egypt in 1798 has led most historians to imagine that Muslims rejected the Revolution from the outset, or simply neglected its importance, until it arrived armed to the teeth on their doorstep. But the decade from 1787 to 1797 deserves a re-examination from the viewpoint of 1789 rather than that of 1798.

Prologue

From the end of the fifteenth century until the last quarter of the eighteenth, Islam remained on the fringe of a French consciousness preoccupied by victories and disasters; religious struggles; the privileges of towns, provinces, and orders; the rhythms of the agricultural year; and the difficulties of everyday survival. In this sense, it was not very different from the world inhabited by subjects of the Ottoman Empire. Religious denomination, local allegiances, and the struggle for subsistence dominated the lives of the great mass of Muslims and Europeans alike.[1] Islam was principally understood by the ancien régime as a heresy, a distorted version of Christianity. With the global geopolitical shifts of the later eighteenth century, these matrices of religious understanding were fundamentally changed.

From the mid-sixteenth century onward, France joined a loose alliance with the Ottoman Empire, fostering ongoing contacts in diplomacy, military training, and trade with a Muslim power. Beginning in the 1720s, philosophers began to investigate the life and teachings of the Prophet Muhammad in new ways that undermined older theological understandings. Trade and diplomacy produced travelers' accounts that shaped the ideas of Enlightenment thinkers. Radical philosophical ideas about Islam came together with diplomatic and commercial knowledge of Muslim societies to produce a sea change in conceptions about Muslims and Islam that would become entangled with the revolutionary transformation.

Few of the 28 million people living in ancien régime France would ever meet a Muslim, but Islam circulated and was made meaningful in other ways. Words to denote Muslims were many—Turk, Arab, Saracen, Barbaresque,

Ottoman, Oriental, Mogol, Persian, and Mahometan, as well as Muslim (*musulman*)—and punctuated the landscape of the everyday: the sign of the "Grand Turk" hanging over a Versailles inn; fears of Barbary pirates and the slave trade across the Mediterranean that surfaced in novels and popular culture; the "Great Mogol" boutique of Rose Bertin, Marie Antoinette's favorite dressmaker; Montesquieu's *Persian Letters* and Galland's *Arabian Nights*; the *Oriental Encyclopedia* of d'Herbelot; and the anonymous *Abdeker; or, the Art of Preserving Beauty*, offering cosmetic advice from a Yemeni doctor.

Connections could be more intimate. Places and families across France carried names like Le Turc and Sarrazin, traces of medieval Muslim presence in Languedoc and Provence, or the Ottoman fleet that wintered in Toulon in 1543.[2] Members of many French families—among them the Rousseau, Chénier, and Laclos families—spent extended periods living in Muslim cities for trade or diplomacy. Some—like Louis XVI's foreign minister, the Count de Vergennes, former ambassador to Istanbul, and Louis de Chénier, father of revolutionaries André and Marie-Joseph Chénier—brought Ottoman Christian wives back to France. Others, like the famous Count de Bonneval, moved to Istanbul and converted to Islam. At the other end of the social ladder, convicts and Protestants sentenced to serve in the galleys of Marseille and Toulon found themselves laboring alongside "Turks"—Muslims purchased from slave traders in Malta or Italy. Muslims were, in the words of a recent historian, Europe's "familiar strangers."[3]

At the same time, Islam remained a looming presence on France's doorstep. Marshall Hodgson, the great world historian of Islam, considered that until the seventeenth century, Islamic society was the most expansive and influential in the Afro-Eurasian hemisphere: a visitor from Mars visiting at that time "might well have supposed that the human world was on the verge of becoming Muslim."[4] Muslim societies stretched from the Atlantic to the Pacific, from the Caucasus to the Cape of Good Hope. The three great blocs of Mughal, Safavid, and Ottoman empires straddled the junction of Europe, Asia, and Africa. Although Cemil Aydin has recently argued that a unified "Muslim World" is a myth, these societies nonetheless shared practices such as prayer, fasting, and the hajj pilgrimage that promoted what others have called a "Muslim cosmopolitanism."[5] After the Ottoman defeat at the gates of Vienna in 1683, the tide gradually turned in favor of Europe and its expanding American colonies, but the influence of the Muslim empires remained immense.

Muslims were a powerful and often threatening presence across the Mediterranean in North Africa. In 1689, through a combination of gunboats and diplomacy, the French state concluded treaties with Algiers, Tunis, and Tripoli that ensured the protection of French merchant shipping and French subjects' right to observe their religion unobstructed, as well as advantageous tax arrangements. In return, Muslims were officially permitted to observe their religion in France. Like most arrangements involving foreigners, these were reciprocal privileges legally contracted between sovereigns, not "rights" inherent in the individuals, let alone universally valid. Thus, if Muslims were "fairly" captured by a hostile power under the code governing corsair activity in the Mediterranean, they could be stripped of rights and treated as slaves. Even these Muslims were the object of diplomatic intervention and had their own Muslim cemetery and prayer room provided in Marseille and later in Toulon. In the same way, French subjects carrying the wrong papers or traveling on a foreign ship might find themselves enslaved in the *bagnios* of Algiers or Tunis: Jean-Jacques Rousseau imagined just such a destiny for his hero Émile, in the incomplete final volume of his famous book.

Islam was increasingly regarded as a distinct religion and not a heretical variant, ripe for rediscovery in the intellectual ferment of the Enlightenment. Jonathan Israel has argued that the followers of Spinoza—a stream he calls the "radical Enlightenment"—shaped a new vision of Islam "as a pure monotheism of high moral calibre which was also a revolutionary force for positive change and one which from the outset proved to be both more rational and less bound to the miraculous than Christianity or Judaism."[6] If these thinkers considered Muhammad in a new light, and used an idealized version of Islam to highlight the failings of Christianity, they were more damning about Muslim believers, considering them just as superstitious and inimical to philosophical thought as Christians, with the added element of fatalistic resignation to the will of God. The article *Alcoran* (Koran) in the *Encyclopédie* of Diderot and d'Alembert hardly differed in tone from traditional Christian polemics against Islam, employing freely such terms as "ridiculous," "extravagant," and "superstitious," and setting the "book of so-called revelations and the doctrine of the false prophet Mahomet" in contrast to "the sacred truths of our religion."[7]

The most influential representation of Islam in the early eighteenth century was an epistolary novel by the aristocratic writer the Baron de Montesquieu. His 1721 *Persian Letters*—a book that launched a thousand imitations—employed the perspective of fictive Muslims on French society to render many of its structures amusingly unfamiliar. Montesquieu's imagining of the Persians Usbek and Rica was influenced by philosophers such as Sale and Boulanvilliers, but equally by contemporary travelers' accounts and the 1715 Persian embassy to France. The choice of Muslims was not innocent. Following the death of Louis XIV, Montesquieu dressed his aristocratic critique of Bourbon absolutism in Muslim clothing, suggesting—as he argued more explicitly in his *Spirit of the Laws*—that despotism was an "oriental" system whose apparent stability concealed a servitude that stifled social development and encouraged arbitrary violence. For Montesquieu, the oriental despot exercised total authority over all of his subjects, regardless of rank, raising slaves to be ministers, and reducing prominent notables to slavery or, worse, sending mute assassins to strangle them. The object of the lesson was France: in letter 37, the French king was reported to "esteem the politics of the East" and to emulate the government of the sultans above all others. At the other, positive pole of Montesquieu's political analysis was the "English" system, in which the constitutional monarchy was balanced by a Parliament composed of elected "Commons" and hereditary "lords." For philosophers like Voltaire and Montesquieu, the English system offered stability and freedom, and the Turkish one insecurity and tyranny.

The real and invincible attraction of the *Persian Letters*, however, lay in its irresolvability of perspective—and Montesquieu was reported to have disavowed it later as a youthful folly.[8] Through it, Muslims became a positive point of identification, in a way that coincided with the hugely popular and influential *Thousand and One Nights*, translated from Arabic by Antoine Galland a few years earlier. Conceptions of Muslim difference—and equally of Muslim similarity—were shaped and reshaped across a space populated by many intermediaries. Edward Said famously argued that this "Orient" functioned as a projection of Western imaginings, and a way of exerting power over the Muslim world. This, however, was a far more mutable "orient" than the one suggested by Said's critique.[9] Lady Mary Wortley Montagu, for example, was uniquely able to visit the famous "harem" at the heart of these imaginings, and her insistence that women exercised greater freedom in the Turkish system was furiously debated by the adepts of Montesquieu. Jean-Jacques Rousseau—son of a poor watchmaker who had spent seven years living in Istanbul—could admire the ostensibly radical social mobility of Muslim societies as a source of greater tolerance and reciprocal social relations.[10] The scholar Abraham Hyacinthe Anquetil Duperron set out to reverse Montesquieu's assumptions about "Asiatic" societies and their governments in his 1778 *Oriental Legislation*, claiming they showed superior rationality and justice. A new interest grew in the Islamic model as one in which multiple religions were able to exist in toleration: even Voltaire, who penned a play casting the Prophet Muhammad as an evil fanatic, could elsewhere describe him as powerful and courageous, and the religion that he founded as "indulgent and tolerant," in contrast to Christianity, "the most intolerant [religion] of all, and the most barbaric."[11]

By the late eighteenth century, the growing intellectual interest in the Ottomans and other Muslim societies led to the dismantling of many of the conceptions that had sustained the "specter of despotism."[12] The collapse of Montesquieu's opposition between English and Turkish models was hastened by the beginnings of the revolutionary era, as the brutal repression of the independence struggle in the American colonies undermined admiration for the English system. The "debate on despotism" brought questions about Islam and Muslim societies into the heart of early revolutionary debates, as Thomas Kaiser has shown.[13] As we will see in the next chapter, Muslims were thrown into new prominence by the war against the Ottomans by Russia and Austria beginning in 1787. As the first stirrings of the French Revolution emerged in the late 1780s, these significant shifts in the political, religious, and cultural mappings of Islam were evident in a series of new works appearing in France.

The years 1788–1789 saw a new translation of the Persian poet and political theorist Saadi; three new books on the Turkish war; books on Senegal and the African peoples; Abbé Poiret's account of his mission to North Africa; and a book titled *Révolutions de l'empire ottoman* by Louis de Chénier. Most important were two works: the first, the *Tableau général de l'empire othoman*, published by an Ottoman Armenian intellectual, Mouradgea d'Ohsson, examined Ottoman history and Islamic law—a subject largely neglected by the *philosophes*.[14] Mouradgea insisted that the present problems faced by the empire were not the result of Islam itself: they derived only from "popular prejudice" and misinterpretation. All that was needed to reform the empire, he argued, was "a superior spirit, a wise, enlightened and enterprising Sultan" who would make use of the power offered to him by religion.[15] Similarly, Abbé Giambattista Toderini's *Della letteratura turchesca*—on which Abbé Grégoire explicitly modeled his later *De la littérature de nègres*—set out to demonstrate the Ottomans' high regard for science and civilization: it was hailed across Europe as at last providing an account free of the "religious bigotry and the pious animosities . . . those artificial barriers, which ignorance and priestcraft have erected against the nobler principles of humanity." One reviewer drew the conclusion that in this book the differences of Frenchman, Spaniard, and Turk had disappeared, so that "human nature appears, under every disguise, essentially the same in its virtues and defects."[16] In the 1789 French translation by Abbé Cournand—a Marseillais cleric, reader to the king, and future revolutionary—Toderini's conventional refutations of the errors of Islam were carefully excised.[17]

These changes, however, did not emerge simply from disembodied ideas: they were the fruit of multiple journeys and crossings, undertaken for a host of reasons—commercial development, military assistance, diplomacy, exile, religious missions, leisure travel, scientific curiosity. The authors were themselves caught up in the currents of exchange and mobility that were helping to transform the world and carry it forward into the age of revolutions. The late eighteenth century also saw Muslims "on the move" in new ways that anticipated the transformations in mobility that Julia Clancy Smith has described in the nineteenth century.[18]

Muslim presence in eighteenth-century France was limited; however, there are signs that it was increasing in this period. More Muslims were traveling to France than ever before. Marseille was the center of a roaring trade with the Levant and North Africa: France's involvement in the American War of Independence had accelerated the establishment of peace with the "Barbary" powers, bringing them into the emerging international contract, and promoting trade from both sides of the Mediterranean. These Muslims rarely appear in the archives or the printed record, unless they were entrusted with some official mission, appealed for assistance, or found themselves caught in an incident reported by the authorities.

Muslims enslaved in Spain, Italy, and Malta were purchased by the French Crown as slave labor in the arsenal of Marseille, building and rowing man-powered warships. When the galleys were relocated to Toulon in 1748, Muslims laid claim to the cemetery under the stipulations of treaties between France and the North African powers assuring Muslims of the free practice of their religion. They were successful in reclaiming the keys to the facility in the 1770s.[19] In 1777, the local chronicler Jean-Baptiste Grosson noted in his annual "Almanac of Marseille" that "since then, every Friday, one frequently encounters Muslim travelers returning from or going there."[20] The facility for rapid burial was a necessary condition for any potential extended residence by Muslims; other requirements like prayer, halal slaughter of animals, and celebration of festivals could be sustained by individual Muslims or private groups. Public worship by non-Catholics was prohibited in France, yet Muslim practice was de facto tolerated as a result of reciprocal treaty obligations. By the early 1780s, in correspondence over this same Muslim cemetery, the Chamber of Commerce in Marseille made reference to "the large number of Algerians who are in Marseille at present."[21]

Muslims who moved through France without encountering difficulties rarely left much trace in the registers. Consular correspondence and local records bring some of those journeys to light. In 1783, "a certain Aly Ibu Chaban, Algerian, arrived in Paris and requested funds to assist him in returning to his country."[22] In 1784, a man named Salem, from Tripoli in North Africa, arrived in Paris, requesting assistance in traveling to Alexandria. The ministry discovered that he had already received money 18 months earlier to return home. "I can only remark with astonishment the fact that he is still in France," wrote the minister.[23] In 1785, the ambassador in Istanbul provided a recommendation to allow "a certain Haggy Aly, Algerian," passage to Marseille to enable him to board a ship to his homeland.[24] In 1787, the Chamber of Commerce in Marseille complained of "the escape by eight Algerians who were part of the crew commanded by Raïs Ahmet."[25] These sailors, quarantined in the lazaret of Marseille, became angry at the unwillingness of their captain to pay for the provisions necessary to feed them and escaped into the French countryside during the night, creating a panic that they might endanger the whole region with plague.[26] In the same year the chamber reported that "the Marechal de Castries has directed toward our Chamber a certain Mehemet Cheliby, who says he is Algerian, and has been in Europe for three years."[27]

Cheliby's case points us to the insight offered by historians of Freemasonry, such as Xavier Yacono and Pierre-Yves Beaurepaire, into Muslims passing through Masonic lodges in France in this period. The Marseillais lodge Saint-Jean d'Écosse established chapters in Istanbul and Izmir, and the order's records refer to "the dissensions brought to our attention by the lodge of Algiers."[28] There is no further record of an official lodge in Algiers, but the presence of French merchants along the Algerian coast, and captives from different origins including Britons and Americans, may have made Masonic practice possible. Kenneth Loiselle suggests that "atheists, Jews and

Muslims continued to be *personae non gratae* " in Masonic lodges throughout the century and into the Revolution, although Xavier Yacono found at least seven names of Muslim Masons in this period.[29] A lodge in Marseille in 1767 specifically forbade the admission of "any individual who has the unhappiness of being a Jew, Negro, or Muslim," and other lodges in France declared the centrality of Christian belief. That explicit exclusion may itself point to the new constituencies seeking entry into the Masonic establishment. Beaurepaire records an Algerian requesting entry to the lodge Saint-Louis des Amis Réunis in Calais in 1785: after demonstrating with his certificates, signs, and passwords that he was truly a Mason, he was received "with the usual applause" and given financial assistance by his brethren. Two months later he arrived in Toulouse, where he was described as "brother Ibrahim Sherid, of the Respectable Lodge of Algiers."[30] In contrast, Mehemet Cheliby was rebuffed from the lodge in Nantes because of "difference of religion."[31] His attempt to seek redress in Paris suggests that some Muslims were beginning to assert rights beyond the boundaries of the religious and dynastic communities in which they were born, as we will see in chapter 3.

Muslims were present in France's colonies too. Ibrahim, a "Moorish merchant and Algerian subject," was reported to have been trading in the French colonies, where he "attracted the esteem of all the inhabitants."[32] His case only appeared in the archives when he was unlucky enough to lose all of his merchandise after the counterrevolution in Martinique. In 1787, a young Senegalese Muslim named Amrou arrived in Paris, after more than a decade of enslavement on the island of Tobago. At the age of 11, he had convinced his mother to allow him to accompany an English ship's captain, who promised to take him to London, "where he would learn all the language and sciences of Europe." The moment they left the port, the young boy was clapped in irons and taken to the Caribbean to be sold. In 1783, the island was transferred to French rule, and the new governor, Arthur Dillon, was made aware of Amrou's predicament by his assistant Philippe-Rose Roume de Saint-Laurent. Amrou still remembered his childhood Islamic education and spoke good Arabic. Several enslaved former servants of Amrou's uncle testified to the veracity of his story (needless to say, they were not freed from their captivity). The young man was brought to France in 1787 and was entrusted to the interpreter Pierre Ruffin, who noted that "he seems deeply attached to his religion, and he was delighted to arrive at my house and see Ishak Bey and his valet, both professing the same religion: their embrace was very touching."[33] These trajectories were one consequence of a world in the grip of revolutionary shifts that found their epicenter in France: they would take on new significance as they intersected with the rapidly changing events of the French Revolution.

As a consequence of treaties with North African powers, Muslims theoretically had the right to practice their religion in France. As we will see, these "rights" were reclaimed in new ways in the 1780s, at the same time other religious minorities in France were beginning to call for toleration. Pressure was growing on the French monarchy to put an end to the increasingly threadbare fiction that all French men and women were Catholic—a considerable irritant to France's new and very Protestant ally, the United States. In the wake of the Treaty of Paris in 1783, which officialized the outcome of the American war and restored French prestige—while doing little to repair the royal finances that had been drained to a disastrous extent in the process—pressure grew from the American side to offer toleration to Protestants. Yet even the smallest movement in that direction was decried by clerics as heralding a return to the bloody years of religious war, and betraying the legacy of Louis's ancestor, the Sun King. Meanwhile, the closest royal advisers, and Malesherbes in particular, were pushing him to regularize a situation that produced chaos in administration. The result was characteristic of the "reforms" of the monarchy before 1789: starting out with grand ideas, then whittling them back to a meager minimum, or, even worse, a further retrenchment of the existing situation. The so-called Edict of Tolerance of 1787 did no more than formalize the de facto recognition that non-Catholics existed. By refusing to recognize Protestantism as a religion, it created havoc for Protestants, who were expected to formalize their marriages with a priest or judge—allowing some to repudiate their spouse instead. The problem applied to Catholics too, since curés were now expected to act against their religious convictions, as secular agents of the state, or hand the job over to non-ordained functionaries. By seeking to preserve Catholic privilege (and guard against critics from within), the church and monarchy unwittingly made the first steps toward secularization, while simultaneously provoking a new wave of religious tension. What is important for our purposes is that, although they hardly knew it, on the eve of 1789, Muslims had, for the first time in a century—indeed, perhaps since the end of Muslim presence in the eighth century—a political existence in France.

1. Paris Turned Turk

"A vast scene is unfolding at this moment before the eyes of all who claim to follow the important political revolutions of which we may be witness," wrote a journalist in May 1788, as calls to summon the Estates General resounded across France.[1] The months that followed would transform France and shape the course of world history. But the "revolution" the journalist described was not unfolding in France. It was looming at the edge of Asia—a war that threatened to change the balance of power in Europe and across the globe. In 1783, the Russian annexation of the Crimea—strangely paralleled by events in the twenty-first century—shook the foundation of the eighteenth-century world order and provoked powerful responses that were crucial in creating the conditions for revolution in 1789. The incapacity of the French monarchy to respond to this and other external crises—along with the collapsing finances that underpinned that weakness—was as important a catalyst for radical critiques as the problems at home. As historians have recognized in recent times, these external and internal crises became intertwined in a snowballing politicization, fueled by the explosion of new forms of media, that gave new meanings to long-existing conflicts in towns and rural areas.

The word "revolution" did not yet refer to the overthrow of a political system—something as yet unimaginable—but rather to turbulent events with global significance.[2] The journalist saw no irony in declaring the word "most naturally applicable" to the war between the Ottoman Empire and Russia, into which Austria had rushed precipitately, looking to tear eastern European territories away from the weakened Muslim empire that stretched across three continents.[3] Many saw this as the prelude to a new European order in which France would forever lose its place. The geographer Brion de la Tour evoked the terrible precedent of Poland. "Should we not fear that this scene will be even more tragic than the first?" he asked. "That we will see torrents of human blood spilled?"[4] He demanded to know if the supporters of the war were seeking to "renew the Crusades" in launching a great holy war, seeking the total destruction of Muslims in Europe. Meanwhile, another newspaper reported, the rulers of Morocco, Algiers, Tunis, and even Mecca had sent money to the sultan, "and a large number of their subjects are departing every day for Constantinople in order to fight in his armies. . . . We have never seen the degree of ardor for the defense of the Mahometan faith that can be seen today among the inhabitants of the Muslim states."[5] Historians have noted the importance of this mobilization in the emergence of modern political Islam; this great shift also contributed to the mounting crisis in France.[6] Foreign policy debates that involved the Muslim world were critical to the period leading up to the Revolution, as Thomas Kaiser has shown.[7] As this chapter will suggest, the presence of high-profile Muslims in Paris during these months—coming from both the Ottoman capital and from Muslim powers in India—proved a lightning rod for anger over the government's failure to assist France's Dutch, Ottoman, and Indian allies in their struggles against hostile powers, allowing the rise of predatory new European alliances, the English and Prussians on one side, and the Austrians and Russians on the other.

A wave of support for the Ottomans swept through Paris in 1787–1788, as had been the case for the American colonists and their struggle for independence a decade earlier. Books and newspapers discussed the question furiously and drew connections and parallels with the internal situation in France. Most of all, they took the king's inaction as a sign of his impotence and the power of the cabal of aristocrats who surrounded him, led by his Austrian queen. It would become a common claim against Marie Antoinette that she exacerbated the debt crisis by secret transfers of money and material support to her brother, the emperor, for his war against the Turks.[8] The Parisian bookseller Prosper-Siméon Hardy wrote in his diary that since the war was declared by Russia and Austria "everyone in our capital has turned Turk, so to speak, so strong is the feeling of sympathy for the cause of the Ottomans, and the desire for their success."[9] He deplored "our inaction and our silence" that seemed to be assisting the belligerent designs in the East.

Few historians today would suggest that the origins of the French Revolution were purely internal. In economic, military, and cultural terms, the

France of 1789 was connected into wider Atlantic, European, and global networks. Newspapers and correspondence circulated widely in Europe and beyond, along with luxury goods and technical expertise. Since the voyages of Cook in the 1770s, mapping of the globe had taken a precipitous stride. Philosophers drew on comparisons with Old and New World societies to question received ideas. Novelists, playwrights, painters, and composers made imaginative leaps into these new and distant places. News of events taking place on other continents now traveled quickly enough to appear in the newspapers before those events had become part of the historical past. For the first time, it was possible to imagine a world in which global events were occurring simultaneously. The "revolution" looming in Europe's eastern borderlands was a case in point. The influential French-language *Gazette de Leyde* (running to 7,000 copies per edition, not counting the many pirate editions) featured news of the Turkish War on its first page in more than half the 26 editions produced in the first three months of 1788.[10]

The pro-Turkish party faced off in the press with those who would become known as the "Austrian Committee." A volume of secret correspondence sent to Russia in this period recorded that everyone in Paris was talking about three new books: one on "wit and morals" by an opponent of Necker, another on the revolt of the Dutch patriots, and lastly Constantin François de Chasseboeuf, Comte de Volney's *Considerations on the War with the Turks*.[11] The former consul and *philosophe* Charles de Peyssonel castigated the pro-Russian Volney, who argued that the Turks were better pushed out of Europe.[12] "I belong to the nation," Peyssonel wrote. "I have the right to denounce to the nation a work that in my opinion contains principles opposed to the nation's interests."[13] When Volney—who was elected to the Estates General in 1789— did ultimately betray the Revolution by accepting a royal buyout, his "manifesto for Joseph II against the Turks" was recalled with bitterness by Camille Desmoulins.[14]

The "Muslim question" appeared in many different forms in the pamphlet war of 1788–1789. Under the absolute monarchy, open critics of the royal government had risked arrest and imprisonment.[15] Then, unexpectedly, on 5 July 1788, a royal decree invited all "scholars and educated persons" to offer opinions on the procedures to be followed in the Estates General.[16] At least 6,000 pamphlets appeared in the four years before censorship was re-established.[17] Dozens of these pamphlets drew on Muslim themes. One pamphlet drew a contrast between the navel-gazing aristocrat, fixated on the power struggle in France, and the cosmopolitan monarchist who cites "the foreign wars, the domestic struggles, the Turks, the Russians, the Emperor, the Ministers, the Parlements, the Exiles, the non-Catholics" as key issues of the time.[18] Jean-Louis Carra—a journalist who had a decade earlier called for France to participate in the dismemberment of the Ottoman Empire—now denounced the "unjust war" against the Turks.[19] Another pamphlet praised the sultan's conclusion "after his own enlightened wisdom" that France could offer precious little support for the Ottomans in their present predicament. "The good sense of some of these Turks that we so despise," the pamphlet continued, "would not be out of place in the Estates General."[20]

In fact, as a result of these changing geopolitical circumstances, Muslims were indeed passing through Paris, and some had real connections to the revolutionary ferment. Mahomet Benal, reportedly "one of the most important men in the Empire of Morocco," was in Paris in January 1788 ostensibly seeking redress over illegally seized ships.[21] His accommodation was arranged by a former attaché of the Duke of Orléans—the noted physiocrat author Nicolas Baudeau, who was seeking to create a new "Royal Atlantic" company venture with the Moroccans.[22] Another envoy from the North African city of Tripoli, Mahomet Berabinabinan, stayed for a week in Paris on the way to The Hague in June 1788. He and the nine "slaves" in his entourage were described as "all favored with unpleasant features, a bad reputation and looking much like beggars."[23] The fact that the envoy was on his way to congratulate the stadtholder William V on his restored rule after the crushing of the Patriot revolt by a Prussian army probably played a part in this derogatory description. These figures of real—and already politicized—Muslims were appropriated, caricatured, and ventriloquized in the pamphlet literature and on the stage.

The Ottoman Patriot

The most significant of these visitors was a handsome young Turk who, according to the English traveler Lady Craven, contrasted *"Paris Paradise"* with London, "which he dislikes of all places in the world, because the common people would not let him walk along the streets without calling him, *French dog of a Turk."*[24] Ishak (the Turkish equivalent of Isaac) had already visited France twice, and had found there a set of cosmopolitan cultural possibilities that would bring him for his last visit to France in 1786. Ishak was neither a diplomat nor a traveler; his presence in France was in part the result of the connections he had previously established, and in part a consequence of the informal political mission with which he had been entrusted.

Ishak had begun his life as a noble in the royal palace, rising to the ceremonial role of *peşkir ağası* (towel valet) to Selim, the son of the former sultan and nephew of the ruling sultan Abdul Hamid. Attracted to military pursuits, he chose to abandon the charmed life of the harem to join the navy, and served in the Russo-Ottoman War under the daunting admiral Hassan Pacha, who became his mentor. However, his unusual and burgeoning friendship with a Russian officer, whom he impudently smuggled into the grand mosque in the former Byzantine church of Hagia Sophia, provoked Hassan's wrath, and he left Istanbul in haste. This was the explanation Ishak gave the French for his departure: it is clear that in the aftermath of the war and the death of Sultan Mustafa III, complex factional struggles in the Ottoman capital were intensifying.[25] French officials saw in Ishak a promising bridge for French interests, since "the impossibility of finding Mahometans who know European languages" forced them to employ Greeks they considered unreliable.[26] This idea was taken up with gusto by the foreign minister, the Comte de Vergennes—himself a former ambassador to Istanbul. Ishak arrived in Paris for the first time in 1776, a month after the American Declaration of Independence was adopted in Philadelphia. Handsome, suave, and arresting in a dashing scarlet uniform he had specially tailored to replace his Ottoman robes, Ishak proved more interested in Parisian society than French science, and acquired a reputation with his dalliances at the opera. Justifying Ottoman polygamy to a French lady, he was said to have quipped, "Madame, it would take 10 Georgians to offer the same set of delights I find in a single Frenchwoman."[27] Such repartee won him renown, but did little to improve his reputation: the sexual exploits of this "lustful Turk" were widely recounted and exaggerated.[28] "The genteel Turk became the fashion in Christendom," wrote the English novelist Thomas Hope, "and everybody wanted to see a Frenchified Moslemin, who eat [sic] an *omelette au lard*, drank champaign, and wore a miniature of his Circassian mistress."[29]

It is apparent that Ishak was growing uncomfortable in this guise of the "Frenchified Turk." When an embassy arrived from Tunisia in 1777, he donned Islamic dress to welcome them. When they departed, Ishak accompanied them to Algiers and Tunis, where he stayed for some time while seeking to discover whether a return to Istanbul could be possible. In Algiers, he sought the support of the *vekil hardji* (admiral) Hassan, who would become the ruler of Algiers in 1791, and—as we will see in chapter 6—a close supporter of the French Republic. After a stay in Tunis, he traveled to Smyrna, where he was warned against returning to Istanbul, and went instead via Italy to Russia, hoping to receive the repayment of a large sum he had lent to his friend. Not only were these hopes disappointed, but during his stay he received word from his brother in Istanbul that the Russians had invaded the Crimea, betraying the treaty signed in 1774.

Ishak was becoming a patriot. Prince Potemkin offered him money and properties to join the Russian camp and persuade his fellow Muslims to submit to the empress. Ishak "took the liberty to tell them that he had but one faith and one country [*patrie*] to which he remained faithful, and that if his stay in Russia had become suspect, he wished only to bring it to an end."[30] Bachaumont recounted a conversation with a Turk passing through Paris in 1783 who can only have been Ishak. The pseudonymous "Ali" declared of his time in Europe: "I admit that my morality is no more austere than before, but my religion is more relaxed in its principles, and my politics is completely changed. I want to go home to my motherland: I will live an unknown and obscure life, or try to, or I will sacrifice myself for her: I will open her eyes to her real interests."[31] These interests, he insisted, could only be achieved with the ascension of the young prince Selim to the throne; yet this possibility remained distant, and a war loomed on the horizon. The new meaning of the Ottoman conception of *vatan* (homeland) was not simply a borrowing from Europe, but a response emerging in the broader dynamic of the revolutionary age.[32]

Ishak soon discovered that his projected return would not be easy.[33] In 1785, a group of notables had attempted to overthrow the sultan. Selim was henceforth confined to the palace, and the coup leader, Grand Vizier Halil Hamid Pasha was executed. These factional conflicts should not be imagined as pro- and anti-Western: they had more complex roots and emerged in response to the existential threat to the empire.[34] Refugees from the Crimea were stirring up the population against a "surrender" widely viewed as a betrayal of Islam; they pushed for immediate war.[35] Meanwhile, other members of the ruling divan believed that more time was needed to modernize the army, and that a precipitate war might lead to total defeat. At stake was the very survival of the empire.[36]

It was a different Ishak who arrived in France in 1786. "I have become a grave and thoughtful man," he wrote to an official, "and, if I may venture, wise and sensible."[37] Retaining his Islamic dress, he no longer sought to blend into Parisian society. Like other Muslim patriots across the Ottoman Empire, he dreamed of regaining the Crimea from Russia, but feared that war could equally bring about the collapse of the empire, the conquest of its capital, and the total expulsion of Muslims from Europe. It was well known that Catherine spoke of creating a new Orthodox Christian state centered on Constantinople: the danger was clear and present.

Ishak was bearing a locked box containing secret letters to Louis XVI and Minister Vergennes written by Selim from his prison in Topkapi Palace, reproaching France for its part in pushing Selim's father, Sultan Mustafa II, to go to war with Russia in 1772.[38] "You who have eyes, make good use of them," Selim quoted from the Koran. "We are secretly meditating the fittest way to repair these evils," he continued, broaching the possibility of an "opportune circumstance"—by inference the replacement of the current sultan.[39] Louis responded with avuncular homilies, urging Selim to study the art of government, and assuring him that Ishak would be bringing back the most modern and enlightened ideas from France.

The open secret of Ishak's presence in France exposed the weakness of the French monarchy and helped shift public perceptions of the Ottomans. He did not reside at court, but in Chaville, frequenting the liberal aristocratic household of the Count de Tessé, along with the Marquis de Lafayette (whose wife was the countess's niece), and the American ambassador Thomas Jefferson.[40] Like other foreigners in France, Ishak was both outsider and insider, visitor and resident, supporter and critic of the revolutionary transformation taking place. In his later position in the Ottoman reforming regime of Sultan Selim III he would remain, like Jefferson, Francophile yet opposed to the radical elements emerging after the fall of the Bastille. Ishak was not a revolutionary: he was a patriotic reformer whose commitment was both imperial and religious. He went further than most Muslims of his time in his exploration of Europe, yet he reaffirmed his commitment to the stability and defense of his own society and religion. His presence in the France of the pre-Revolution was a symptom of the wider shift taking place in the geopolitical structures of the world, one which stretched into Asia as well as into the Middle East and North Africa.

The Muslim Ambassadors

In July 1788 a carriage drawn by six horses pulled into the courtyard of a house in the fashionable quarter of Paris, until recently the residence of Jacques Necker, the popular minister recalled to Versailles as a result of the financial crisis and popular discontent. Its passengers, dressed in simple robes and white turbans, were Muslims, ambassadors sent by the sultan of Mysore in south India to negotiate with Louis XVI. They were Mohammed Dervich Khan, a *sharif,* or descendant of the Prophet Muhammad, and military commander; along with his son, the second ambassador, Akbar Ali Khan—"a man of letters aged 70, who carries a copy of his complete works in his luggage"; and Mahomet-Osman-Khan, "in charge of speaking and answering questions"; accompanied by his nephew, Ghoulam-Sahib. "They are Muslims, like their master Tippo-Sahib, and not Hindus," explained Pierre Monneron, the captain of the ship that brought them to France. "Their language is Moorish [Urdu] but they also speak Persian."[41]

If Paris had "turned Turk" in response to Austrian aggression, the burgeoning threat of British expansion in India was also on many minds. French losses in the Seven Years' War were still ruefully remembered, and British imperialism was much in disfavor after the American independence struggle. France had managed to cling to a tiny foothold in India and the Mascarene Islands (today's Réunion and Mauritius). That hold had been strengthened through the French alliance with Haider Ali of Mysore in southern India, whose growing influence was a thorn in the East India Company's side. The success of the American struggle for independence undermined Britain's global prestige and revealed the possibilities of a united resistance. In a book on "Muslim power in India," published in 1789, an Indian author wrote that the Americans, "displeased with the new imposition, refused to obey the king's commands; and [they] . . . revolted from their authority and set up for themselves, spreading full open the standard of rebellion and defiance." He emphasized the assistance they received from the French, "who have an enmity of some hundred years' standing against the English of Europe."[42]

It is unsurprising, therefore, that Haider Ali's son Tipu Sahib—or as he would soon be known, Tipu Sultan—would seek French assistance to drive the English out of India. Louis XVI, however, had no stomach for such resolute action. One of the king's ministers would later recall that during the Revolution, Louis declared of Tipu's proposals: "This resembles the affair of America, which I never think of without regret. My youth was taken advantage of at that time and we suffer for it now. The lesson is too severe to be forgotten."[43]

Like the Ottoman Ishak Bey, these Indian Muslim allies, arriving at such a moment, served to underscore France's geopolitical weakness, which compounded French financial and social problems. It was not

Figure 1. Elisabeth Vigée-LeBrun, *Mohammed Dervich Khan, Ambassador of the Sultan of Mysore*, 1788. Peter Horree / Alamy Stock Photo.

only the religious difference but the physical one that made an impact, their high status complicating the conventional associations between skin color and slavery. A newspaper reported the confusion of crowds gathering in the rue Bergère to see the ambassadors: "They are not white like us," said one; "They are not black," said another, "and everyone was curious to see these extraordinary men come from so far away to bring magnificent presents for the king."[44] Elisabeth Vigée-LeBrun, the court painter to Marie Antoinette, produced a portrait of the ambassador Mohammed Dervich Khan as a handsome, powerful figure, towering over the viewer, wielding a huge scimitar (fig. 1), despite the visceral distaste she expressed in her memoirs for the ambassadors' dark skin and Indian manner of eating with their hands.[45]

Figure 2. *Almanac for the Current Year, 1789: Homage of the Indians to Louis XVI*, [1788]. Bibliothèque nationale de France.

The ambassadors were generally described as strikingly thin: an engraving entitled *Almanac for the Current Year, 1789* depicts the meager ambassadors festooning the king's bust with garlands, with a caption reading "Homage of the Indians to Louis XVI," in case of any doubt (fig. 2). This was pure propaganda: the ambassadors were not at Versailles to crown the king with laurels, but to request assistance that the king had refused. Their failure would cost them dearly: at least one would be executed after his return to India. Rumors circulated of fabulous offers of cash if the king was willing to lend French support to the Indian ruler and his fight against the British.

A small plaque on the frame of Vigée-LeBrun's painting declares that the ambassador at first refused to have his portrait painted on religious grounds, and only the king's command had been able to overcome the ambassador's prejudices. This too was nonsense. Tipu Sultan himself was painted in numerous likenesses, and his palace walls are covered with portraits of his numerous allies: Kate Brittlebank has underlined the importance of portraits and other visual symbolism in establishing political legitimacy in Tipu's court.[46] In this sense, the portrait accomplishes more artfully the same end as the engraving: bolstering the king's prestige through the homage paid to him by these prestigious Muslim visitors, particularly Mohammed Dervich Khan, a sharif claiming descent from the family of the Prophet.[47]

The body of the ambassador, invested with a potent patriarchal masculinity, thus served to supplement the failing role of the king. Lynn Hunt saw the collapse of faith in the "family romance" of the monarchy and the wider crisis of paternal authority as central to the revolutionary cultural crisis.[48] Pamphlets of this period excoriated Louis for impotence, flabbiness, drunkenness, stupidity—every form of feebleness that could be imagined. Antoine de Baecque has noted the "ontological vehemence" of these metaphors, which attacked the king's body as unworthy of the sovereign power invested in it.[49] But the alchemy of these pamphlets was also transforming the terms in which global relations were understood.

The *Friendly Letter of the King of India, Tipoo-Say, to the King of France* presented Louis XVI as the innocent or foolish dupe of nobles, "imams and derviches" around him, and warned against allowing women close to the throne. *The New Epiphany; or, Liberty Adored by the Magi* recast the Christian nativity story with three kings—Louis XVI, George III, and "Tiposaïb"—attending the birth of a new Messiah, Liberty, born from the Third Estate.[50] The *Conversation of the Tippoo-Saïb's Ambassador with His Interpreter* of 1788 presented the Muslim as representative of a wisely governed, patriarchal state, observing the "ridiculous folly" of France. While criticizing the monarchy, it also expressed alarm about the shifts in relations between men and women.[51] As in Vigée-LeBrun's portrait, the Muslim offered a solid patriarchal figure, one that the pamphleteer could exploit to criticize the public role of women and the effeminization of men.[52] By 1789, however, this was changing. In the *Letters of One of the Ambassadors of Typoo-Saïb*, what had previously appeared as stability was criticized as enslavement: this pamphlet presented the revolutionary changes as transforming Muslims too. Insisting that "men are more or less the same, even across such great distance," the ambassador in this pamphlet declared that he had "become a philosopher by breathing the air of your country."[53]

In this context, Muslims were increasingly cast as brothers in a sentimental narrative of revolutionary emotions. The Marquis de Caraccioli's *Letters of an Indian in Paris to His Friend Glazir*, published in two volumes in 1789, features a citizen of Tipu's state of Seringapatam, depicting him as a sentimental traveler drawn to Paris by the accounts of a Frenchman he encountered. Caraccioli foregrounds the emotional sensibility of the Muslims: "It is believed in distant lands that we other Indians never weep. Oh! Who has a more tender heart than the disciple of Mahomet! The Alcoran is admirable solely because it recommends on every page kindness and hospitality."[54] This "fraternalization" of the Muslim was already well advanced by the crisis of July 1789.

The Bastille and the Seraglio

In an engraving by the neoclassical painter Nicolas-André Monsiau, *The Revolution of 1789; or, The Conquest of Liberty*, the Bastille is in the course of demolition, oddly blanked out by white puffs of smoke; a giant empty suit of armor—the aristocracy?—has tumbled down from the battlements (fig. 3). Improbably moored nearby is the great "ship of state" with broken masts, emblazoned with the achievements of the Revolution. Its crew of laurel-wreathed deputies clamor solicitously around the figure of Liberty, while the smaller boats of the provinces defend the endangered ship against monstrous enemies rearing in the shallow waters. The king and queen and the royal family approach from the shore, shepherded by Lafayette and Sieyès, and acclaimed by cockade-wearing crowds from the terraces in front of the Hôtel de Ville.[55]

In the lower right corner is an odd scene (fig. 4). A soldier chases away a bearded Turk at the point of a bayonet, his turban decorated pointedly with an Islamic crescent. A second turbaned figure flees in front of him. Nearby, a familiarly curly-wigged Mirabeau appears to be ordering the soldier to dispose of these Muslims. The Turk brandishes chains, manacles, and a paper reading "Lettre de Cachet": symbols of the arbitrary power of imprisonment formerly wielded by the monarchy.[56] Yet there is little else to distinguish these Turks from the crowds around them. It seems that these figures are intended to incarnate the despotism put to flight by the Revolution, thereby "de-despotizing" the monarchy, but this symbolism only recalls the violence that the image attempts to erase. The presence of these terrorized

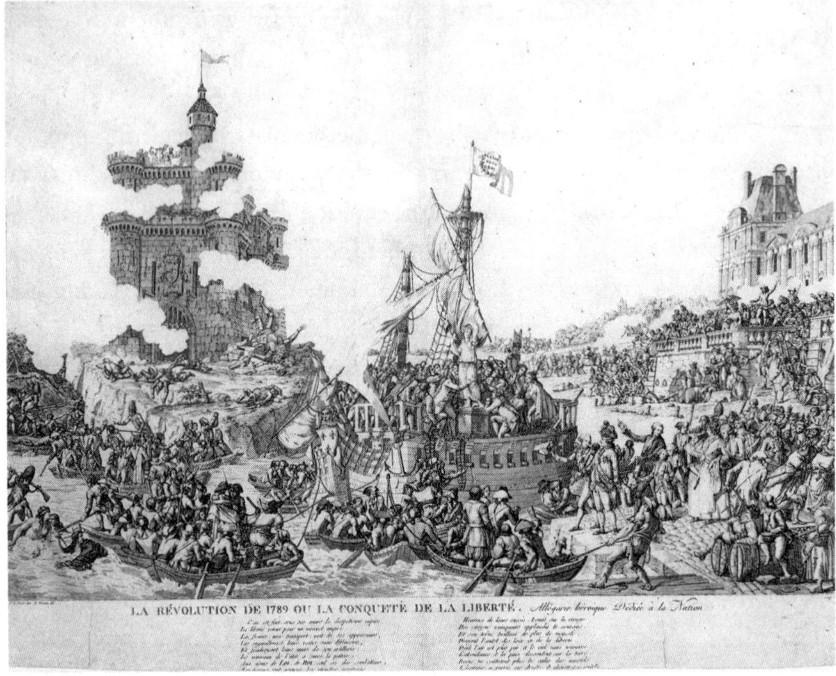

Figure 3. Nicolas-André Monsiau, *The Revolution of 1789; or, The Conquest of Liberty: Heroic Allegory Dedicated to the Nation*, 1789. Bibliothèque nationale de France.

Muslim bodies seems utterly at odds with the monumental glorification of the mise-en-scène.

This image is part of a wider crisis of representation that speaks both to the difficulty of finding forms to represent the revolutionary transformation that was taking place, and to the entanglement of Muslims in that crisis. We see here, as elsewhere, how Islam could be politicized in the attempt to control the implications of revolutionary events; yet the Muslim was not a stable "orientalist" trope, but a real category that was already shifting in the events leading up to the revolution. Muslims could no longer function as mere allegory: they were implicated in the whirlwind of politicization that this image sought and failed to tame.

It was the new sentimental conception of the Muslim that came to the fore in the immediate wake of the seizure of the Bastille. William Sewell describes the days from 12 July to 23 July as "an extraordinary period of fear, rejoicing, violence, and cultural creativity that changed the history of the

Figure 4. Nicolas-André Monsiau, *The Revolution of 1789; or, The Conquest of Liberty: Heroic Allegory Dedicated to the Nation* (detail), 1789. Bibliothèque nationale de France.

world." Its transformative potential lay not in the events themselves, but in their conjunction with larger structural tensions that gave way in a sudden rupture. Sewell suggests that these shifts led to "redefining and renegotiating" social relations, including those between "priests and parishioners, seigneurs and peasants, municipal officials and townspeople, masters and journeymen, husbands and wives, fathers and children."[57] He might have added: French and foreigner, Catholic and non-Catholic, Christian and Muslim. These wider resonances were not incidental. The occupation of the Bastille was not in itself a body blow to the old regime. Casting the events of July 1789 on a world-historical scale allowed them to transcend the long history of popular contention in town and countryside, and transform the structure of France itself. But from the first this process was racked with violence, fear, and anxiety, and the new ways that Muslims were imagined among the violent events of the Bastille betray the difficulty of representing the changes in a stable form.

The anonymous *Turkish Letter* of 1789 featured a fictional Selim writing to his friend Nadeth in a style similar to that of Caraccioli's Indians: "How happy the climes where the guiding spirit has sown the seed of philosophy! How happy the nation that this precious plant, fortified by cultivation, covers with its sacred reeds and feeds with its healthy fruits. O my dear Nadeth! I live here among men."[58] Expressing his profound emotional response to witnessing the release of the prisoners of the Bastille, Selim moves from sympathy to vengeful wrath, declaring his regret that the "corde" (the Ottoman version of the garrote) was unavailable to the French to dole out instant death to the enemies of the people. The discourse of vengeance in 1789 has been interpreted by some historians as demonstrating that the Revolution was violent from the very outset.[59] There is no doubt that the anger expressed in pamphlets and popular songs was real, and the urge to violence considerable. Yet alongside the roiling passions at the local and national levels, with their heroes and villains, self-sacrifice and revenge, was the awareness of a larger, world-historical stage upon which the events of the Revolution were being acted out, an important balancing force against the immediate desire for vengeance, which thus appeared petty and below the gravity and dignity of events.

Another Selim, this time the "real" sultan, figured as the protagonist of another pamphlet, the *Letter of the Grand Turk to the King of France*, "Written at the Sublime Porte in Stanboul, on the 15th of the moon of Rhamazan, 1789"—a surprisingly accurate Islamic date, translating to 10 June 1789— which bluntly criticized royal foreign policy, while insisting that the king had been "tricked" into acting against the interests of France. "You have a wife to give you children and not advice, and brothers to obey you," the Grand Turk declared.[60] A pamphlet written in direct response, entitled *The Parisians to the Grand Turk*, used this figure of despotic patriarchal authority, not to criticize the king, but to lay a competing claim to his sovereign power. Too busy to reply to Selim, the pamphlet declared, the king had been replaced in his function by the Paris Districts. These new divisions of the city had been created temporarily for elections to the Estates General, but remained in place and grew in power during the July crisis. The sultan should not be offended by this substitution, the pamphlet continued, "because, if you compare carefully what you are and what we are—your power, your rights, your honors with ours—your pride will soon be forced to recognize that a District may be placed on the same level as you."[61]

What had been a figure of undesirable despotism to be chased out was now brought back in the struggle to give concrete form to popular sover- eignty. "Our laws are the simple emanation of our will, as the effect and the measure of our power," the pamphlet asserted. "The law is the child of all, and this child is a Hercules in his crib." The Hercules figure, Lynn Hunt suggests, served to reorganize the confusing power of a multitude into a single potent and virile body.[62] Here, set in an incongruous calculus with this Greek demigod, was a powerful Muslim ruler. The power of popular sovereignty is greater than that of the sultan, the pamphlet insisted, since "you only reign for yourself, your Divan, your Seraglio and your eunuchs: we, on the other hand, rule for the good of all, and we even know how to make men out of our eunuchs." The explosively virile force of the Hercules-people thus gives a literal potency back to once emasculated Frenchmen.

This spoke to the euphoria but also to the anxieties of the moment. If the king's sovereignty was transferred to the "People-King," so was his weakness, including the disastrous international position of the monarchy. In the face of that anxiety, Selim no longer represents a figure of sovereignty to be emulated, but is an inconvenient reminder of French weakness to be disavowed. The pamphlet turns viciously against the sultan, telling him to save himself from the Russians by appealing to the Prophet, or taking a pilgrimage to Mecca. Still better, it declares, "turn your eyes toward France and Spain; they will have forgotten that the disciples of Mahomet kept the former [sic] under its yoke for eight centuries, and fertilized parts of the latter with their blood."[63] This syntactical confusion over the length of Muslim presence in France only compounds the strangeness of this sudden turn to religious vilification. It is the visceral gesture that serves the point here; yet despite the praeteritio reminding us of this sanguinary history, the pamphlet still offers a potential conciliation.

The hostile dimension of these responses to the Islamic religion can be seen in a more vituperative, satirical form in the *Letter of the Mufti of Constantinople to the Abbé Maury*, printed ostensibly "in the Seraglio, at the Press of the Favorite Sultana." This "letter" was in fact a comic dialogue between a Muslim cleric and a French slave, who addresses his master as "monseigneur" (traditionally reserved for high clerics). The mufti responds that he is "neither monseigneur, nor eminence; my name is Mahomet Dervich."[64] The pamphlet thus entangled once again the name of the ambassador of Tipu Sultan. The satire was an attack on the abbé Maury, the most prominent leader of the Catholic antirevolutionary faction in the National Assembly: it used the mufti as a mouthpiece to shower Maury and the royalist faction with salacious insults.[65] Receiving news of events in France, the pamphlet's sultan exclaims, "By the beard of Mahomet . . . your Abbé Maury is some kind of Muslim in disguise, and I wager ten Viziers' heads that if you examined his foreskin, you would find it has been whipped off." The mufti then promises to send his assassins to kill various revolutionaries, but if this should fail, he promises to make the abbé "the first Eunuch to the Validé Sultan [the sultan's mother] in charge of providing her with pleasant sensations through his cunning oratory."[66]

Characteristically, this blackly comic fantasy tumbles rapidly into obscenity, offering to castrate Maury and submit him to the sexual desires of a powerful woman. Earlier pamphlets had associated Islam with a stable patriarchal structure, which had been used to instruct the king on his duties to his people. Here Islamic religious elements were commandeered in a more violent attack associating female power—both sexual and political—with emasculation.

In the early months of the Revolution, Muslims were politicized from above by the entanglement between external and internal questions, disturbed by volatile refigurings of race, gender, and religion in the revolutionary turmoil, sliding unpredictably between the satirical and the serious, as words and ideas changed rapidly in meaning and value. But this crisis of representation cannot be understood apart from its entanglement with bodies—in this case, the Muslim bodies that were present in the space, or imagined elsewhere, and their relations to power and sovereignty. The strategies of what has become known as "orientalism" created a relatively stable separation between fiction and reality, allowing the oriental observer or observed to function as a mirror reflecting society. In 1788, the representations of the Indian ambassadors still sought to draw upon the reservoirs of meaning around sovereignty and despotism to defend or instruct the monarchy. In the revolutionary pamphlets, by contrast, this reality was cannibalized, disfigured, reconceived, in the rapidly altering events and realities of the revolutionary crisis. In 1789, the underlying structures of orientalist fantasy collapsed—as Monsiau's queasy attempt to figure "despotism" in the form of Turkish bodies shows only too clearly. The revolutionary violence from July to October 1789 would introduce new figures of Islam as a force that carried both threat and promise, and would clear the ground for the shift that allowed Muslims for the first time to be conceived, not as "other," but as potential citizens.

2. The Turban and the Axe

In the early morning hours of 14 October 1787 a bloody confrontation took place aboard a barge winding along the green-clad banks of the river Yonne. The water coach, as it was known, set out from Paris on Saturday, 13 October, for the town of Auxerre, with onward connections to Lyon and Marseille. The more affluent passengers disembarked from the crowded barge at Montereau, where the Seine meets the Yonne, to take the faster diligence by road. Those who stayed aboard were drawn from the bottom of the heap: the lower classes, rabble, street girls, troublemakers, according to a newspaper report.[1] It was an uncomfortably intimate journey. Some 60 passengers were crammed into a small space over several days: soldiers, seasonal workers, and young women nursing babies they were likely bringing from the Paris foundling hospital. Among them was a man variously described as Achmet Bender, a North African, or as Ali Mustapha, a Turk from Crete, and accompanied by an interpreter, or by two servants, according to different accounts. Almost the sole point on which all observers could agree was that this man was, "in a word, a Muslim."[2]

On the night of the 14th, a few miles beyond the town of Sens, an altercation took place in the congested quarters below deck. It was later alleged that while Achmet was asleep, other passengers set fire to his beard—a form of religious violence employed elsewhere against Jews. In the melee that followed, Achmet reportedly stabbed two of his fellow passengers with a knife and, seizing the axe that the boatman wielded against him, wounded several others. The local guards were called, and a pistol was fired, smashing the Moroccan's lower jaw. Achmet died of gangrene in the prison of Sens six days later, just as soldiers arrived from Paris to take him back for judgment. Instead, they carried back to the Châtelet the axe used in the attack, an object that would have a strange revolutionary afterlife.

It is difficult to determine with any certainty what took place aboard the boat, since, as we will see, multiple and conflicting accounts appeared in the local and Parisian press, as well as in sensational printed images hawked through the provinces by *colporteurs*. A letter from the *intendant* of Provence, Gallois de la Tour, in 1785 suggests that harrassment of Muslims was not uncommon in this period. A "Turk" named Cagiali (most likely Hajji Ali) traveling to Morocco complained that sailors had tried to kill him during his quarantine in Marseille: after his release, standing in the Place de la Comédie with another Turk, he was attacked by a local who spat in his face and assaulted him, leading him to draw his knife. Three days later he was attacked at his place of residence by several men. He then went with other Muslims "to demand justice" at the Hôtel de Ville, fruitlessly, as it transpired. La Tour reproached the authorities in Marseille for their torpor: "He made his complaint, and you responded that you had no knowledge of those responsible. It was on this apparent refusal of justice that this Turk departed for Paris."[3] He now informed them that Cagiali would shortly return to Marseille. It is likely that he traveled by the same route that "Achmet/Ali" took in 1787. The combination of "Ali" and "Turk," along with the connections to Morocco, may help explain the confusions around the story of 1787. It is possible that Ali and Achmet were the same, and that he had deferred his travel for longer than expected. Alternatively, "Achmet" could well be one of the other "Turks" mentioned in the story: his violent reaction might then be explained by these earlier attacks. What is clear, however, is that the violence previously confined to the streets of Marseille and to the correspondence of local authorities was about to become a big news story. Where Cagiali disappeared from view as only a consular concern, Achmet would be thrown into prominence by the religious and political crises of the pre-Revolution.

In October 1787, in the midst of a mounting political and financial crisis, preparations were taking place at the royal court in Versailles for the promulgation of what is often inaccurately described as an "Edict of Tolerance" that would recognize for the first time in a century the existence of non-Catholics in France. It was primarily intended to offer a mechanism for legal and economic reintegration of the large Calvinist minority scattered across France, which previously had no legal existence.[4] The edict itself sought to minimize its innovation by claiming it was only recognizing natural rights that already existed. However, rather than simply recognizing the validity of Protestant marriages, the edict insisted they must be legalized by a judge or curé. In doing so, the monarchy itself launched the beginnings of the revolutionary clash with the church by asking clergy to perform paid service for heretics. At the same time it undermined the church's monopoly over marriage by permitting non-Catholics to solemnize their vows through a secular state representative. Reception of the edict was ambivalent at best: Mallet du Pan wrote that it had revived "all the old fears and stupidities."[5] Protestants were both elated and disappointed by the decree, and increasingly frustrated by its halting and clumsy implementation.[6] As Louis Mazoyer wrote, when we see "quarrels building up, hatreds awakened, hopes appearing and boldness growing, we understand that the Edict of 1787, far from putting an end to the old religious struggles, re-animated them, as a clumsy breath fans the flames it sought to extinguish."[7] Yet Louis XVI, apparently pleased with the result, told Malesherbes to concern himself next with the Jews.[8]

This could only add more fuel to the fires of Catholic reaction. Tens of thousands of Jews resided in France, principally in Alsace, where politicized and violent local struggles had already broken out over the forging of false receipts for loans by Jewish moneylenders, resulting in arrests, riots, killings, and destruction of property.[9] Malesherbes, the principal architect of the edict, sought to allay these fears by dissolving the real religious minorities of France into an imaginary plurality encouraged by Enlightenment interest in the variation of religions. In his tract *On the Marriage of Protestants* he insisted that "if the new law exercises the positive attraction to foreigners that it should, people of all religions will come into the kingdom." He imagined a future when "colonies of Chinese" and "industrious Indians" would come to settle in France. In the meantime, the new law would allow the registration of the "deaths of those other heretics and schismatics, Jews, idolaters, and Muslims deceased in France."[10] The official "tolerance" offered by the edict replaced the older "fiction of a Catholic France" with a new fiction of a multiplicity of faiths into which the troublesome Protestant minority would be dissolved and forgotten, and which would in no sense challenge Catholic predominance. In this sense, the presence (real or imagined) of other faiths in France became a political expediency. As we see from Malesherbes's comments, Muslims figured prominently in this new and expansive conception of "toleration."

In this sense, 1787 can be said to have launched the imaginary "Muslim minority" in France. It was needed as a means of universalizing the notion of "natural rights" to which the monarchy appealed in order to defuse Catholic opposition. Far from a radical or revolutionary notion, this conception of rights inherent in human nature was here set *against* the rights accorded by citizenship. In doing so, the monarchy opened for a moment a gap between citizenship and Catholicity, and then slammed it shut again. For Mazoyer, 1787 was less an error than the "prologue of the civil and religious wars of the Revolution in the French Midi."[11] Not only the bitter quarrels over Jansenism, but older and deeper religious divisions—Catholic and Protestant, Christian and unbeliever—played a role in creating the conflicts of the Revolution.

It is in the radically different responses to the story of the violence on the boat to Auxerre that we can detect these different and conflicting understandings of the nature of religious diversity in France. The most conventional version of the story was that spread by the *complaintes*, cheaply produced prints that had been sold by traveling booksellers for centuries, alongside the almanacs and devotional materials that formed the bulk of the total print trade.[12] With images and songs, this was a form designed for a largely illiterate population. Here Achmet was presented as a moral lesson on the evil of unbelievers: "Christians, these facts / Keep well in your head, / The blackest of acts / Performed by Achmet."[13] But despite this moralizing refrain, the ballad characteristically identified with the criminal who found himself embattled and alone aboard the boat—and attributed his survival to "divine permission" even as it called at the end to "remember God, but not Achmet." Another ballad accompanying the engraving (to be sung to the familiar tune of "I Am Coming, Dear Adélaïde") declared that "everyone knows the cruelty of an angry Turk" yet insisted more sympathetically that on his arrest, "they grabbed him and hustled him, without the least compassion."[14] The caption on one of the engravings repeated the story that while Achmet/Ali was asleep, "several miscreants took advantage of his position to cut off his beard" (fig. 5).[15] Michel Foucault has noted how such "black heroization" and reversal of the moral order of punishment emerged in response to the suffering of the accused: "instead of remorse, torture sharpened pride, [and] the justice that brought the sentence was rejected."[16] These representations, according to a local source, along with the newspaper reports, were "sold and peddled throughout the provinces," popularizing this strange, antiheroic Muslim figure at a moment of spreading religious disquiet.[17]

Figure 5. *Portrait of Ali Mustapha, Born in Candie in 1734,*
[1787]. Bibliothèque nationale de France.

The story could not have been more different in the version reported
by the revolutionary journalist Nicolas-Edmé Rétif de la Bretonne—a native
of Auxerre—who claimed to have been among the crowd waiting at the
Quai St. Bernard in Paris for the arrival of the barge that brought news of
the massacre. Rétif claimed that "an Algerian, . . . having received several
insults from some imprudent and idiotic soldiers, pretended at first not to
notice, but when an obscenity regarding Mahomet was uttered during the
evening, this unfortunate fanatic, like all the others, decided to avenge
himself and perish as a martyr. He awaited his moment, put out the light in
the grand cabin, and armed with the boatman's axe, struck out in the dark,
imagining that if he did not see his victims, he could not be accused of
targeting anyone, and would thus be innocent of the crime of murder. He

spared only the women nursing babies, proof that he was not mad, as the owner of the ferry line claimed in his inept letter in the *Journal de Paris*."[18] Rétif did not explain the illogic of a suicide attacker attempting to escape potential prosecution. Most telling was his remark that in this violence the perpetrator was "like all the others," leaving the question of whether this referred to fanatics or to Muslims. Rétif was deeply anticlerical, and it is easy to see here the influence of Voltaire, who used the figure of *Mahomet* as a mask to attack clerical "fanatics."

The letter Rétif chose to interpret as a cover-up was written by the director of the water-coach company to the *Journal de Paris*: it declared that the supposed "Turk" was in fact a Moroccan in his thirties, named Achmet Bedeer, beardless and unarmed, traveling in the opposite direction toward Marseille with an interpreter around eighteen years old.[19] The director insisted that Achmet was ill, suffering from epilepsy, and that the other passengers in the boat had done their best to assist him. The violence was the result of a hallucination in which Achmet imagined he had been taken captive on a ship, and sought to defend himself, seizing the axe brandished at him, and using it to kill the men, while stripping naked for no apparent reason, and sparing the women.[20] The deletion of Achmet's beard in this version seems to over-egg the pudding, a little too consciously defusing the act of religious violence against the Muslim that was widely reported elsewhere.

The letter to the *Journal de Paris* was likely responding to a third version of the story, reported in Bachaumont's *Mémoires secrets pour servir à l'histoire de la republique des lettres*, a well-known publication of Enlightenment leanings. According to this version, the man, "a Turk or Algerian, in a word, a Muslim in full costume," was traveling with an interpreter and a black domestic servant. The other passengers in the coach, "generally made up of a lot of common people, rabble, prostitutes, and troublemakers," began to mock and abuse him. During the night, while he was asleep, some of these people set fire to his beard. Waking in terror, the man unsheathed his scimitar and struck out at his tormentors, reportedly killing and injuring several, but avoided harming any of the women. Finally, the conductor of the boat fired a pistol, wounding the man in the face. He was then caught in a stranglehold and dragged to the prison in the town of Sens. "When this news arrived in Paris," the author continued, "it provoked a great deal of rumor: the question was raised whether this Muslim was not in a position to be pardoned. If his beard was a symbol of his honor, according to the tenets of his religion, did he not have the right to avenge himself by annihilating his enemy, like a man who has received a slap in the face? While this matter was being hotly discussed, we learned that he had died of his wounds."[21] A British newspaper reporting the events stretched the connection with the situation of non-Catholics in France, suggesting that the violence was due to "unguarded expressions, wanton jests, or inhospitable insults on a peaceful stranger, because he happened to wear an African or Oriental dress, a long beard, and to deny the Pope's infallibility."[22]

These contradictory versions of the story reveal its currency as a repository for competing understandings of religious toleration. This notoriety may explain the presence of "the head of a certain Turk, called Mustapha" in the wax museum of the Palais-Royal in 1788, a popular amusement that figured in the events leading up to the storming of the Bastille, when crowds seized the wax head of Necker and promenaded it in the Tuileries gardens on 12 July. According to the satirist F.-M. Mayeur, Mustapha "had very unjustly massacred some jokers who amused themselves by setting fire to his beard and moustache on the boat to Auxerre." Perhaps as an ironic comment on the refabrications of the story, Mayeur marveled that it had been possible to reconstruct a face well known to have been half shattered by the gunshot.[23] It was not, however, the head of "Mustapha" but the axe of Achmet that would figure in the events of October 1789.

The Barbarian's Axe

On the morning of 5 October 1789, hundreds of Parisian women set off toward the seat of royal government in Versailles. For weeks, patriotic speakers at the Palais-Royal had been calling for a march: on 30 August, a "frenetic" named Camille Desmoulins sparked a failed first attempt by claiming (incorrectly) that the Austrians, having concluded a peace with the Turks, were about to invade Alsace.[24] In late September, rumors spread like wildfire that royal guards, incited by the queen, had insulted and trodden on the tricolor cockade, while the band played what would become the counter-revolutionary anthem: "O Richard, O My King!" from André Grétry's opera *Richard the Lionheart*.[25] The tangled relationship of the French monarchy with the Muslim world, in its crusading past and its disappointing present, was present in the background of these events from the outset.

As the populace gathered to search for weapons on 5 October, among their first targets was the Hôtel de Ville, where the newly constituted municipality of

Paris had been established. The procès-verbal of Commissioner Grandin on 28 October 1789 "recording the damage committed by the people" lists the objects taken by the intruders: several guns, a ceremonial pike, an old flag, and several objects held in evidence, including "the axe with which the Turk Achmet Bender killed and wounded several people on the Auxerre barge in October 1787."[26] Armed with these weapons, a band of market women made their way across the city, following a religious tradition associated with Saint Genevieve, allowing them to pass through the city relatively unobstructed.[27] Behind them, in the drizzling rain, followed a larger crowd whose ragtag character was said to have first given rise to the disparaging description "sansculottes."[28]

During the night, the crowd of 20,000 remained relatively calm, although deputies were shocked by the wet and bedraggled women invading the hall where the National Assembly was deliberating. The Assembly dispatched a deputation to meet the king, who, apparently astonished that his people were lacking bread, sent out guards to order the preparation of rice, which was all that could be found. The gates of the palace remained closed. But in the morning, the relief guard, having been given no different instructions, opened the gates as usual at 5:30 a.m. The crowd poured into the open courtyard, and groups fanned out in the park, opening doors into the palace compound itself. According to some accounts, a man began climbing one of the pillars toward the royal apartments, leading a guard to fire. The climber fell bodily onto the pavement, shattering his skull.[29] After a moment of stunned silence, the crowd exploded with fury, rushing at the gates of the royal courtyard. They overwhelmed and trampled the guardsman, named Deshuttes, and then dragged his dead body into the square.

At this moment, according to numerous accounts in the inquiry conducted by the Châtelet, a man with a large black beard made his way through the crowd with an axe and struck off the guardsman's head. A second guardsman was killed in the same fashion, and their heads were fixed to pikes, carried by the crowd as a menacing sign of the punishment of traitors. According to one report, the man was not only bearded in a manner associated with Muslims, but dressed in the clothing of a slave from North Africa. "This monster!" wrote the revolutionary journalist Louis-Sébastien Mercier some years later. "I have seen him: he was for a long time a slave in Morocco, where the sovereign counts among his daily pleasures to have five or six heads chopped off before breakfast. That is where he exercised by necessity the horrible vocation that he later employed by choice in Paris."[30]

Mercier insisted that this "cutter of heads"—known as Nicolas—had not only decapitated the two guards at Versailles, but boasted of having gouged out the hearts of Foulon and Berthier in the days after the fall of the Bastille.

The uses of Roman antiquity by revolutionary actors have been well cataloged, but here it was a new kind of "barbarian" that was imagined in the struggle to define the new order. Michel Foucault saw this figure as the inverse of the "noble savage" who learns to sacrifice freedom and live in reciprocity. "The barbarian, in contrast, has to be bad and wicked, even if we have to admit that he does have certain qualities. He has to be full of arrogance and has to be inhuman, precisely because he is not the man of nature and exchange; he is the man of history, the man of pillage and fires, he is the man of domination."[31] This description well suits the way inhabitants of the "Barbary Coast" of North Africa had long figured in the French imagination: the literal "barbaresques" associated with piracy on the seas and raids on the shores, with enslavement and arbitrary power. At this very moment the larger transformations brought about by the Revolution were bringing Muslims, and these North Africans in particular, more closely into the French political, economic, and cultural sphere.

The decapitation of these men in front of the king's apartment was a symbolic performance that transformed their otherwise incidental deaths into a powerful political act, one that the "barbarian" was needed to accomplish. The ritual beheadings repeated and amplified those that had followed the fall of the Bastille, but now they served to demonstrate a shift of what Foucault called "the right to take life or let live" from the monarch to the people.[32] Foucault saw the *sword* as the symbol of that royal sovereignty; in the hands of the people it became the *axe*, a symbol that would resurface at the center of the fasces of the French Republic. Thus, even today, the chief symbol of republican sovereignty carries an axe at its heart. Far fewer lives were lost during these two days of confrontation than had been lost at the Bastille, yet their consequences were both greater and more divisive, moving the center of power from Versailles to Paris, and rupturing the inviolability of the king. Muslims were imagined in multiple ways in this shift that some saw as concluding the "revolution of liberty" and beginning a new, more radical revolutionary movement for equality: the "first days of the rise of the Jacobins," according to Germaine de Staël.[33]

The conception that the "coupe-tête" Nicolas was a former captive in North Africa may have drawn upon religious echoes of the march itself. In

1785, a procession of 300 freed French captives from North Africa—the largest procession of the late ancien régime—traveled across France, arriving in Paris on 17 October, where disheveled and drunken former slaves roamed the streets during a three-day festival replete with much food and wine.[34] Gillian Weiss describes the reactions of spectators to the frightening former slaves who performed their captivity, noisily dragging chains and cracking whips.[35] One witness later claimed that they were not slaves but local riffraff, "rented out and made up to fill this role." Some observers described the march of 5 October in terms that recalled the ambivalence of that procession four years earlier. While royalists sought to blame the violence on the Duke of Orléans and his cronies, some moderate and constitutional revolutionaries cast the violence as the work of foreign elements. Several claimed that the men carrying pikes, axes, and sharpened sticks were foreigners—"worthless rabble, bandits from all corners of the world," declared one pamphlet; "vagabonds of various nations," insisted another.[36] Jean-Paul Rabaut Saint-Étienne complained of "strange faces" that were alien to the physiognomy of Parisians, and blamed these "savage bands" of foreign brigands for all the violence of the following day.[37] The *Patriote français* insisted that the only legitimate course of action was protest to the authorities: "Insurrection is the resort of slaves, or those who fear enslavement."[38] A shift was taking place from a moderate to a radical revolution that would overturn all categories, even those of free and unfree. The consequences would be felt most intensely in the Caribbean, but they were also important in North Africa, just as the region was emerging as critical to the subsistence crisis that underpinned and energized the revolutionary transformation.

Muslims and the Subsistence Crisis

In 1689, following bombardment by a French fleet, the powerful North African city-state of Algiers signed a 100-year treaty with Louis XIV, which was confirmed in 1719 after the accession of Louis XV. Following Algiers's lead, Tunis and Tripoli signed similar treaties at the same moment. Thus, in 1789—of all years—France's long-standing treaty protections from piracy in the Mediterranean were coming to an end.

In the late eighteenth century, the states of North Africa were undertaking major shifts of their own. Just prior to the Revolution, Morocco undertook a significant change in its policy. Unable to compete militarily with his rising Algerian neighbor, the sultan of Morocco developed a "soft power" approach: in early 1790, French newspapers reported that the sultan intended to purchase all the European slaves in Algiers and exchange them for Muslim captives in Europe, thus winning kudos both from Europeans and the Muslim world.[39] "The Moroccans," wrote the *Courier français*, "are perhaps not as distant as one imagines from true civilization. Piracy has come to displease them, and if they now disdain to live at the expense of their enemies, they will take up trade, industry, the cultivation of the arts; and this fine region of Africa inhabited by the Barbaresques will become as flourishing as the states of Europe."[40] These hopes were disappointed when the sultan died the following year, leaving a country divided between his warring sons.[41]

Tunis was the spearhead of a different kind of shift, as the traditional spheres of "Muslim" and "European" commerce opened mutually in the 1780s. Khalifa Chater's figures suggest a spectacular transformation, as Tunisian trade with Europe rose from under 6 million livres in 1785 to well over 22 million in 1792: close to a quadruple increase in seven years. Two-thirds of this trade was with France.[42] Marseille remained the principal European port of all trade with the Muslim world, with 35–40 percent of ships arriving there.[43]

If Morocco and Tunis thus seemed to offer new paths toward civilizational unity, Algiers was considerably less conciliating.[44] In 1785, the Algerians had signed a treaty with Spain, meaning that Spanish warships no longer provided a check on Algerian corsairs in the Atlantic. The ambassador of the new United States, Thomas Jefferson, refused to conclude the expensive agreement necessary to protect his country's shipping, exposing American ships to raids, loss of cargo, and enslavement of crews and passengers. France gained from the system of piracy: the minister of the marine, La Luzerne, pointed out that the "terror" inspired by Algerian pirates reduced competition from foreign shipping and aided French interests.[45] Yet the monarchy seemed to be frittering away this advantage through inaction.

In the lead-up to 1789, the French monarchy tried to argue that the 100-year term had been renewed in 1719; the Algerians insisted that the treaty they had signed was ending, and a deadlock ensued. As a result, as 1789 approached, Marseille faced the threat of piracy against its ships as never before, at a moment when the lack of foodstuffs was felt most intensely. The Comte de Mirabeau made this clear in a pamphlet he wrote in March 1789 following riots over food prices. Everything came down to bread, he told the inhabitants of Marseille. There was enough grain in the city for more than three months, and "more should be arriving from Africa, Sicily, the Adriatic, Cagliari, Livorno, the Roman Campagna, from the North, and from New England."[46] Why was bread so expensive? he asked. The bad harvests were one factor, and that was something only God could decide. But there was another reason: "because New England is at war with the Algerians, fewer ships are arriving from there, and thus we see how war is bad for everyone, since the Turks who are also at war are buying up the grain from North Africa."[47] Even in Paris, the crisis of Franco-Algerian relations contributed to the bread shortage, as wheat purchased from Sicily, Sardinia, and the Papal States, shipped to Rouen and Le Havre, was blocked by the presence of hostile Algerian corsairs.[48] On 3 October—two days before the people of Paris revolted—the minister of foreign affairs wrote from Versailles to the consul in Algiers, calling desperately on the Compagnie d'Afrique to undertake "the most vigorous activity in the provision of grain, and increase purchases in its concessions as much as may be possible." Even beyond the treaty crisis, France needed the backing of Algiers to ensure that the ruler of the city of Constantine would give preference to the French in purchasing grain: "I am sensible just how necessary it will be, in order to ensure the success of these operations, to resolve our differences with Algiers."[49]

But this was not so easy. The French government was embroiled in several unresolved disputes with Algiers that threatened the nonrenewal of the peace. According to the treaty, French authorities were responsible for protecting Algerian ships within the firing distance of a cannon off the French coast. In 1787, an Algerian ship was sunk by Neapolitans close to Toulon. The dey of Algiers refused to accept monetary compensation and insisted instead on a replacement vessel. The crisis faced by the Ottoman Empire, under attack from Russia and Austria, meant the Algerians had been compelled to send ships to Istanbul to assist in the defense of the empire. When no replacement was forthcoming, the situation became increasingly dire.

Versailles had been extremely ham-fisted in resolving this crisis: preoccupied with internal crises, Louis XVI's government had left the Algerian issue unresolved.[50] Rumors began to spread in Algiers that France was in fact planning an invasion with the assistance of Morocco and Spain. The rais (corsair captains) clamored for a complete rupture, which would provide them with rich new targets. The recognition in mid-1788 that France lacked the military strength to force a resolution of the issue led to the dispatch of a mission under the auspices of the interpreter Venture de Paradis—who spoke fluent Arabic and Turkish—furnished with expensive jewels to win over key supporters. In May 1789, at least eight French ships were seized by Algerian corsairs on the pretext that they were partially owned by Austrians: a menacing sign of the consequences of any rupture of the treaty.[51] Their crews and passengers were all placed in chains as captives. In August, reports arrived in France that the Algerians had sent ambassadors to Morocco to discuss the possibility of forging a hostile alliance against a France "enfeebled by interior problems."[52]

The connection between Algerians and the subsistence crisis was made explicit in Necker's *Mémoire instructif* to the Committee of Subsistence, published widely in July 1789. Grain destined for Provence was redirected toward Le Havre, he noted, but "by one of the many misfortunes that seem to be heaped upon France this year, an unexpected conduct on the part of the Algerians is spreading alarm in the Mediterranean and intimidating shipping."[53] The *Correspondance littéraire secrete* reported that the situation was worse than Necker claimed, and that he was well aware that "the Algerians have captured a number of our boats carrying grain . . . but kept it secret out of prudence."[54] Other newspapers linked the Algerian actions to the French betrayal of the Ottomans: the influential commentator Peyssonel insisted that the Ottoman Empire, "outraged to see France doing it so much harm under the disguise of a former friendship, wants to know definitively whether it should consider and treat France as one of its friends or one of its enemies." He saw in the Algerian actions a wish to declare war on France "because they consider us an ally of their enemies."[55] Thus, the Algerian imbroglio linked the subsistence question to the failures of royal foreign policy and the larger crisis of the regime.

Marseille, the French city closest to North Africa, was already in the throes of revolution. Months before the events of July in Paris brought political crisis to the heart of French power, the Mediterranean city had been rocked by revolutionary action. One pamphlet blamed this unrest on the foreigners who flocked to the port: "Before the general revolution of July, the people of Marseille, if not rather the horde of foreign sailors who flock there from the ports of every nation, rose in insurrection against the excessive price of basic foodstuffs."[56] Among these "foreign sailors" were a number of Algerians and other North Africans. In the months that followed, these Muslims would play an important role in resolving part of the crisis that was exacerbating the food shortage.

In May 1789, the newly established revolutionary municipality of Marseille took an approach that seems to have been on their own initiative rather than under instructions from Versailles. They decided to deal directly with "the Algerian merchants settled in Marseille in order to prevent the problems and difficulties that may arise in the case of shipwrecks or any other accident."[57] For the first time, they called together a representative of these Algerian merchants, along with the head of the sole French company trading with the Algerian coast. The Marseille Chamber of Commerce had previously resisted strenuously the municipality's attempts to open the Mediterranean trade to foreign merchants, which had been expressed in the *cahier de doléances* they had drawn up for the Estates General. But now they took a more active role: "To assist in the same object from our side, we have called upon Hassan Ben Karaly, representative of the Moors of Algiers, on one side, and the Gimon brothers—who are almost the only company dealing with Algiers—on the other."[58] They noted that they had instructed Ben Karaly "that nothing prevented him, or any other Algerian, from using French ships for his own commerce with Algiers . . . that our treaties gave him that freedom." Just a few years earlier, the Chamber of Commerce had been in conflict with these local Muslims over the provision of religious facilities in the city. Now, however, the revolutionary shift, combined with the diplomatic crisis, made it necessary for the first time to call upon Muslims to play a public role.

It would take months for the new regime to get its affairs in order and send an envoy to Algiers to conclude the renewal of the treaty—an extremely expensive and delicate affair. The ministry was forced to apply to Istanbul for the dispatch of an Ottoman envoy who could lean on the Algerians to renew the treaty. In shifting revolutionary circumstances, however, this treaty could not restore the stability the crown had hoped for. Instead, it was almost immediately ruptured in early 1790 by a series of new contentions that suggested the new regime's difficulties in establishing control over border regions.

On two successive occasions, freighters seized by Algerian corsairs and brought into French waters were seized by Neapolitan and Genoese crews, who also took prisoner the Algerian sailors aboard. More troublingly, questions arose as to what role French citizens and even the local authorities might have played in these events, which left one Algerian dead, two others injured, and a dozen more captive in Italian ports. The Neapolitans claimed to have received permission from the municipality to seize the ship, and even to have been assisted by the National Guard. The Chamber of Commerce in

Marseille insisted that "if some Frenchmen were in fact present, they were engaged entirely in the attempt to save the lives of the Algerians, after vainly attempting to prevent the act of violence that the Neapolitans were guilty of committing."[59]

This "Algerian affair" posed very delicate questions, as the officers of Toulon recognized in a letter praising Paris's positive engagement with local Muslims as "careful conduct truly befitting of patriotism . . . in a moment when public order is still so precarious and unstable."[60] Yet this "patriotic" engagement with Muslims remained under the shadow of religious violence, as was made clear in the dey's official protest to the French monarch. "Is it befitting of the dignity of your court," he demanded, "to leave unpunished such ill treatment of our people in your own ports? One man's arm was cut off, another received 15 or 16 wounds, a third was killed, and the rest strangled, including one whose beard was burned. There is no insult or injury that was not carried out against them. We have all been so shocked in Algiers, from the highest to the lowest, and above all the members of the Divan, who cried, 'No! We cannot believe our former friends could be involved in such things. Only God who knows and sees all can decide on this!'"[61] This burning of the beard echoed the anti-Muslim religious violence in the reports around Achmet Bender in 1787.[62]

Despite this religiously inflected conflict, the dey accepted the appointment of local Muslims as intermediaries in France. The parties who had been damaged in the incident, he declared, "have named an Algerian merchant who is on the spot, Sidi Hassan [Ben Karaly] Khoja, as their representative, along with the captain in command of the ship that was seized. These two Muslims will sell the ship and its cargo through the intermediary of M. Gimon, and will send the proceeds here through his agent."[63] This was a significant departure from the older reciprocal arrangements between courts. In tandem with the municipality in Marseille, the government of Algiers allowed Algerian merchants in France to take a role once restricted to high envoys of diplomacy between courts.

For the first time, then, in 1789–1790, the previously invisible Muslims of Marseille not only emerged into the light, but found themselves drawn into the political stakes of the Revolution, as arbiters, agents, and intermediaries in the resolution of serious contentions between France and Algiers. In Marseille, this action remained discreet, but was continued on the margins of revolutionary activity whenever needed to resolve problems in an ongoing collapse of the old diplomatic practices. Hassan Ben Karaly himself died in Marseille in July 1791, and the Chamber of Commerce requested the French consul in Algiers to summon his heirs to Marseille to wind up his estate.[64] As we will see later in this book, with the advent of a new dey in 1791, the engagement with the new regime changed in form and became more direct; there is also evidence that Algerian Jews, with their more expansive Mediterranean networks and larger communal structures in Marseille, became the privileged agents of this new engagement between Algiers and revolutionary France.[65] Nonetheless, as late as 1797, when the first permanent Ottoman ambassador arrived in Marseille, and discovered to his chagrin that he was required to spend more than a month in quarantine, several Turks of the city were persuaded to visit him "in the hopes of lessening [his] resentment and boredom."[66]

The Respectable Turk

At the same moment that, in Marseille and Toulon, Muslims were emerging from the shadows at the edges of the subsistence crisis, another Muslim was present much closer to the heart of the political crisis in Versailles. Ishak Bey, the "gallant Turk" whose adventures had inspired so much fantasy, found himself a direct witness of events. Indeed, he was drawn directly into the political contention over the meaning of the October Days. Those who sought to undermine the authentically "popular" dimension of the march insisted that it was a plot by liberal nobles, funded by the duc d'Orléans to replace the reigning royal family with his own branch of the Bourbon line. Such accusations surfaced frequently in the swirling confusion over these events, and had a long afterlife. The most exhaustive historical account, by Albert Mathiez, largely scotched any suggestion that Orléans was really an *eminence grise*: the duke had little more control than anyone else over the direction events were taking.[67]

Nonetheless, the events of October were much more than a bread riot. The leading role played by women lent the crowd authenticity as an expression of true popular feeling, provoking royalists to claim that the leaders of the march were men in disguise. The duc d'Aiguillon, a leading liberal aristocrat, was said to have travestied himself as a fishwife on the orders of the duc d'Orléans in order to whip up the crowd. The ultra-royalist and conservative Catholic Abbé Maury, passing d'Aiguillon on the terrace of the Tuileries palace, was reported to have said, "Passe ton chemin, salope" (On your way, slut!). The misogynist claim was repeated elsewhere, particularly in an anti-revolutionary pamphlet attributed to Antoine-François-Claude Ferrand in the form of a letter describing the "horrible scene of the 5th and 6th October" and insisting that "you [d'Aiguillon] were disguised as a fishwife, and you directed the actions of these overexcited females." Ferrand based this account on four witnesses "worthy of respect" who had recognized d'Aiguillon under his "tragico-burlesque" disguise: "of this number is a Turk, very well known at Versailles under the name of Isaac Bey, who was revolted by it, and could never speak without horror about this aspect of your life."[68]

Of the four putative witnesses to this carnivalesque scene, Ferrand cited only the "Turk" by name. A number of French witnesses in the inquest of the Châtelet had reported suspicious behavior and men dressed as women. Did Ferrand feel that this Muslim testimony bore greater weight than that of a French observer? During this time, Ishak was indeed living in the town of Chaville, which straddled the road taken by this revolutionary crowd. Whether he really saw d'Aiguillon disguised as a fishwife, or whether this was a convenient fiction attributed to him because by mid-1790 he was no longer in France and so was incapable of being called to account, the credibility of such an assertion was reliant on the fact that his presence throughout the events of this time was well known.

We saw in the last chapter how critics of the monarchy invested representations of Muslims with an aura of patriarchal stability in order to critique Louis XVI's weakness and impotence. Here, it was the defenders of the monarchy who adopted these "patriarchal" uses of Islam. Ishak became the locus for the projection of the political and gender anxieties of the collapsing regime, the "necessary Turk" who could serve as a buttress of patriarchal heterosexuality.[69] Some conservative opponents suggested that d'Aiguillon was so feminine that he could easily be taken for a woman (with coded intimations of homosexuality), claiming that it was "as difficult for him to prove that he is a man today as it is to prove that he was not a woman on the night of 6 October."[70] This concatenating "gender trouble" was not simply the action of revolutionaries: it was generated on both sides, accelerating the collapse of confidence in the patriarchal model.[71]

It seems likely that Ishak was also the inspiration for the "Ibrahim" of another pamphlet, *The Dialogue between Ibrahim Pacha and a Municipal* of 1790, which purported to be narrated by a Frenchman who had spent two years in Egypt, but had hastened back to France on hearing news of the Revolution, "to enjoy the regeneration of my *Patrie*." While staying at a hotel in Marseille, the author writes, he encountered an Ottoman envoy who (like Ishak) had come to seek French assistance in the war against Russia and Austria, and who described to him an encounter with a "municipal"—a member of the Paris revolutionary districts. Here, Louis XVI's failure to support the Ottomans was blamed on a revolutionary "despotism" that weakened the monarchy, turning the accusations of 1789 back upon the revolutionaries themselves.

In the dialogue imagined by the pamphlet, the revolutionary hurriedly warns his Turkish interlocutor against even mentioning the king out loud. In a sardonic note, the author approves this advice: "Poor Ibrahim, be careful— you'll be denounced to one of the Districts, and despite your character, you'll be very lucky if you're not accused of crimes against the nation."[72] The Turk no longer functions here as an outside observer, but as a potential participant in and victim of revolutionary politics. Thus, in response to the municipal's laudatory description of the fall of the Bastille and the killing of Foulon and Berthier de Sauvigny, Ibrahim asks: "And what is it that you want from these atrocities?" With a kind of burlesque innocence, the revolutionary replies, "We want to be happy."[73] Ibrahim lets loose a diatribe against the revolutionaries as brigands, barbarians, cannibals: those who wish to help humanity, he declares, must do everything *for* the people, and do nothing *through* them. Predictably, given the counterrevolutionary tone of the pamphlet, the municipal swiftly confesses that he too is terrified of the people, and asks to accompany Ibrahim to Turkey. "Come then, traitor!" the Turk declares. "When you arrive, I'll have you impaled." The Turk has here been drafted into a struggle between revolution and counterrevolution that is no longer bounded by France's borders: it is notable that Thomas Jefferson owned a copy of this pamphlet, and bound it in with the Châtelet report on the October Days.

Like the fictional Ibrahim, Ishak left France after the October Days. In April 1789, the sudden death of Sultan Abdul Hamid brought about the very "revolution" that many Ottomans had been waiting for, the advent of the prince Selim—Ishak's childhood friend—to the Ottoman throne. Yet Ishak did not depart at once for Istanbul: he remained through the surprising and frightening events of June and July. To explain this, we must consider Ishak, not as an exotic curiosity, but rather as a reforming Muslim notable, who had established close connections with liberal aristocratic circles prior to the

Revolution, and continued to engage with the project of constitutional reform until this moment of sweeping political violence against the established order. It was then that he departed from France, like many disillusioned French and foreign admirers who turned away from the Revolution.

The Comte de Ségur described in his memoirs encountering the "educated, tolerant, spiritual" Ishak, and congratulating him on his acquisition of European knowledge that would be so useful to his homeland. According to Ségur, Ishak demurred, insisting that his travels and studies were only for himself. "When I go back to Constantinople," Ségur reported him as saying, "I will take great care to hide everything I know, to appear to despise the arts and the learning of Christians that we consider the fruit of the devil . . . in a word, I will be as stupid and ignorant as my compatriots, since otherwise my head will not stay on my shoulders for more than a week.[74]

Whether these are really Ishak's words, there is no doubt that his attempt to return to Istanbul placed him in enormous danger. The sultan, his childhood friend, refused to see him. He was placed under arrest and taken in a boat toward Lemnos. This cannot but have recalled the fate of his friend the reforming minister Halil Hamid, who had been taken to an Aegean island and executed in 1785. The boat stopped in the Dardanelles, and Ishak was able to communicate with the French consul through the intermediary of two Jewish dragomans who came aboard the ship. They alerted a group of Algerian officers commanding the fleet stationed in the Dardanelles, and through their intervention he was able to leave the ship, and accompany them on their campaign. On his return, he sought the protection of the French consul, Amoreux, and remained in Smyrna for the three years that followed.[75] Amoreux, a convinced royalist, emigrated after the execution of the king in 1793. Ishak was reported to share his convictions. According to one author, he maintained a "religious devotion" to the memory of the king, and "detested all the French for the crime of 21 January."[76] Another, however, described him as "entirely French by his feelings and his character" and as the force behind the new administration's "marked preference for the French on all occasions."[77] These French accounts failed to understand Ishak in the complex Ottoman social and political context in which he was embedded, interpreting his responses entirely in relation to French realities.

Ishak returned to grace with the appointment of his childhood friend Küçük-Hussein as Capudan Pasha, marking a new era of change. Ishak, according to another account, "contributed more than anyone to this reform."

He "encouraged Hussein's taste for all the arts of Europe, and contributed greatly to that revolution that the admiral wished to introduce in Turkish customs."[78] Much remains to be revealed in his story. More than simply an accidental observer of the French Revolution, he was a direct witness and participant—but as a Muslim and an Ottoman. He offers a crucial line of connection between revolutionary ideas and the first reforms of the Ottoman Empire, the "new system" (*nizam-i-jedid*) of Selim III and the *tanzimat* reforms of Mahmud II that would give a new shape, dress, and organization to the empire.[79] Ishak's place in those reforms remains largely unclear. A tantalizing suggestion emerges in the works of Thomas Walsh, who encountered Ishak later in Egypt, and suggested that the motivation for Ishak's disgrace was theological and not simply moral or political. "His stay in France having enlarged his ideas," Walsh wrote, "he attempted by his writings to reform many parts of the Mahometan religion; at which, as may well be supposed, the Mufti took great offence, and got him proscribed."[80] The abbé Grégoire, in his *History of Religious Sects*, regretted that Walsh had not offered more details on this project.[81] It is crucial to think of Ishak not simply as a "westernizing oriental" but as a Muslim Ottoman whose primary commitment was to his own society and traditions. He might well have said to the French—as he did to the Russians who sought to employ him against his countrymen—"I have but one faith and one fatherland." Some 12 years later, on 28 June 1801, Ishak Bey would be the Ottoman signatory on the convention ending the three-year French occupation of Egypt that also brought the Revolution itself to an end.[82]

Ishak left no direct account of his reaction to the moments he witnessed on the days of 5 and 6 October: it was as endlessly refracted and distorted as the story of Achmet Bender. The events of those days altered the direction and meaning of the Revolution, from a reform still conceived within the patriarchal order of the "good family" of the kingdom, to a more radical fraternal order of equality. The figure of the Muslim—both real and imaginary—became entangled with these shifts, and in the process emerged in new ways. The older religious and political framings of the Muslim—as infidel and despot—were giving way to a much more fluid set of conceptions. Muslim presence in France was no longer employed simply as comparison or analogy, but engaged as part of the struggle to redefine the Revolution in France as part of a universal transformation. Less than three months after these events took place, as the next chapter will show, Muslims would become eligible for the rights of citizenship.

3. The Rights of Muslims

On 24 December 1789, the French National Assembly awarded full civil rights to Muslims. The decree passed on that day qualified Muslims—along with other non-Catholics—as eligible to occupy all civil and military offices in France, to vote and stand for election if they qualified as active citizens. That this shift should mark the first Christmas Eve of revolutionary France seems too symbolic to have been an accident. In a France where only a handful of Muslims could be identified as conceivably fulfilling any of the conditions to become citizens, we must ask why they were so prominent in the framing of the decree, and what significance, if any, it held for the future conception of the Muslim citizen.

The deputies of the National Assembly, elected in the spring of 1789 to the Estates General, were decidedly men of the ancien régime, and hardly a propitious group to make such a fundamental shift. One-quarter of them were clergy, including bishops and curés, whose views rarely extended to enfranchising non-Christians. Of the Third Estate deputies who formed half of the chamber, Timothy Tackett suggests that their religious views fell on a spectrum from pious Catholicism to philosophical agnosticism: most felt some antipathy toward clerical excesses, but also saw religion as a crucial element in ensuring social order.[1] A minority of noble deputies espoused an anticlerical skepticism, but the aristocracy by and large regarded orthodox Catholic faith as an essential pillar of their status and identity.

For more than a century, the position of the French monarchy had been that France must be and remain Catholic, to prevent a descent into religious anarchy, and ensure morality and social cohesion.[2] The so-called Edict of

Tolerance of 1787 did little more than officialize what everyone knew—that non-Catholics existed in France, and not only as "foreign" communities. In rupturing what it explicitly described as a "fiction," however, the monarchy opened the Pandora's box of plurality of religions. Fearing a violent backlash against Protestant emancipation, the authors of the edict insisted it was intended to recognize the rights of all non-Catholics, including Jews and Muslims, hoping thereby to dilute its offense to the church. In doing this, they made a step toward recognizing multiple religions rather than a single, true "religion" against which other erroneous or misguided practices were tolerated.[3] This process would take a great leap in the confused and sometimes violent struggles to define the place of religion in the new order after July 1789.

The rights offered to Muslims were not a vacant utopian gesture but an integral piece of the new society revolutionaries were seeking to build. The debate over how Muslims, Jews, and other non-Christians could participate in the French state would become, as we will see, a furious battleground in defining the break with the ancien régime, and the complexion of a new France. Making a new citizenship was neither simple nor straightforward but a tug-of-war involving multiple interests, not only in the National Assembly, but in the provinces, in the emerging political clubs and newspapers, and in the political action of religious minorities themselves. Were it not for these conflicts, the Muslim question might have remained implicit, in the realm of potentiality. Instead, it emerged as an explicit proposition in late December 1789, in the debate over the admission of non-Catholics to full citizenship.

The direction from which this proposition came was surprising: François de Hell, deputy of Alsace, and one of the most strident opponents of Jewish emancipation. "The National Assembly," ran his proposed decree, "conscious of the strong and friendly relationship between France and the Ottoman Porte that has lasted for over a century, declares and decrees that all Muslims, and particularly the subjects of the Turkish emperor, in Europe as well as in all other parts of the world, will enjoy, in every part of the French Empire, all the rights, honors, and advantages enjoyed by French citizens."[4]

We have seen that concerns over France's relationship to the Ottoman Empire were widely disseminated at this moment, yet the rights of Ottoman subjects in France were not at issue, since they were governed by reciprocal treaties still in force. Moreover, the proposed decree would apply to all Muslims, and not only Ottoman subjects (who of course included many Christians and Jews). Why would an opponent of Jewish rights espouse those of Muslims? In the October Days, the Muslim emerged as a "barbarian" figure in the violent shift from royal to popular sovereignty. Yet here, just a few months later, Muslims reappear, not as barbarians, but as prospective citizens. To understand why this should be the case, we must investigate the changing conception of rights that emerged almost immediately in the aftermath of the Bastille, in July and August of 1789, as the new National Assembly set about preparing the Declaration of the Rights of Man and Citizen. We must recognize that the unexpected legislators imagined themselves adumbrating rights not only for French men and women, but for the human race. They thus hurtled directly into the confrontation that many deputies hoped to avoid with the centuries-old, deeply entrenched power of the Catholic Church.

Religion and Revolution

On 1 August 1789 the Comte de Castellane dramatically opened the debate on the Declaration of Rights with an invocation of the vast unfriendly "surface of the terrestrial globe" upon which this universal project dared to burst forth. Even in Europe, just a tiny handful of places recognized the existence of rights, "without needing even to mention the whole of Asia, nor the unfortunate Africans who discover in the islands [of the Caribbean] an even more terrible enslavement than they suffered at home."[5] Some historians have located the origins of the Declaration in imitation of the bills of rights in the American colonies.[6] But the Comte de Montmorency was clear on the difference: "Let us follow the example of the United States," he exhorted. "They gave a great example to the new hemisphere: let us give one to the universe."[7] This was a conception of rights conceived from the first in a universal frame. As Adrien Duquesnoy suggested, the revolutionary party looked to the future, seeing that the "present generation might not gather the fruits of the revolution; but what are men and years in the light of centuries and empires?"[8]

When opponents insisted that a declaration was unnecessary, since these "rights" were already carved in the hearts of men, whether by God or nature, the deputy Target retorted: "Are they [known] by the peoples of Asia?"[9] Extending the National Assembly's vision to the lands of Islam and beyond offered the demonstration that what had been identified as "natural" values were not yet universal: they had to be *made* through a great, world-historical act of legislation.[10] This was not merely an intellectual intoxication: as Marcel Gauchet has observed, the universalism of the revolutionaries was neither genius nor folly. Conditions dictated that "only the universal could answer their problem."[11] But the universal was not a monolithic conception: it was a terrain—like the nation—contested in a multiplicity of ways by both the proponents of the Revolution and their adversaries. It could be a grand vision, a strategic ploy, or a code in which certain parties sought to defend their particular interests, claiming they were supporting pragmatic compromise in the name of the larger goal.

On 3 August, a rather timid parish priest whose name was not recorded rose to announce with a rustic proverb that he wanted to talk about something that concerned his vocation. This provoked laughter. When the three orders joined together, he asked, had they not planned to erect a chapel in the Assembly? To what god would it have been consecrated? "To an unknown god, *deo ignoto?*" Laughter broke out again. No, he pursued, "we are still the true children of the Catholic, apostolic, and Roman Church."[12] This statement was met with silence. He was called to order by the president. This clumsy interaction revealed a sea change. The curé clearly imagined his invocation of God would find broad consensus, but instead it brought to the surface the great shift that had taken place. In the debate over religion it was no longer *at all* certain which god was in question.

On the following night of 4 August, in the wake of extreme unrest in Paris and the "great fear" of peasant insurrections spreading across the countryside, the Assembly voted to dismantle the bulk of the seigneurial underpinning of French power and property.[13] Article 11 of the August Decrees declared that all citizens, whatever their origins, were eligible to hold any ecclesiastic, civilian, or military post, removing the restriction of opportunity based on birth. But they did not define *who* was eligible for citizenship, still limited by default to those who professed the accepted religion. Non-Catholics remained governed by the Edict of 1787, which offered the barest official recognition of their existence and reinforced exclusions from office. To alter these arrangements threatened to stir up the ghosts of centuries of religious strife.

The night of 4 August, had only made the deputies more aware of the world-historical nature of the Declaration they were debating. Adrien Duquesnoy, acknowledging concerns that it could be seen as "an attempt to replace the religious ideas that have always been so dear to the People," asked that the Declaration begin with "a great and majestic religious idea, applicable to all religions, to all beliefs, and all climates."[14] Universalism here functioned as a strategy to circumvent head-on confrontation with popular

Catholicism. His tactic was echoed by other deputies such as Lally-Tollendal, who insisted that any clause on religion should be "applicable to all beliefs and all religions."[15]

On 22 August the Assembly began to debate the three articles proposed in the draft project of the 6th Bureau:

> XVI. Since the Law cannot punish offenses committed in secret, it must be supplemented by religion and morality. It is thus essential for the good order of society that both of these should be respected.
> XVII. The maintenance of religion requires public worship. The respect for public worship is thus indispensable.
> XVIII. Any citizen who does not trouble the established religion should not be disturbed.[16]

This draft was still anchored in ancien régime ways of thinking—hardly surprising since so many of the deputies coming to Versailles as representatives of their local communities felt intrinsically bound to the traditional structures of church, parish, and congregation. They looked primarily to religion as a means of governing the population and assuring morality and good order. For the new order, however, the draft failed to articulate positive rights, and instead prescribed duties to respect "religion"—meaning (only) the Catholic religion and its public ritual. Those who fell outside the Catholic fold would not be persecuted as long as they remained "discreet" and offered no challenge to the established system.

In the wider forum of the Assembly, however, these traditional ties seemed to evaporate quickly. This was not because the majority of deputies were enlightened freethinkers—few of those elected to the Estates General had any previous relationship to Enlightenment circles.[17] It was the opponents of reform who were most wont to employ erudite references derived from an aristocratic education. Instead this shift unfolded from the political process itself. As deputies first debated the need for a Declaration of Rights, and then established its opening articles, a logic emerged that began to break sharply with the structures of the ancien régime. The emphasis on natural liberty and equality, argued from first principles, tore up the ground on which religious privilege rested. The night of 4 August certainly demonstrated that these were not just principles, but could be put dramatically into action.

The shift in ways of speaking about religion can be detected even among the defenders of the status quo. The bishop of Clermont declared that "religion is the foundation of empires; it is the eternal reason that watches over the order of things." Yet in doing so he made reference to Plutarch and the necessity of the "worship of gods."[18] The abbé d'Eymar—vicar-general of Strasbourg and arch-defender of church privilege—arguing confusingly for the "right" to exercise a religious duty, declared, "I do not ask for the proscription of all religions" (presumably other than Catholicism); "I myself have preached tolerance on more than one occasion."[19] Here religion in the singular meant Catholicism, and in the plural presumably meant anything else.

It was the proponents of religious toleration who took the clearest position regarding pluralism. M. de Laborde, painting a picture of a Europe ruled by despotic states demanding religious homogeneity and thus torn by war, insisted that persecution only multiplied sectarian difference. The powers of the earth should have nothing to do with religion, and certainly not by violence, since "Jesus Christ and his apostles preached gentleness." Religious toleration was a *reciprocal* duty: "Let us respect foreign religions, in order that they respect ours in turn."[20] Such principles of reciprocity and tolerance were based on the assumption that the French state would remain Catholic, while tolerating other religions as foreign. Toleration, then, according to this argument, was in the interests of society, since it best maintained the existing national order.

Mirabeau immediately rejected the terms of this argument. Toleration, he exclaimed, was not liberty; indeed it was "in a larger sense itself tyrannical, since the existence of an authority with the power to tolerate obstructs freedom of thought."[21] Moreover, he argued, toleration could not be construed as a right, it could only be prescribed as a duty, and therefore had no place in the Declaration. Instead, the article must be reconfigured to express the right of each individual not to be troubled in the expression of his religion. "In fact there have always been different religions," he observed. "Why? Because there have always been different religious opinions . . . which result from the diversity of characters."[22] The phrase "religious opinions" was not new, but in Mirabeau's use it went much further than simple plurality of religions. In effect it erased the very nature of religion as collective worship by assimilating it to abstract *individual* opinion. This was not a separation between religion and politics, but a radical politicization of religion, tumbling it from the realm of transcendent truth into the fallible domain of human ideas.

The first day of debate ended in a cacophony of cries and expostulations that prevented the discussion from progressing any further. The following morning, Pétion de Villeneuve rose to remind the Assembly of its grand vocation. "It is not a question here," he declared, "of making a declaration of rights for France alone, but for men in general."[23] This reminder of universalism was in fact made in the hope of deferring the bulk of the vexed religious question to the constitution, and debating only a basic individual right to protection from persecution on the basis of religious belief. To this end, the Comte de Castellane proposed to eliminate the three clauses on religion and substitute a single article: "No man may be persecuted for his religious opinions, nor troubled in the exercise of his religion."[24] This offered a clear statement of religious freedom for the individual, both in belief *and* practice, separating it from the question of religion's place in the state. A majority of the deputies agreed that such a simple formulation, understandable by all, should form the basis of rights on religious matters. Yet this was not to be. In the screaming match that followed, this straightforward article was mangled beyond all recognition, truncated and altered in a way that would profoundly shape the future of the Revolution.

In this debate, both radicals and conservative defenders of religion contributed to unseating Catholicism as the undisputed basis of French society. The revolutionary deputy from Aix, Charles-François Bouche, called in his speech for the word *culte* to be altered to "all beliefs and religious opinions."[25] Talleyrand, the bishop of Autun, shouted at his conservative opponents: "Religion? Which religion? Do you mean all religions?"[26] From the other side, Mirabeau's archconservative younger brother—familiarly called "Tubby Mirabeau" (Mirabeau-Tonneau) for his corpulence—took the tribune. "Is it your intention then," he intoned sardonically, "to create a religion of pure circumstance by permitting every shade of belief? Each man will henceforth choose the religion dictated by his passions. The young will take on the religion of the Turks; the moneylenders will turn Jewish; and women may well opt for the religion of Brahma."[27] If this cliché-ridden vision of a free market of religious, economic, and sexual convenience was intended to lampoon the immorality of his opponents, it perversely hinted that in the absence of external compulsion Catholics would rapidly abandon their faith.

Castellane answered Mirabeau-Tonneau's assertion in kind: "Do you really believe that those who are so feeble in their faith would bother taking on a new one, and submitting themselves to all the exhausting rites of the Muslim faith?"[28] In this version, the barrier to adopting Islam was not its truth or falsity, but rather the strenuous requirements of its observance—implicitly, circumcision.[29] He renewed his motion to pass a simple article protecting individuals from religious persecution.

He was drowned out by a storm of shouts and cries that the president of the Assembly found impossible to silence. An exasperated editor of the *Moniteur* explained that it was impossible to record the events "in a sitting governed by the greatest degree of disorder, where partisanship ruled, where the cry of nature, the voice of reason, the rights of man were treated with contempt, where the President, unable any longer to stave off the demands of his conscience, sought twice to resign. . . . The motion of M. de Castellane was amended, re-amended, broken up, rejoined, twisted around in a hundred ways. One could hear from every side, *I propose an amendment. I demand to speak. . . .*"[30]

The level of emotion here was at a height not seen since the night of 4 August, but here chaos, not unanimity, ruled. Half the house was seeking to pass the motion, and the other half to exclude the discussion of religion altogether from the Declaration. Since the first part of Castellane's motion, declaring the freedom of religious opinion, seemed accepted, he strategically withdrew the second part of his motion, since a freedom from persecution should protect religious nonconformity.

Jean-Paul Rabaut Saint-Étienne, the pastor and deputy, suddenly took the floor to speak for the first time openly as a Protestant, pleading passionately for protection not only for individual religious beliefs but for their public exercise. Rabaut put his argument forcefully, not only on behalf of Protestants, but for "all the non-Catholics of the kingdom," insisting upon "what you demand for yourselves: liberty and equality of rights." Speaking on behalf of Jews, he demanded the same rights "for that people torn from Asia, always wandering, always proscribed, always persecuted for more than eighteen centuries, who will take on our manners and our customs if they are incorporated by our laws, and whose morals we have no right to reproach, since they are the fruit of our barbarity and of the humiliation to which we have unjustly condemned them."[31]

Rabaut declared passionately that even if the word "intolerance" had been "banished from our language, where it will remain only as one of those barbaric and antiquated words that is no longer used, because the idea that it represents is destroyed,"[32] its inverse was equally unacceptable. "It is not tolerance that I demand," Rabaut insisted. "This word implies an idea of pity that is humiliating."[33] "Tolerance! Forbearance! Pardon! Clemency! These ideas are utterly unjust toward dissenters, wherever it is the case that religious difference, the difference of opinion, is not a crime. Tolerance! I demand that this word also be banished, this unjust word that presents us as citizens worthy of pity, like guilty men who need to be pardoned, those who have come to think differently from us through education or accident."[34]

Rabaut was so carried away by his outrage that he had to apologize for his tone. This confrontation of the Assembly with the impassioned political voice of non-Catholics did little to dampen opposition. He insisted on returning to the tribune to clarify that religion was a question of *collective* rights, since no authority could in fact prevent individual opinion. Yet in the tumult, this statement sounded mistakenly like a suggestion that "freedom of opinion" was the formulation all could agree upon.

Gobel, the bishop of Lydda who would later become archbishop of Paris, leaped upon Rabaut's point to agree that it was impossible to police opinion, and proposed that men "can be free in their opinions, even in expressing them, with the sole condition that they do not disturb public order."[35] This appeared to converge with Mirabeau's diametrically opposite reasoning—he had been arguing that the only role of the police in relation to religion should not be to enforce religious conformity, but rather to "ensure that no religion, not even your own, disturbs the public order: this is your duty."[36] These confused principles were suddenly put to a vote, and article 10 of the Declaration of the Rights of Man and Citizen was suddenly, astonishingly, agreed—in a form that nobody recognized.

The final article now read: "None shall be troubled for his opinions, even religious ones, as long as their expression does not disturb the public order established by the law." The addition of "even" had made a statement defending the rights of religious dissenters to practice their religion into a toothless protection for thoughts. Any *expression* of those opinions would now be subject to the policing of public order. In other words, French citizens had a right to believe what they liked, as long as they did not cause any problems by making it public. This was in fact *less* freedom than already existed in practice, and did nothing at all to enfranchise religious minorities.

As Castellane lamented, "The Assembly, which seemed at first to unanimously approve the new wording, then added various amendments that made it utterly opposed to my principles."[37] The religious party that had moments earlier sought to suspend the discussion of religion now applauded wildly, "above all," according to Mirabeau's *Courrier de Provence*, "on the benches of the clergy and the majority of the nobles," while their opponents "trembled to hear principles that might serve as the base for a Declaration of the Inquisition."[38]

The victory for Catholics would be a Pyrrhic one. The debate in the Assembly had unmistakably altered the terms in which religion was understood. From an established Christian faith underpinning the legitimacy of the French state, religion had become a free-floating "opinion" that was subject to the same freedoms, and the same constraints, as other forms of political association and expression. In the clash between the defenders of religion, who insisted that it must figure in the Declaration, and the defenders of liberal freedoms, who insisted that the Declaration must deal only with rights, religion was officially "politicized" in the sense of becoming a form of expression of opinion. Where religion had once been understood as a birthright offered through revelation, it was now understood—and partly as a result of the action of the religious Right—as a form of variable political choice. It would be the defenders of traditional Catholicism themselves who would fall victim to their own trap in the years to come, as later chapters will show. Moreover, it mattered less what the Declaration said than what people believed it said. In spite of the recalcitrant wording of article 10, the doors had been opened to a more radical shift.

Muslims and the Demand for Rights

Article 10 offered cold comfort to religious minorities in France. Yet to treat the text alone in abstraction from the wider social context would be a mistake. As was the case after the August Decrees, popular understandings of what had been legislated were often very different from the strict legal interpretation, and local actors implemented it in more radical fashion. Moreover, where gaps emerged that ill suited the overarching logic of the revolutionary transformation, groups and individuals taking up new roles in the emerging political structures often pushed changes from below. Sometimes these actions were conscious and concerted, and on other occasions they simply involved the decision to participate at a local level.

From the late 1770s, Jews in Alsace had been compelled to begin a degree of political participation in response to the forces unfurled against them. During the 1780s, they had sought interventions from the famous Moses Mendelssohn and Christian Dohm, a German Enlightenment writer.

Mirabeau had contributed to the popularization of philosemitic ideas in France, with his book *Sur la réforme politique des juifs,* published in London in 1787. French Jewish notables had consulted on those of Mendelssohn and Dohm; by 1789 they were well placed to take up opportunities for political participation, and did so with remarkable rapidity. In Bordeaux and other parts of southern France, Jews were more integrated into local power structures than their coreligionists in eastern France, and had more to lose with the advent of the Revolution. Yet they too took up participation in citizen militias, wrote petitions, and demanded rights. Like the Protestant deputy Rabaut, they rejected the condescending "tolerance" offered by the ancien régime, which, as their petition to the National Assembly declared, "no longer suits a Nation that wishes to base its rights on the eternal base of justice." They sought equality of individuals regardless of religion: "it would be contradictory that one should claim a right of preeminence over another, relative to the exercise of citizenship."[39] The Jews of Paris, as David Feuerwerker notes, rose above the differences of origin to claim a place for all Jews in the patriotic fraternity.[40]

Like many other groups, from people of color to women and actors, Jews did not simply wait for their fate to be decided from above by the National Assembly. They worked in local municipalities and communes, and particularly with the commune of Paris, to elaborate their own political language, and shape that of their interlocutors. Can the same be said of Muslims? We have no evidence that Muslims sought any intervention at the National Assembly or in the capital during this period. The population was certainly small, and is unlikely to have been long established: medieval Muslim presence in southern France had left no continuous legacy. Moreover, it was located primarily on the southern coast of France, in Toulon and Marseille, the principal ports of trade with North Africa, which had burgeoned in the years prior to the Revolution.

We have seen earlier in this book the evidence of Muslim participation in Freemasonry, and this may well have offered a line of communication for ideas later taken up by the Revolution. Masonic notions of equality, brotherhood, and enlightened progress were certainly a key source of revolutionary thought, symbolism, and ritual. Yet the evidence suggests the Masons were not always willing to suspend the older prejudices of religion. The register of the Grand Orient of Paris on 7 April 1786 recorded the complaint of "Brother Méhémet Çelibi, Algerian Mason," who had been rebuffed in a provincial lodge: "on arriving in Nantes, and wishing to fraternize with French Masons, he presented himself at one of the lodges of the region, the Lodge of La Parfaite, but although he was known to the president of the lodge, the brothers refused to let him enter, declaring that the difference of religion prevented them from allowing him entry to their ceremonies."[41] Mehmet requested that the Grand Orient in Paris endorse his Masonic patents in order to forestall similar problems elsewhere. Although he insisted upon his right to be admitted to the lodge regardless of his religion, he did so by seeking a special dispensation rather than by seeking enforcement of the principle itself.[42] Still, it does suggest that Muslims, too, were asserting their rights in the shifting climate of the 1780s.

In 1782, when the last parts of the former Arsenal were sold off, the Marseille Chamber of Commerce opposed the sale of the Muslim cemetery, insisting on its retention on behalf of "the large number of Algerians who are in Marseille at present."[43] In 1784, a Muslim notable in Marseille, Hadji Ibrahim Aga, addressed a petition directly to the minister of the marine, the Marquis de Castries, requesting, "in the name of the Turks settled in Marseille, the use—which he declares to be contested—of the terrain located near the ramparts and designated for the burial of Muslims."[44] No copy of the original petition survives, but Castries's response indicated that the claims of the Muslims were taken seriously: he asked the municipal authorities in Marseille to determine "for how long this terrain has been allocated for the burial of Turks, on what basis, and whether they are really being deprived of it."[45]

Here Muslims resident in France sought to assert their rights, but as *Muslims* rather than residents, subjects, or citizens. These were not the kind of "natural" rights that were understood to inhere in the humanity of the individual, but reciprocal rights assured by treaties. Nonetheless, they did not claim the rights as subjects of the dey of Algiers or the sultan of Morocco, but rather on the basis that, because they were Muslims, their right to practice their religion was ensured by the reciprocal rights of Christians in Islam. In this sense, they drew on their own tradition of rights, one deeply rooted in the *umma*, or community of believers. Islamic law gave certain rights to non-Muslims, but those rights were distinct from, and in significant ways inferior to, those of Muslims.

The late ancien régime had already begun to move toward a new model of rights, one that no longer identified the royal subject, the Catholic, and the French citizen as a single unit. The Edict of 1787, while recognizing that non-Catholics could have civil status in the kingdom and enjoy legal marriage and inheritance, reinforced a litany of disabilities and exclusions. Similarly, while the Letters Patent of 1784 accorded to the Jews of Alsace abolished the humiliating "body tax" that assimilated Jews to livestock, it reimposed a raft of exclusions and limitations on Jewish life in the region. While acknowledging the "natural" rights that inhered in all human beings, the monarchy was nonetheless incapable of dismantling the sacralized conception of hierarchical privileges that underpinned the entire social structure.

The king's sacred role was the most important element in a structure legitimated by religious tradition and extending from privileges down to disabilities and exclusions. All French subjects belonged to categories determined by this structure, and many participated in confraternities and other professional associations, alongside their place in parish and congregation. French identity *was* Catholic identity: non-Catholics had no place in this structure except through fictions of conversion or as protected foreigners. Certain professions too were excluded from civic participation. It seems bizarre today that actors should be excluded from civic rights because their profession involved deception, or that executioners, performing a function ordered by the state, should have been forbidden from ordinary social contact with their neighbors.[46] These exclusions were not simply "prejudices," but part of a system of power that proved extremely difficult to reform. The extreme resistance of the stakeholders pushed the revolutionary movement to ever-greater confrontation and overthrow of the system.

The late ancien régime had already seen moves against the existing system of hierarchy and exclusion. Liberals formed political groups to lobby for the most excluded. The most notable of these was the Society of the Friends of Blacks, founded in 1787, which agitated for the recognition of people of color as equal in humanity and therefore in rights. In April 1789, Pierre Victor Malouet, slave-owning former governor of Guiana, and now *intendant* of Toulon, protested the "prejudice" that slavery could not be improved and made more humane. If other abuses like the *gabelle*, the hated salt tax, could be reformed, then why not the plantation system? Malouet mockingly asked the Amis des Noirs why they did not form another society of Amis des Maures (Friends of Moors) in Marseille, to call the bey of Tunis to account for his part in the slave trade.[47] This comparison was obviously specious, and a respondent from the Amis des Noirs was quick to point out the flaws in the argument: "Marseille has no power over a foreign government," whereas France exercised sovereignty over its colonies.[48] Undaunted, Malouet would continue to employ such comparisons with Muslim societies freely in his arguments against the universalism proposed by his opponents.

An anonymous pamphlet titled *Le danger de la liberté des nègres* used Muslim societies in a cruder and simpler way: "in the Declaration of the Rights of Man it is said: all men are born equal and remain equal in rights. The word 'man' means 'Frenchman,' since you cannot pretend to make a Turk believe he is equal to the sultan, or tell an African outside French sovereignty that he has no right to sell his prisoner to whomever he chooses."[49] The anonymous author described the partisans of humanity as a "sect" whose real motivation was political and "Machiavellian." He warned "Negrophiles" that the blood about to be spilled would change their vaunted humanity "into an eternal monument of shame and reproach."[50]

The threat of disorder and violence was frequently used in attempts to put a "brake" on the speed of revolutionary change. In Alsace, during the rural violence of the Great Fear in 1789, crowds attacked Jewish establishments along with local monasteries and châteaus. Many Jews suffered violence and saw their shops destroyed and their letters of credit burned. Hundreds fled toward Basel and Mulhouse. Most returned within a few days, but the violence was widely reported. On 3 August, the abbé Grégoire protested the violence taking place, and for the first time raised the Jewish question in the National Assembly. On 14 August, the Jews of Bordeaux wrote a letter to thank him for his intervention, but also to remind him, and the new government, that they did *not* seek special actions on behalf of Jews, but rather the simple application of constitutional rights. They emphasized the illegitimacy of any law specifically applying to Jews "that established restrictions on the fundamental principles of the Constitution."[51] The Sephardic Jews of Bordeaux—a wealthy and privileged minority—had little historical connection to their poorer Ashkenazi coreligionists in Alsace, but they were quick to see the common dangers that now faced them. They responded with strong language that emphasized fraternity between Jews and Christians in their common political participation in the elections to the Estates General, and the formation of the National Guard. The Jew, they declared, "embraces in you his fellow citizen, his brother, and his friend."[52]

Crucial here is the role played by Jews themselves from the outset of the Revolution, not as outsiders seeking participation in revolutionary citizenship, but as revolutionary citizens-in-waiting presenting their own complaints against corporate privileges, both those traditionally employed against them, and those now seeking to position them as a group distinct from other citizens. Jews, in other words, did not simply wait for the deputies in Paris to think about them: they pushed constantly for inclusion, not only through words, but through active participation.

We have seen that in the 1780s Muslims were exerting claims for rights in France, yet those claims were made as Muslims, and not in the political language of equality and fraternity that Jews were beginning to exercise. There is no evidence in 1789 that Muslims responded to the shifting landscape of rights: their small concentration in Marseille left them far from the center of debate. Nonetheless, they emerged in a remarkable fashion at the heart of these debates, when François Hell proposed the framing of a decree to enfranchise Muslims distinctly as a group.

The Decree of 24 December 1789

On 21 December, the deputy Brunet de Latuque insisted that the National Assembly revisit what it had so far failed to declare: the eligibility of non-Catholics for all elected offices. Roederer added his voice in favor of actors, who had also been excluded from public functions in the old regime, because their profession involved falsehood. The Count of Clermont-Tonnerre went further, to insist that no profession should exclude a citizen from office. A heckler shouted out sarcastically, "And the executioner!" Clermont-Tonnerre took the heckler at his word, as he later described it: "Following my principles, I had to talk about the executioner too."[53] Characteristically, conservatives suggested an extreme case to subvert the notion of equality, only to find it taken up and adopted as part of the dismantling of ancien régime structures. Like Muslims, executioners were a handful of men across France, hardly a significant population, yet here they could play a key role in tearing the old fabric of sacral belonging. The Alsatian deputy Rewbell immediately declared that Jews did not consider themselves citizens, while the liberal aristocrat Custine insisted that the Assembly at the same time declare "the liberty of all religions."

In response to Custine's proposition, Thiébault, a priest and deputy from Metz, sought to raise the specter of foreign religions invading France, claiming that this project would apply not only to Jews and Protestants, but to atheists, deists, Muslims, animist Africans in the colonies, and Chinese (French Jesuits had an important presence in China). His description of a potential "Pacha who flees to France escaping the fatal garrote" described rather well the case of Ishak Bey, who had fled to France from the threat of political assassination in Istanbul.[54] He concluded his long submission with a demand that the Assembly not declare freedom for any religion, "neither the Jews, nor the Calvinists, nor the Ubiquitarians, nor the Puritans, nor the Anti-Trinitarians, nor the Socinians, nor the Armenians, nor the Gomarists, nor the Quakers, nor the Anabaptists, nor the Turks, nor the Persians, etc. etc.: all sects implied by the expressions of M. de Custine."[55] Thiébault depicted Calvinists as a dangerous and rebellious sect, and claimed that Jews were nihilists who believed nothing; Turks and Persians represented the two strains of Islam, Sunni and Shia, here denominated as foreign nationalities.

Two days later, on 23 December, Clermont-Tonnere gave the powerful speech regarding the extension of rights to Jews that has often been understood as a model of republican assimilation. "We must refuse everything to the Jews as a Nation," he declared, "and accord everything to the Jews as individuals." But Clermont was criticizing the application of collective laws and rights to Jews—an old regime practice—not their cultural and religious distinctiveness. Under the ancien régime, each local group of Jews was officially referred to as an extraterritorial "nation," with its own regulations, special taxes, and restrictions. This system of tolerance, Clermont insisted, "with its degrading distinctions, is so iniquitous in itself that the man who is forced to tolerate is just as discontented with the Law as he who can obtain nothing more than this kind of tolerance."[56] As Maurice Samuels has argued, in its place he did not propose a new *intolerance* of difference, insisting on cultural assimilation, but insisted that this difference was completely irrelevant.[57] "As for their unsociability, it is highly exaggerated. Is there a law that requires me to marry your daughter? Is there a law that requires me to eat hare, and to eat it with you?" Such differences, he expected, would likely disappear once barriers were removed, but even if they did not, "they are not crimes that can or should be dealt with by law." Jewish petitions had already vehemently rejected the idea that any law be applied to Jews distinct from other citizens. Clermont was following in the same line of universal citizenship. Jews must not be treated as a separate corporation—but this did not mean they would cease to be Jews. If they did not wish to be citizens, then they should not be tolerated but banished, but he cited the clear evidence of their own requests—their participation in voting, patriotic gifts, and enrollment in the National Guard—to refute the claims of Alsatian deputies like

Rewbell. Clermont-Tonnerre insisted that Jews must be offered citizenship *without* any preconditions—a fundamental and crucial statement of the nature of revolutionary citizenship.

As the wind changed, and enfranchisement of Protestants and Jews began to loom on the horizon, conservatives began to shift their position. Just days earlier, Protestants were being anathematized as a heretical and troublesome "sect." Now the abbé Maury, leader of the clerical party, made a stunning reversal. "Protestants," he declared, "have the same religion and the same laws as we do." The only difference, he continued, was in their practice (*culte*). In contrast, he declared that Jews were not a "sect" but a "nation with its own laws that it has always followed and wants to continue following." He elaborated a series of clichés about Jews as greedy exploiters of honest peasants, comparing them—tellingly—to North African pirates. In this way, Maury sought to reconstruct the singular conception of religion by identifying it with Christianity and excluding all other religions—particularly Judaism and Islam—as foreign. Speaking disingenuously in the language of fraternity, he kindly declared they should not be persecuted, but protected "as individuals, and not as Frenchmen, since they cannot be citizens."[58]

In response, a young and relatively unknown deputy, Maximilien de Robespierre, took the tribune to declare that the principle of citizenship allowed no exclusions. Any faults the Jews might have, after accounting for exaggeration by their enemies, were the result of the persecutions they had suffered, persecutions that he denounced as "national crimes." "Let us well understand," he declared, "that it can never be politic, whatever may be said, to condemn to humiliation and oppression a multitude of men who live among us."[59] Robespierre and Adrien Duport, the leader of the liberal wing, asked the Assembly simply to decree that all laws restricting admission to citizenship were invalid pending approval of the constitution. In a narrow vote, the Assembly chose to vote instead on Brunet de Latuque's decree specifically naming non-Catholics.

In some sense, this was a victory for the conservatives, since it stepped back from the full decree of enfranchisement abruptly separating the new from the old regime. Instead, it employed the same terms as those of the Edict of 1787, and implicitly offered simply to extend the boundaries of admission without establishing a principle. Opponents of Jewish enfranchisement began to push back strongly, demanding that the term "non-Catholic" be replaced with the narrower "Christian." Others, however, recognizing the unwillingness of the Assembly to grant religious privileges, sought a more subtle politics of "limited universality" driven by racial and religious prejudice.

The Prince de Broglie warned of "cosmopolites" to whom it would be dangerous to accord citizenship, and raised threats of invasion by a "Jewish colony that is constantly multiplying." He claimed if citizenship was accorded immediately, "it is to be feared that the people's hatred, excited by this decree, would lead to the most terrible excesses against the greater number of these unfortunate Jews."[60] Rewbell, a member of the Jacobin Club and deputy of Colmar, also raised the threat of violence against Jews because of "incurable" hatred on the part of the population. In an earlier statement he had suggested that the Jews themselves did not consider themselves citizens. Rewbell would later show himself one of the most implacable opponents of Jewish emancipation, but it is striking that in this debate he offered no expansion of his views that would reveal his full divergence from the position taken by his fellow Jacobins. His position defending the rights of free people of color would be strikingly different, and opponents in the Assembly would heckle him about the contradiction.[61]

The Right found itself even more divided: some still wished to block rights for all non-Catholics, while others, like Maury, supported limiting them only to Christians. Broglie, like Rewbell, opposed the notion of Jewish citizenship, but was unwilling to deny it entirely. It is in this context that François Hell, deputy of Alsace, suddenly called for a special decree of the National Assembly declaring the admission of Muslims. He drew attention to the vulnerability of French Christians in the Ottoman world: noting the recent storming of Belgrade—an Ottoman fortress—by the Austrians, he insisted on the pressing need to assure "all Muslims, and particularly the subjects of the Ottoman Porte, all the *droits de cité* in France."[62] Hell, from the easternmost province of France, was certainly in a closer position to be conscious of the Russian and Austrian war against the Ottomans: the Austrian Netherlands was just across the border, and rocked by precarious revolutions in Liège and Brabant.[63] One of the instigating factors on 5 October—surely at the very moment that news of the fall of Belgrade was arriving—had been Camille Desmoulins's claim that the Austrians had concluded a peace with the Turks, and were on the point of invading Alsace. In this sense, Hell's proposition made direct connections to French geopolitical concerns in 1789; yet it is clear that this was not the real tenor of Hell's motion.

This grand proponent of Muslim rights was the same François Hell who had been at the heart of the affair of the "false receipts" in 1778—the forgery of Hebrew documents that almost ruined the Jews of Strasbourg, leading both to murderous riots and to the mobilization of Jewish demands for change. His proposition on the rights of Muslims came at the end of what Rita Hermon-Belot has aptly called "an unusually violent attempt to impose conditions of complete inequality on Jewish citizenship."[64] Hell drew attention to the ostensible origin of Jews in Asia, while declaring he would not pronounce upon it. He called in the language of humanity for French-born Jews to "enjoy all the rights exercised by other French citizens, in conforming to the prescribed duties" but then subjected this citizenship to a series of drastic conditions: payment of taxes in addition to the current "protection"; prohibitions on all organization or petition as a group; regulations on marriages, limited to one-sixth those of other religions in any area; and bans against moneylending and property speculation. He noted that his project had been elaborated several years earlier in response to the royal *Lettres patentes* of 1784. This, he claimed, would achieve the dual goal of eliminating usury while "making all the individuals who are born and reside in the French Empire equally happy." Equally happy, but not equal—this was the protocolonial formula for second-class citizenship.

It was after this that Hell added his proposition for Muslims. The few historians who have made any reference at all to this debate of Muslims have qualified it as mere window dressing.[65] Ronald Schechter has argued that it was "only the need to appear inclusive" that can explain this "otherwise bizarre" proposition, since there was no "Turkish question" to be resolved in France. Schechter suggests Hell's gesture could be nothing but a feint "to display his generosity as a member of the French nation."[66] Yet when we look carefully at Hell's propositions, they are not so contradictory. Indeed, they demonstrate a strong continuity—as Hell himself emphasized—with the ancien régime structures for maintaining religious minorities in subordinate positions. "Toleration" of Jews meant permitting them to live in France—without persecution, but without the same rights as other French citizens. In the same way, Hell drew upon the ancien régime structures that offered reciprocal rights to Muslims to assure the safety of French citizens in the Ottoman Empire. In other words, while Muslims would obtain equivalent rights to those of French citizens, in recognition of the powerful alliances that protected them, it was by no means clear that they could actually be citizens. This differentiated form of citizenship would link rights, not to true equality, but to the pragmatic necessities of reciprocity and toleration.[67] In other words, Muslims would have rights *as Muslims* and not as citizens.

Making a separate decree of rights for Muslims would resolve the question before it arose. It would establish the precedent of dividing the question of "non-Catholics," making it easier to make a similarly distinct pronouncement on Jews as Jews rather than as French citizens. Instead, the Assembly ignored Hell's propositions, and passed the decree admitting all non-Catholics to active citizenship. Yet, fueled by the fears whipped up by the deputies of Alsace, the Assembly added a clause that maintained in place the suspension of application of these decisions to Jews.

In passing this decree that made no reference to such limitations, the National Assembly rejected the attempt to link reciprocity and rights. Instead, it pursued the path to the conception of equality that Bernard Gainot has termed "isonomy"—not simple removal of barriers to advancement, but a more absolute insistence on the equal value and rights of all citizens.[68] This citizenship was not simply based on national boundaries: it was also much larger and more universal. Ironically perhaps, we must conclude from this analysis that it was in *failing to mention Muslims* in their decree that the National Assembly accorded rights to Muslims. The decree on non-Catholics allowed them to be citizens without restriction, and not just protected foreigners. In doing so, the Assembly established a principle separating citizenship decisively from any form of religious identity, one that could not for long permit the exclusion of Jews.

This sense was clear in a report by the *Courrier de Lyon*: "For the past two days the question has been debated to decide whether Jews—who, like Muslims, have the good fortune to recognize the unity of God—and Protestants—our brothers, our compatriots, who do not believe in the transubstantiation of the host—in a word, whether any citizen, regardless of his beliefs, should share in all the dignities and the offices of the French Empire."[69] The newspaper depicted the differences between Christians, Jews, and Muslims as purely theological, and folded them into a single word, "citizen." Crucially, it did not suggest that they must abandon these beliefs, or any other difference, in order to be considered brothers and compatriots.

On 27 September 1791, as the new constitution came into force, Duport proposed that the Assembly strike down the last remaining suspension of Jews from the exercise of citizenship. The preceding two years had seen the piecemeal admission of the "Spanish and Portuguese" Jews of western France, in January 1790, then the abolition of the punitive taxes on all Jews in July. In Paris, Jews had been awarded rights by the commune, but still remained in suspension from the National Assembly. In his speech, Duport drew, not on these precedents, but rather on the admission of other non-Christians on 24 December 1789. Freedom of religion, he declared, "no longer allows any distinction to be placed between the political rights of citizens on the basis of their beliefs. And I believe also that the Jews cannot be the single exclusion from these rights, when pagans, Turks, Muslims, even the Chinese—in short, men of every sect—are admitted."[70]

This powerful universalizing logic helped persuade the Assembly to overcome the fears fanned by Alsatian deputies that local peasants would riot and massacre Jews if they were given equality. Once the principle was established that "non-Catholics" also included non-Christians such as Muslims, there was no possibility of permanently shutting out Jews from citizenship.

Maurice Samuels has recently argued that Jewish participation was not peripheral but critical to the new definition of citizenship. Revolutionaries, he suggested, "used the Jews to define a new type of nation."[71] In parallel, I would argue, revolutionaries used Muslims to help define a new type of universality, one intimately linked to the new conception of the nation as an open political community, and rendering it fundamentally different from the closed dynastic, ethnic, or confessional nation. The rights of Muslims came to form a vital element in the articulation of the revolutionary conception of equality—and therefore of the new formation of rights itself. This would become clear in June 1790, when the appearance of turbans in the National Assembly set off a remarkable sequence of events.

4. The Turbans of Liberty

In the evening sitting of the National Assembly on 19 June 1790, deputies were greeted with the unusual sight of men in turbans and long robes at the bar. The group of foreigners that had arrived to request the right to participate in the Festival of the Federation, to be held on 14 July—the first anniversary of the fall of the Bastille—was no ordinary deputation.[1] It was a coup de théâtre that produced a shockwave of emotion, an "allegorization of the human race," as one historian has aptly described it.[2] Contemporaries described the hall filled "with loud acclamations; the galleries, intoxicated with the joy of seeing the universe in the middle of the National Assembly, clapped their hands and stamped their feet."[3] The *Journal général de l'Europe* called it "even more deeply moving" than the tributes by French provinces and religious orders—and even the appearance of the victors of the Bastille— that had preceded it.[4] "These scenes," wrote Adolphe Thiers later, "which may well appear ridiculous when reading their details coldly, are among those that have the privilege of profoundly moving those who experience them."[5] Jean-Baptiste Cloots, the leader of the deputation—which was variously described as a "delegation," an "embassy," or a "committee of foreigners"— gave a rousing oration that was printed in all the major newspapers. It was not the words so much as the gestalt of the Revolution's global vocation that provoked this overwhelming response.

The consequences of this emotional shock were remarkable, similar to the emotional force of fraternity at the height of revolutionary factional struggles, which Robert Darnton has described.[6] Electrified by what appeared to be concrete proof of universal fraternity extending into the Muslim world and beyond, the deputies first voted to remove the humiliating statues of Louis XIV crushing the provinces that dominated the Place des Victoires in Paris. Then, astonishingly, radicals unexpectedly called for the abolition of noble titles. After a loud but brief exchange, deputies voted to obliterate the inherited order of rank that had structured French society for centuries, clearing the ground for a new landscape of equal citizenship. William Doyle has underlined the profound shock experienced by those who considered their nobility as much a biological as a social fact, a reality written in their blood.[7] Rafe Blaufarb has described it as a shattering of the initial revolutionary consensus based on the noble belief that the Third Estate shared "a common vocabulary of merit."[8]

For supporters, it was a major victory: 19 June was "the image of the night of 4 August," wrote the *Courrier français*, "the same patriotic fever, the same zeal, the same enthusiasm for the public good, the same sacrifices by the generous representatives of the French nation."[9] Even the royalist Comte de Paroy, who called the deputation a "grotesque masquerade," commented sardonically on its emotional impact: "It is impossible to describe the cries of joy and noisy applause provoked by the speech of the Prussian Cloots," he wrote. "The deputies imagined themselves already in a Paris that was the capital of the human race, the peoples of the earth rushing forth to admire the victors of the Bastille and listening in mute and astonished silence to the sublime and eloquent stakeholders of the Palais-Royal" (figs. 6 and 7).[10]

The deputation succeeded in its immediate political project of securing a place in the immense Festival of the Federation for 1,000 foreigners, amid the 300,000 participants from Paris and the French provinces. "This civic ceremony," Cloots declared, "will not be only the festival of the French, but the festival of the human race."[11] The very notion of "foreigner" was already in flux. By a law of 30 April 1790, foreigners born outside France had been offered French citizenship "by swearing the civic oath . . . after five years of continuous residence in the kingdom; if they have, in addition, acquired properties, married a Frenchwoman, established a business, or received letters of bourgeoisie in a town."[12] The deputation pushed even further, requesting rights not just to naturalization as Frenchmen, but to revolutionary participation *as* foreigners. In this sense, they challenged the conception of national citizenship as the underpinning of the Revolution.

The rights accorded in abstract form to Muslims six months earlier were here put into concrete form in the bodies and dress of these visitors.

Figure 6. Jean Duplessi-Bertaux, *Jean Baptiste Anacharsis Clootz, Orator of the Human Race at the National Assembly, 19 June 1790,* [1799]. Bibliothèque nationale de France.

Now, however, they went further: Muslims were not only symbols, but part of a *demand for inclusion* on the part of those on the edges of the revolutionary transformation, in ways that continued the demands formed by marginal groups in the process of the widening of rights.

From the first, responses to the deputation betray a global confusion. It was clear that those who had appeared were foreigners, but no one seemed certain what groups had been represented or in what manner. The official *procès verbale* of the session listed the participants in the deputation as "English, Prussians, Sicilians, Dutch, Russians, Poles, Germans, Swedes, Italians, Spaniards, Brabançons, Liégeois, Avignonnais, Swiss, Genevans, Indians, Arabs, and Chaldeans, etc." The *Mercure de France* added "Hindus and Turks, Tripolitanians and Moors," and observed that "this Congress declared itself charged with powers by the foreigners of all nations residing in or passing through Paris."[13] *L'espion de la Révolution française* added,

Figure 7. Jean Duplessi-Bertaux, *Jean Baptiste Anacharsis Clootz, Orator of the Human Race at the National Assembly, 19 June 1790* (detail), [1799]. Bibliothèque nationale de France.

"Negros, Syrians, Indians," and insisted that some of these had "the stamp of the galley slave on their shoulders."[14] In *Les révolutions de France et de Brabant*, Camille Desmoulins added Persians, Africans, and Ethiopians.[15] Others, from ignorance or a spirit of mischief, tacked on Chinese, Mongols, and Tartars. One enthusiastic description called it "the representation of the whole world."[16] It was so perceived, regardless of the detail of those involved.

The confusion extended equally to the status of the deputation. In his speech, Cloots presented the group not as foreign residents in France but rather as representatives of oppressed sovereign peoples, an argument he would later develop in his extended pamphlet on the "Universal Republic." The session's president, the Baron de Menou, responded in contrast to the petitioners as representatives of "other Nations," whom he exhorted to "return to the places that gave you birth" after the Festival of the Federation, and instruct their monarchs to emulate the example of Louis XVI, "the restorer of French liberty."[17]

Nowhere is this confusion more pertinent than in the case of the two North African Muslims whose scrawled names and signatures on the petition constitute the sole evidence of their presence, with no further corroboration of their identity, the reasons for their presence in Paris, or even the correct transliteration of their names. The two signatures on the document—written in a similar hand—were deciphered by John Goldworth Alger as "Si Lamr de Tripoulé" and "[Hage] Monakmeti de Tounisie."[18]

These names make some sense in Arabic: "Si" is short for "Sidi," or "Sayyidi," an honorific title, the North African equivalent of "Mister"; and "Hage" (Hajj) is the title given to those who have performed the pilgrimage to Mecca. The names "Hamro" or "Hamza" are possible, but it seems more probable that it is some transcription of "h-m-d": Hamed, Hamdu, or Hamida. Similarly, "Monakmeti" is not recognizable as an Arabic name, but could be read instead as "Abou Ahmet," a common form of honorific address known as *kunya*, based on the name of a man's firstborn son.

Ultimately, the only really salient fact about these two signatures is the illegibility of the principal name, while their Islamic titles (Si and Hage) and cities of origin (Tripoli and Tunis) are quite distinguishable. This is not the case with the other names associated with the Muslim world: "Jh. Cazadour Chammas Caldéen"; "Dom Chavich arabe," who added in Arabic *al-qass Chawich*, making explicit his title as priest; or the Greek from Istanbul who signed himself simply with the inconspicuous cognomen "Stamaty." This Greek-speaking Christian from Istanbul, who had arrived in France in 1788, wrote rapturously of the reception he had received in Paris, but noted that he took care to lie about his origins, and pretended to be a "Hellene from Argos," as inhabitants of Istanbul were despised.[19]

Early modern identity was as much a work of art as a truth-claim: studies of the ancien régime nobility suggest that origins were frequently reinvented in line with ambition.[20] The world of the Enlightenment and the salons encouraged the reinvention of lives. As Jean-Jacques Rousseau performed a new kind of "authentic" self in his *Confessions*, he recounted a series of false conversions, assumed names, and costumes, including the "Armenian" dress he assumed toward the end of his life. The revolutionary remaking of identity sat at the turning point: Vincent Denis's work suggests that the concrete practices of identification that locked identity into a single verifiable passport emerged only in early 1792.[21] From that moment onward we are able to identify individuals in the archives with greater certainty, a corollary of the actions of the state. In 1790, these practices still remained nebulous, and this not only enabled individuals to alter and exchange their identities, but allowed others to challenge the reality of the identities claimed by revolutionary actors.

Indeed, imputations of imposture swirled around the deputation from the first. Some of the wilder allegations are easily disproved: the members wearing turbans and robes were not simply actors from the Paris Opera, and the men of color were not domestic servants hired for the occasion. Yet like many such allegations, their very existence shed doubt on the authenticity of the deputation, and many later historians have therefore simply dismissed it as a "farce": a presumption facilitated by the elision of nonwhite historical agency from the Revolution.[22] Yet while we should not fall into the trap of such "unthinkability," we must recognize the possibility that elements of fiction and manipulation were at work. Like François Hell in December 1789, Cloots was not averse to using Muslims for political effect, seizing upon the ambivalent trajectories of universalism that they represented. The story of the deputation and its Muslims—and equally its people of color—is more tangled than any simple opposition between veracity and imposture might suggest. To get closer to the blank space at the center of this piece of revolutionary theater, we must investigate the populated areas around it: the meanings attached to the Muslim symbols that dominated the mise-en-scène, the ambivalent projects of Cloots himself, the juxtaposition of questions about race and enfranchisement, and the role of identifiable non-Muslim Ottoman subjects in the deputation. As we unravel the stories that were spun around this embassy, we begin to see how little effort was made by its supporters or detractors to identify the Muslims involved. Instead, it was the turban, as a signifier of religious shift, that became a point of crystallization for debates about the universal and national limits of the revolutionary transformation.

The Universal Turban

"You ask me if the Jews are admitted to the Society of the Friends of the Constitution?" wrote Edmond Géraud, a young student from Bordeaux, in April 1790. "Yes, and we would equally admit Turks, if they were aflame with the love of patriotism, with the reputation of good conduct."[23] Even before the deputation of June, sentimental gestures of universalism were preparing the ground to read Muslims as proof of the universal destiny of the Revolution.

This anticipation is evident in the tour de force by the master engraver Philibert-Louis Debucourt: his *National Almanac Dedicated to the Friends of the Constitution* from 1790 presents the coming order of the constitutional monarchy through a classical architecture studded with portraits of the king and heroes of the Revolution. Beneath this figure is a blank space onto which the calendar for the new year could be pasted (fig. 8).

On the right side of the pedestal, a crowd gathers to applaud: according to the legend beneath, the figures in the foreground are a Frenchman and an Englishman who, "united by their common love for the *patrie*, invite a crowd of residents of various countries to a fraternal confederation, among whom

Figure 8. Philibert-Louis Debucourt, *National Almanac Dedicated to the Friends of the Constitution*, 1790. Bibliothèque nationale de France.

can be seen a Turk and an Indian who stand in ecstasy at the sacred words 'Liberty' and 'Constitution'" (fig. 9). The "patrie" of this image is not co-extensive with the "nation": it is a universal idea that can unite Frenchman and Englishman, Turk and Indian. Richard Taws suggests that this "invocation of an ongoing global fraternity" speaks to a time and space of "permanent revolution."[24] If so, it is in an emotional sense rather than a political one, which finds its visual index in the "ecstasy" of the faces beneath the turbans and hands folded in a gesture of awed contemplation. At the same time, the prominence of the "Turk" Ishak Bey and the Indian ambassadors that we saw in chapter 1 suggests that this pairing was not inadvertent. The Muslim was no longer a signifier of a despotism to be hunted out, but of a fraternity to be invited in.

Figure 9. Philibert-Louis Debucourt, *National Almanac Dedicated to the Friends of the Constitution* (detail), 1790. Bibliothèque nationale de France.

Imagining the scene in the Festival of the Federation in similar terms, the writer Caraccioli employed the personified voice of "Lutèce" (Paris): "A Turk cried out in all the fervor of his soul, 'I would give all that my trade can bring me in a year to see our sultan present at this festival, and to ask him if the joy spread across so many faces is not worth as much as the ignominious glory of chopping off so many heads.'" Caraccioli's Indian regretted being born so far from Paris, even if the weather was better on the Ganges than on the Seine. His Arab improbably yearned to die on French soil, since only France could serve as the "vestibule of heaven." Meanwhile, "a Negro clapped his hands, crying that in French eyes there are no more slaves."[25] In 1789 Muslims had been drawn into the struggle over emancipation of religious minorities; in 1790 they would be linked to the struggles over color and the institution of slavery.

Such visions had become common in Paris and the provinces. In a play entitled *The Turkish Assembly*, a playwright of the rural town of

Clermont-Ferrand dressed the Revolution in Turkish costume.[26] Fatima, a young orphan, selflessly sacrifices her dowry to help poor Muslims, renouncing the possibility of marriage in order to work in the interest of the nation. At the Comédie-Française, a trilogy of short plays on the theme of past, present, and future imagined a future "Universal Federation of Peoples": its vision featured a "savage" from the Americas, a Turk, and a former slave as witness to the sentimental reconciliation of noble, peasant, monk, and bourgeois in a village. "Every people in its turn will break its chains, and France serve as example to the universe," proclaimed the mayor.[27]

A publication entitled *The National Guide* suggested a similar vision with a poem entitled "Great Prophecy." The world would soon be changed if the "philosophical senate" had its way: "We will see other laws, other tastes, other customs, and men of different kinds. The two worlds will soon at last be one, and will work together in the interest of all. Turks, Kaffirs, Canadians, under the two hemispheres, will all form just one people of brothers."[28] A pamphlet widely reprinted in the newspapers declared that the revolutionary cockade "will travel all over the world," once again citing Muslims and people of color as its first destinations.[29]

Even the most iconic of revolutionary songs could be reshaped in this universal light. "Ça ira" became popular as a work chant when thousands of ordinary Parisians participated in preparations for the Festival of the Federation in 1790. In 1791, a new verse was added to the song by a "patriot of the Savoy," a largely French-speaking province on the edge of France that remained until 1792 under the control of Piedmont. "Ah! ça ira! ça ira! ça ira!" ran the verse. "Père Gerard's almanac will be read everywhere. The Muslim, as soon as he sees it, will sell his Koran to buy one."[30] In several later songs, like "Le bonnet de la République," and "Les voyages du bonnet rouge," the idea of swapping the turban for the bonnet of liberty would appear as a trope of universal revolution.[31]

An engraving entitled *Sorceress Consulted on the Revolution of 1790* shows the three estates responding differently to a vision of the "union of the four corners of the world" (fig. 10). Women representing the continents dance in a circle: Europe is represented by a crown, America by a feathered headdress, Africa by a black slave, and Asia by a turban. It is in this heavily iconographic style of universalism—one familiar from imperial imagery of the continents bowing to Europe—that Cloots conceived his deputation. Its outcome was more powerful and more transformative than he had imagined.

Figure 10. *Sorceress Consulted on the Revolution of 1790*, 1790. Bibliothèque nationale de France.

As the engraving of the sorceress suggests, the vision of global harmony was not shared by all. Opponents at first undermined the deputation by attacking the role of foreigners. A pamphlet of September 1790 complained that provincial deputies protesting the decision to issue paper *assignats* to resolve the financial crisis had "in vain demanded to be admitted to the same tribune where every day we listen to the victors of the Bastille, the Avignonese, the Liégeois in revolt against their sovereign, the Jews, the Turks, the Arabs, even the galley slaves from Fribourg."[32] Similarly *Les actes des apôtres* ridiculed the "Genevans and Arabs, Avignonese and Jews, Paris-born Persians as well as Chaldeans and many other deputies of the globe, who have taken seats in what is doubtless the most august assembly in the universe."[33] Later, as France was threatened with war on its borders, the *Correspondence patriotique* recalled in a rather sinister fashion "the perhaps too active part that the Prussian M. Cloots, the Piedmontese M. Rotondo, and a number of other foreigners have played, without any right, in the events that have accompanied our Revolution."[34]

The royalist *Gazette de Paris* insisted that the peoples of the world gathered in the deputation should either have offered honest testimony to the advantages of traditional monarchy or have been banished as troublemakers. The Russians should support their empress, and the Poles and Belgians flee back to their countries. In the case of the Arabs, the author suggested that by supporting the actions of the National Assembly, they were apostates to Islam. "Arabs!" cried the editorial. "Ah, men raised in the fortunate climes of Arabia Felix revere the chiefs of their various tribes. Their paternal government was the very model of the monarchical government, and those Arabs who applauded were infidels to their law."[35] The "gentle" Indians, "so submissive to the leaders of their castes," were governed by law "that prohibits the mixture of races." Thus, these Indians who applauded the abolition of the aristocratic racial caste must be "cowardly and ignorant impostors."[36] The Chaldeans, the author suggested, were only too well known in Paris, but it was oddly implied they were in the pay of rich planters from the colonies.

The *Gazette* archly suggested that the whole deputation was an inversion of the famous burlesque of the Great Mamamouchi at the end of Molière's play *Le bourgeois gentilhomme*—in which the middle-class Cléonte pretends to be a Turkish prince—here with aristocrats pretending to be commoners. It was only three months after the deputation that the conservative *Mercure de France* closed the circle by suggesting that members of the delegation were paid actors. Reporting on a later deputation by Swiss residents in Paris who claimed the right to represent the interests of their people in the style pioneered by Cloots, the journal's Genevan editor, Mallet du Pan, rejected his compatriots' claims as "burlesque" and added a note comparing them with the deputation "of the universe." Now he claimed that "all Paris knows, and it is an undeniable fact, that due to a mix-up with names, the man who played the Turk in this masquerade went several days later to M. de Biancourt, deputy at the National Assembly, to collect the payment he had been promised."[37]

None of the accounts in the newspapers following 19 June contained the suggestion that the turbans worn in the deputation had been borrowed from the Paris Opera, nor did Mallet du Pan suggest this. These accusations were amplified by hostile foreign critics like Edmund Burke, who sought to discredit the participation of their compatriots in the deputation. Cloots responded to Burke, "It has been said that our Arab was a Turk borrowed from the Opera and that the Chaldean had never seen the Euphrates. These scholarly Orientals are too well known at the royal library and the royal college to bother refuting such absurdities."[38] Cloots made no reference to the two Muslims in the deputation, but this was not his only omission. Describing the "Dutch officials in flight from the prisons of the stadtholder, Vonckists from Brabant, and Swiss democrats," he mentioned three well-known names that were not present: one had "expressed his regrets" the next day for not being able to appear, and the other two (Olavidès and Trenck) were used only in illustration. It appears that Cloots was loath to name the actual members of the deputation, most likely because of their relative lack of celebrity.

Thus, the deputation both was *and* was not an imposture. While it appears clear that the members were real revolutionaries from the margins of the political scene, Cloots habitually massaged the reality of its members in hopes of enhancing its political significance. In the same way, his opponents, and particularly those outside France, insisted upon the fraudulence of the deputation to deny its claims to universality.

A German magazine of 1793 went to the trouble of engraving Cloots dressing up his "Turk" in a back room, while others donned pantomime Chinese and Native American costumes, and a monkey clapped in symbolic appreciation. A pamphlet entitled *The Foreign Deputation on the Champ de Mars: To the French Confederates* described the reception of the petitioners as "more ridiculous than flattering" and constituting a "stain that this magnificent Assembly will never wash away." The pamphlet proclaimed what would become a constant of nationalism: foreigners must obey the law of the country that tolerates them. It condemned their "absurd and inappropriate pretension" to offer approbation of those laws. At one moment it portrayed the Assembly as at the mercy of a "horde of foreigners swept up from the streets of Paris." At another it accused the radicals of xenophobia, asking of the foreigners: "Have they forgotten the gross insults heaped on them by the Lam[eths]? . . . Have they forgotten that the emissaries of a certain party in this Assembly . . . had insulted them on numerous occasions in the Tuileries, in the Palais-Royal, on the bridges, and everywhere they met them?" Although describing the foreigners as "scum," the "sewer of nations," and "the cloaca of the human race," the pamphlet did not suggest they were impostors, and even noted the presence of "several men of good faith [who] did not belong to the class of foreigners with which they appeared."[39]

The accusations of actors dressed in costumes from the Paris Opera make for an entertaining story that historians have enjoyed recounting, but they remain entirely unproven. On the other hand, it is perilous indeed to take the inimitable Cloots at his word.[40]

Cloots and the Politics of Islam

Jean-Baptiste, Baron de Cloots (or Clootz, as it was so often written by his enemies) has attracted applause and ridicule in almost equal measure. French historians from Michelet to Jaurés and Soboul—and above all his early, admiring biographer, Georges Avenel—depicted him as an innocent, almost saintly visionary, while Anglophone historians have nearly unanimously assumed that he was either mad or a charlatan or both. His claim to be the "Orator of the Human Race" has appeared to some as far beyond its time, and to others as ridiculous bombast. The prolific and scattershot nature of his writings, combined with the absence of other documentation, has favored polemical views, despite the appearance of more subtle biographies.[41]

Born in the castle of Gnadenthal near Cleves, a Prussian subject from a Dutch family, Cloots attended the Parisian Collège de Plessis, alongside the future general Lafayette and the revolutionary journalist Gorsas. At fourteen he was sent to the military college in Berlin, which he loathed. The early death of his father unexpectedly liberated him from his painful cadetship, and he returned joyfully to Paris with a large income, a copious library, and ready entry to the salons of his aristocratic acquaintances. A maternal uncle, Cornelius de Pauw, was an influential and erudite philosopher, the author of books on the Americans, Chinese, and Egyptians, and Cloots was similarly ambitious for philosophical fame. A devoted disciple of Voltaire, he set out to emulate or outshine his idol. Parisian philosophy was a crowded marketplace in which wealthy aristocrats eager for prestige jostled with Grub Street hacks desperate to make a living.[42] The Enlightenment, as Daniel Roche has shown, was not confined to *philosophes*: it drew in reforms in transport and trade, agriculture, and military technology, and even the church sponsored works that affirmed the truth of Christian doctrine through the use of reason.[43] Cloots's first target was an eminent figure of this "Catholic Enlightenment," Nicolas-Sylvestre Bergier, whose *La certitude des preuves du Christianisme* was published in 1767.[44]

Under a pseudo-Islamic anagram of "Bergier"—"Ali Gier-Ber"—Cloots produced a satire entitled *La certitude des preuves du Mahométisme; ou, Réfutation de l'examen critique des apologistes de la religion mahométane.* His gambit was simple and fairly crude: replacing Jesus Christ with "Mahomet," Rousseau with "Hakim," and Christianity with Islam. The final volume, as it appeared in 1781, had swollen into a vast and unkempt tangle of footnotes—and even footnotes to the footnotes—many running over numerous pages, and frequently banishing the main text to a single line: an apparatus worthy of Sterne, but without any detectable humor. At moments the book seemed to be condemning Islam alongside other revealed religions as a superstitious fallacy, at others admiring the progress of Islam in the world, and even declaring Islam superior to Christianity. "I can give only the most general indication of the principal countries that follow the Koran," runs one footnote, followed by a long and detailed list of the vast extent of Muslim lands. The Islamic religion, he declared, "makes great strides with every day that passes, in Tartary, China, India, Guinea, in the heart of Africa, Europe, etc." Cloots seemed to be vaunting this progress as a victory over Christianity. "The Russians and the Greeks say: *better a Turk than a Papist.* I say: *better a Muslim than a Christian.*"[45]

Where other philosophers, such as Montesquieu, Rousseau, and Voltaire—along with Cloots's uncle, de Pauw—had used Muslim societies as an opportunity to relativize, critique, and challenge European mores, Cloots did more than just "think with" Muslims. Despite his eighteenth-century fascination with encyclopedic knowledge, he seems to have been caught between the idealist progressivism of the eighteenth century and a more radical, even nihilistic materialism. Unlike many of his atheist counterparts—for example, in the d'Holbachian circle described by Allan Kors—he did not reject the Revolution, but instead took the opposite path, becoming a fervent, even fanatical revolutionary.[46] In contrast to pro-revolutionary thinkers like Condorcet or Paine who saw only fanaticism as inimical to the rule of reason, and called for full toleration of religion, Cloots argued for the destruction of *all* religion, and its replacement with philosophy.

But Cloots still found himself on the margins of French intellectual life. His second book claimed the title of "Gallophile," a term he coined to describe his aggressive cultural alignment, directed against the Anglophilia so prevalent among many French thinkers. Cloots depicted Paris as the center of all that was great, but as the capital of the *world* and not just France, a new Rome for atheists and deists of all countries. The Muslim world took a subordinate place in this European cosmopolitan unity that vaunted civilization above freedom: "Enlightened kings are never wicked; ignorance is the mother of tyrants."[47] Like other Enlightenment philosophers, Cloots was quick to condemn the "pirates" of Algiers as a "gang of thieves, assassins, scum-suckers," and willing to donate to any "subscription to exterminate these pirates in their hideout." He declared too that France must "leave Tipu Saib to be crushed by the Marattas" so that the latter could rid India of the

British.[48] He hailed Catherine's annexation of the Crimea, declaring that it would "awaken the Turk, and put him on a more respectable footing" and predicted that Crimea would soon become an independent power, a flourishing "republic" from which France would benefit.

Like his hero Voltaire, the young Cloots felt confident to pronounce on the world without having seen much of it. In the late 1780s, however, he set off on an extended grand tour, passing from Greece to Turkey and returning via Italy and North Africa. Visits to the Muslim world had become more frequent in the grand tour of the 1780s: Jeremy Bentham traveled to Istanbul around the same time, as did Lady Craven, who published her *Journey through the Crimea to Constantinople* in 1789. In the same year, the Welsh radical Richard Price received a letter from his friend John Howard, who was undertaking a similar journey, which he never completed, as he fell ill and died in the Crimea.[49]

Cloots left no record of the African leg of his journey, other than a brief reference in a letter to be published in Camille Desmoulins's newspaper in 1790. "Liberty," he wrote, "belongs to the entire human race, and I would have come from China to serve as a sentinel to your admirable constitution. I was visiting glorious Greece, when the first Assembly of Notables shed a ray of hope on a France in chains; and the south wind sped me toward this promised land. Alas! The aristocracy of the *parlements* pushed me back into Africa. I did not return to Gaul for good until the second Assembly of Notables: I crossed the Tagus, the Ebro, and the Pyrenees, thanking the God who had secured you a double representation, a sure presage of the prodigies that were to come."[50] We cannot know whether Cloots made connections in North Africa that would bring him into contact with Muslims traveling through France in 1790, or whether this journey helped instead to spur him to imagine North Africans among his deputation. It is characteristic, however, that in his brief account, Cloots subordinated the journey to his own personal drama that pitted his atheism against the forces of the religious establishment.

While appearing as the "ambassador of the human race," Cloots saw his role equally as ushering in a new age of reason in which all religion would be banished from the earth. His speech opened with a reference to the emperor Julian the Apostate, who renounced Christianity in the fourth century CE. Despite his grand rhetoric of universal fraternity, at the heart of his project was the religious question. In the same way that he believed his book on "Mahometism" was a kind of anti-Bible, he also conceived of the presence of Muslims in the deputation as the chief demonstration that the reign of religion had come to an end with the new era of the Revolution.

In October 1790, Cloots wrote again of his work on his "Muslim book" of 700 pages, which had cost him 15 hours of work per day. "But the circumcised will no longer hold me captive," he joked, in his characteristically off-color fashion. "I would rather give up my foreskin." He was now working on a new tome driven by his "patriotic zeal and [his] hatred for the aristocrats." He claimed this hatred was an "innate idea" contradicting the theories of Locke and claiming—at least in a gestural way—the existence of absolute and natural principles prior to human social experience. Yet at the same time he flattered himself on a style that "could win over the people with images that seemed drawn from the pages of the Koran and the Bible."[51] He would never deliver such a grand work—his revolutionary writings ultimately amounted only to jottings, correspondence, and speeches, which he would bundle together hastily into pamphlets. Instead he would rebadge the "Muslim book" as his antireligious masterpiece—a revolutionary bible.

The unexpected success of the deputation also transformed Cloots from a peripheral figure to a household name. Prior to 19 June he had spoken twice at the Jacobin Club, and written a few short letters to newspapers. Suddenly he emerged as a revolutionary voice, publishing 10 articles in the *Chronique de Paris* alone in 1790, 13 in 1791, and 21 in 1792.[52] He no longer carried his title of "Baron" since the abolition of noble titles: the measure did not apply to foreigners, but Cloots thus "naturalized" himself by ideological sacrifice. He went a step further and "debaptized" himself "in order to be logical," he wrote later.[53] Cloots was the first to adopt a revolutionary pseudonym: Anacharsis, after a Scythian philosopher and the hero of a popular novel of 1788.[54] This practice was later taken up by radicals under the Republic, from Anaxagoras Chaumette to Gracchus Babeuf, and by many ordinary French men and women.[55]

We may see in this the foundation of Cloots's politics, which was religious in its antireligious fervor, evangelistic in its atheism. His self-styled "civic crusade" was primarily against Catholic Christianity, yet in this struggle it was Islam that figured most frequently as reference, weapon, tool for satire, model, symbol. Cloots did not wish simply to abolish religion but to replace it with his own universal system, a morality "for all times and places," that would render the Koran obsolete, along with the Gospel and the

Zend-Avesta. In a 1791 pamphlet, Cloots presented the hostility toward the deputation as a purely personal struggle between himself and the "satraps." Long before the revolution, he declared, he had prepared an "arsenal": a repertoire teeming with viziers, janissaries, muftis, sultans. Islam was Cloots's stock-in-trade, a weapon in his assault on Christianity, and a tool in his revolutionary political ascent.[56]

Cloots openly embraced this kind of instrumentalization, which he exercised most egregiously in the case of people of color, who found themselves excluded from citizenship in the early period of the Revolution.[57] The whites of the colonies saw an opportunity to resist colonial reforms and reinforce their autonomy and racial privilege, on the model of the American Revolution. The representatives of people of color formed a lobby group under the leadership of Julien Raimond, a Saint-Domingue planter of mixed descent. While claiming equality, they did not at first oppose slavery, as some of them were slaveholders themselves.[58] They sought alliances with white planters, but met with no success, and Raimond was refused accreditation from the National Assembly as a colonial representative.

Raimond was not present in Cloots's deputation, but a number of other "gens de couleur" were among the 36 deputies. In one sense this might appear strange, since they were subjects of the French king, and not foreigners. On 28 March 1790 the National Assembly had accorded them, in principle, the rights of active citizens, but those rights were contested by the colonial authorities. Thus, their presence suggests that for Cloots, "foreigner" meant not exactly foreign, yet not fully French: he harnessed into his political theater various vectors pushing for greater inclusion in the revolutionary settlement. Cloots presented these Caribbean French as "Americans" in his description, at the same time offering the visual éclat of the black African alongside the turbaned Muslim of Asia and the Europeans, appearing to bring to life the iconography of the "four quarters of the world."

Attacks on the deputation also mixed in elements of racist vilification. Antoine-Francois Bertrand de Molleville, Louis XVI's minister of foreign affairs, claimed in his memoirs that "M. de Boulainvilliers, who was there in the Assembly on that day, recognized in the deputation the negro servant of one of his friends. 'Ah, Azor!' he exclaimed, 'what are you doing here?' 'Sir, I am playing the African,' replied the negro." The following day, Bertrand continued, "we learned that this embassy of all the peoples of the earth . . . was entirely composed of vagabonds and foreign domestic servants, paid 12 livres a head."[59] If the putative "Azor" was really a Parisian servant, then he was neither a vagabond nor a foreigner; but the word *nègre* was enough to render him unfit for political participation.

The people of color in the deputation were certainly not Cloots's paid dupes: a year later, after Cloots had written in support of Barnave and the colonial lobby, the "Citizens of Color and Free Negroes" wrote him an open letter in Brissot's *Patriote français* and the *Moniteur*. "Monsieur," they wrote, "you announced yourself as the ambassador of nations and the Orator of the Human Race; it is in this quality that you appeared last year at the bar of the National Assembly. Several of us accompanied you. By what strange opposition of principles have you therefore improved the decree of France's legislators that accorded us the eternal rights of liberty that you claimed for all the inhabitants of the earth?" They insisted that Cloots must choose between "admitting that you have betrayed your mission, or proving that we are not members of the human race."[60]

In the *Patriote français*, Cloots responded to the accusations made against him characteristically by denouncing his accusers as hypocritical slave owners. He compared the "clamor of certain moralists against your colonial regime" with that of the pacifist Quakers against "our murderous and conservative artillery." The first duty of a state was to self-preservation, he argued: "this is so true that if this survival required barbaric sacrifices to Moloch, to Brahma, to Toutatis [a Celtic god], we would have to tolerate the sacred butchery like so many other religious absurdities." His system of "general liberation," he declared, admitted "neither colonies nor metropoles, neither differences of color nor differences of nations," and only a little patience and prudence were needed to arrive at this goal. He refused to attach himself to any "fraction of humanity" in his commitment to the absolute sovereignty of the human race.[61] Cloots's universalism was sincere, yet he deployed it here to paper over the inconvenient claims of particular groups.

The citizens of color themselves in their reply in June revealed similar contradictions, insisting that while they did not actively support slavery, the unfree blacks were "not yet ripe for liberty, and must be led there with wisdom." They should become the "pupils" of their free brothers. Moreover they made numerous dubious references to Cloots's foreign origins, to "German nobles," and compared him to the counterrevolutionary Hertzberg. Finally, leveraging a belief in his probity, they exhorted him to "consult your great principles, they will always be worth more than this mysterious politics, which is no more than the seal of ignorance."[62] The sense of a "politics" that no longer represented the values of the revolution, but rather a set of byzantine competing interests, would help alienate many in the revolutionary party.

Marisa Linton has shown how personal friendships and interests interacted with ideological positions in the factional divisions of Jacobin politics.[63] These dynamics worked a little differently for Cloots, an outsider who found himself propelled to the heart of revolutionary politics, first as a writer and orator, and later as a naturalized Frenchman and deputy to the National Convention. Cloots sought to integrate himself so fully into revolutionary politics that he refused to belong to any faction—or, more accurately, sought to belong to *all* of them at once. Noting this fence-sitting indecisiveness, Albert Mathiez memorably remarked that Cloots "had no fixed position but his redemptive atheism."[64]

The new political alignments were not only personal: they were formed and broken in the storm surge of a revolutionary politics racked not only by war, famine, and counterrevolution, but also by the revolutionary demands of newly politicized individuals and groups pushing in from the margins—a "revolution from below" coming not only from the popular movements in Paris and the provinces, but also from people of color, the enslaved, women, peasants, and others. These struggles are imperfectly illuminated, since the documentary record here is so much sparser than for the debates and experiences of elites; even fainter is any account of what Muslims—if indeed the participants in the deputation of 1790 were what their signatures suggest— might have felt or demanded from such participation. The closest we can come is through the supposed "Turk"—in reality a Christian Arab from the Levant—who, remarkably, delivered an address to the National Assembly. His trajectory can tell us something about the space of Muslim participation that remains blank in our account.

The Turkish Deputy

It is a disappointing fact that the first speech delivered in the National Assembly by an Arab was left unrecorded for posterity. Just over a year after the Assembly came into being, and with it the history of the modern French Republic, the man who signed himself in French and Arabic "Dom Chawich, Arab" seized his opportunity to speak. Yet from the first, it appears that this historic moment was shadowed by ambiguities. Firstly, no one in the Assembly, whether journalist or stenographer, was able to comprehend his words: the acoustics of the indoor riding academy where the Assembly met were notoriously bad, with a cavernous roof above a wooden floor and noisy galleries overlooking serried ranks of benches beneath. Indeed, one account claimed that he spoke "half French, half Arabic, so that he was only understood by experts."[65] Bertrand contemptuously wrote that "the Turkish deputy, or supposedly such, then took the floor, and stammered a phrase in such bad French that no one could understand anything."[66] Newspapers nonetheless speculated that he expressed "the grand idea he had formed of the French Nation" and the "constitution destined to ensure the happiness of the universe."[67]

This was the understanding of the session's president, the Baron de Menou, who replied that "it was Arabia that once gave Europe lessons in philosophy; it was she who, having guarded the treasure of scientific knowledge, spread across Europe the sublime conceptions of all parts of mathematics."[68] Menou invited all the foreigners, to the number of 1,000, to attend the Festival of the Federation, but asked that they return to their countries afterward and instruct their monarchs to follow the example of Louis XVI.

Menou here read "Arab" as "inhabitant of Arabia." In fact, Chawich was born in the Palestinian city of Acre. Moreover, he had come to France in 1786, had married a Frenchwoman, and therefore, according to the new laws, was entitled to be a citizen—perhaps the first to consider himself a French Arab. "Chaviche, rue du Petit Lion 7" figured on the list of the first Parisians to join the Jacobin Club in December 1789 along with Chénier, Desmoulins, and Robespierre.[69] Few foreigners had been so quick to join the new radical movement, and this is perhaps what gave Chawich the particular distinction of speaking in the National Assembly.

Chawich's early money-making efforts had been tied to the counter-Enlightenment entrepreneur Jacques Cazotte—self-styled member of the "illuminati"—who employed him to produce new versions of "The Arabian Nights," through newly discovered or invented tales.[70] Chawich had already argued with Cazotte over the latter's excessive adaptation of the Arabic texts: Cazotte joked that he had been guilty of "*lèse-Arabie*"—offending against the dignity of Arab culture.[71] By 1789, the partnership was over, and Cazotte reported that "I have split entirely with my Arab, who has taken all the money and left me to pay for all the supplies . . . after delivering a number of unfavorable opinions about my way of thinking and acting to the *nègre* called Chamay, who has decided to take him on."[72] This use of the term "negro" appears to have been a racial slur against Chawich's employer, Joseph Chammas, who also participated in the deputation of 19 June. Cloots declared that he had given Chammas a civic certificate in his capacity as "Orator of the Human Race at the National Assembly of France," declaring to "all the free men of the earth" in the "Capital of the Globe," that Joseph Cajadaer Chammas, "member of the oppressed sovereign of Mesopotamia, had the honor to attend the Federation of the 14 July, by virtue of a decree emanating from the august French Senate on 19 June of the Year 1."[73] Chammas had been living in France for decades: his uncle, "Ciriac Cazadour Chammas, native of Mesopotamia," was naturalized French in 1741 and adopted his nephew from Diyarbakir in 1763, giving him French nationality.[74] Cloots was not at all averse to dissimulating such details in order to bolster his claims to speak on behalf of a global constituency, claims very much focused on securing a place in the French political scene.

On 14 September 1790, a letter from Chawich appeared in the *Chronique de Paris*, responding to the accusations of imposture in the *Mercure*. The embassy, he wrote, "which gave rise to the famous decree of the same day, is one of those great events that good citizens applaud and aristocrats curse." He cited the story of the *Mercure de France*, and deplored its lies. "I am the Turk who appeared at the bar of the National Assembly under the banner of M. de Cloots," Chawich declared. "I knew this Prussian only from his writings on Muslims and Jews, until the abbé Delaunay, my colleague at the Royal Library, introduced him to me personally. I admired the great thoughts of this orator of humankind, and I acted in consequence." Chawich denied the reports that he had asked for alms from M. de Biencourt. Was it likely, he asked, that he would ask for money from deputies when foreign millionaires were among the deputation? Turning to the accusation that he was dressed in a false costume, he declared that the occident would soon tire of Du Pan, and "the orient will be the refuge of the apologist for despotism. Let him come to my house the day before his departure, and I will clothe his nakedness in an old dolman and an old turban, and he will see whether my wardrobe is borrowed from the opera." He held no grudges, he declared, "I call on Mahomet and all the prophets in witness."[75]

This invocation of the Prophet of Islam by a Christian priest was hardly probable or acceptable even in a Muslim society. It speaks to the importance given to Islam in the deputation: Chawich's presence as an "Arab" was not enough to achieve the necessary degree of political significance. Instead, he had to describe himself as a "Turk" and surround himself with references to Islam. Was this merely the work of Cloots, writing under the name of his protégé? We cannot know for sure, but we may see that Chawich had his own political voice. On 13 May 1791, a debate raged in the Jacobin Club around the rights of free people of color, in which Cloots had taken the side of Barnave and Lameth against the Amis des Noirs, who supported emancipation for free blacks and enslaved Africans. The society's records indicate that "an Armenian, or Turk, appeared at the tribune, and spoke in favor of the free people of color. He gave MM. Barnave and Lameth a small lesson, through the story of a father who said that a single false step can spoil the fruits of fifty years of virtue."[76]

If this was Chawich, as all indications would suggest, he had marked his rupture with Cloots—who surely would never forgive him—for reasons we do not know. It is striking that he should choose this question of the universality of rights to make his statement. It speaks to the powerfully different motives of those who participated in the deputation of 19 June 1790, and suggests that for this Arab "Turkish deputy" that moment had been one of presenting and demanding a set of universal rights that would rise above religion and color. We do not know whether the signatures that lie alongside his on the petition were really those of visiting Muslims from Tunis and Tripoli. In the story of Chawich himself, and the analogous struggles of the citizens of color, we can sketch something of what that participation could have meant.

At this same moment, in May 1791, the *Journal des clubs ou sociétés patriotiques* published its reflections on the Jacobin Club, which, it argued, was still the "temple of liberty" despite the entry of more ambivalent figures: fanatics, hypocrites, republicans. The editorial insisted that this was the moment for unity, for common citizenship, for reconciliation—even with aristocrats. "Although this word may burn the ears of a patriot," the editorial continued, "we must accustom ourselves to listening to and forgiving him, just as a Catholic must learn to see a man and a citizen in a Protestant, in a Jew, in a Mahometan."[77] The journal placed no condition or exclusion on such citizenship: it accompanied this statement with no trappings of exoticism or orientalism, or byzantine strictures concerning Islam. Instead, it asserted a universal conception of citizenship that could bridge the gaps between Muslims, Jews, and Christians of various confessions. This articulation came at a moment when the struggles within the church itself were on the brink of eruption into outright schism: an explosion that would alter forever the place of religion in the revolutionary landscape.

5. The Constitutional Mosque

In the course of 1791, as France, struggling to forge a new constitution, was torn apart by religious conflict over the relationship between church and state, a strange new landscape took shape in the imagination of revolutionaries and their opponents. If their words were to be believed, mosques and minarets were springing up all over France like mushrooms, markers of the Revolution's utter sacrilege of the Christian order, or of a new, regenerated France in which intolerance was banished, depending on the viewer's perspective. Yet it was all imaginary: apart from the small and relatively unknown prayer spaces connected to Muslim cemeteries in Marseille and Toulon, there were no mosques in France and none would be built for more than a century. On both sides of the deepening political and religious divide, mosques and muftis, the Koran and the Prophet, emerged as staples of speeches, petitions, satires, sermons, dialogues, songs, cartoons, and engravings, invoked to attack, defend, or explain the new order.

At the eye of this storm was the clerical oath: as Timothy Tackett has shown, across this period the oath became a "veritable obsession" that spread into all the forms of popular consciousness, so that by 1792 "even young children might be seen re-enacting the oath ceremony as they played in the streets."[1] Its consequences shaped the course of the Revolution itself, not just in the heated atmosphere of the Assembly and the Paris clubs, but in villages and towns all across France. The oath was not simply a matter of loyalty to France or to the Revolution. It marked a radical split in the conception of religion itself. It is this shift that was often imagined in Muslim clothing, in a landscape of the imagination strangely dotted with minarets, pagodas, temples, and synagogues. Tackett notes the "strikingly similar language" of clerical protest that included references to Protestants, Jews, and Muslims.[2] But this language was shared, even more surprisingly, across the revolutionary spectrum.

In April 1791, the department of Paris declared that all religious edifices should be marked with exterior indication of their usage. In the National Assembly the abbé Couturier protested that the intent of this decree was to establish "every kind of sect in our former churches . . . to convert them into mosques, into synagogues, into temples for Lutherans and Anabaptists, into pagodas where the Armenians, the Chinese, the Turks, and the Persians will come to worship their false divinities." If two years earlier, he cried, "someone had dared propose that you convert by decree a single church into a mosque, or into a Protestant temple, would you not have rejected indignantly such a proposition?"[3] The speech was interrupted by "prolonged laughter."[4] Yet rumors that Jews and Muslims were about to acquire disused religious buildings continued: it was said that the Jews had "fixed their eyes on the Jesuit Church of Saint-Antoine," and the Muslims were about to turn the former convent of the Feuillants into a mosque.[5] *L'ami du roi* called on the municipality to protect churches leased by refractory congregations in the same way that the people supposedly protected Jews and Muslims: "The department must be aware that the people will let the Jews and Muslims exercise their religion publicly in Paris, but turn in fury on the churches of the Roman Catholics."[6]

Later the same year, discussing the question of whether priests who had refused to swear the civic oath should be allowed to open their own churches, the Breton deputy Sylvain Codet declared that if it was simply a difference of "religious opinion," then they should certainly "have their temples, as the non-Catholics have their chapels, the Jews their synagogues, and the Muslims their mosques."[7] On 21 October, in a furious debate regarding the non-juring priests, the deputy Davigneau defended their right to dissent by insisting that no single religious doctrine could dominate over another: "Can you prevent Paris," he asked, "from having its temples, its churches, its rites, its priests, its synagogues, its mosques?" If not, he insisted, "you cannot prevent the nonconformists from remaining peacefully attached to their rite."[8] In a letter, an octogenarian priest explained in despair that he was reduced to a choice between abjuring his faith and dying of hunger. "Cruel!" his letter cried. "While you open temples to Protestants, to Jews, to Mahometans, you close the churches to me, and you take from me even the consolation of celebrating the sacred mysteries."[9]

In this sense, in the course of 1791, Muslims came not only to represent the constitutional protections offered to religious minorities, including non-Christians, but to play a more intimate role at the heart of the agonizing struggles over the clerical oath. Muslims had been admitted to largely hypothetical rights of active citizenship at the end of 1789; along with Protestants, Jews, and a panoply of other groups, they became symbols of the breakdown of the traditional Catholic order. At the same time, they could play the inverse role precisely as demonstrations of a new, tolerant, universalist France, as we saw in the deputation of 1790. However, in the religious struggle of 1791 provoked by the institution of the clerical oath, different dimensions of Islam's meaning and uses came most intensely to the fore. "Freedom of religion"—once anathema to the defenders of Catholicism—was now invoked by the very parties who had furiously rejected it. The rights accorded to Muslims—since Jews remained incompletely enfranchised until September 1791—were brandished, and exaggerated, as a convenient example. This increasingly elaborate but useful fiction of a Muslim France was also enlisted by revolutionaries themselves, in order to position Catholicism, not as the majority or dominant religion, but rather as one religion among others.

As a quantitative indication of the amplitude of the phenomenon, an analysis of the collection of pamphlets at the Jesuit Library in Lyon (digitized through Google Books), which is particularly complete for the religious struggles of 1791–1792, reveals that out of a sample of 60 pamphlets dealing explicitly with the clergy, the clerical oath, and the Civil Constitution of the Clergy, 15 (25 percent) mention Muslims, and 31 (52 percent) mention Jews. Indeed, the references to Muslims in this literature around the oath are so numerous that we can only investigate some of them here.

Revolutionary images of the period also drew on these meanings in surprising ways. In a monumental engraving by Louis Le Coeur to celebrate the new constitution, massive stone tablets are affixed to a giant fasces of the 83 departments bound around a club (the symbol of Hercules-People), topped by a liberty bonnet and a French rooster seeing off a vulture (fig. 11). The muscular figure of the Nation is writing a half-finished Constitution, her pen poised on the line referring to the king, who, in June 1791, with his family and servants, had attempted to flee toward the border. Arrested and returned under the fiction that he had been saved from "kidnappers," Louis was reinstated only on condition of accepting the constitution: he is otherwise nowhere to be seen in this image.

Figure 11. Louis Le Coeur, *The French Constitution*, 1791–1792.
Bibliothèque nationale de France.

The column sits atop a plinth built from the blocks of the Bastille. On one side of the column, a priest raises his arm fervently to swear the civic oath; on the other, citizens gaily bedecked in tricolor cockades dance in a merry circle. In front of this celebration of constitutional joy is an Englishman in a brown traveling coat who, according to the caption, "is wasting his time" attempting to explain the constitution to a "rich slave of Asia" in his white turban and red dalmatic coat (fig. 12): "In his country, this unfortunate man does not even know the name of Liberty!" But, the caption adds, "his turn will come. In the meantime, how happy everyone is, especially this troop of children already soldiers of the *patrie*!"

This image speaks to a more complex set of concerns than the euphoria around the "turbans of liberty" we traced in the last chapter. The Muslim's reluctant enlightenment serves as a counterweight to a peasant family—the

Figure 12. Louis Le Coeur, *The French Constitution* (detail), 1791–1792. Bibliothèque nationale de France.

mother wearing an ostentatious cross, and the father kneeling obediently, clutching the pope's condemnation of the Revolution, which had been issued on 10 March 1791. The constitutional *curé* points out their misunderstanding. The resistance of the Muslim is in some sense parallel to that of the ignorant villager: his inevitable recognition of the Constitution projects and prefigures that of these good but backward peasants.

Here, the universalism that Muslims had come to symbolize was being used for quite different ends: to resolve the religious contradictions that threatened to upend the constitution before it was even promulgated. The opponents of the constitution too would wield their own Muslims, mosques, and Korans in their attempts to discredit the new order.

Islam and the National Religion

Tous les cultes seront permis,
Et même celui de Moïse.

> De Mahomet le paradis
> Sera vanté dans mainte église.
> Comme à présent dans ces cantons
> D'être conséquent l'on se pique,
> De toutes ces religions
> Nous exceptons la catholique.
>
> Every sect we'll tolerate,
> Even the one that Moses led.
> Many a church will now promote
> The paradise of Mahomet.
> Since nowadays in all these regions
> We all pursue the same logic,
> Of all these various religions
> We just reject the Catholic.[10]

As this sarcastic ditty from a counterrevolutionary newspaper suggests, the conservative vision of France in 1791 was one in which the rights accorded by revolutionaries to Jews and Muslims were understood as leading not only to the loss of Catholic privilege, but to the destruction of Christianity in general. As early as 1789, pamphlets began to attack the new arrangements of the church as unholy: *Le naviget-anticyras; or, The System without Principle* opposed the toleration of other religions. Acknowledging that "all men are free" in mere questions of ideas and feelings, the author insisted that this freedom did not apply to religious faith. Giving even social rights to non-Christians, he argued, invalidated the church's teachings: "If it were free for men to follow whatever religious opinion they considered appropriate; if it did not matter whether they were Christian, Jew, Muslim, pagan, deist, or atheist, depending on the country in which they were born; if they could go to heaven by error or falsehood, as well as by the truth, why announce the contrary?"[11] The author called upon French Protestants to forget their differences and join Catholics in fighting these dangerous unbelievers, the Muslims, Jews, and atheists who were responsible for divorce and the marriage of priests. He warned that Dutchmen, Turks, and Jews would be moving in next door.[12]

The *Parliament's Thanks to the National Assembly* opened in a satirical vein by heaping ironic congratulations on the "sacred patriotic orgy" of the new regime.[13] Religion, it declared, is the foundation of empires: remove this pillar and the whole edifice comes crashing down. The pamphlet predicted that unrestricted freedom of religion would lead to a new Saint Bartholomew's Day massacre and a "holocaust" of corpses. Religious prejudices are necessary, since "a Jew, a Lutheran, a Mahometan, a Catholic, and a Mandarin will never sympathize with one another."[14] The pamphlet nonetheless reflected the outcomes of the struggles over the Declaration of the Rights of Man and Citizen: "Far from forcing each citizen to accept our way of adoring God, we can close our eyes to his beliefs, without allowing him to preach his dogmas in public." In what country, the pamphlet asked, "can two ministers share the pulpit to preach J[esus] C[hrist] and Mahomet, Jupiter and Diana?"[15]

At least one minister appears to have done just this. During Easter 1790, in the Parisian church of St-Germain-des-Prés, the vicar Isaac Jean Joseph Cassius delivered a "patriotic sermon." "If there was ever a time when we needed the precious peace sent from heaven," he declared in the opening of his sermon, "it is in this moment that we are living. What troubles we face, what agitation of spirits! Where are the friends of peace today? We are Christians, as we would be Mahometans."[16] Quoting Mésenguy's *Exposition de la doctrine chrétienne*, he left off the completion of the statement: ". . . as we would be Mahometans, if we had the misfortune of being born in a country professing the religion of Mahomet."[17] The Jesuit version emphasized the importance of religious instruction. The vicar Cassius agreed that a faith determined only by accident of birth was "weak," and now believed faith should be a conscious ideological choice. French Christians could accept the Revolution by recognizing that God's purpose was at work through it. Cassius lauded the model of a Jewish Maccabee "dying for the salvation of the Republic," and cited Jupiter, Apollo, Minerva, and the nymph Egeria as precedents for gods adopted by the state.[18]

The day after this sermon was delivered, a Carthusian monk, Christophe Antoine Gerle, unexpectedly raised a motion in the National Assembly to recognize Catholicism as the national religion. Dom Gerle had become a deputy in December 1789, and was appointed to the Ecclesiastical Committee tasked with reforming church organization. Although a member of the Jacobin Club, he was under intense pressure from the conservative clerical party; abruptly interrupting a discussion on church finances, Gerle insisted the Assembly should act to defend itself against accusations that the committees were under liberal control: "To silence those who slander the Assembly, saying that it wants to destroy religion, and to calm those who fear that it will accept all religions in France, we must decree that the Catholic, apostolic, and Roman religion is and will always be the religion of the nation, and the only one authorized for public worship."[19]

This was not the first time the issue had been raised. In February, a speech by Garat on the "barbarity" of those who renounce their civic responsibilities to enter religious confraternities led to cries of blasphemy and provoked the bishop of Nancy to raise a motion to decree Catholicism the national religion.[20] A counterrevolutionary pamphlet declared that "the sudden explosion provoked by this motion is exactly what would have been produced in an assembly of zealous Catholics by a proposition to accept the religion of Mahomet."[21] The record suggests, however, that it was the attempt to *legislate* the dominance of the Catholic Church that was rejected: at this point, at least in their language, deputies—even Garat—insisted that the dominant and national character of the Catholic Church was supremely obvious, and thus did not need legislative approval. The conservative Catholic wing was torn by a paradox: although denying that the Assembly had any jurisdiction over the church, they demanded it legislate the dominant status of their religion.

Like the earlier motion, Dom Gerle's was disallowed for its failure to follow process. By the time the motion was presented in due order the following day, both "patriotic" and "aristocratic" resistance had solidified. The deputy Bouchotte rose to protest that the Catholic religion was self-evidently the "first" religion in France, and any decree declaring it the national religion would be superfluous and an act of fanaticism. "Is not religion independent of the actions of the human spirit?" asked the Baron de Menou, proposing a somewhat disingenuous countermotion: "The National Assembly declares that out of respect for the Supreme Being, out of respect for the Catholic, apostolic, and Roman religion, the only religion funded at the state's expense, it cannot pronounce on the question submitted to it."[22] Dom Gerle immediately renounced his own proposition and embraced Menou's logical but meaningless formulation. A furious and convoluted discussion then ensued. Just prior to the recommencement of the debate, the deputies of Alsace had presented a new petition against admitting Jews in their region to the rights of citizenship. Duval d'Eprémesnil now warned against an outbreak of religious violence against minorities: "Beware of the terrifying comparison that will be made when the Jews want to . . ."[23] At this, the "murmurs" of the Assembly became so loud that he was forced to take his seat.

The decisive moment finally came when Mirabeau rose and made a wild and theatrical gesture in the direction of the Louvre. Pointing to a window of the manège, he declared chillingly: "From this very tribune at which I speak, I see the dreadful window from which a king, the assassin of his subjects, mixing earthly interests with those of religion, gave the signal for the Saint Bartholomew's Day massacre."[24] It was a true coup de théâtre: all of the deputies turned toward the window (which of course had no actual connection to the massacre two centuries earlier). A master orator, Mirabeau marshaled the whirlwind of emotion in the Assembly and gave it structure, so that many deputies interpreted their confusion of sensations as a heroic resistance to tyranny and intolerance.[25] As the leaders of the clerical party— Abbé Maury, Duval d'Eprémesnil, and the younger Mirabeau—left the Assembly, they were threatened by angry crowds.

In July 1790, the Ecclesiastical Committee reported on its deliberations regarding the reform of the church in France, and proposed a new civil constitution that would transform the clergy into functionaries of the state. At the same time, the state would not recognize the Catholic faith as having any special status in relation to other religions. In response, the conservative clerics began to fulminate against the supposed consequences of this new religious policy in destroying the catholicity of France. The bishop of Toulon wrote in his *Lettre pastorale* of July 1790, "This is the triumph of the philosophy that dreams of annihilating all religions by setting one against the other." He imagined the sacred majesty of the Catholic Mass interrupted by "the chants and yells of the most impious sects . . . the Protestants, all the heretics, the Muslims, the deicide Jews, even the pagans will henceforth hold up their heads, spread their doctrine and insult yours, try to make you swallow their poison, and if they cannot, to push you into indifference for your religion, a fate worse than death itself."[26]

In responding to this "scandalous publication" in August of 1790, the deputy de Sillery reminded the Assembly of its duty "to punish those who arm themselves with the sacred weapon of religion to obstruct your work." He read aloud a summary of the letter provided by the municipality of Toulon, which declared: "The Muslims, the deicide Jews will now come, their heads held high, to insinuate their fatal poison, and insult the sanctity of our religion by the public practice of their errors."[27] Here the Protestants and pagans had disappeared, and only Jews and Muslims remained, no longer merely as ideas but imagined as real and present religious minorities practicing in the city. In the southern port city of Toulon—where the last Muslim galley slaves had lived out their lives after 1748—this was not entirely inconceivable.

The journal *L'ami du roi* protested the new regime's elevation of political authority above religious truth. "We are a National Convention," the Jansenist Armond-Gaston Camus had threatened in a debate. "We can certainly change religion, but we do not."[28] "If thus using this unhappy power," the journal protested, "[the Assembly] decided to raise as a constitutional law the profession of Judaism or the Mahometan religion, do they imagine that the priests and bishops, bound by the oath to maintain the constitution, would be forced, on pain of perjury, to take the turban or to be circumcised?"[29] As frustration grew among patriots with the hesitation of the Vatican to pronounce on the legitimacy of the new order, a pamphlet mockingly declared: "Hurry up, Holy Father, come on! Choose your party / Or if you refuse I will ask the mufti."[30]

In March 1791, Pope Pius VI finally delivered his long-awaited response to the revolutionary reforms. The brief *Quod aliquantum* was a rejection, if not an outright one. While condemning the attacks on the independence of the church in France, it still sought to find a compromise that would prevent a schism in the church and stave off the seizure of the papal enclave of Avignon.[31] In September, as the constitution was about to be promulgated, the pope repudiated Loménie de Brienne, who had sworn the clerical oath and accepted election as constitutional bishop of the Yonne. In his instructions, he declared that Loménie's attempts to "reconcile the Gospel with the new constitution" would lead to "the election of priests by the people: elections in which Jews, Mahometans, Calvinists, in a word, every sect, will have the right to vote."[32] If the pope did not approve the innovations of the Revolution, it appeared that he validated the more bizarre fantasy of Muslim infiltration into French religious life.

The pope's accusation was of course a consequence of the decree of 24 December 1789, which had given Muslims a hypothetical right to admission as full citizens. The Comte d'Antraigues—a former supporter of the Revolution and friend of Voltaire and Rousseau—drew that direct line in a pamphlet he published in London: "On 21 December 1789," he suggested, "it was proposed to the Assembly that actors should be admitted to the ranks of active citizens. M. de Clermont-Tonnerre, seeking to curry favor with the dominant party, decided that they must also admit the Jews, Mahometans, idolaters, and executioners." Indeed, how could the Assembly have excluded executioners, d'Antraigues declared, when it had "presided over the murders of 6 October, and pulled the strings of all the brigands in the kingdom since the first of July."[33] It was the Jacobin Club, he insisted, that avidly took up the motion to admit non-Catholics, "which gave them the hope that by passing the Civil Constitution of the Clergy one day, and giving all active citizens the right to elect bishops and priests, they could have the ministers of the church elected by Protestants, Jews, Mahometans, actors, executioners, and thus to heap onto these ministers of the church every possible kind of humiliation and ignominious torture."[34] In the counterrevolutionary mind, the Jacobins not only *favored* but were in some sense increasingly *identified with* Jews, Muslims, executioners, and other proscribed groups.[35]

The abbé Augustin Barruel took up this counterattack that would ultimately result in his full-fledged conspiracy theory accusing the Jacobins of leading a consortium of Freemasons, Protestants, and Jews in a concerted attack against the Catholic foundations of Europe. Part of this vision was the projection of Islam as a component of the new political religion. The report of the Ecclesiastical Committee in July had claimed to be returning the church to its "primitive," purer state: in response, Barruel's *Journal ecclésiastique* denied that any "secular tribunals" (*tribunaux laïcs*) like those the Assembly was proposing had ever governed the primitive church. When, it asked, was the interior regime of the church ever decided by the multitude? "In what period was the bishop or priest elected by provincial deputies, Catholic deputies, heretic deputies, Jewish or Muslim deputies, without the least exception?"[36] In Barruel's feverish imagination, the Muslims had moved out of the church and into the Assembly itself.

"I see in the decrees of the month of July," a pamphlet declared, "the same profanation of our temples by a purely political ceremony: I see Jews, Turks, Calvinists, actors introduced by force into the sanctuary."[37] The vision of the future here seemed to blend into a vision of the present, as though Muslims were already firmly ensconced in the pews. "Is it necessary to be Catholic to become an elector?" the pamphlet asked. "Nothing could be further from the case. The pagans, the Mahometans, the Jews, the Lutherans are very worthy electors, and will therefore be responsible for giving us bishops and priests."[38]

In December 1790, the cathedral chapter of Autun defied their bishop, Charles Maurice de Talleyrand-Périgord, one of the few to support the civil constitution. They declared that participation of non-clergy in elections of clerical personnel "would add, on top of its radical stupidity, a scandalous innovation" and would be even more monstrous "if Protestants, Jews,

Mahometans—essentially enemies of our religion and thus hardly scrupulous (to say the least) to ensure worthy ministers—were admitted freely among the electors."[39] This was no satire: they appeared serious in contemplating the possibility of Muslims voting in clerical elections alongside Jews and Protestants (who would indeed gain that right). The invocations of pagans and devotees of the Grand Lama had disappeared, but Muslims remained obstinately among these potential participants in clerical elections. The archbishop of Auch suggested the same unholy trio of Jews, Protestants, and Muslims in his *Lettre pastorale* of December 1790: "In effect, my brothers," he wrote, "heretics, Jews, fanatical Muslims, if they present themselves, will elect our priests and bishops, and who can say what degree of liberty we will have one day to accord or refuse them the canonical institution itself?"[40] Thus, from the simple, and largely hypothetical, according of rights to Muslims, they had leaped in imagination from voting to becoming deputies, and to a phantasmagorical seizing of the bishop's miter.

Islam, like other religions in France, was caught up in the whirlwind of political culture that the Revolution unleashed. For revolutionaries, the exercise of rights by Muslims served to demonstrate that those rights were truly universal. For those opposed to the revolutionary reform of religion, even the hypothetical exercise of rights by Muslims demonstrated the utter ungodliness of the new administration and the falsehood of its claims to have the interests of Catholics at heart. Shared across both of these otherwise opposing tendencies was a discursive constant: the fiction of a Muslim France. From late 1790, as the struggles over the clerical oath divided the Catholic Church in two, far from disappearing from the increasingly internecine struggle, Muslims only appeared with greater frequency on both sides of the divide.

The Koran and the Civic Oath

In December 1789, as the National Assembly debated the admission of non-Catholics to civic status, Louis-Simon Martineau delivered his report on the Civil Constitution of the Clergy, which would be ratified in July 1790, placing the legal seal on the radical transformation of the Catholic Church that had been undertaken over the preceding year.[41] The civil constitution instituted elections of bishops and parish priests, and provided them with salaries to replace the nationalized properties of the church: as civil servants, they were expected to swear an oath "to be faithful to the nation, the law, and the king, and to defend with all his power the constitution decreed by the National Assembly and accepted by the king."[42] Martineau insisted that this oath was not a political subordination of the church, but a recognition of the supremacy of religion, "since without religion, an oath is a word empty of meaning."[43] Commenting on Martineau's report, the curé and deputy Thiébault complained to the committee that it was not clear *which* religion was meant: "You have not explained whether you will swear on the Gospel or on the Koran, by great Jupiter or by the three-times sacred God of Isaiah."[44]

In November 1790, the Assembly went further, instituting a new compulsory oath for all those gaining election to clerical positions; although in essence similar to previous oaths, the new civic oath rapidly came to be viewed as inconsistent with the higher allegiance to God and the apostolic succession in Rome. Accepting or rejecting the oath would soon become the formal sign of belonging to one of two camps, effectively creating two parallel churches: a Constitutional Church and a "refractory" church. Timothy Tackett has concluded that the schism over the oath was driven less by theological disputes than by regional diversity and local religious cultures, exacerbated by the proximity of religious minorities.[45]

After police reports revealed that in some sections of Paris, refractory Catholics had failed to register the births of their children at the parish church and had instead arranged secret baptisms by non-juring priests, the mayor of Paris, Bailly, took action to prevent the refractory church from performing civic functions. While the Declaration of Rights had enshrined the liberty of religious opinions, Bailly suggested, this was a question of "public order" and in particular the keeping of appropriate records. Moreover, he argued, liberty of religion demanded that registering births should not occur exclusively through baptism, since Jews and Muslims did not follow such a practice. "We cannot force any Catholic priest to register the birth of a child whose parents do not wish him to be baptized, any more than we can force Jews or Muslims to baptize their children."[46] This was an extension of Malesherbes's arguments intended to permit the registry of Protestant marriages and births; here, however, it served as an argument for establishing a secular *état civil* for all citizens—a radical diminution of the church's centrality in society.

Several days later, a proposition was put to the Assembly that "births, deaths, and marriages of citizens will be recorded by civil acts."[47] A number of speakers opposed this motion, including the notoriously anti-Jewish Alsatian deputy Rewbell, who claimed that this motion was a ruse by refractory

Catholics themselves. "From whom does this petition on which you are deliberating emanate? Is it from the Protestants, from the Muslims, from the Jews, from the Anabaptists? No—it is from the nonconformists, from the refractories."[48] In his haste to prevent Jews from obtaining equal civil status, Rewbell spoke as though Muslim petitions were an everyday phenomenon, without raising an eyebrow.

In September 1791, the Constitutive Assembly was dissolved, and elections brought a wholly new group of deputies to the Legislative Assembly. The *Courier de l'Europe* described the scene as the new deputies swore their oaths to uphold the constitution: some dissolved in tears, while others kissed the sacred book "that certain mischievous jokers have called the Koran of the French."[49] This comparison of the constitution to the Koran was not just a witticism: as a written document that governed both civil and religious structures of the state, the Koran was a common touchstone. In 1790, *L'ami du roi* reported a long discussion in which Malouet argued against the proposition that France already had a "constitution" on the basis of its tradition. In contrast, he continued, "the Turks have a constitution; it is the Koran."[50] Both Condorcet and the abbé Maury could—surprisingly—agree that the Koran was a kind of constitution.[51] Other comparisons were less judicious. In 1792 *Journal de la cour et de la ville* mocked "the laughable fury of a certain troop [the Jacobins] who have just solemnly declared anathema any firebrand who would commit the slightest offense or insult to our sublime Alcoran."[52] Describing the sansculottes, the *Mercure de France* declared: "Listen to them in public; *they want only the constitution, nothing but the constitution, the constitution or death.* Gullible innocents take them at their word, and bellow back in response, as the Muslims cry, '*The Koran, nothing but the Koran, the Koran or death.*'"[53] "The new constitution," a pamphlet declared, "tramples on the sacred laws, tears all rights from the clergy, to give them to heretics, Jews, and Mahometans, if they decided to establish themselves in France and take up the title of active citizens."[54]

As the traditional church came into direct conflict with the state, Catholics who refused the constitutional order found themselves constituted as a religious minority alongside Protestants and Jews. One counterrevolutionary pamphlet imagined Gros-Jean, a local villager, asking the local curé where he should celebrate Easter. In a "tolerated" church, the curé replies. If you belong to the constitutional religion, he explains to Gros-Jean, you are not a Catholic, and you have no more right to go to a priest "than to a Protestant minister, a Jewish rabbi, or a Turkish mufti, since you are not of their religion." The curé tells his parishioner that "they have tried to introduce Jews, Calvinists, Lutherans, Huguenots, Muslims, pagans in all of France," and that the curé of Saint-Laurent in Paris had printed pamphlets declaring "that the religion of Jesus Christ is no more respectable than that of Mahomet."[55]

Soon, however, resisting Catholics began to draw upon Islam as a model, comparison, and example for a new, entirely unaccustomed assertion of "religious rights" against the state. The *Annales monarchiques* insisted that if Catholicism rejected the civil constitution, so did Protestantism. Moreover, it added, "the Mahometan who enjoys [such rights] in France, if he wants to benefit from a full and entire freedom of religion, will not allow his mosque to be supervised by the Sieur Gobet [i.e., Gobel, the first constitutional bishop], and the Jew who curses the ministers and muftis in his synagogue enjoys this right in peace."[56]

A pamphlet from Rouen made the same point, but from a constitutionalist position: "The law in the civic order can and must demand that all the subjects of the state, Christians, Jews, Muslims, should be subject to the same rules of police and administration, and governed by the same political arrangements."[57] Like other religious minorities, dissenting Catholics must remain free to exercise their faith, and if other minorities were not forced to swear an oath, then neither should Roman Catholics.

On 29 November, the royalist *Journal de la cour et de la ville* published on its first page a supposed citation from the *Bibliothèque orientale* of d'Herbelot. After the terrible and bloody schisms following the death of the Prophet Muhammad, it claimed, one of the Abbasid caliphs had declared the Koran "was only the work of man, and it was permitted to each to adapt its maxims and believe as he chose. Are the Muslims more free than the conquerors of liberty?"[58] The journal seemed to be suggesting that the French should follow this model of religious freedom and allow refractory Catholics to decide on their own interpretation of religious duty.

As the struggles over the civic oath continued, the civil rights accorded to non-Catholics, and their freedom to practice their faith in France, were marshaled as an argument for permitting non-juring priests to continue their vocation. The fact that Catholic clerics had been singled out for a special oath was presented as contrary to the Declaration of Rights. The safeguard of "public order" that the clerical party had inserted into the redaction now provided the legal framework for a crackdown on the refractories.

Disturbances reported from all over the countryside as well as in major cities offered a powerful corroboration that the refractory priests were troubling public safety, and provincial deputies began to push for stricter action.

In Montpellier, the two parties came to blows on a Sunday in October, as local patriots tried to close the "unconstitutional" churches, while defenders of the refractory priests now cried for "freedom of religion"; the municipality replied that all religions were tolerated, but retired in confusion "uncertain whether these dissidents from the law should be regarded as citizens of a different religion."[59] The poet André Chénier wrote a letter to the *Moniteur* declaring that the refractory priests indeed belonged to their own religion, based on "the Gospel, a book where one can find anything one looks for," and called for the National Assembly to offer everyone "full freedom to follow and invent any religion he likes."[60] Like Chénier, many revolutionaries believed that complete freedom of religion was necessary, not only from the principle of rights, but also to prevent the establishment of a constitutional Catholic church in the new regime in the dominant position the traditional church had held in the old regime.

Le cri de l'humanité; ou, L'ami des vieillards published a plea to forgive those priests who had refused the oath, whatever their motives. "We permit Protestants and Jews," it declared, "and we will permit Mahometans and idolaters to exercise their religion freely among us. The diversity of these religions can never disbar them from our aid, our care, our friendship. Do we not owe even more, in all reason, to our compatriots, to our old friends? . . . The words *Peace* and *Liberty* should be written in every heart, and serve to unite all the subjects of the French constitution."[61] From the threatening figures of a religious freedom that would allow infidels to vote for priests and bishops, Muslims had become exemplars for the freedom claimed by refractory Catholics.

"Moi qui suis Mahométan"

Under attack from the Catholic Right's allegations that Muslims, along with Protestants and Jews, would be voting in elections for priests and bishops, becoming deputies, building mosques, and forcing France to adopt Islam, the revolutionary party did not reject Muslims or insist that they would renounce their faith in order to become citizens. Instead they reinforced their assertion that the new constitutional order was for everyone, including Muslims. The "constitutional mosque" now joined the symbols of universalism in the new order. This could lead at moments to extraordinary forms of emotional identification across the religious divide.

In January 1791, the popular newspaper *La feuille villageoise* described a ceremony for the clerical election held at Sainte-Chapelle in Paris. One of the electors mounted to the tribune and gave a moving speech, then swore the sermon of allegiance to his parish and municipality. Following his example, a number of pastors and other ecclesiastics hastened to make the formal declaration of their submission to the Civil Constitution of the Clergy. "Today seems to be the festival of religion," the journalist wrote, describing the joy and warmth of mutual affection. "Such a spectacle could convert prejudice itself!" he continued. "One of my neighbors cried out: 'If I were a Turk, I would become a Christian right now!'"[62] In this real or imagined scene of passionate support for the constitutional reforms of the church, Muslims seemed to leap quickly to mind. The "prejudice" of religion here was incarnated by the "Turk"—also a proverbial expression in French for obstinacy—whose conversion would heal the divisions of French religion.

Where Muslims had once been consistently depicted as "fanatics," the accusation of fanaticism was now preferentially directed toward the non-jurors and their supporters, and Muslims could even be conceived as their innocent victims. The mayor of Strasbourg compared the cardinal de Rohan to Peter the Hermit, "commanding, in the name of heaven, the massacre of Muslims."[63]

From the pamphlet literature, Muslims moved into the mainstream of political debate. On 21 October, the Assembly allowed a free discussion on the measures to be taken against refractory priests. Speakers made repeated reference to Islam in different ways. The deputy Davigneau, replying to Lajaune's ramped-up proposition of a decree that would sequester non-jurors in the departmental capitals, asked whether the real goal of this proposed legislation was to make the opinion of the "conformists" a new dominant religion, and emphasized the freedom of religion given to Muslims and Jews as an argument for allowing different practices of Catholicism.

The deputy Baert insisted that to treat Catholicism differently from other religions only pushed it back to the center of French life. Either priests must be treated the same as other citizens, or Catholicism must be recognized as a religion with special status. If it was just another religion, he insisted, "then you cannot be preoccupied by priests in regard to spirituality, any more than with Jewish, Protestant, or Muslim ministers."[64] There were indeed fanatical priests, he acknowledged, but they must be fought only with contempt and ridicule, and punished for any infraction of the law like any other citizen. Apart from questions of salary, he declared, "you have no more right to concern yourselves with them than with Protestant ministers, with rabbis or Muslims."[65]

The deputy Roujoux sounded the tocsin about the revolt in the countryside, warning that the open insurrection in the Vendée would be imitated in every one of the 83 departments if the "fanatics" were not dealt with. He drew a distinction between the religious opinions and the social obligations of priests, separating their sacerdotal from their political functions. Nonetheless, he insisted that the most crucial measure must be to "repeat to the people that the citizens are all equal in the eyes of the law, that it assures and protects equally the freedom of opinions of the Catholic and the Muslim, and that if the freedom of one is attacked, the freedom of the other is compromised." Yet he also declared that any religion that troubles social harmony and "isolates the citizen from the happiness of the *patrie*" is ineligible for such protection.[66]

On 26 October, as the debate continued, Ducos made a speech in which he insisted that the role of a religion in the state should not be judged by its truth or falsity, since "what is evident to me as a Catholic, is not so to a Protestant, and for the same reason, the Muslim could claim to write at the head of all the laws: There is only one God, and Mahomet is his Prophet."[67] Thus, he declared hopefully, he had resolved the problem: "Separate all that concerns religion from all that concerns the state; treat the expression of religious opinions as we treat all other opinions; treat religious assemblies as we treat other assemblies of citizens; allow every sect the freedom to choose a bishop or an imam, a minister or a rabbi."[68] For Ducos, then, the freedom to be both a Muslim *and* a citizen in France represented the essence of the separation between church and state.

By March of 1792, a deputy could take the tribune, outraged by the cost of the funeral rites of Mirabeau, to declare, "Are you trying to force me—I who am a Calvinist or Mahometan—to pay for a Mass I don't believe in?"[69] A representative of the French people could now position himself rhetorically as a Muslim—but crucially as a French Muslim, a citizen, and a taxpayer—in order to insist upon the equality of treatment of all religions. The philosopher of religion Pastoret insisted on 19 June that marriage must henceforth be secular: "one must be allowed to take a wife as one chooses, from the different sects of Christianity, among the disciples of Moses or Mahomet, and circumcise or baptize one's children as one chooses."[70] Yet beneath this egalitarian vision, the explosive force of religious schism was building.

Fueled by the violence in the provinces, and the reactions by local authorities, revolutionaries sought to find ways to force the priests to swear the oath. A number of projects were presented: the deputy François de Neufchâteau, in the project he presented on behalf of his committee, drew upon the subjection of freedom of religion to "public order" that had been inserted into article 10 of the Declaration of Rights. He distinguished between the opinions of the refractory priests and their duty as public functionaries to swear the oath. "Religion," he declared, "for the enemies of the constitution, is only a pretext that they abuse."[71] The defense of the liberty of religion, he argued, necessitated an attack on the "invisible empire" of the priests. Therefore, within a week, priests would be required to swear the oath to municipal authorities, who would publish lists, and those who refused would be excluded from their positions and salaries, placed under surveillance, exiled from their district, and imprisoned for a year if they disobeyed.

Most of the deputies agreed, but many feared that the uncompromising nature of the articles would only harden resistance against the constitution and widen the schism. The deputy Lemontey proposed therefore that priests compelled to swear the oath might preface it with any reservation (a word that provoked outraged cries, and which Lemontey quickly replaced with "declaration") they required for their conscience. From the moment the priest had sworn loyalty to the constitutional law of the state, he insisted, "he is certainly master of reserving his own belief, since you will not demand more from him than from a Muslim who, before swearing the civic oath, reserves the right to make a journey to Mecca."[72]

Here, the observant Muslim slipped in as a more acceptable figure of religious devotion than the fanatical Catholic. Supporting Lemontey's amendment, another deputy, Castel, proposed that, in order to reduce Catholic resistance to the oath, the oath should be sworn in common by "every priest and superior minister of any religion whatsoever," removing any reference to Catholic "ecclesiastics." The law must be general, he said, and "if it is your duty to support every religion, that duty imposes another, to ensure that no religion is contrary to the constitutional laws of the state." No priest or refractory Catholic, he argued rather naively, "could believe that this oath is linked to religious ideas, once he sees that you demand it of a Jew or a Muslim."[73]

Others saw this development quite differently. They were neither the revolutionary politicians, nor the refractory opponents of the constitution, but the new prelates of the Constitutional Church, seeking to grab power in what was still a mighty institution of French society. They declared themselves the leaders of a regenerated Catholic faith that would take its rightful place at the center of the state. The *Instruction pastorale* of the bishop of Lyon, Antoine-Adrien Lamourette, was clear in distancing the true faith from the other religions with which it had been associated. Unlike other faiths, he argued, the Catholic religion was inherently revolutionary, ideologically allied to the notion of universal fraternity, and opposed to tyranny. "Despotism," he declared in contrast, "is the essence of idolatry and Mahometism. A pagan and a Muslim cannot fight against oppression without becoming apostates to their faith. All resistance is sacrilege where servitude is a state commanded by religion. Thus it is that the first sigh for liberty that these slaves utter must be the beginning of a determination to abjure their gods and their prophet, and that the first movement that brings them to us is also a first movement toward the Gospel."[74] In his *Délices de la religion*, he quoted a fictional work that ventriloquized a Muslim to laud Christianity: "It does no injury to veracity," he wrote, "to place this discourse in the mouth of a disciple of Mahomet, because a Turk can say reasonable and appropriate things, and esteem an order of religion and ideas that has made those who adopt it truly happy."[75]

Claude Fauchet, the constitutional bishop of Calvados and deputy to the Legislative Assembly, who had participated in the attack on the Bastille and blessed the tricolor flag of the National Guard, wrote a long diatribe against Islam in his *De la religion nationale*.[76] He called Islam "absurd and inhuman," yet insisted that it did what religion was supposed to do: "it binds the ties of conscience tightly between those who believe in it; it is the very constitution of their government, and what gives it all its power." Islam, he insisted, was utterly intolerant of religious difference, though tolerant at the civic level. It was this "religious intolerance that is the force, and the civic tolerance that is the weakness, of the Mahometan states." According to Fauchet, since Muslims could neither seduce nor dominate with their "nonsensical doctrine and brutal fanaticism" nor "cut the throats of all the inhabitants," they were forced to tolerate religious difference on a civic level. Even as he execrated its principles, its adherents, and its social structures, Fauchet treated Islam as an ideal model of "religion," seeing "an invincible nerve of power in the immovable principles and the inviolable union of believers."[77] For Catholicism, the glory of the comparison was in its reversal: the church won believers by the "pure attraction of its Truth." Christians tolerated individual unbelievers but not their religions, which they would seek to dissolve through active zeal. This notion central to the Constitutional Church has often been attributed to revolutionaries in general, but as we will see, it was opposed by Jacobins in the struggles to come.

By 1792 the refractory Catholic party had come increasingly to present the rights given to Muslims less as an outrage to the church than as a precedent for the rights they demanded should be granted to them as a dissident religious minority. The pro-Revolutionary party, working toward the establishment of the constitution, presented the inclusion of Muslims as a fait accompli that was now essential to the universalism of the new order: they drew upon a hypothetical Muslim population of citizens in the present or the future in their resistance to any attempt to restore religious dominance in the state. Nonetheless, there were already those among the more radical party who imagined a state without any religion at all, whether official or individual. In contrast, it was the Constitutional Church, struggling to regain its strength and legitimacy as the dominant state religion, that insisted upon the toleration of Muslims and Jews only as individuals, and the rejection of their religions and their communities of belief. If Fauchet, Lamourette, and Gobel would all go to the guillotine, the great survivor of the Constitutional Church would be Talleyrand, whose role would outlast the Revolution, and in many senses betray all that it stood for.

Robert Darnton has celebrated the "kiss of Lamourette" on 7 July 1792, in the midst of the debate on the dangers faced by a France at war, as a counterpoint to revolutionary violence, and an expression of "possibilism" and the deep currents of fraternity. The language that inspired the deputies in the National Assembly to rise and embrace one another across parties and factions was a centrist motion to "reject and hate" both political extremes. Yet many saw this moment as orchestrated for other reasons, as a "Judas kiss" sealing a great conspiracy against the Revolution. One recent historian has asked whether it cannot instead be seen as a transposition of "missionary rhetoric" from the sacred to the political context.[78] Just a month after this solemn repudiation of the republic, the popular invasion of the Tuileries and the overthrow of the monarchy would force the National Assembly in a different direction, away from both the constitutional monarchy and the Constitutional Church. As we will see in the next chapter, this shift was accompanied by a new set of relationships with a North Africa whose importance was growing as France entered into the war in Europe.

6. The Muslim Republic

In May 1793, the North African city-state of Algiers was the first power to make an unambiguous declaration recognizing the new French Republic, established on 21 September 1792. In the wake of the "second revolution" of 10 August, and the storming of the Tuileries palace, the Legislative Assembly had been dissolved, and a new National Convention elected. At war with much of Europe and Britain after the execution of Louis XIV in January 1793, the republic had few friends. Algiers was in rapid transformation, a kind of "republic" analogous to France, adapting to the new geopolitical context, and negotiating the Spanish cession of Oran that would form the space of modern Algeria. North Africans were crossing to France with greater frequency, so much so that the Algerians hoped to establish a passenger ferry between the two countries. As republican France articulated a new openness to Islam, Algeria began to view the republic as a friend and partner rather than a religious enemy. In France, older fears of the barbarian pirates were giving way to the new conceptions of Muslims, but could still exert considerable force.

On 5 July 1792, Mathieu Blanc-Gilli, a deputy from Marseille, published a pamphlet addressed to the citizens of Paris, warning them that thousands of men, including Muslim North Africans, were on the march from the Mediterranean toward the capital. "The city of Marseille," he wrote, "due to its port on the Mediterranean, surrounded by a hundred nations, must be considered as the sink into which the dregs of a large part of the globe drain, attracting all the filth of the human race." With the kind of venom that had become characteristic in this period of ever-rising passions, he spoke of this sewer "fermenting with the infected scum of crimes vomited from the prisons of Genoa, Piedmont, Sicily, all of Italy, Spain, the Archipelago [Greece], and Barbary [North Africa]." The Marseillais, he claimed, were victims of the "deplorable fatality" of their geographical position, and the "furies" attributed to its citizens were in fact all to be blamed upon this "plague" spread by the foreign 2 percent of the population.[1] Blanc-Gilli claimed that this horde of "stateless brigands" was in the pay of France's enemies, seeking to massacre its monarchy and carve up the country between them. The royalist Jean-Gabriel Peltier drew on Blanc-Gilli to suggest that those who had stormed the Tuileries were foreigners, including North Africans. "This collection of outcasts," he declared, "Barbaresques, Maltese, Italians, Genoese, Piedmontese, numbering 250, protected by Pétion and Santerre, were suddenly the masters of the National Assembly and the capital."[2] If the specter of the Muslim barbarian/Barbaresque of October 1789 seemed to re-emerge here, the context on both sides of the Mediterranean had changed considerably, and Muslims could be imagined differently—or perhaps more "indifferently"—in the new revolutionary context.

An Algerian Founder of the French Republic?

In a much-cited line, an American diplomatic historian once wrote that "in an indirect sense, the brutal Dey of Algiers was a Founding Father of the Constitution."[3] Confrontations with North African powers revealed a weakness in the fledgling United States' foreign relations that encouraged the American public to back a federal Constitution in 1789. If this is so, then we may say that in a rather different way, another dey of Algiers—no more "brutal," however, than his predecessor, or the slave-owning authors of American independence—might be counted among the founding fathers of the French Republic.

The announcement of Algiers's recognition of the French Republic was reported widely in newspapers across Europe. The *Moniteur* published the text of the decree as follows: "The object of this deed is that in the year 1204, at the beginning of the month of Rajab, our predecessor Muhammad Pasha, of fortunate memory, renewed the former treaties of friendship and peace with France and promised to ensure their execution without any infraction; and the consul having now requested that these treaties be renewed, under the same title as in the past, with the Republic of France, this renewal has been signed today, 9th of the month of Shawwal, the year of the Hijra 1207, so that in the future we may have recourse to it and act in conformity."[4]

The date 9 Shawwal 1207 in the Islamic calendar translates to 20 May 1793. This was just two days after the reception of citizen Genet in Philadelphia by President Washington marked the reluctant de facto recognition of the French Republic by its nominal ally, the United States.[5] No European ruler would recognize the republic until 1795. The *Moniteur* made the point explicitly: "While Europe forms a coalition against free France, an African power, more loyal and more faithful, recognizes the republic, and swears friendship for it, despite the most sinister news from France."[6]

This "African power," Algiers, was a strange quasi-democratic anomaly in the largely monarchical world of the eighteenth century. Until 1792, European observers described Algiers as a "republic" or a "regency" with roughly equal frequency. Although overemphasizing the autonomy of these "regencies," they were correct in observing that Ottoman sovereignty in Algiers was vested not simply in the dey, the ruler, but also in the *divan* (ruling council) and the *ojak* (militia) of Algiers, bringing it closer to a republican than a monarchical structure of power.[7] In the early eighteenth century, in all three major cities of the Maghreb, the authority of the Ottoman pasha (governor) had been monopolized by local elites. Where in Tripoli and Tunis power passed into the hands of a ruling family, in Algiers the traditional structure of the *ojak* continued along the lines favored by Sunni Islam, through a process of election of a "dey"—a Turkish word for "maternal uncle."[8] From 1710, the dey was invested with the functions of the pasha by the Ottoman sultan, who sent an official caftan of office.[9] The sultan, as the caliph of Islam, ensured the dey received religious support from the *ulama*, the Muslim clerics. The nationalist historian Ahmad Tawfīk Madanī considered this the first Algerian state—the "Algerian Ottoman Republic."[10]

Algiers was described not only as a republic but as a peculiarly *democratic* one. Algiers, alone among Muslim states, and unusual even in eighteenth-century Europe, elected its ruler by a limited democracy.[11] Rousseau celebrated this in his unfinished sequel to *Émile*, admiring a dey who "arrived in the position of supreme power by the most honorable route that could take him there: from a simple sailor, passing through all the ranks of the navy and the army, he was raised step by step to the highest functions of the state, and on the death of his successor he was elected to succeed him through the unanimous suffrage of the Turks and the Moors, the men of war and the men of the law."[12]

This was a rather idealized picture. Algiers was in no sense a modern *political* democracy, based on competition between individuals or parties, majority rule, and alternation of power. It rested on the principle of consensus (*ijmā*) legitimated by Islam and particularly by jihad, the defense of the faith against the traditional Spanish enemy. The ruler was elected for life, and could only be replaced on his decease. In principle, any member of the militia—some 10,000 men—could aspire to become dey. In 1789, the abbé Poiret visited Algiers, and wrote of the city that in contrast to Tunis— "a monarchist state that passes successively from father to son"—Algiers is a republic "whose government is elected and extremely unstable."[13] When a dey was to be named, he explained, the principal chiefs of the militia would meet and conduct the election, which usually appointed one of the existing ministers. In effect, the dey was named by acclamation, and for life. Rivals could achieve power only by overthrowing the reigning leader. In 1754, the assassination of the dey by a soldier who declared himself the new ruler was followed 15 minutes later by the execution of the usurper: surely the shortest rule on record.[14]

The violence and instability of this system led a number of early eighteenth-century European observers to use Algiers as an illustration of the inherent dangers of democracy. As Ann Thomson has written, the main characteristic of Algiers for travelers in the early eighteenth century was "its penchant for bloody revolution."[15] For most enlightened Europeans, monarchy seemed the "natural" form of government, despite the apparent classical precedent for democracy. Montesquieu explained the Roman state as "a kind of irregular republic, rather like the aristocracy of Algiers, where the militia, which has sovereign power, elevates and deposes the magistrate that they call the dey; and it is perhaps a fairly general rule that military government is in certain respects more republican than monarchic."[16] Edward Gibbon cited Montesquieu's comparison at length, and queried whether the epithet of "aristocracy" was really applicable to Algiers. "Every military government," he insisted, "floats between the extremes of absolute monarchy and wild democracy."[17]

As the political situation worsened in France, references were frequently made to North Africa as a kind of dark mirror of the French Republic. When the commune of Paris began to exert ever-greater power in the provinces, the commissioners sent by the Convention called it a "Regency of Tripoli" and warned that it would soon become "Algiers fused into Tunis."[18]

Malouet—who so often employed Muslims in his rhetoric—declared the Jacobins to be the equivalents in France of the Turks who dominated in Algiers: "Our situation," he declared, "is very like that of the Regency of Algiers, minus the dey."[19] Edmund Burke, responding to his compatriots who argued that the British government should placate France just as it did in paying an annual tribute to Algiers, acknowledged sardonic similarities between the "janizarian republick" of Algiers and the "jacobin republick" of France: "[Algiers] has a constitution, I admit, similar to the present tumultuous military tyranny of France by which a handful of obscure ruffians domineer over a fertile country and a brave people." Yet Algiers was far away: he trumpeted the danger of "Algiers transferred to Calais," whipping up the racial threat of the "very scum, scandal, disgrace, and pest, of the Turkish Asia" on England's doorstep.[20]

From Marseille, Algiers was the same distance in a straight line as Paris, and far closer than London. Across the eighteenth century the relationship between France and Algiers was gradually shifting. In the second half of the century, the Algerian regime had found new ways of ensuring peaceful transitions of power by limiting possible candidates and grooming them for rule. It was said that during his 12-year rule, the dey Baba Ali II summoned an ordinary soldier, Muhammad ben Othman, into his presence by mistake, and took the accident as a sign from God: the soldier eventually succeeded him as dey, ruling peacefully for a quarter century until his death in 1791. Whether true or not, the story indicates the emphasis placed on Muhammad's humble origins as a form of legitimacy confirmed by divine ordination.

Shortly before Muhammad's death, in October 1790, a powerful earthquake brought down the fortifications around the city of Oran, which had been reoccupied by the Spanish since 1732. The bey of Mascara, the western province under the command of Algiers, besieged the city with 40,000 men. Under pressure from the revolutionary wars in Europe, the Spanish chose to cede the city to the rule of the new dey, Hassan, who thus became the most powerful figure in North Africa, uniting a large territory stretching from the city of Constantine to the border with Morocco.

A vignette from a cheaply produced sheet of colorful revolutionary figures, probably produced around 1797, depicts Hassan Pacha as a hero of the revolutionary wars (fig. 13). One red-sashed French general holds the tricolor flag of the republic bunched overhead while another proffers a purple wreath of honor; the dey crosses his arms in front of his chest in a gesture suggesting

Figure 13. The Dey of Algiers, from *Imagery* (detail), [1798]. Bibliothèque nationale de France.

humility and religious piety. There is nothing here to suggest oriental despotism or any of the other exoticizing conventions around Muslim rulers.

How did Hassan emerge, even briefly, as a revolutionary hero? In the course of 1791, a series of diplomatic standoffs had arisen between France and Algiers, partly as an ongoing consequence of the uncertainty that had been allowed to flourish in 1790 prior to the confirmation of the treaty, and partly as a result of concurrent shifts on both sides of the Mediterranean. The ink on the new treaty was hardly dry when it was put to the test in mid-1790 by engagements between Algerian and Italian ships in French waters near Toulon and La Ciotat, resulting in the capture and imprisonment of Algerian sailors. The compensation of losses and the return of the Algerians taken captive to Naples and Genoa—particularly the captain Ali Reis—were key demands of the Algerian government.

The demands from Algiers included reimbursement for the Italian slaves who had been captured and released by the attack, but many found it outrageous that the French government should pay the notional ransom of Christian captives who had already been liberated. Moreover, among those taken to Algiers and enslaved in retaliation were Frenchmen who had been serving aboard Italian ships. The Marseille Chamber of Commerce wrote to the consul in June 1791 reporting the concerns of the "patriotic circle of this city," which had become deeply interested in the fate of a certain Carrière, "who is believed to be one of the Frenchmen who were part of the crew" and had commissioned the chamber to write on their behalf.[21] Gillian Weiss has investigated the plight of other Marseillais enslaved in Algiers in this period, deprived of the support of the religious orders that had specialized in redeeming captives.[22] One revolutionary proposed exchanging two "seditious priests" for each remaining French captive in Tunis and Algiers, provoking roars of laughter in the Jacobin Club.[23]

When the new consul, Césaire Philippe Vallière, arrived in Algiers in January 1791, he was greeted with dissatisfaction by the dey, since the promised reparations were still lacking and the Algerian captives not yet repatriated. A few months later, in another confrontation with Genoese sailors near Saint-Tropez, an Algerian captain died and a sailor was taken captive, with seven others forced to take refuge in Toulon. The consul wrote with concern to the French government warning that these continued violations of French territory were feeding the impression that France could no longer control its borders.

The second anniversary of the fall of the Bastille was celebrated by the small French merchant community in Algiers "with the greatest patriotic intoxication," according to the consul. In Paris the mood was far more muted, given the king's attempted flight several weeks earlier. Two days before this celebration, the consul continued, the dey Muhammad had succumbed to his long illness, and the *khasnadgi* (treasurer) Hassan, his nephew and adopted son, was elected to take his place. The operation was carried out smoothly, as much of the executive power in Algiers had already been handed to Hassan. Certain officials who had made their opposition clear were swiftly exiled to the distant provinces, but none were executed. This "modern antidespotic maxim," the consul wrote, was the new dey's policy: the abolition of the death penalty for criminals, and a willingness to promote the redemption of captives for reasonable sums.[24] This suggests a greater shift on questions of crime and punishment than that in Europe; even

Beccaria, Voltaire, and Rousseau did not balk at execution in the name of national security.[25] Hassan Dey would come to regret the decision to grant exile to his opponent Ali Burghul, who returned from Istanbul to lead a coup in Tripoli, seeking a new power base in North Africa.[26]

The *Mercure universel* reported the death of Muhammad, noting his origins as a simple soldier, and his rise to the position of a despot, who had nonetheless "carried his country to the greatest degree of glory, wealth, and power to which it was susceptible." Its only criticism seemed to be his mercantilist insistence upon enriching state coffers: "the treasury was his idol and he filled it with enormous sums, pushing economy to a sordid degree." This conception of Algerians as fabulously wealthy would also play a part in French imperial designs.[27] The editorial congratulated Hassan as the second dey to be elected without bloodshed: "it is a great step toward civilization and philosophy. The friendship of the new dey toward the French presages the respect and advantages that France will so deservedly enjoy in Algiers, under the double title of commerce and politics."[28]

The picture of a calm transfer of power was illusory: in fact the structure of sovereignty in Algeria on the eve of the cession of Oran was fragile, as events in the following months demonstrated. Suspecting that Salah Bey of Constantine was preparing a push for greater autonomy in the east, Hassan dispatched a replacement, Ibrahim Bey. Salah took advantage of Ibrahim's generosity in releasing him from prison, and had him murdered in his sleep. Hassan sent a new governor, who had Salah publicly hanged. In the mountainous regions of Kabylia, and in the desert, tribal groupings violently resisted the imposition of taxation from Algiers.

Hassan was better versed in European affairs than his predecessor, having spent years in Spain, briefly as a captive in 1777, and then as ambassador. However, he quickly declared his predilection for the French. "For me," he declared, according to the new consul, "I have always been a friend of the French; now I am master, I can treat them as my heart would wish. Consul, let us tie up the old affairs as quickly as possible. Let us leave no vestige of times past; make sure that on your side all is in order. I promise from my side, on the faith of a prince, that as long as I reign, the French will be well loved and considered in my country and treated as well as they could desire."[29]

This friendship seems to have been not only sincere, but also personal. The dey wrote to Louis XVI specifically requesting to send him a certain

Captain Doumergues to carry presents to the sultan in Istanbul.[30] The document was dated a week before the death of Mohammed was officially announced, suggesting the urgency of this mission to gain the sultan's official investiture. While the request for a ship was not unusual, this direct nomination of an ordinary merchant captain to command the ship was a surprise. But much was on the line, and Hassan may have feared betrayal. In April 1791, with rumors of the dey's illness swirling, the Spanish suddenly changed their minds about their decision to withdraw from Oran.[31] It was vital to establish the legitimacy of the new dey, but also to offer the Spanish an attractive deal.

Faced with looming war in Europe, and the ever-mounting cost of holding Oran, the Spanish government chose to trade military presence for commercial privilege, establishing a company similar to the French Compagnie d'Afrique that held significant concessions on the coast around Annaba (Bône). The Spanish wished to retain the port of Mers el-Kebir as a fortified concession, but Hassan refused. On 12 September, he signed a convention with Spain to allow the Spanish to evacuate Oran and Mers el-Kebir "freely and voluntarily"; in return, the Spanish were offered peace, commercial privilege, and freedom of Algerian ports.[32]

As these negotiations were progressing, the government in Paris, on the cusp of the new legislature, failed to move quickly with regard to the dey's request for a ship to carry his ambassador to Istanbul. The king's letter of congratulation was dispatched two months after Hassan's accession, and there was no sign of the ship the new dey had requested. Hassan turned now to the Spanish, who rushed to take up this important symbolic task, which promised to place them in the superior diplomatic position in Algiers. On 8 October, a Spanish ship arrived to carry the dey's ambassador to Istanbul, the French ship having been unaccountably delayed. Hassan had lost patience with the French, and threatened suddenly to imprison the French consul if the Algerians detained as a result of Italian infringements on French territory were not repatriated. The dey prohibited all commerce with the French, and issued an order to all Algerians—"Turks, Moors, and Jews"—to leave France at once. [33] Such an order suggests that the Algerian population in France, though small, was still substantial, and also diverse in ethnic and religious origin.

An engraving from the middle of 1792 by Debucourt—creator of the *Almanach national* discussed earlier in this book—offers a lively panorama of Paris society in the critical months after the declaration of war, before the

Figure 14. Philibert-Louis Debucourt, *The Public Promenade*, 1792. Bibliothèque nationale de France.

republic, the trial of the king, and the *patrie en danger*: a "public promenade" in the gardens of the Palais-Royal, associated with luxury and vice, but also with revolutionary ferment (fig. 14). The figures were not simply satirical types: the Goncourt brothers insisted that many of the individuals depicted were clearly identifiable to contemporaries.[34]

The Goncourts, for all their perspicacity, did not point out in the very far distance a head distinct from all the others, with a beard and turban that clearly mark him to be a Turk, analogous to the figure in the *Almanach national* of 1790 that we noted in chapter 4 (fig. 15). This time, however, the figure of the Turk does not serve to give meaning to an imagined political space, a future calendar of revolutionary time, but instead populates the intensely sociable space of the palace gardens. He appears to be conversing with two men in wigs, and there is no suggestion of a link with the scenes of vice and display in the middle distance.[35] Indeed, the difficulty of making him out in the picture would rather suggest that he had no iconic function at all. This marked "indifference" in both senses of the term is important for thinking about how a visible Muslim presence was becoming normalized in France.

Figure 15. Philibert-Louis Debucourt, *The Public Promenade* (detail), 1792. Bibliothèque nationale de France.

We know that Algerians were in Paris during this time from one case in particular because it involved a theft and a violent disagreement that provoked great consternation in Paris and in Algiers. On 3 April 1791, a visiting Algerian notable, Sidy Hadj Omar—the soon-to-be Dey Hassan's brother-in-law— was robbed in his *hôtel garni*. When he moved to another hotel, a second robbery was attempted against him during the night, and "an Algerian captain in his suite arrested one of the thieves, after having had his clothes ripped by a knife attack that, fortunately, did not wound him."[36] The conseil reported that Sidy Omar was in understandable haste to leave the city where his presence had attracted so much attention—not because of his dress or religion, but because "he fears not without reason that the reputation of wealth that has been given him now exposes him to pressing dangers."[37]

Unfortunately, the Algerian could not leave, because the 25,000 francs that had been stolen from him were already engaged for purchases from a jeweler, who now threatened, according to the report, to "use violence against him and have him arrested." The mayor of Paris, Bailly, was engaged to intervene on Sidy Omar's behalf. Finally, the royal treasury, already over-burdened with the issue of assignats and food shortages, advanced to Sidy Omar the sum that had been awarded by the court, although the decision was still under appeal.

Other Muslims had melted into revolutionary society. On 16 September 1792—just a week after the September massacres in which Parisian crowds invaded prisons and tried and executed prisoners—a Turk named Ali-Bacha, originally from Smyrna, was "grossly insulted" by a cook, who "called him a rascal, a rogue, a spy of Lafayette, and even spat in his face." The cook, arrested and interrogated by the local police commissioner of the Buttes-de-Moulins district, confessed to having drunk "a bit too much brandy" and regretted his actions. He was released after Ali-Bacha, "having consulted his heart, withdrew his complaint."[38] This episode may have been no more than a drunken dustup, but it speaks to the anxiety about espionage and conspiracy in the wake of the Brunswick Manifesto, and the arrest warrant issued against Lafayette, who had fled into Belgium. At the same time, it shows how this Turk could be imagined at once as a revolutionary participant, if an ambivalent one, and could himself adopt a kind of patriotic magnanimity in forgiving a quite serious verbal and physical insult. This behavior was characteristic of popular justice: in revolutionary discourse, as Sophie Wahnich notes, "it was the heart and not just the mind or reason that guaranteed the defense of the project."[39] Here, an ordinary Muslim seemed to perform the sentimental alignment with revolutionary ideals imagined by the pamphlets and writings of the early Revolution.

Ali-Bacha might well be the same individual recorded in the registers of Marseille as Ali Aga Serriu Basaglou, "Ottoman subject from Crete." In late 1792 and early 1793, probably as a response to the same set of anxieties about the foreign conspiracy, registers were kept for foreigners arriving in Marseille, and among the many Ligurians, Piedmontese, and Spaniards, we can see names such as Osman, "Tunisian merchant," and his presumed traveling companions Sidi Momet Sulagi and Sidi Alagi [al-Hajji] Mamet Placasby; Sidi Kilil Bou Hagi Braan, Turk from Morea, and Kiris Marguerity, Ottoman; Sedy Hady Mamet Elmisrery and Mamet di Moustaffa, Tunisians; and even Magmou, "blind Moroccan beggar."[40] We know nothing more of these visitors, and even the orthography of their names remains uncertain, but this small snapshot can give us some sense of those moving back and forth between France and the Muslim world during those months.

Barbary and Revolution

At the end of 1791, the mood in France was increasingly bellicose, and Algerian hostility fanned rumors of conspiracy stalking the streets. Some saw the Algerian threat as a counterrevolutionary plot to allow a Russian-controlled Swedish fleet into the Mediterranean.[41] The *Révolutions de Paris* accused Hassan Dey of being a "creature" of the Spanish who aped their "haughty disapproval of the French constitution."[42] The *Journal politique* similarly accused the dey of being "the enemy of the French constitution."[43] The *Journal politique des empires* despaired that these problems with Algiers, combined with the insurrection of the colonies and the French troops in India, and the fracturing relationship between monarchy and Assembly, demonstrated that "we can no longer have any doubt of the counterrevolution, and we can declare that the sublime Assembly is at the end of its tether."[44]

The imbroglio with Algiers tore the veil off the fracturing French government, still attempting to prop up the tottering edifice of constitutional monarchy. The minister of the marine read out loud in the Assembly the dey's declaration that "the French are not what they used to be, that they have become liars, that one can no longer rely on their word." Deputies began to murmur when they heard the dey's remarks to the consul "that there was no need to write to the minister, and that he could even less write to the king, since we did not have one."[45] When the minister's response to the dey was read aloud, deputies sniggered at the words "most illustrious and magnificent Lord," which were repeated ironically by the deputy Lacroix, and in several newspapers. One unnamed deputy declared that "of all the means of obtaining peace, the worst of all is cowardice" and asked the diplomatic committee to investigate a declaration of war "so that we can destroy for all time this nest of brigands."[46] Indeed, for some, an offensive and popular war might offer a way of saving the monarchy, and preventing a descent into anarchy. Revolutionaries feared that the offensive position of Algiers was a plot to give other European powers "a disguise and a pretext for arming themselves."[47] It was no longer clear, however, exactly who had the right to declare war.[48]

The apparent rupture with Algiers threw into further doubt the authority of a king who could control neither the Assembly nor his own brothers. The émigré princes were harbored by neighboring monarchs who, the newspapers insisted, no longer considered France a power worthy of consideration: "some of the responses of these states have been dismissive, and others are insolent and ironic; a number have not even responded, and the dey of Algiers manifests hostile intentions."[49] At a moment of crisis, the Algerian affair did not simply remain as an external question of foreign relations: it was drawn into European and French domestic politics and the rising fear of counterrevolutionary conspiracy.

The anti-Jacobin newspaper *La rocambole* denounced "that little beggar of a dey of Algiers, who has the impudence to believe himself a great lord, when he is no more than the chief of a handful of brigands."[50] The *Journal de la cour et de la ville* blamed the French themselves for lacking patience: "a virtue that we never cease to test in all other peoples, and (who would have guessed) even in the Algerians, who have, however, finally reached the point of losing patience with us."[51]

The *Journal général de l'Europe* expressed more seriously the popular anxiety about the position of the Assembly confronted by a situation where "everything conspires against [France] and her sublime constitution." The editorial blamed "these detestable émigrés . . . who keep in the heart of the capital itself followers who preach scandal and revolt."[52] These traitors had recently posted on walls all over Paris a threatening letter from the émigrés, causing alarm throughout the population. "What contributed even more infinitely to the disorder," the editorial continued, "was that the very same day, the minister of the marine had recounted to the Assembly the hostilities committed against France by the Algerians, and the brave Parisians believed that they would see the aristocrats and the Algerians arriving at the same time." These aristocrats might well arrive, the newspaper opined. "As for the Algerians, there seems to be little likelihood that they would push as far as Paris, but they begin to harass us, and these harassments could become extremely serious."[53]

A caricature of early 1792 depicts General Lafayette as a scarecrow propped on the edge of the Rhine by two poles, the "Congrès Américain" and the "Commune de Paris," vainly swatting with his sword at a stream of winged heads, including the dey of Algiers along with the Grand Turk, the king of Congo, and the emperor of China, amplifying the troubles on a global scale (fig. 16).[54]

In fact the rupture with Algiers was so brief that some called it "the fifteen-hour war." After a week, the French rushed a ship to Algiers carrying Captain Doumergues and the naval officer Missiessy. At first, the boat was refused entry to the port, but Doumergues was summoned personally to the dey and gained permission for the ship to enter. The dey received Missiessy "in a favorable manner . . . and tasked him to write to the king of the French that he had placed his envoy next to him like a friend. He expressed the interest he had taken in the troubles of France, insisting that if he had believed it in his power to help, he would have spared nothing to prove his attachment to the nation and to the person of the king."[55]

The language of friendship was key to the dey's relationship with France, both in the close relationships he maintained with individuals and in the shift in the forms of reception and address. He had protested to the French consul that "this is not the way friends behave; that the Spanish had a very different way of acting."[56] Hassan grumbled about Vallière, who

Figure 16. *Scarecrow of the Nation*, 1792. Bibliothèque nationale de France.

consistently hedged and promised without explaining the realities of the situation, but when the ministry decided to recall the consul, the dey intervened and requested that he be allowed to continue in his post.[57] Nabil Matar has analyzed the confusion between diplomacy and *mahabba* (loving friendship) by a Moroccan ambassador in the late seventeenth century: "his inability to recognize the difference between the public and state and the private and personal in his negotiations."[58] Sanjay Subrahmanyam has argued for a more nuanced view of "incommensurability" in the relations across cultures.[59] Questions of "sensibility" taken in a larger cultural sense can help us see these encounters not as mutually incomprehensible worldviews, but as diverse emotional styles. Nonetheless, we can see in Hassan's highly personal engagements some echoes of the centrality of friendship in Marisa Linton's analysis of revolutionary politics: it was a powerful force, but also one that was highly unstable.[60]

The dey's change of heart came so rapidly that some began to suspect the whole thing was a fabrication. Bertrand noted that the dey's letter expressed concern for the position of the king, and "offered to help him subdue his rebel subjects and completely re-establish his authority." The minister omitted this phrase in presenting the letter to the National Assembly, since it would have been "inevitably cited in the newspapers as the final proof of a terrible plot against the liberty of the nation."[61] In this sense, eager to bolster the king's failing stocks, the minister helped present Hassan as a friend of the people rather than of the state.

On 20 May 1792, a month after France declared war on Austria, two Algerian ships were attacked by a Neapolitan frigate and pursued into the port of Cavalaire, near Fréjus. As the authorities in Toulon reported in a letter to the National Assembly, the local customs official raised the French flag and signaled to the Neapolitan captain that the Algerians were within range of French protection. This was ignored, and the Algerians were forced to abandon ship under fire. "The municipalities, alerted by the sound of cannon fire, arrived rapidly at Cavalaire with a large detachment of National Guard."[62] The Neapolitan captain began firing grapeshot at the Algerians who were leaving the ship; the National Guard became involved in attempting to save the Algerians, but also to prevent them from mixing with the local population for fear of plague. The captain of the Neapolitan ship claimed that he had been given orders not only to fire on Algerian ships in French ports, but to pursue their crews onto French soil; "but the lieutenant of the port having observed to him that he would be greeted by two thousand national guards who would repel his landing, he apparently abandoned this project."[63] In the end, 350 Algerians were taken to quarantine in Toulon, where they were given food and lodging while awaiting repatriation to Algiers. The *Journal de l'Assemblée nationale* reported that the Algerian captains were remarkably philosophical about the attack and the reparations they would receive from France. They declared that they had not bothered to defend themselves, and now declined even to participate in the repair of their ships, since "this arrangement was not their business, and that it was up to the French nation to do what was appropriate."[64]

The dey's response to the captains was furious: he was said to have had one of them executed and the other beaten on their return. His reaction to the French was equally angry. He conveyed to the consul that "he would no longer keep the peace with the French if they allowed his ships to be attacked on their coasts." In a letter to the king, Hassan thundered: "What can one think of a sovereign whose territory is so disrespected, and whose flag is treated as a contemptible rag? Is this not the lowest humiliation for the emperor of France? How low the high opinion we once held of you has sunk!"[65]

Hassan demanded the surrender of the peace treaty and a reparation of 200,000 sequins. The consul, aware of France's precarious financial situation, refused, and a rupture seemed in the offing. Then, suddenly, the dey changed his mind. "Then the dey appeared to calm down," the *Moniteur* reported. "He called the consul to him, and told him with an air of frankness that the Republic [of Algiers] being at peace with France, he did not wish to declare war, and gave him back the treaty. He demanded, however, that the French provide two ships in place of those that had perished, and said that they could claim their reimbursement from Naples."[66]

The *Moniteur* suggested it was fear of French warships that inspired the change, but something else appears to have been happening. On 7 December, at the sitting of the Jacobin Club in Paris, the representative of the affiliated club in Marseille, Dorfeuille, made an impassioned speech regarding the revolutionary sentiments of his city and its support from Algiers. He began by declaring that the Marseillais had charged him with expressing their feelings of fraternal attachment to their Jacobin brothers in Paris. "If it is a crime to be a Jacobin, the Marseillais are profoundly criminal," he declared. Then he moved to "announce to the society that the dey of Algiers, aware of Marseille's needy situation, has sent assistance, announcing that as long as he has grain, he will always share it with his brothers the French." Amid thunderous applause, he continued, "And thus we see that as all the kings of Europe conspire against the liberty of peoples, we see one king becoming human!"[67] This language of fraternity is key to understanding the articulation of a new Algerian relationship to the Revolution.

Islam, Equality, and Fraternity

By mid-1793, as one historian put it, France had "the whole of Europe for an enemy, and the Regency of Algiers as its only friend."[68] The republic was in a terrifyingly vulnerable position. After the execution of Louis XVI in January, Britain had joined the coalition against France, which now counted every power in Western Europe. As battles were fought in the east, western France rose in counterrevolution. Provincial cities, from Bordeaux and Caen in the west to Marseille and Nîmes in the south and Lyon in the east, rebelled against rule from Paris. In Toulon, rebels handed the city over to the British, cutting off the main French port on the Mediterranean.

Algiers supported France, not just morally but materially. Not only did the dey encourage trade with France, he advanced considerable sums of cash to enable French merchants to purchase grain, which would otherwise have been impossible given the shortage of hard currency in France. In 1793, after the capture of Toulon by the British, he refused to allow supplies to be shipped there from Algiers, as the *Moniteur* noted: "The dey of Algiers, who demonstrates the most positive disposition toward the French, has refused to deliver grain to the English and the Spanish, despite the most spectacular offers. They are all the more disappointed, since they were counting upon this resource to end the state of extreme famine reigning in Toulon."[69] In late 1793, the Committee of Public Safety sent a copy of the Law of the Maximum to the consul, and instructed him to circulate it to all the merchants in Algiers, encouraging them to "continue their speculations" in the purchase of grain that would be crucial for French survival.[70]

When a French "traitor" called Bartero fired on Algerian ships, claiming to have mistaken them for Dutch vessels, the dey momentarily threatened to declare war, but retracted the threat when the two chebecs that had been attacked the previous year arrived fully restored in Algiers. The dey responded to the consul, according to the *Moniteur*, "You are honest and sincere; I will ratify our treaties; I am ready to give you the sums that you need; come at the harvest and find all the grain you want; we will cement our friendship and our most affectionate attachment."[71]

This language of emotion is central to the comprehension of the relationship between North Africans and the French Revolution. Recent historians have seen a far greater role for personal friendships and enmities in the politics of the Revolution.[72] At a time when French men and women were turning away from traditional structures for making sense of their world, and from deeply felt loyalties to faith and the monarchy, these personal ties helped maintain moral confidence amid chaos and often shocking violence. In Algiers, too, great changes were taking place. External and internal crises threatened the Ottoman sultan, who was also caliph of the faithful. Algerians could no longer be certain that this centuries-old anchor of their world would endure. Old enemies now became allies: Spain, Genoa, Russia established treaties and commercial relations. New adversaries emerged, including the United States, itself in the process of determining its destiny.

Algerians sought to make sense of this new world. In the newly Algerian city of Oran, the governor, Muhammad Bey al-Kebir, drew a circle of intellectuals and writers around him, seeking to push forward the new state. One of them, Ahmed Ben Sahnun, composed a *qasida,* or epic poem, to record the feats that had led to the Algerian conquest of the city. In his notes to this poem, probably composed in 1794, he described the events of the French Revolution: "In this year the people known as the French [*faransis*], who are Franks [*ifranj*], rose up against their clergy [*'ulama*] and forced them into exile in Spain and other countries. They killed their king and precipitated the country into anarchy [*fawda*]." Ben Sahnun interpreted the Revolution as primarily religious, and may well have received his reports from Spanish clergy in Oran. "They remained without any religion and each person does exactly as he pleases in religious matters," he noted. However, he went further than most Arab observers, to describe the ideological shift: "They agreed that no inhabitant should be superior to any other, and that all are equal; there would be neither noble [*sharif*] nor commoner [*dana*] and all should address one another by the name 'citizen' [*akh*]."[73] It is striking that this conception of citizenship should be rendered by *akh*, the Arabic word for "brother," a very familiar form of address in the Muslim world.

This assessment accords with a more general disapproval felt by many across the Muslim world toward *fawda* (anarchy). The conception of a republic was not alien to Islam, but a government without a stable and permanent head was difficult to comprehend. Islamic politics called for *ijma'* (consensus), not *fitna* (disorder). French politics was seen by many Muslims as a chaos of meaningless chatter and bickering, offensive to the ears. As Giuseppe Gorani, who had spent time in North Africa, suggested in his *Lettres aux français:* "These barbarians are not *chatterers* like you, but at base they are much more philosophical; one never hears them speaking in profanations and I find a great deal more philosophy in their indifference than in your furies."[74]

The idea of political liberty did not appeal to traditional Muslim thought, since according to Islamic political and juristic principles, it was God that remained at the center of human action, not the free individual. The right to insurrection against an unjust leader was recognized in Islamic societies, but it emanated from divine justice and not from the native entitlement of individual humans. The royalist *Gazette des cours de l'Europe* reported in September 1791 that after the peace with Spain, 11 Frenchmen who had traveled to Algiers to offer their service were arrested. "They had with them an Algerian who had been living in Paris, once an honest man, but now infected to the bone with the principles of liberty in the French style of 1790 and 1791. This unfortunate tried to raise his countrymen against the dey because he was making peace with Spain." The newspaper blamed this on the "cunning Jacobin propagandists" who could not live without disorder, and reported that he was to be "impaled or burned alive."[75] It is hard to know if there was any basis at all to this story, but if true, it suggests that currents of radicalization were crossing the Mediterranean in this period.[76]

Equality, in contrast, was an underpinning of Islamic thought, but once again this was equality before God, an equality of submission. Muslim societies were intensely patriarchal and hierarchical: in Algiers, the "uncle" (dey) wielded power invested in him by male "active citizens" of the *ojak*. "Fraternity" was a key term in the structures of North African Islam, and new Sufi confraternities were emerging across the region at this time, part of a larger "neo-Sufi" development.[77] One of Hassan Dey's architectural legacies was a grand mausoleum in Algiers for an influential Sufi *marabout*, Sidi 'Abdul-Rahman, who died in 1794.[78]

The dey employed this conception of fraternity in his understanding of the Revolution, frequently referring to the French as "brothers," and showing himself willing to forgive infractions of treaty obligations when there was a personal approach by intermediaries he considered honest and sincere. French observers, including the consul, repeatedly described this behavior as erratic and capricious; the colonial historian Henri de Grammont wrote of Hassan: "Later he lent 5 million livres to the Directory, without any interest . . . he was by nature chivalrous. . . . Unfortunately for him, he suffered the worst form of the mental illness common to all the deys, a complete lack of balance in the brain, which made him act under the influence of the moment, without reflection, and which subjected him very often to unmotivated outbursts of anger."[79]

This of course was a profoundly colonial reading of the history of French relations with Algiers. French observers of the time, as well as later historians, consistently misinterpreted the relationship between emotion and politics in Algiers, just as the dey misunderstood in key ways the changes in France. The consul rarely invoked concrete political conditions in Algiers: the dey's competing need, for example, to satisfy the corsair captains, the *ulama*, and the chiefs of surrounding tribes, while avoiding conspiracies against his authority. The dey, in turn, seems to have taken at face value

many revolutionary expressions, particularly those of simplicity and fraternity, reading them as compatible with Muslim values, and abstracting them
from the political culture in which they were generated.

By 1794, the relationship between France and Algiers, these two rising
republics on opposite shores of the Mediterranean, was closer than ever
before. Just a few weeks after the coup of 9 Thermidor brought down
Robespierre, the Committee of Public Safety wrote to the dey (using the
familiar "tu" in which all citizens were now addressed) to thank him for his
support: "The Government of the Republic feels the greatest satisfaction and
proposes to show its gratitude to you through an unalterable friendship and
by offering every service that you might request, and that circumstances
permit it to render." As an example, the committee declared, they "had no
sooner been informed that you wished to see established in the future a ferry
line between France and Algiers, than they rushed to issue a decree in line
with your wishes, and in a short time this establishment will be formed for the
mutual benefit of the two countries."[80] The establishment of these passenger
boats would suggest not only a new degree of communication and trade, but
a voluntary end to piracy.

This tranquility was ruffled by the case of Pierre-Joseph Meifrund, a
former vice-consul in Algiers. On his return to France in 1782, Meifrund
became active in politics: in 1789 he was elected to the Estates General as a
deputy for Toulon.[81] A committed revolutionary, in 1791 he became unhappy
with the radical direction of politics both in Paris and in Toulon. Denounced
by the municipality in late 1792, he was elected president of the general
committee of the sections in a royalist takeover, and his name appeared prominently on the declaration that handed Toulon over to the British. When the
British were expelled from the city in December 1793, Meifrund fled with his
family to Cartagena in Spain, where he was denounced by compatriots from
Toulon as a dangerous revolutionary. Like many families of the time, the
Meifrunds were caught between two fires. Surprisingly, however, a boat
suddenly arrived from Algiers with express instructions to carry them across
the Mediterranean.

Meifrund had played a central role during an earlier episode in which
Hassan had been detained in Spain. He was married to the sister of Vallière,
the French consul in Algiers. In 1791, in the period of the dey's frustration
with Vallière, it was Meifrund he requested as a substitute. Hassan was now
determined to use his credit with the French government to have Meifrund

reinstated and exonerated, with full return of the property he had lost as an émigré. Vallière was horrified: already suspect in France because his son had emigrated, he was now expected to lobby on behalf of a family member accused of treason. The Committee of Public Safety sent a representative, citizen Ducher, to investigate the consul, but he found no reason to believe the request had come from him. Indeed, Vallière had refused any contact with Meifrund—and, one assumes, his own sister—to avoid any blemish on his reputation. Hassan Dey, however, was adamant. As Vallière reported to his superiors, he went to discuss trade arrangements, but he was cut off in mid-sentence by the dey, who declared, "Consul, listen to me, don't say any more, don't offer anything. I want nothing. I have done a little for your country, and I will do all that I can. Here is the great favor I ask and which will be worth more to me than millions in silver. See that Meifrund, this unfortunate and virtuous old man, can return to France and receive his property and pension. He is here, I hold him in my heart. He is an old man, my best friend, and I watch over him. I will restore his fortune—I owe it to him. But to repay all my gratitude, all my friendship to him, I must get him back to his country."[82]

Hassan wrote to the minister of his demand, "which is a personal one for us," regarding his "close friend" Meifrund: "he is not one of the class of traitors—we are absolutely sure of that. There is no man without faults. We ask for grace that Meifrund's should be forgotten. He deserves your esteem and your consideration; we guarantee it by our testimonial."[83] He sent back the gifts that Vallière had presented to him, as well as those of the Compagnie d'Afrique, instructing the bey of Constantine to sever relations with the company.

After Thermidor, fearing a rupture that might lead to new shortages of grain in the Midi, the new Committee of Public Safety gave in, writing to the dey that they would "search for every way to reconcile this sentiment with the respect that we owe to the law."[84] The Directory sent a new envoy, Herculais, who declared not only Meifrund, but Vallière, the chancellor Aston Sielve, and various others to be suspect and suspended them from their duties. Eventually, however, he too came to see that the dey was immovable, and the French Republic finally accorded Meifrund the restitution of all of his property, despite his notoriety in the betrayal of Toulon. Sweetening this illegal decision was the loan of a million piastres from the dey to the cash-strapped republic.

The dey, by now an actor entangled in the Revolution, compelled the revolutionaries to compromise their own principles in exchange for this crucial friendship, in the context of a war that was shifting the ground on which the Revolution stood. Hassan became a player in revolutionary politics, and a powerful one. He refused to adapt personal friendship to political necessity in the ways that revolutionary politicians learned to do: a kind of compromise that came to disgust many in the French polity. Yet in investing Algerian resources in a revolution in which his stake was so limited, he also created a situation that ultimately dragged Algeria into the struggles of postrevolutionary France.

The debts that France owed to Algiers remained unpaid during the three decades that followed: neither Napoléon nor the restored Bourbon monarchy bothered paying off a former ally left far behind in the arms race of the early nineteenth century. By 1820, the debt amounted to 7 million francs. When the dey Hussein discovered in 1827 that the middlemen had been paid off at a discounted rate without informing Algiers, and all the money seized by French creditors, he was so angry that he struck the French consul. That blow became the pretext for the French invasion of 1830, leading to the occupation and ultimate annexation of Algeria by France, and the deaths of hundreds of thousands in the bitter struggles against the colonial occupation over the next 130 years. To understand how this friendship between France and the Muslim world descended into violence, we must investigate the shifts taking place in the most radical moment of the Revolution, which has become known as "the Terror." The Year 2 of the new calendar, with the rise of the Jacobins to power, and the new energy of the attack on the church, brought a new shift in the understanding of Islam and its relation to the Revolution.

7. Islam in the Temple of Reason

On 20 Brumaire of the Year 2 (10 November 1793), in front of the cathedral renamed a "Temple of Truth," the deputy Joseph-Marie Lequinio announced to the assembled citizens of Rochefort that there was no God. "No, citizens, no!" he cried. "There is no future life! The celestial music of the Christians and the beautiful houris of the Mahometans; the majestic face of the Eternal and the potency of Jupiter; the Tartary of the ancients and the Hell of the moderns; our paradise and the Elysian Fields of the Greeks; Satan, Lucifer, Minos, and Persephone are nothing but chimeras equally worthy of the contempt of the thinking man. Nothing will be left of us but the scattered molecules that formed us and the memory of our past existence."[1] The assembled crowd did not seem overly perturbed by this uninviting assessment of their destiny, judging by the festival of dancing and singing that followed.[2]

In late 1793, some radical Jacobins came to believe that the reign of religion on earth had come to an end. All religions would be dissolved happily into the republic, and out of the "Temple of Reason" would emerge a new, regenerated ideal man. All the wars of religion would be over, the barriers to the unification of the human race would be brought down, and the ideals of liberty and equality would sweep the earth.

"The Protestant, the Jew, the Catholic, and the Mahometan will disappear in the temple of reason," Lequinio wrote. "You will see only the man, the republican, the sincere friend of equality, liberty, and general happiness."[3] In the conventional view of the Revolution, this "dechristianization" was a mainspring of Jacobin ideology, adding fuel to the flames of "the Terror." Yet as Bernard Plongeron reminds us, the word "dechristianization" itself never really formed part of the revolutionary vocabulary.[4] Lequinio's utopian statement comprehended more than mere Christianity: it envisioned a millennial end to all religion. It was published in the Year 3, *after* the fall of Robespierre, "by order of the National Convention." The religious politics of "the Terror"—a term that in itself deserves rethinking—were more diverse than many historians have imagined.

There is no doubt that the church was centrally at stake in these struggles. Yet if Jacobins largely concurred by 1793 that Christianity—and not only Catholicism—should be rejected, they differed vastly over what should replace it. We might therefore speak not of a single "dechristianization" but of multiple "*dechristianizations*"—not in Michel Vovelle's distinction between a long-term secularization and the short, violent episode of 1793–1794, but rather in recognizing that there was no single revolutionary, or even Jacobin, answer to the problem of religion.[5] It is better understood as what Michaël Culoma has called a "politico-religious confusion" that was not the effect of radicals alone, but a more widespread and diverse social experience in towns and the countryside.[6] It was a confusion that split the Jacobins down the middle, with the radical commune of Paris on one side dominated by atheists like Hébert and Chaumette, and on the other the "Mountain" led by Robespierre, seeking to establish a new, official deism of the "Supreme Being." But even these parties were not unified: some atheists sought a new cult of nature or reason, while others wanted no religious observance at all. Similarly, deists were divided among those searching for a new universal civic religion, and those who aspired merely to a modernized Christianity stripped of "superstition." In this struggle, Islam was not swept aside, but on the contrary drawn to the forefront in a number of ways.

If atheists saw Islam alongside Christianity and Judaism as a religion to be eliminated, they nonetheless maintained the figure of the Muslim as a test case for the universal vocation of the Revolution. In an image from 1796, a vision of liberty trees, fraternal banquets, and rejoicing peasants is pitted against another landscape of massacre, execution, and auto-da-fé (fig. 17). Here the Orthodox, the Muslim, and the pagan savage no longer join the dance of the four parts of the world, but stand aghast learning the lesson of the evils of religion. The caption appears to refer to the work of the constitutional Catholic bishop Fauchet, in his sermon on the accord between religion and liberty in 1791.[7]

Figure 17. "Yes, when we really have our say." Frontispiece from B.-G. Manuel, *La Parole, poème en quatre méditations* (Paris: Dufart, 1796). Bibliothèque nationale de France.

For deists, too, Islam—strictly monotheistic and universalist—could seem much closer to their vision of a purified religion. Rousseau had declared Islam "the most logical" of the three principal religions in Europe.[8] Condorcet agreed that of all religions, Islam was "the simplest in its dogmas, the least absurd in its practices, the most tolerant in its principles," even as he condemned Muslims themselves as locked in "an eternal slavery [and] . . . an incurable stupidity."[9] Samson, in his *Crimes des empereurs turcs*, regretted that the Prophet Muhammad had not used his ascendancy to "bring Asia and Africa back to the simplicity of the independent and pastoral morals of the children of Ismael." In such a way, he might have "brought back to life the century of the patriarchs."[10] In the *Mercure de France*, an author explained that Muslims "are devotees of deism, as good Christians are of the incarnation: that is to say, because the unity of God was revealed to them by their prophet Mahomet, they are extremely proud of this belief, and attribute it to themselves alone, treating all other peoples as polytheists and idolaters, and particularly us [the French] because of our Trinity and our worship of images."[11] This abstract vision of Islam neglected actually existing practices of Muslims, which varied widely from devotion to marabouts through the syncretic piety of peasants and Shia ritual in Iran.

Contemporary shifts in Islam offered an analogue that helped drive the sense of a world on the brink of religious transformation. In a report dated 25 November 1793, the *Feuille du salut public*, a semi-official mouthpiece of the ruling committee, wrote of a "formidable enemy" arising in Arabia that "threatens nothing less than the overthrow of the Mahometan religion and the caliphate, in the very places where it was born. It is a certain hyabi [Wahhabi] who is at the head of a great horde of Arabs, between Mecca and Bassora. He denies the divine mission of Mahomet, the revelation of the Koran, and the need for mosques. He invokes god with his fellows in the open air, and with patriarchal simplicity."[12] Europeans perceived the Wahhabi movement as "a deistic revolution in Arabia," as a recent scholar has described it.[13] The suggestions made by earlier travelers, such as Carsten Niebuhr, had been transformed by Volney—an important influence on revolutionary thought—into a conviction that Asia was on the brink of a "great religious and political revolution."[14] Based on a conversation with two Bedouin tribesmen, he became convinced that "the Arabs live without worrying about the Prophet or the Book. . . . Each of us lives by following his conscience."[15] Guillaume-Antoine Olivier, sent on a mission to the Middle East in 1796, described Wahhabi belief as dispensing Muslims from all "the puerile ceremonies of Mohammedanism" and bringing them back to "the pure and simple belief in a God who is always just, always good, always ready to pardon the faults committed in this world of imperfection and weakness."[16] The conception of a "pure" or "primitive" Islam here paralleled and accompanied the struggles that moved from a desire for "primitive" or rational Christianity to a dechristianized "natural religion." The Wahhabi shift seemed to demonstrate a larger movement back to a basic and universal religion like that imagined by Rousseau.

This inaccurate conception of Wahhabi doctrines—which certainly stressed the radical oneness (*tawhid*) of God, but did not deny the revelation of the Koran—was shaped, consciously or unconsciously, by the religious shift happening in France. Those opposed to the changes, too, saw connections between the movements: the Austrian ambassador in 1794 referred to the rebels in Arabia as "Wahhabi Jacobins."[17] In fact, Wahhabis would show themselves the most ferocious opponents of the values propagated by revolutionaries.

Islam was thus caught up in complex ways in a global vision of the end of religion. "If God and kings are tyrants," declared a pamphlet, "we no longer want them; if dogmas are the cause of discord, we reject them. We must be neither Muslim, nor Christian, nor Jew, nor Brahmin, nor Bonze, nor Shintoist, nor Chinese worshipper of Fô, nor Siamese worshipper of Sammonokodon, nor Tibetan. We must be free, we must be sane, we must be at peace."[18] Yet as this chapter will show, this antireligious vision was far from the unified and peaceful global vision projected here. It was just as riven by personal, political, and factional hatreds as the struggles over the Declaration of Rights and the civic oath, this time from within the radical movement itself. If religion divides, as some revolutionaries insisted, then the rejection of religion was no less divisive.

"Dechristianization" is a term that both simplifies and muddles the complex religious politics of the Year 2: the term itself was coined—of course—by the self-declared enemy of religion, Anacharsis Cloots, in his *République universelle*.[19] It conflates a widespread anticlericalism—the hatred of priests—with the larger debate over religion, morality, and society. At the end of 1793, it would have been extraordinary to find a Jacobin with the slightest sympathy for priests of any persuasion. But the agreement that the Catholic Church must be destroyed did not mean that there was any agreement on what should replace it. Dale Van Kley has written of the "religious origins" of the French Revolution, yet by this he meant "Christian origins," as he made clear in arguing that "the 'dechristianization' campaign and Terror of 1792–4 remained largely within forms bequeathed to [revolutionaries] by the history of French Christianity."[20] Suzanne Desan has shown that these religious experiments were considerably more diverse, folding elements of anticlerical revolutionary ideology into ancien régime rituals.[21]

Other historians have emphasized the "cult of Nature": Dan Edelstein has concluded that a "Jacobin project" configured around an absolute belief in the divinity of Nature as a source of law underlay the Terror.[22] The search for a unifying ideological cause neglects the diversity of responses among the Jacobins, and the agonizing struggle over religion that leaves any such conception of a "Jacobin project" speculative at best. Moreover, in reifying the shifting factional groupings according to a largely retrospective analysis, it misses the powerful veins of anticlericalism among Girondins and even some monarchists. Religion in the Year 2 was not a theory, or a project. It was a terrain upon which a great struggle for the soul of the Revolution was taking place. Islam, too, had its place in this struggle, along with Christianity, Judaism, atheism, nature, and reason, and a host of other ideas that swirled in the void left behind by the sudden and cataclysmic disappearance of a church that had organized French life for a millennium.

The Revolutionary Culture of Islam

In the struggles over the constitution and the civic oath it had become commonplace to represent France as a multifaith society containing Catholics and Protestants, Jews and Muslims—and sometimes Hindus, Buddhists, Confucians, and pagans. Jeanbon Saint-André, sent by the National Assembly on a mission to Cherbourg, insisted that all congregations must be given equality: "Jews, Christians, Muslims, disciples of Confucius, or worshippers of the Grand Lama, you are all equal in the eyes of a free people."[23] Some constitutional priests like Alexandre de Moy, curé of Saint Laurent in Paris and standby deputy at the National Assembly, rushed to assure his parishioners that "thus the priests of any individual religion, of any confession, of any sect, whether Imams, Rabbis, Bishops, Muftis, are in [the nation's] eyes, only constitutional citizens if they observe and respect the laws."[24] Theology was not the job of the government, he insisted. "Let some annotate the Koran, some the Veddas, and others the Talmud; let some learn to baptize, and others to circumcise." Officials could not show preference to any religion: "they may not go today to a church, unless they go tomorrow to a temple, the following day to a synagogue, and then to a mosque."[25] In Paris, Charles Villette denounced "the clowns and imbeciles" who had placed a large crucifix on the Pont de Sèvres: "Since everyone has the right to preach for his saint, I demand a place for a Mahomet, a Confucius, a Zoroaster, etc., since without that, the Turks, the Chinese, the Persians, the Indians, coming and going across the bridge, will have the right to complain."[26] In provincial Troyes, the district declined the petition of the "Friends of Liberty" against the nuns in the Hôtel-Dieu, observing that "they have shown the spirit of tolerance necessary in a hospital where a Muslim has the right to be treated like a Christian, a Jew, a Quaker, or any other individual."[27]

Some constitutional priests protested that freedom of religion could not be so easily combined with equality, since religions were, by nature, mutually exclusive. A petition of the curés of Paris insisted that religious liberty should mean that each religious collectivity had the autonomy to determine its own conditions, membership, and governance: "Is there freedom of religion in a country where a Jew could be forced to welcome in his synagogue, or even recognize as his minister, the disciple of Mahomet; or the Lutheran or Calvinist compelled by the civil authority to confide the supervision of his worship to a Roman Catholic?"[28] Here the counterrevolutionary fantasies of 1791 were inversed: now they presented minority religions as the victims of revolutionary religious equality. Constitutional Catholics insisted that equality between *members* of different religions did not mean the equality of the *religions themselves*, which should remain apart from and clearly subordinated to the official religion.

With the collapse of the monarchy, a new constitution was urgently needed. But as new propositions poured in, few could agree on what place it should give to religion. In his project, the deputy of Paris, Antoine-Joseph Thorillon, reminded his readers that "we must fraternize and invite into all civic offices the Jew, the Mahometan, as well as the Christian of all confessions."[29] But this did not mean an abandonment of religion. "A school that brings together at the same time a Roman Christian, a Greek, a Jew, a Mahometan, etc., will need to create institutions for each religion, and separate the classes." What power, he wrote, "can legitimately prevent me from assembling with my brothers in a temple, a synagogue, a mosque, or a church to sing praises to the God I worship!"[30] Another deputy, Lanthenas, offered a more poetic "declaration of duties" to replace that of rights: its first articles dealt with the "relations of man to God" and declared that by the use of his reason, every man would recognize the fundamental truth of the author of the universe. "What does it matter," he wrote, "in what clothing or color we dress the mother-idea of all perfection? What does it matter in which language we speak the name we give him? Or the names of his apostles, Jesus Christ, Confucius, Plato, Mahomet, or others in whom one trusts?"[31]

Muslims were central in the language of toleration, the official vision of a France in which religion was free and presented no obstacle to social harmony. "It matters little to us," declared Chaumette, the driver of the antireligious movement in the commune of Paris, "that someone should be Deist or Atheist, Catholic or Greek, or Calvinist, or Protestant, that he should believe in the Koran, in miracles, in werewolves, in fairy tales, in hell—that is none of our business, if he is republican."[32] In the Parisian section of William Tell, Étienne Barry declared that "Jews, Christians, Turks, Deists, polytheists, all may worship in their own way, as long as they don't want to force us to do the same, don't disturb the social order, and above all that they do not compel those who don't think the same way to contribute to the cost of their religion; it is not fair to owe the fiddler so others can dance."[33] This vision was embodied in the town of Bayonne, on 30 November, when before young women attired as Liberty and Bellona, four young men dressed as "the European, the Asiatic, the African, and the American leaped about each in his own fashion."[34] At a nearby village, Monestier declared "friendship and fraternity to all the French, Catholics, Jews, Protestants, Muslims, as long as they defend the unity and the indivisibility of the Republic and equality and liberty."[35] These colorful and imaginative festivities belie the "utopian platitudinousness" that Mona Ozouf saw in drab festivals of Reason.[36]

While some deputies asserted that all religions were equally true, others contended they were all equally false. In Marseille, Sébastien Lacroix declared before the Popular Society that all the "thousands" of religions in the world were "the products of ignorance or tyranny" and all their promoters "born enemies of humanity" from Jesus to Brahma and Muhammad. "Tear from the hands of our children the Bible and the Koran," he thundered, and turn them instead to bountiful nature itself.[37] Others rose in the National Assembly to denounce religion more viscerally. "Citizens," J. B. Harmand, deputy of the Meuse, proclaimed on 3 September 1793—the day that crowds in Paris began to storm the prisons—"the hand of history has followed with the trace of human blood the steps of all religions and all priests: there is no corner of the earth that does not present to an appalled humanity and philosophy the bloody remains of the gallows and pyres erected in the name of the divinity." He cited as evidence the classic St. Bartholomew's Day massacre and the Spanish Inquisition, as well as "Moses cutting the throats, in the name of the god of Sinai, of 47,000 Jews in the desert of Oreb; Mahomet putting to the sword, under the walls of Mecca, all those who refused his horrifying apostolate." Moreover he linked this religious violence to "the torches of incendiary fanaticism under our eyes, the deplorable department of the Vendée."[38]

This violent rhetoric reflected and fueled real violence. In many villages, political and religious motives could not be separated.[39] Even before the September massacres began, lynchings and murders of priests had been taking place across the country.[40] While the killings in Paris were often explained as a reaction to the Brunswick Manifesto, which threatened the people of Paris with annihilation, and the news of the capture of Verdun, they were equally understood by many witnesses as religious violence. "What is the motive of this butchery?" asked Rétif de la Bretonne in his *Nuits de Paris.* "They wanted only one thing, to rid themselves of the refractory priests." He claimed that the other killings were carried out merely as cover for this attempt to annihilate the non-juring clergy. The greatest horror of all, he wrote in May 1793, "is that we see that this massacre was relatively successful."[41] Rétif was torn between his empathy for individual victims and his conviction that these priests were his "most cruel enemies; in my eyes the most despicable of beings."[42]

These words can tell us something about the nature of anticlericalism in 1793: more than a political position, it was a passion that evoked many of the same emotions and even the same language as religion itself. Despite the acknowledgment of widespread attacks against priests, this has rarely been understood as a form of religious violence in itself. Similar episodes of killing between neighbors, in other settings, have often been interpreted as solely religious, and as demonstrating a fundamentally different line of development. Where counterrevolutionary violence is often read in terms of religion, the violence committed by revolutionaries has been understood in terms of class, discourses of "natural right," repressive state mechanisms, or crowd psychology. It is crucial, however, to confront the religious dimension of this violence, and how it fueled—both as motivation and as reaction—the political positions of the period known as the Terror. Revolutionaries themselves were powerfully aware of the need to offer some new solution to the religious question: this violence made it all the more urgent.

After the execution of Louis Capet on 21 January 1793, the regime sought to expunge all reference to kings and queens. An enterprising publisher rushed in a patent for playing cards sporting figures more appropriate to the new Republic of Virtue. Other designs had been attempted, but these—conceived by Henri de Saint-Simon, one of the most important precursors of socialism, and reputedly designed by Jacques-Louis David, the greatest of revolutionary artists—rose above the ephemeral, to offer powerful new ways of imagining this world.

The former queen of hearts found her replacement in the goddess representing "Freedom of Religion" (fig. 18). Against Liberty's muscular

Figure 18. "Freedom of Religion," revolutionary playing card, 1794. Bibliothèque nationale de France.

leg stand scrolls of the Talmud and the Koran, capped with tiny liberty bonnets. The heavy tome of the Gospels appears, but it is slipping sideways, displaced by her twisting pose. The Koran is the only text that is open, a scroll revealing the illegible writing on the manuscript. Liberty is flanked on one side by the pike and red cap, with a banner reading "Dieu seul"—only God—and on the other by a pair of palm trees, situating her, as the description suggests, in the prophetic reaches of the desert, not in France. Her hand, although apparently placed on her heart, appears to palpate a breast, suggesting a different, rather less abstract conception of female fertility, reminiscent of the Egyptianesque "Fountain of Regeneration," from whose breasts poured the elixir of liberty, erected for the festival of 10 August 1793. It also pointed to a radically diverging path forward, in which Islam could play one of two roles. The volumes of the Talmud and Koran could be used to "correct" Christianity, removing its privilege or restoring its monotheistic purity. Alternatively, they could be used to destroy its claims and substitute a different religion altogether, embodied in the powerful female figure of Nature.

Islam constituted a precedent for the great religious shift France had experienced, as a Swiss writer noted: "History only offers two examples of a people forced in the course of one year to change both government and religion. The first was performed not by a man but by a saint, by a prophet sent for this purpose by God: in a word by Mahomet."[43] Not only high philosophical texts but ordinary popular culture featured similar ideas, if reduced to a simpler level. The words of "Ça ira" were adapted by a "patriot of the Savoy," newly annexed to France, celebrating the constitution and declaring that "the Muslim, as soon as he sees it, / Will sell his Koran in order to buy it."[44] Another song, "The Bonnet of the Republic," included a verse that declared, "We'll go and find in old Turkey / The follower of Mahomet. / He must now join with our party. / We'll share with him our secret / If he swears our civic oath. / If he abjures the Alcoran / I'll give him for his old turban / The bonnet of the Republic."[45] This vision of universalism was reprised in a song called "Les voyages du bonnet rouge," which joyfully announced: "The enslaved child of Mahomet, / Free in receiving this bonnet, / Will strike down all his despots. / Neath the eyes of the Sultan, / He now blesses the turban / Of the French sansculottes."[46]

The most remarkable example comes from a pamphlet of 1794 entitled *The Origin of the Three Revolutionary Religions*. It concerned not, as we might expect, the three principal religions in France (Catholic, Protestant, Jewish) but the three that offered precedents for the construction of a new revolutionary faith. The citizen P.B.T declared that "the reconciliation of Christians, Mahometans, and Jacobins" would assure the success of the Revolution. "A citizen of Nazareth, called Jesus," he continued, "was the first legislator to push the love of democracy to the point of considering the poor citizen, the sansculottes, as a member of the sovereign." Similarly, he argued, "the true Mahometan feels transported with fury at the prospect of the crimes that cover the earth," leading him to "work efficiently for the regeneration of the human race." The pamphlet compared Christianity and Islam and saw the latter as more effective in promising sensual delights in the afterlife, but also divided by "Tartuffes" into the "two sects of Ali and Omar" (Shia and Sunni).[47]

Only the Jacobins, however, could combine the Muslim's indignation against injustice with the Christian's love of democracy. In the citizen's description, however, the Jacobins—"delivered without restraint to this holy anger that creates enthusiasts"—resembled indignant Muslims more than peaceful Christians. The Jacobins' distinction was their indifference regarding the afterlife and their more radical universalism: "They even appear to be the enemies of the God of the Christians, and the God of the Muslims, in that these two divinities accord privileges to their believers, while the Jacobins abhor these privileges, and pursue them mercilessly."[48]

The tone of this pamphlet is difficult to discern: it seems less satirical or triumphalist than ambivalent. It speaks to the uncertainty of the new religious landscape unfolding in 1793. Among the Jacobins, some leading figures felt that the promotion of a society without religion was a dangerous experiment that would unite Europe against France, and leave little basis to create the virtuous, regenerated society they hoped for. Popular violence presented a great challenge to their visions of this new republic: rather than the Stoic qualities of the classical heroes they admired, it presented hellish visions of heads on pikes, carnivalesque processions, and the frightening force of the crowd. For those who believed that morality could be established voluntarily and without "superstition," this violence threatened their claims that human beings were naturally good. In such contradictions, however, some saw an "all or nothing" moment for the elimination of religion itself.

Cloots: Mahometanism against God

On 27 Brumaire (17 November 1793), Anacharsis Cloots rose in the National Convention to gloat over the recent execution of the constitutional bishop Fauchet, joking in a gruesome fashion about "the bishop of Calvados, of guillotinous memory," and seeking the "reparation of an outrage committed against reason by the Legislative Assembly." In January 1792, Fauchet had blocked Cloots's attempt to obtain the endorsement of the National Assembly for the book *The Certitude of the Proofs of Mahometanism*, which he had written a decade earlier. In an Assembly still agonizing over the issue of the constitutional clergy, Fauchet could easily sideline a work "in which the Gospel is directly attacked."[49] Now the self-styled "Orator of the Human Race" exulted that a "philosophical explosion" was laying waste to "all the false revelations" and making way for the "conversion of a great people."[50]

Producing the book from his pocket, he declared: "This work, unique in its method, its strategy, and fascinating in its details, and its developments, saps in a single blow all the revealed sects, ancient and modern. It is entitled *The Certitude of the Proofs of Mahometanism* because I hurl a Muslim at the legs of the other sectarians, who fall down one after another."[51] In 1790, Cloots had ushered in Muslims as figures of the Revolution's global vocation. Now he brandished them as weapons in his war against religion.

The Convention officially approved Cloots's book as a "work that demonstrates the nullity of all religions," and sent it to the Committee of Public Instruction to be distributed throughout the country.[52] Most deputies had certainly not read the long and laborious satire, and probably assumed it was actually promoting Islam, which makes their approval all the more curious. Georges Duval wrote later in his *Souvenirs,* "In truth, it seemed to suggest something of a contradiction, since, logically speaking, this work by the Orator of the Human Race could not prove at the same time the falsity of all religions and the certitude of Mahometanism, unless he did not consider Mahometanism a religion."[53]

Cloots has been of interest to recent scholars for his cosmopolitan vision of human rights, a vision that certainly included Muslims.[54] But this cosmopolitanism was subordinate to—or even instrumental in—his larger project for the abolition of religion. In his 1792 pamphlet *The Universal Republic*, he included Muslims in the global revolutionary transformation, given "the experience of Boston and Charlestown . . . the patriotism of the Indians of Pondicherry, . . . the Africans of Bourbon [Mauritius], . . . the Americans of Saint-Domingue."[55] In Greece, the Declaration of the Rights of Man and Citizen would bring liberation both "to the conquered Greeks and to the conquering Turks." He presented as evidence "the civism of the Pagan and Mahometan National Guards of Pondicherry and Chandernagor."[56] These Muslim citizens, Cloots insisted, would abandon their religious "prejudice" in joining the universal republic—and voluntarily, since man was everywhere the same, and "feels . . . [or] is susceptible of feeling the same sensations everywhere."[57]

At first, it was a question of equality and coexistence for atheists with those who "who will swear by the Koran or the Zend Avesta."[58] But this tolerance was accompanied by a visceral anticlerical hatred that extended to all religions. "Religion," he declared elsewhere in the same work, "is a social illness . . . a religious man is a depraved animal."[59] Reason, he insisted, demanded all or nothing. Yet Cloots still put limits on his universal vision: a "premature" insistence on colonial independence would anger potential allies like England and Holland. The French should deal with internal problems before attempting to "extend the concordat of Saint-Domingue to the people of color in all climates."[60] He welcomed the dispossession of the Knights of Malta, not as the opportunity to recruit ordinary Muslims to the revolutionary cause, but rather to welcome the alliance of the "brave Ottomans, our faithful allies."[61] Like other Jacobins, he was not willing—yet—to call Muslims into open revolt against their rulers.

On 24 August 1792, Cloots was one of the foreigners given French citizenship by the National Assembly.[62] Before he could take his seat as a deputy in the Convention, the massacres of September 1792 challenged his claim to the essential wisdom and goodness of individual humans that would make religion obsolete and serve as a natural foundation for his "universal republic." Like other revolutionaries, Cloots was faced with a choice: to embrace or reject this violence.[63]

By 1793, Cloots was not only excusing the bloodshed, he was applauding it. "Had it pleased God," he wrote, "that the massacres of the 2nd September extend across all of France, we would not see today the British invited into Brittany by priests who should not be deported but *septemberized*."[64] This new term (formed from the word *briser*, "to break") he claimed to have coined. He gleefully deployed this violent corporeal repertoire against the people's enemies. A purifying "holy hatred" rather than a brotherly love was the driving force for his vision of fraternity: "The people is rarely wrong," he wrote. "It does not hate in vain."[65]

Cloots's increasingly religious fervor for the universal republic was in part driven by the millenarian emotions unleashed by that violence. He called upon the Assembly to declare that sovereignty resided not in the French people but in the totality of the human race, the federation of all individuals. Cloots's universal republic would be a global politico-religious power taking on "the catholicity of a sacerdotal catechism" for the world's peoples. "Error," he declared, "makes Muslims prostrate themselves toward Mecca; the truth will lift all men's eyes to gaze upon Paris." Those, he continued, "who want to exclude from our fraternal association, from our truly catholic church, those individuals who live outside Europe commit an injustice by geographical error, since there are many parts of Europe much more distant and less accessible than parts of Asia and Mauritania."[66] The *Archives parlementaires* mentions

12 bursts of applause from the Assembly during this speech, including "lively applause" and a "double round of applause." Cloots presented himself as a new messiah in rhetoric seething with religious references. He argued that the human race was not only universal and sovereign, but in its regenerated form it was also a "political divinity." The universal republic would replace the Catholic Church, with the deputies in the place of saints. The word "foreigner," *étranger*, "barbaric expression that makes us blush," would no longer exist.[67] Cloots declared that he recognized no border except that between the earth and the sky.[68] Laughter broke out in the Assembly, and one deputy loudly demanded a union between the earth and the moon. But Cloots, undeterred, continued with his vision of universal liberation: "If somewhere a slave exists, then somewhere a tyrant exists; my freedom is not whole, it is compromised—it demands the total extirpation of tyranny and slavery."[69] He compared his program with that of the prophets, the "zealots of Mecca and Jerusalem" who had spread their religion across the globe.[70]

The "cult of Reason" was a religion without God. It had little to do with actual reason; in practice it was centered on various forms of iconoclasm and inverted religious ritual.[71] The proponents of "reason" did not sponsor essay competitions, set up academies, or send out volunteer teachers, as Enlightenment rationalists had done. They invaded churches, substituted the Mass with their own rituals, marched in processions with new hymns, burned symbolic offerings, and created shrines to sacrificial martyrs.

Cloots did not engage directly in violence, but he took a radical step into coercion in the early hours of 6–7 November, when he went with his collaborator, Jacob Pereyra, to the home of the constitutional bishop of Paris. The "public officials" were announced, and Gobel rose from his bed to receive them. They told him that this was the moment for him to sacrifice himself for the republic, to resign his functions and declare the abjuration of his faith. Gobel responded that he "knew no error in his religion, that he had nothing to abjure, and would stick to it." They responded, according to Gobel, that "it has nothing to do with the question of whether or not your religious principles are or are not sound; it is simply a question of resigning from your post." Gobel claimed he had agreed on this basis, since "the people appointed me, and the people can dismiss me; this is the fate of a servant under the orders of his master."[72]

Once again, Cloots was looking to a theatrical gesture to advance his politics: he did not care that Gobel was not actually abjuring his faith so long as it appeared that he was. And indeed, in the Convention on 17 Brumaire (7 November), Gobel's abdication opened the door to a series of abjurations by Parisian clergy. Momoro, interim president of the département, announced that these priests had come to "strip themselves of the character that superstition had lent them. . . . It is thus that, very soon, the French Republic will have no religion but that of liberty, equality, truth, a religion derived from the bosom of nature, and which, thanks to your work, will soon be the universal religion."[73] Julien de Toulouse, a Protestant pastor, declared that Gobel had "shown the same feelings that were engraved in my soul, and I imitate his example"; in his provincial upbringing, "the ministers then called Catholics heard me praise the justice of the Supreme Being, in preaching that the same destiny awaited the virtuous man, whether he worshipped the God of Geneva, the God of Rome, of Mahomet, or of Confucius."[74] These abjurations did not assert the renunciation of religion Cloots hoped for but rather an acknowledgment of a radical religious diversity, even equality between religions. Nonetheless they inspired a wave of resignations from the Constitutional Church all across France, as Michel Vovelle has shown, with more than half the clergy abandoning their vocation, and many subsequently marrying.[75]

Two days after this new piece of radicalizing revolutionary theater, Cloots was elected president of the Jacobins, and on the day after his election, 10 November, the Festival of Reason was celebrated in Notre-Dame. A week later the Assembly acknowledged Cloots's "Muslim book": the Orator of the Human Race was riding high. But this ascendancy was illusory: behind the applause of the Assembly, forces were at work to dismantle the radical antireligious project. On 21 November, as the commune prepared to close all the churches in Paris, Robespierre gave a speech at the Jacobin Club calling for reinforcement of freedom of religion, and accusing the "new fanatics" who, "on the pretext of destroying superstition, want to make a kind of religion from atheism itself."[76] On 12 December, in the midst of the regular "purge" of members, he denounced Cloots, who was unanimously expelled. Robespierre showed himself more than willing to exploit the widespread fear of foreigners to discredit his opponent. The Assembly passed a new law on 18 Frimaire (21 December) prohibiting "all acts of violence and measures contrary to freedom of religion." A week later, Cloots was arrested, along with the other supposed "Hébertists"; on 24 March they went to the guillotine. Gobel and Chaumette followed on 13 April. Cloots stayed true to his antireligious faith until the end, choosing to be executed last, and exhorting his co-condemned not to waver in their faith that death was an eternal noth-ingness. If Robespierre appeared to have won this war against atheism, that victory was equally illusory, as we will see later in this book. Cloots was not by any means an isolated crank: his meteoric rise, and his equally rapid fall, were driven by much larger dynamics, which continued after his death, as the case of Joseph Lequinio reveals.

Lequinio: Cosmopolitanism against Islam

Coming from a small hamlet in Britanny "in a still savage region" to Versailles in 1789, Joseph Lequinio was at first dazzled by the National Assembly, but quickly became disillusioned by the cynicism of politics.[77] Devoting himself to the cause of agriculture, he wrote in May 1790 a book explaining the bene-fits of the Revolution for Breton farmers; he began a newspaper and agitated for their cause. Soon, however, his devotion to and belief in the peasantry was shaken by the refusal of priests to accept the constitution, and the stub-born support they found in the countryside.

In 1791, Lequinio addressed local peasants in the department of the Gard, suggesting that religion was a necessary attribute of all people, and explaining that since each people adored God in their own way, it was illog-ical to hate one another for those differences. "Understand once and for all what freedom of opinion in religious matters means—go to the Mass of a juring or non-juring priest, practice the religion of a Jew or a Turk, be Chris-tian or Muslim, adore god in one way or another—you are free . . . it is up to your conscience and your conscience only to decide."[78] Live and let live: Lequinio believed that opposition would drain away over time, and the constitutional order would be solidified.

The tempestuous battles over the Constitutional Church profoundly altered this belief that the salvation of the Revolution lay in the extension of freedom of religion to all, including those refusing to swear the constitutional oath. In *Les préjugés détruit*, published in November 1792, Lequinio described his mounting horror at the "mutual hatred" that had emerged between the two parties in the religious schism of 1791. There were fanatics and hypo-crites in China and Turkey, he observed, but "no other religion had so great a spirit of intolerance as that of Christian priests." As someone who believed sincerely in the goodness of the people—he edited a newspaper for the local farmers, and worked ardently to establish a canal—he was shocked to the core by the murderous hatred of peasants toward priests who had sworn the oath. He added a note hoping that these conditions were purely of the moment, and that "it will all seem so puerile and ridiculous in a few years."[79]

Lequinio found a way to rise above this internecine violence through universalism. "I am a man," he declared, "and the earth is my *patrie*. I do not know the human species in terms of height or color, and the blood of a European is no more precious to me than the blood of an Asiatic, the blood of a white man than that of a redskin or a mulatto or a black; the enslaved man is always my friend, a friend in misery over whose fate I shed tears, and his master in every land is a tyrant whom I abhor." On the title page, Lequinio identified himself as a "Citizen of the Globe" and declared that he preferred this "precious title" even to that of deputy of the National Convention. "Whoever you are," he wrote, "your friendship is precious to me: Christian, Mahometan, Jew, Indian, Persian, Tartar, or Chinese, are you not a man, and am I not your brother?"[80]

Yet if he valued Muslims as individuals, he opposed their religion. Lequinio used Islam to condemn religion in general, depicting all religions as "monstrous absurdities that, until now, have degraded man, stifling his intelligence and compromising his reason." "Mahomet," he wrote, "this audacious monster, so arrogant as to publicly order massacres in the name of heaven, made ignorance an explicit article of his religion, and the greatest obstacle faced by the virtuous men who seek to call the Mahometans to liberty will be to make them violate the precept that prohibits them from education." He lamented that African and Asian slavery would be so much more difficult to end, because "most of them are subject to the religion of Mahomet," and claimed that the Prophet—"the charlatan of Mecca"—had outlawed all forms of education.[81]

Lequinio's cosmopolitan commitment was not an abstract Enlightenment ideal, but a concrete response to the violence occurring around him. Nor were his dechristianizing actions in the Year 2 the program of a fanatical atheist: they can be better understood as a search for a larger order in the context of violent religious schism, which raised the terrifying specter of the bloody civil wars that had riven France for centuries. Appointed as a representative on mission to the Vendée, he reputedly killed at least one prisoner with his own hands, and issued orders for pitiless repressions. In his speech on happiness in Rochefort in November 1793, he invoked the "sacred love of the *Patrie*" paired with intractable hatred of "tyrants of all kinds, political or religious," calling upon this love to "force" humans toward dignity. He repeated this word "force" four times; this coercion would lead to a world where "all hypocrisies will disappear . . . all thrones will fall . . . all limits will be erased, and . . . at last, in several centuries, the human species will reach a point where it is nothing but one single family, and the globe it inhabits one single *patrie*."[82]

The decree of Frimaire declared that the French people and its representatives abhorred intolerance and persecution of any kind, including "the extravagances of philosophism, like the folly of superstition and the crimes of fanaticism."[83] In Rochefort, Lequinio interpreted the freedom of religion quite differently. On 1 Nivôse he declared that of course "all religions are free," but only as "opinion," insisting that "any man, whoever he is, who goes about preaching any religious maxim at all is, by that alone, guilty before the people." Religious practice was now a violation not only of the constitution but of "social equality, . . . which does not allow any man to raise publicly his ideal pretension above those of his neighbor."[84]

Equality of religion thus meant no religion at all. Lequinio was berated by the Committee of Public Safety, but wrote back on 1 Pluviôse, acknowledging "the inconvenience of the violence provoked in the name of religion," but seemed genuinely mystified as to how he had differed from Robespierre's vision. "Freedom of religion," he observed, "is that of practice, and not that of using magic and a deceitful eloquence to force people to practice it."[85] His decree against all religions had been welcomed all over the region, he suggested, and Paris was out of touch with the mood of the provinces. Lequinio was not defying the Committee of Public Safety; Aulard is wrong in suggesting that he continued in a "Hébertist" politics of dechristianization. Instead, he believed that he was waging the same struggle as that of the committee in Paris, the attempt to defeat "fanaticism" and extirpate the enemies of the republic. Enveloped in the local context, he failed to see the shifting ground of religious policy, and came close to losing his head.

Claudy Valin, in a recent biography, has underlined that the term "dechristianization, so often used in his case, does not correspond to his mind-set nor to the dispositions he put in place."[86] Indeed, Lequinio was capable of describing Jesus Christ as a good sansculotte, even as he rejected Christian mysteries. On 10 December 1793, at the opening of a temple of truth, Lequinio's Jewish protégé Alexandre Lambert made a speech in which he welcomed into union with the religion of nature "the three sects that have most dishonored it." "Let us no longer be Jews, Christians, Protestants," he exhorted. "Let us be citizens, and let us fulfill our duties."[87] He called on "rabbis, curés, ministers" to renounce their functions, and particularly "the absurdities of the Jewish religion, that dominating religion that gave birth to Mahometanism, to Christianity, to Protestantism, in short to all the absurdities that have for so long desolated the four corners of the earth."[87] Lequinio ordered the publication of this speech, which, he declared, "proved the progress of one of the peoples fanatically attached to the ideas originating from its religion."[88]

In March 1794, Lequinio was recalled to Paris. On 18 Floréal (7 May) Robespierre delivered his great speech in the Convention on the internal politics of the republic, denouncing those who "suddenly attack all religions through violence, and . . . set themselves up as the fiery apostles of nothingness, and fanatical missionaries of atheism."[89] These extremists, Robespierre declared, had relegated reason to the temples in order to drive it out of the republic. In the Jacobin Club, Lequinio responded to this speech with an outburst of sycophantic praise, calling it one of the "most beautiful and sublime days of the republic," which had confounded the calumnies directed against its representatives. This articulation of support for Robespierre was well timed. Brival rose shortly afterward to accuse Lequinio of hypocrisy, and of denying the existence of the Supreme Being in his books and speeches. A few days later, Lequinio produced a page of his book *Les préjugés détruits* to argue that it did recognize the Supreme Being. He declared, moreover, that if his book contained any errors, he would burn it with his own hands. Robespierre intervened to say that no one doubted Lequinio's patriotism. "What does it matter to us what one man has written or said?" he asked. "What interests us is to know who is a conspirator, who has provoked the ferments of discord in civil society, in a word who is attached to the foreign faction."[90] This timely remark saved Lequinio from the guillotine, when Cloots, Pereyra, Gobel, Chaumette, and many others lost their heads.

Yet when the wind blew the other way following Thermidor, Lequinio turned like a weather vane against his savior, explaining these changes of direction as the result of the monstrous evil of a man he had praised to the skies just weeks earlier. He claimed that the Robespierrists had sought to recall the *représentants* and substitute their own agents, "brutal, capricious, cowardly, and cruel men who thirsted like their masters for human blood. . . . who did not blush to become the subaltern ministers of a new superstition that the new Mahomet was in the process of establishing on the ruins of the old, and . . . proclaim themselves everywhere the new kings, the new gods of France, and their power without end."[91]

The attack on religion in 1793 was not simply a question of "dechristianization"—a term invented in the later struggles over secularization at the end of the nineteenth century. It was a much larger collapse of faith in religion as a stabilizing force in society, and the desperate struggle to find some way to replace it. Cardinal de Bausset wrote later that although we may think that this was simply a question of the struggle over the clerical oath, "it was equally intended to destroy the Protestant religion, the Jewish, the Constitutional, the Muslim, since all these religions were proscribed during this deplorable period."[92] The reality was more complex even than this. It was neither a single destructive impulse from the center, nor a grassroots response emerging from a weakened religious faith at the periphery, but a chaotic field of battle involving many actors. At stake was the question of how religion, with its enormous power to marshal the most fundamental emotions, would relate to the state and the new civic, national, and universal passions. De Bausset was right, however, that Islam too was dragged into this struggle.

What could this mean for Muslims themselves? Were they to be considered as foreigners to be distrusted and banished, as fanatics to be cured of their superstitions, or as potential allies to be welcomed in revolutionary France? The arrival of two Indian Muslims in 1793, and their trajectory through a France in the grip of what has become known as "the Terror," can reveal much on these questions.

8. The Muslim Jacobins

In the first weeks of Floréal of the Year 2—April 1794—at the height of the period that has become infamous in history as "the Terror," an Indian Muslim arrived in Paris and applied for assistance to the Committee of Public Safety.

On 2 Floréal, he was referred to an official who proposed boilerplate language for a decree to the effect that the Committee of Public Safety, "wishing to fulfill the duties of hospitality, authorizes the commissioner of External Relations to furnish him with a sum of 1,200 livres to allow him to continue his voyage, and to provide him with a passport." When the order was finally delivered, on 21 Floréal, new wording had been added: "The Committee of Public Safety," it read, "*considering that the French nation honors misfortune*, authorizes the commissary of external relations to provide provisional assistance, as an act of hospitality, to Ahmed Khan, Indian."[1] It was signed by Barère, Collot d'Herbois, Robespierre, Billaud-Varenne, Prieur, Couthon, Carnot, and Lindet.

On 18 Floréal, while he was deliberating on this case as a member of the Committee of Public Safety, Maximilien Robespierre pronounced the same words in an address announcing the long-awaited religious policy of the Jacobin regime. That phrase had never previously appeared in his speeches or writings. "*We honor misfortune*," he declared, "misfortune, which humanity cannot entirely banish from the earth, but which it consoles and alleviates with respect."[2] We cannot know how the presence of this young Muslim in France shaped Robespierre's thinking about revolutionary hospitality and the universal destiny of the Revolution, but the coincidence of language is too significant to be ignored. The committee altered the tenor as well as the wording of the decree, which said nothing about the continuation of his journey or a passport. The Committee of Public Safety had decided to ask Ahmed to suspend his journey and remain in France. This can tell us something about revolutionary hospitality at this moment: it was not passive charity but a more active form of political engagement. Its effects were striking. In the months that followed, Ahmed Khan began the first project to translate the Declaration of the Rights of Man and Citizen for the Muslim world.

The Muslim partisans of the Revolution have almost been lost from history.[3] The rupture between France and Islam that followed just a few years later rendered such a convergence unthinkable in retrospect, and brought to the fore a chorus of Muslim voices that condemned the Revolution as anarchy and atheism.[4] But during this brief moment of the mid-1790s, that posterity had not yet been written. There is another history to be rescued from its logic.

Though the French, shaped by their own revolutionary uses of Islam, easily imagined Ahmed Khan as a naive, exotic traveler blown off course into a political storm, he was more than he appeared. As Adrian Carton has argued in relation to Pondicherry, the question of Indian radical participation in the revolutionary ferment has been overshadowed by the dominance of British imperialism and the racial politics in the French Caribbean.[5] C. A. Bayly too has traced a new lineage of Indian liberalism from the revolutionary age.[6] Most of these studies have focused on Bengal, Calcutta, and South India; the story of Ahmed Khan is one that brings Bombay, Gujurat, and the Deccan into the picture.

But Ahmed's story can tell us something too about the French Revolution and its relationship to the foreigner. Despite the shifts in revolutionary historiography, the old notion that foreigners were arbitrarily persecuted under "the Terror" has remained largely in place. Certainly, during 1793, after Britain joined the coalition against France, and as fears of conspiracy grew among elites and nonelites alike, the foreigner became a focus of anxiety. The "foreign plot"—part imagined, part real—came easily to the minds of many in this moment. From the perspective of this Indian Muslim, that history looks different. Instead of suspicion and distrust, he found support and encouragement. By the time he arrived in Paris, the republic had abolished slavery and welcomed people of color as full citizens. Although the fall from cosmopolitanism into xenophobia has been a key component in discursively driven understandings of the Terror—as an inevitable working-out of the Manichean conception of friend and enemy—the real picture is more complex, and goes to the heart of the struggle over definitions of citizenship and rights.

Ahmed Khan and his elder brother Nawazish Khan were sons of the nawab of Bharuch, a small city on the coast of Gujarat that became independent with the fragmentation of Mughal power in 1736. The ruler of the nearby city of Surat continued to claim that customs revenues from Bharuch had been granted to him by the Mughal emperor. In 1771, the British East India Company made a deal with the nawab of Surat to enforce these speculative claims against two-thirds of the revenues. The governor of Bombay, William Hornby, sent an army against Bharuch; it failed, and negotiations ensued. Finally, in November 1772, the East India Company's forces stormed and sacked the city, aided by the intrigues of a disloyal adviser, Lalbagh. The nawab fled to Dehwan, where he died just a few months later.[7]

The company's governors in London instructed their agents in India to return the city to the nawab's sons, but Hornby refused: he maintained company rule in the city until 1783, then used it as a bargaining chip in a treaty signed with the Marathas, ending a long-running war.[8]

The affair had become one of the scandals that were gradually creating the "Company-State" in India, a state exceeding British control, with its own army and bureaucracy. As Nicholas Dirks has shown, these scandals helped form the shape of British imperialism.[9] In a letter to the French minister, Ahmed wrote that he threatened the governor: "If he did not return the hereditary lands of my family, I would go to England and make my case directly to the court. This threat annoyed the governor, and he had us imprisoned, my brothers and myself. At the end of five months of arrest, we managed, all four of us, to escape his vigilance and board an Arab ship without the knowledge of our tyrant, and traveled to Muscat, then to Basra, Baghdad, and Constantinople."[10]

Ahmed explained that on arriving in the Ottoman capital, the four brothers separated, with two staying behind while Ahmed and Nawazish set out on a journey to London. They traveled to Salonika, and took a ship from there to Marseille. In April 1793, just a few months after the execution of Louis XVI, they arrived in Marseille with their domestic servant, and somehow managed to communicate their wishes to the authorities, possibly in English. The Chamber of Commerce which had traditionally dealt with such issues had been dissolved, but the local deputies requested the municipality to authorize the "administrators of the Provisional Bureau of Commerce" to provide the Indians with transport to Paris and letters of introduction to the commissioner of external affairs. From Lyon, they intended to travel onward by road, but on the night before their departure, Nawazish Khan fell violently ill, and the two brothers were compelled to remain in the city for almost a year.

The two Indians had arrived in southern France at a moment of great turbulence. The execution of the king in early 1793, followed by the intrusion of armed Parisians into the National Assembly, forcing the expulsion of the Girondins, had provoked anger and concern across the country. In Marseille, Lyon, and other cities, radical groups and royalists were struggling to seize power from the constituted authorities.[11] Ahmed and Nawazish Khan were staying at the former Hôtel de la Croix de Malte, and soon came to the end of their meager finances. Around them, the city was in convulsion: the passage of the Marseillais regiment through the city in August 1792 had radicalized local sansculottes, and in March 1793 their leader Marie Joseph Chalier was elected to the municipality, enacting radical changes to confront food shortages, along with emergency political measures. In May, after a march by the sections that turned into a riot, the Chalier party was pushed out of power, opening the door for royalists to seize control. Chalier and his followers were imprisoned and executed in the public square on 17 July.[12] Faced with this revolt, which came at the same moment as other regional insurrections in Marseille, Bordeaux, Toulon, and other cities, the National Convention in Paris ordered General Dubois-Crancé, commanding an army in Savoy, to crush the insurrection, and during August and September the Army of the Alps bombarded and besieged Lyon.[13]

As these events shook the city, Ahmed and his brother struggled to survive on their rapidly dwindling resources. On 25 July, just a week after the execution of Chalier, the municipality sent the two Indians to the Hôtel-Dieu, the public hospital, and arrested Arnaud, the courier who had accompanied them. As the fighting in the town intensified, the hospital was evacuated to another area, where facilities became further stretched as wounded from both sides streamed in.

On 2 August, two officers of the counterrevolutionary municipality drew up a detailed account claiming a debt of 4,392 livres for the months the two Indians had stayed in Lyon. The document was signed by Combe-Pachot and Maisonneuve; just a few months later, both men would be among thousands sent to the guillotine by the revolutionary tribunal.[14] The repression in Lyon from October to December was one of the most violent anywhere in

France. The number of those judged guilty far surpassed the means of execution, and Collot d'Herbois ordered mass shootings (the famous *mitraillades*)
using grapeshot.[15]

In November, the administrators of the Hôtel Dieu wrote to Marseille
asking the Chamber of Commerce to pay the costs of the two brothers'
extended stay. The letter was marked *ville affranchie*—"liberated city." A
letter sent in reply scratched out the word "ville" and substituted it with
"commune," since Lyon was no longer to be considered a city, but only an
administrative unit. Marseille, too, had been stripped of its name and status,
designated for several months as *Sans Nom* (Without a Name).[16] This tells us
something about the landscape of early 1794, the sense that the old order
must be destroyed utterly before a new France could emerge from its ashes.

In the midst of this paroxysm, the two brothers and their servant were
struggling to survive in a city on the edge of subsistence; yet they did not
abandon their religious practice as Muslims. The hospital directors complained
that the costs were particularly high because of the need for halal food, "the
religion that they profess not permitting them to eat any meat that they have
not bled themselves, which makes their sustenance very difficult in a hospital
when there is a lack of poultry."[17] They needed clothing "because they have
completely run out of linen, turbans, clothing, and are almost naked."[18] In
spite of the violent conflict over religion, these practices of Islam were
respected.

All communication with Marseille had been cut off since the beginning
of April. Nawazish Khan was extremely ill; though his convulsions had been
successfully treated, his legs were in a state of paralysis, and in the midst of
an increasingly bad winter, he had to be carried in and out of bed. The
hospital, at the center of the city under siege, had been "transferred by necessity to a very cramped and uncomfortable location," and doctors warned that
its infected air would soon prove fatal for the young man. The expression of
concern carried a sting in its tail: given the amount of money owed, the
hospital directors insisted that "if you fail to respond promptly on all the
points of the present letter, there will be no other option to follow but to have
them taken to the poorhouse, where they will have a great deal more to
complain about."[19]

Learning of these threats from the liquidators of the former Chamber
of Commerce of Marseille, the minister of foreign affairs, Deforgues, wrote
to Collot d'Herbois, the National Assembly's representative in "Commune

Affranchie." This letter, of 18 Frimaire (8 December), at the height of the brutal repression in Lyon, is remarkable for its tone of humanity and compassion. Deforgues highlighted "the unfortunate situation in which these travelers find themselves, and their pressing need for your intervention." Suggesting that Collot should find out the motivation of their journey, he added a correction that emphasized the "humanity" that should dictate such an action. The minister hoped to find some "public mission" that could justify the use of his own funds to aid the travelers, but added that in any case, "it is worthy of a great and generous nation to lift from misery strangers that fate has cast upon its mercy, and the French people will no doubt approve the measures you take to fulfill this sacred duty of hospitality."[20] It is striking to note here the emergent conception of the *grande nation*, which would come to take on such different meanings under the Directory.[21]

The brothers were given assistance by order of the representatives, and wrote thanking the municipal council, requesting payment for their interpreter, Holstein, and asking for some warm clothing and medicaments. On 26 Nivôse (15 January 1794), the council formally ruled in favor, "considering that these foreigners have been recommended to them by the representatives of the people, and that humanity and hospitality are sacred virtues for a free people."[22] The Terror has often been imagined as a time when humane sentiments were suspended, when foreigners were identified as suspect, persecuted, imprisoned, or executed. The case of these two Indian Muslims, alone, ill, and penniless in a city under siege, tends to show quite the reverse.

Other forces were certainly at work in a France at war both externally and internally, and we might imagine that these rebellious Indian subjects of an emergent British Empire could be considered potential recruits in a larger war. At this point, however, the background of their situation was not yet known to the authorities, and there is no reason to think that immediate political expediency was the primary motive for this generosity.

Revolutionary Hospitality

Despite the support offered by the new municipality, Nawazish Khan survived only for a few more months. Ahmed arranged the last rites for his brother's body, then traveled to Paris. On 2 Floréal (21 April 1794) he met with the minister of foreign affairs and presented an account of his misfortunes, translated into French by Pierre Ruffin, the interpreter who had often served as intermediary for Muslims in Versailles and Paris. He signed his petition "the servant of God, Ahmed Khan; written today, Thursday, 27th day of the moon of Ramadan, year of the Hijra 1209." The minister engaged with Ahmed in a long conversation, which, he reported to the Committee of Public Safety, demonstrated "indications of an excellent education and a dignified bearing that seem to confirm what he says of his origins and his views."[23] While waiting for the decision of the Committee of Public Safety, Ahmed stayed in the rue Richelieu, opposite the National Library, as Ruffin noted on 15 Floréal. A week later, the decision of the committee was delivered, signed by Robespierre, as well as Couthon and Collot, and six other members of the committee.

This decision was just one among thousands delivered by the Committee of Public Safety in the period of its office: we do not know how much time or consideration was devoted to discussing it. One index of its significance is the sizeable amount of money involved, at a time when the finances of the republic were extremely strained and severe economic measures in place. We will see in the next chapter why Robespierre might have had political reason to concern himself with Muslims; yet even more important than those political calculations was the opportunity to articulate a new form of revolutionary hospitality. Sophie Wahnich has criticized the "myth" of the Revolution's welcome of foreigners seeking asylum, yet elsewhere she notes the centrality of the revolutionary idea of welcoming the pariah and the outcast in such influential works as Bernardin de Saint-Pierre's *La chaumière indienne* of 1790.[24] For Wahnich, the "Indian" element of the work is mere ballast in analyzing discursive structures. This was not the case for the revolutionaries themselves: Ahmed Khan clothed these ideas in physical form— and shaped his own narrative accordingly. What we can see here is that the "encounter" of Ahmed Khan with French revolutionary culture was a mutual exchange, and not a shock of contact between distinct and radically divergent cultures. As Sanjay Subrahmanyam has written of such encounters in Mughal India, "The 'amusing fables' on the basis of which most claims concerning incommensurability are made turn out to be false on closer investigation. . . . What usually happened was approximation, improvisation, and eventually a shift in the relative positions of all concerned."[25] Robespierre's language in his speech and the simultaneous use of the same key idea in the case of Ahmed Khan suggest how the presence of even a single individual can have unexpected ramifications. At the same time, we can see that this hospitality was not an "idea" generated from a discursive structure, but an emotional practice emerging in the revolutionary context.

At the moment that Ahmed was meeting with the commissioner in Paris, his younger brother, Mirza Odudeen (Ahid ud-Din) Khan, was in London, having arrived in Toulon while it was under British occupation. There, it appears, he engaged a lawyer and set about seeking financial redress of 180 million rupees from the East India Company. During the month of Ramadan 1794, while Ahmed remained in Paris waiting for the decision of the Committee of Public Safety, Odudeen demanded the company directors supply him and his suite with foodstuffs for the nightly iftar and a carriage and daily allowance.[26] It seems he hoped to remain in England, living on a comfortable pension; the directors, however, insisted he return to India and accept a payoff on behalf of his family that would nullify claims against the company. Instead of seeking political redress for the company's annexation of their state, Odudeen seemed content with personal gain.

Ahmed's inquiries suggest that he was unaware of his brother's activities in London; it is unclear whether he had planned to pursue a similar approach. It is evident, however, that Ahmed changed course during these months. Instead of continuing to London, he remained in Paris, and then moved to Versailles after the decision by the Committee of Public Safety to support him during his stay. Ruffin emphasized the political significance of Ahmed's decision to remain in France, and his willingness to study French. "This fortunate disposition," he wrote, "is not to be neglected in the light of political relations. The interests of his fortune would push him toward English, the language of his oppressors. Why do we not benefit from the inclinations of his heart, which leads him to study the language, customs, and laws of the friendly nation that pleases and assists him?"[27] The commissioner took up this suggestion, noting that "in the future, his dispositions could in various ways make his services useful to the republic and to the work of the commission."[28]

Over the next few months, Ahmed made rapid progress in the French language. The commissioner of external affairs sent 350 livres in assignats to cover his living expenses, and Ahmed agreed to send his domestic servant back to Lyon, probably to take care of his brother's remains, which he hoped to take back to India. In the meantime, Ahmed was presented to the local revolutionary authorities in Versailles. The president of the municipality assured Ahmed "that he could only rejoice in the welcome and the attitude of all the citizens of this commune, and that he could consider himself taken to the heart of a people of friends and brothers." Ahmed replied with gratitude, but noted that his religion compelled certain alterations in the political customs of revolutionary France: he had taken the habit of wearing his tricolor cockade on the left side of his coat, "as Muslims could not ignore the religious scruples that prohibit all decoration on the turban." The municipal council responded that "he could be quite tranquil on this point as on all the others; in leaving, he was invited to attend the deliberations of the council whenever he chose."[29]

Jacques Derrida has pointed to the contrast between conditional and unconditional hospitality. The unlimited act of welcome that requires nothing of the new arrival, and does not even ask for a name or documents, appears on the surface to be the "true" nature of hospitality. Yet such an approach makes the existence of the bounded community impossible. The transformation of the "gift" into a "contract" is determined not by a limitless expression of acceptance, but instead by the *acts* that "render the welcome effective, determined, concrete . . . put it into practice."[30] The grudging but largely undemanding welcome in Lyon, and even that universal "duty" prescribed by the Committee of Public Safety in this sense, did not constitute the real "welcome" of Ahmed Khan, since nothing at all was asked of him in return. In agreeing that Ahmed might decide on how he manifested his political connection to the Revolution, in conformance with his own understandings of his religion, the municipality of Versailles exercised this concrete hospitality that offered the prelude to a form of citizenship. They demonstrated that the universalizing rhetoric about Muslims that had circulated in preceding years *could* be translated into practice, but also that this conception was not based on the refusal of difference. Instead, the nature of this hospitality was neither to constitute Ahmed as an exotic outsider, the recipient of a unilateral act of generosity, nor to demand that he conform rigidly to the norms and rules of the society that welcomed him: it was a flexible form of dialogue that invited without compulsion. It is crucial to see in this the *experience* of rights, not simply as ideas, but as lived practice.

Ruffin noted that this revolutionary sociability brought great happiness to Ahmed, who had been living in enforced solitude in Paris due to the difficulties of communication, and able to converse only with his servant, which "had thrown this young Indian into a melancholy that the thought of his troubles, and particularly the memory of his brother who died in his arms, so aggravated that he often tells me he feared his reason would not survive."[31]

Ahmed, however, wrote a letter in Persian that suggested a slightly different understanding of his position. He assimilated his gratitude to the republic to his similar experience of hospitality in Muslim countries: "Thanks to the generosity of our friends, we have not experienced any want in our country, in Arabia, or in the Ottoman states. Everywhere we have been welcomed and comfortable." He certainly appreciated the beauty of Versailles, and the walks that offered to restore his mood, and equally the prospect of adding French to his knowledge of Arabic, Turkish, and Persian: "The French are our friends and our brothers," he wrote. "We suffer very much to live among them without being able to understand or talk to them." Ahmed mixed these practical considerations with political expressions of support for France in the war against Britain, calling on heaven to favor his friends and to "confound [the British] and their adherents." Already, it seems, Ahmed was placing himself in political and emotional alignment with the Revolution, through the conception of fraternity, social solidarity, and the common enmity of the British; but he placed this political alignment under the sign of Islam. The letter finished with an apostrophe to the French, invoking Allah in Koranic language: "May He bring you victory upon victory! You will know at the predestined moment how to help us to our goal and to the end of our troubles."[32] Despite British imperialism in India, this outright opposition was unusual: historians have argued that Indian Muslim elites generally "took a dim view of the French Revolution and its principles" and were "preoccupied" by the British political system.[33] Yet this view is too broad; rather than a simple exception, Ahmed may represent a different and less visible underground movement.

Ahmed's progress in learning French was exceptionally (perhaps unconvincingly) rapid. After just 12 lessons, it seems that he was able to express himself in speech and writing, and Ruffin predicted that within two months he would be fluent. The interpreter attributed this not only to memory and determination, but to the emotional character of the "young Muslim," which he considered "happy and susceptible to attachment." In this letter of 12 Prairial, Ruffin wrote to citizen Otto, the chief of the first division of external affairs, that Ahmed planned to come to Paris and "come to see you and embrace you fraternally."[34] A month later, in the middle of Messidor, Ruffin wrote to assure his colleagues in Paris that the "student of the republic" continued to advance in his studies. "His progress, his conduct, and his health are improving in the most satisfying manner."[35] Only his mood had waned, due to the lack of word from his brothers in Istanbul, but also the necessity of procuring a new turban, a vest, and pantaloons as the weather grew warmer. The commissioner wrote sharply back to Ruffin to remind him of the large sums already expended for Ahmed's upkeep.

The Myth of a Xenophobic Terror

The negotiations over Ahmed's new turban were taking place at the very height of the "Great Terror," after the law of 22 Prairial had given the Revolutionary Tribunals the right to judge "enemies of the people" and prescribed death as the punishment for all political offenses, drastically accelerating the pace of executions. Many historians have considered this period the height of xenophobia and suspicion. Yet Ahmed, a foreigner of a different religion, was not only tolerated but actively supported, by the authorities in Paris and by the local municipality.

The thesis of the "xenophobic" Terror is in part the result of a loose conflation of "enemy subjects" with foreigners in general. Where the panic and fear regarding the "foreign plot" (partly imagined and partly founded in reality) certainly led to the inculpation of French citizens who were found to be even loosely connected with suspect foreigners, widespread arrests of British subjects in particular, and a prohibition on the presence of enemy subjects in Paris, it is inaccurate to suggest that this was a blanket exercise of unavoidable "national mobilization" (as Albert Mathiez conveniently suggested at the time of the First World War) or that it implied the projection of the foreigner as an "impossible citizen," as Sophie Wahnich has argued.[36] Michael Rapport showed in his careful analysis of nationality and citizenship that many of those instances that appeared as xenophobic reactions against foreigners were driven by other political calculations, and that large numbers of foreigners remained exempt, including some at the most active levels of political activity in the sections or the committees, yet still concluded that this constituted a "nationalization of citizenship."[37] This is a conclusion we may question.

At no point was Ahmed, a foreign Muslim, placed under surveillance or threatened with arrest, despite his presence in some of the most politically sensitive areas in France. We have no example of a Muslim who was arrested; but we can compare his case with that of the "Turk" who spoke in the

National Assembly in 1790. Dom Denis Chawich, the Syrian priest who had joined the Jacobin Club in its earliest moments, and participated in the deputation to the National Assembly, found himself swept up in the mass arrests of 1793 and imprisoned, fearing for his life for almost a year in the Luxembourg prison, as streams of suspects were taken out, tried, and in many cases executed at the guillotine.

Why did Chawich experience this treatment while Ahmed Khan was assisted and supported by the same authorities? The answer points to a more complex set of experiences for foreigners in France than many historians have recognized.

Historians of the Revolution have struggled to explain why the violence of the Year 2, often described simply as "the Terror"—a denomination that already puts a thumb on the balance—continued toward a crescendo, even though the threat from within and without had ebbed in the early months of 1794. French armies were winning battles to the east, and had crushed both the insurrection in the west and the "federalist" uprisings in the provincial cities. Toulon was liberated from English control, and the republic seemed no longer to be fighting for its life. Yet the functioning of the Revolutionary Tribunals did not slacken, delivering a swelling stream of condemned to be executed by guillotine in many departments across France. Some have seen in this the proof of the original sin of the Revolution—its baptism in violence, its blind devotion to Rousseau—or a fatal "turn" to violence at some point.[38] One widely shared element of this conception has been the view that the violence of the Year 2 was nationalist and xenophobic in nature, and that the figure of the "foreigner" became the scapegoat for France's ills.

Recent historians have challenged this assumption; indeed, they have suggested that cosmopolitanism was as much a part of the politics of the republic as the discourse of nation. As Suzanne Desan has observed, in August 1792, the deputy Marie-Joseph Chénier presented his own deputation at the bar of the National Assembly: this time not a delegation of foreigners seeking participation, but a delegation of French citizens seeking to expand (and in important ways to redefine) the limits of citizenship. On 26 August, after a debate in which deputies such as Vergniaud and Lamourette spoke passionately on the ideal of the republic as a universal conception, defined by political belonging and open to all who professed the same commitments, full political citizenship was accorded to a list of eighteen foreigners: seven British, four Germans, three Americans, an Italian, a

Dutchman, a Swiss, and a Pole. Unlike Cloots's deputation of 1790, this group did not include any names from the Muslim world, nor did it include people of color from the Caribbean.

As Desan suggests, these foreigners "did not represent the whole globe . . . they embodied the European and American Enlightenment, its assertion of cosmopolitanism, and the commitment to certain revolutionary political stances."[39] There were no Muslims, Arabs, or people of color here as there were in Cloots's deputation of 1790. Chénier's petition made particular reference to William Bolts, "persecuted by Lord Clive and by the East India Company for having defended humanity, for having believed that the suffering Indians were not destined by nature to tremble eternally under the yoke of the English ministry."[40] Bolts did not, however, appear on the final list, possibly because of opposition to provoking the British, who were not yet at war with France.

Peter Sahlins has shown that the Convention was in fact responding to a series of requests by foreigners, like the Swede Frederic Hobes, the Englishman William Priestley (son of Joseph Priestley), and the Italian revolutionary Filippo Buonarotti, who had been theoretically granted citizenship prior to 10 August, but without any final decision being made on the nature of that admission.[41] None of these names, however, were included in Chénier's petition, which instead deployed more famous philosophical examples to marshal emotional support for the larger principle. In the list of those ultimately granted citizenship on 26 August, five of those mentioned in the petition were removed from the list, and eight new names were added, including that of Anacharsis Cloots. What began as an attempt by foreign radicals to pry open the limits of revolutionary citizenship became a philosophical declaration of the universality of the Revolution. The list of illustrious foreigners cast the Revolution as an elite act of enlightenment, and not as a common global struggle from below against inequality; in some sense it was also a gesture by the Girondin-dominated Assembly against the rising power of the insurrectionary commune.

On 20 October 1792, a radical Jacobin, Joseph Antoine Boisset, rose in the Jacobin Club to denounce "a foreigner, claiming to be Armenian, and wearing oriental costume, who today insulted a patriotic Jacobin." He insisted that "this Armenian" be expelled from the society, and never again readmitted. François Chabot—later to be implicated centrally in the foreign plot, and married to the sister of an Austrian Jewish banker—responded that such personal quarrels were irrelevant, and since this man was an Armenian, a priest, and "interpreter at the National Library," it was natural that he should "cozy up to the government" that offered him personal gain, in this case the Brissotins. Another, unidentified accuser rose to amplify Boisset's denunciations: "I have always heard this Armenian professing principles opposed to those of liberty," he declared, "and I have already denounced him to my section. On the 12th of this month, I was walking in the Tuileries gardens with one of my friends, when I saw this Armenian talking in a group; as soon as he saw me, he began crying, 'He is an aristocrat, that man is an aristocrat,' and I heard people saying loudly on all sides, 'We should just hang him.' Some citizens came to my assistance, and without them, I can say that this Armenian would have hanged one of the best patriots in the republic."[42]

He added that the Armenian had been heard declaring that "the members of the Society wanted to assassinate Guadet at this tribune"; this remark provoked a tumult in the club. Guadet, president of the Assembly on 10 August, was a strong opponent of the radical wing and the Paris commune in particular, and this accusation of violence against the Jacobins at a crucial moment could have had grave consequences. Both sides seemed to vie to associate this "Armenian" with their opponents in order to discredit them.

Louis Legendre, who had once kept a butcher's shop, and had participated in the storming of the Bastille, the protest on the Champ de Mars, and the attack on the Tuileries on 10 August, rose to deliver an extraordinary affirmation of equality: "I do not know any Armenians or Arabs here, I see only citizens. If you do not rise above your personal hatreds, there will be demands for expulsions every day, one day against a journalist who has said this, another day against someone who has said that; and the personal recriminations will never end."[43]

Legendre's reference to Arabs here, without any obvious connection to the preceding discussion, suggests that he may well have known the identity of the "Armenian" to whom Boisset referred. Two oriental interpreters were employed at the Bibliothèque Nationale, Joseph Behenam and Denis Chawich: Behenam was an Iraqi Chaldean and Chawich a Palestinian Arab. Behenam, born in Mosul, was a politically engaged constitutional cleric who had attended the Festival of the Federation in 1790 as one of the "deputation of foreigners," although at the same time he pronounced himself "naturalized," an adopted Frenchman who had proved his civic virtue, in a sermon given at the church of Saint-Jacques in 1791.[44] Behenam was later cited in a pamphlet as an eyewitness to the imposture of the deputation of 1790, although there is no indication on the signed petition that he had participated.[45]

Chawich, however, was a verifiable member of the Jacobin Club, listed among its earliest members. His oriental dress—to which he made reference in his letters to the newspaper at the time of the deputation—perhaps suggested to Boisset the more familiar Armenian costume. As we noted in chapter 4, the proceedings of the Jacobin Club for 13 May 1791 recorded that during the debate, "an Armenian, or Turk, appeared at the tribune and spoke in favor of the gens de couleur."[46] On another occasion, a month later, an "African" was recorded as giving his opinion on the choice of tutor for the Dauphin, in the wake of the king's arrest at Varennes.[47] These mysterious designations suggest both the participation of a more varied group among the Jacobins than most historians have imagined, and the floating nature of identifiers for those whose chief attribute was their unusual dress, their religious difference, or the color of their skin.

These scattered fragments can give us some suggestion of Chawich's activity in the Jacobin Club; he was active on other fronts too. Both he and Joseph Behenam had been active in seeking redress from the National Assembly for losing their jobs in the reorganization of the library under Roland in November 1792. In his letter of protest, Chawich contrasted the hospitality and privilege enjoyed by French citizens in the Ottoman Empire with his own situation, reduced to penury in France and left for eight months without salary: "Not only the peoples that surround you, but even the savages of Africa would be outraged. Do you want me to portray you to the divan as the most barbarous people, the most unjust toward orientals, while the Ottoman nation is the most humane and the most just toward you?"[48]

In the same letter, Chawich asserted further titles to the gratitude of the republic: he claimed to have played a key role in the discrediting of the French ambassador in Istanbul, Choiseul-Gouffier, by informing a North African ambassador passing through Paris that Louis XVI had given 400 million livres and military support to Austria to make war on the Ottomans. He claimed further to have advised the government on procuring grain in North Africa and the Levant, and offered to act as an intermediary to "turn the powers of Algiers, Morocco, Tunis, and Tripoli against the English." He received support from the minister of the interior, Garat, who noted the contributions Chawich had made to French letters, and "above all since he is himself from a friendly nation where the French enjoy all the advantages that could favor our commercial relations."[49] Chawich risked a great deal by developing an association with Girondin ministers soon to be considered suspect, and revealing his earlier literary collaborations with Jacques Cazotte, one of the first counterrevolutionaries to be executed for treason.

On 15 November 1793, Chawich was arrested by his local section under the recently introduced law against enemy nationals, to which he was not in fact subject, as he pointed out when on 21 Pluviôse (9 February 1794) he wrote to the minister of foreign affairs to protest his incarceration in the prison of the Luxembourg, insisting that "last September's decree against foreigners at war with the Republic does not apply to him": "The citizen Chawich entered the prison as a former foreign interpreter and suspect under the law; everyone knows that the intrigues of the coalition powers did not succeed in making the Ottomans renounce their system of neutrality and their relations with the French Republic; if the Revolutionary Committee of my section was better educated in political affairs they would know that the citizen Chawich, subject of the sultan, is not affected by the law against foreigners. He should not remain any longer the victim of a mistake that makes him all the more unhappy because he has always served the cause of Liberty in every way he can."[50]

To protect himself, Chawich did not argue for his right to be considered French, but instead presented himself as a foreigner, and therefore under the protection of a neutral power, even as he insisted upon his ideological alignment with revolutionary principles.

Chawich was not averse to manipulating religious prejudices, blaming his arrest on the "maneuvers of an intriguing Jew, Pereira." This was the same Pereira/Pereyra who had collaborated to force the bishop Gobel's abjuration, and had been sent to the guillotine along with Cloots—Chawich's former mentor—and those accused of the "foreign plot." A few weeks later, Chawich's defender Chabot was executed along with the Dantonists. In contrast, Chawich was *protected* by his status as a foreigner: the minister wrote to the Committee of General Security on 23 February that "this Arab is a subject of the Ottoman Porte with which the French Nation has always maintained relations of interest and friendship."[51] He asked the committee to liberate "this foreigner" unless there were pressing reasons against it. Chawich would eventually be released from the Luxembourg prison eight months later; the reason for this long detention may well be linked to his having become, through residence, political participation, and marriage, a de facto citizen. A report of the minister of foreign affairs confirmed these complexities of Chawich's situation: "Naturalized French, so to speak, by a residence of nine years, and by his marriage with a Frenchwoman, with whom he has three children, he made himself very respectable before the Revolution, by the services he offered in the post to which he was appointed, and he distinguished himself no less, since the regeneration of the French people, by his attachment to the cause of Liberty, and by the sacrifices he made toward her triumph."[52] By the provisions of the laws of citizenship, Chawich was not a foreigner, but perhaps the first Arab citizen of France.

The case of Chawich demonstrates that there was no blanket xenophobia in the period of "the Terror" or at any other period of the Revolution. He had far more to fear from his political associations with figures who became suspect or actively counterrevolutionary than he did from his foreign status. Indeed, his claim to be the subject of a neutral power *protected* him against violence that took many other lives, yet it did not preclude him from claiming to be French at the same time. In this sense, not only might Chawich be France's first Arab citizen, he also was the first to assert a dual nationality, which, in the event, appears to have presented little problem to the revolutionary authorities.

Ahmed Khan's case, then, was not an isolated one: it fits quite well within the broader picture of the treatment of foreigners in this period. Where there is no doubt that subjects of enemy powers who could not give sufficiently firm proofs of a constant civic loyalty to France and ideological alignment to the Revolution were suspect and liable to arrest or even execution, this was not because they were "foreign" but because they were associated with counter-revolution. Miscarriages of justice took place, and innocent people did go to the guillotine merely for their origin, but this cannot be generalized into any broader picture of either popular or authoritarian xenophobia. Indeed, the path of Ahmed Khan suggests quite the opposite: he would face danger from the British authorities in India because of his association with the Revolution.

On 30 Messidor, a little more than a week before the events of 9 Thermidor brought down the Montagnard government, Ahmed Khan promised, through the offices of Ruffin, to provide "the material proof of his application in the study of our language."[53] During the month that followed, he began a translation of the Declaration of the Rights of Man and Citizen into Persian, the first in any of the major languages of the Muslim world.[54] In just two months, Ahmed had made sufficient progress in French that he was able (certainly with extensive help from Ruffin) to comprehend the language of the declaration and provide a translation.[55] After the year he had spent in Lyon, and the months in Paris and Versailles, we can surmise that his own experience of the Revolution helped him understand the context and struggles encoded in the document.[56] Yet even as he was completing this translation, the political ground was shifting. The declaration that Ahmed translated was the more radical restatement of 1793, rights that remained in suspension along with the constitution, and whose application was rescinded entirely after the coup of Thermidor, rendering his translation useless, if not troublesome.

On 26 Thermidor, Ruffin wrote to Buchot, the commissioner of external affairs, enclosing the first draft of this translation. Ruffin marveled at the rapidity of Ahmed's progress, and declared the product a triumph not just of civilization but of politics. "A Muslim writing in French characters is a conquest for philosophy. I was born in Turkey; I passed a large part of my life there, and since my return to France, my work and my scholarship have brought me into regular contact with Mahometans. Ahmed Khan is the only one I have seen who knows another alphabet than the Arabic one." Recalling his friendship with Ishak Bey, who had been present in France in 1789, Ruffin noted that "the former page of the sultan Mustapha . . . learned to stumble through some French, and after his various travels in Europe he eventually spoke it quite fluently. But he never desired to take it any further." Ahmed Khan, however, offered a riper political opportunity for the French. "The Indians," Ruffin claimed, "have already outstripped the intractable Ottomans in a number of ways along the path of enlightenment. Typoo-Sahib [Tipu Sultan] had the glory of showing the Turks an army of Muslim soldiers armed with bayonets and performing their drill in European style. But our friendship still lacks one thing: for these faithful allies to see a man born in their country and maintaining his religion, who knows how to read and write in our language. This phenomenon was reserved for the republican era."[57]

There is a striking shift in this letter from the language of brotherhood, friendship, and political participation in Floréal, just a few months earlier. Now the emphasis was on Ahmed's *use value* to the republic, with an explicit military context determining the interpretation of his path. As Ahmed was completing his translation of the Declaration of Rights, its provisions were already being ignored as thousands were arrested all over France in the wake of the coup. Between 10 and 12 Thermidor, some 100 members of the Paris commune were executed without trial.

On 1 Fructidor, Buchot sent Ahmed's translation to the Committee of Public Safety with a recommendation that it should be kept in the Bibliothèque

Nationale "as a precious monument of the homage given by an inhabitant of Asia to the true principles of society."[58] On the 4th Sans-Culottide, the second-to-last day of the Year 2, he sent a second copy of the translation to the Committee of Public Instruction. Neither of these copies appears to have survived, but a copy was kept among Ruffin's papers and another by the revolutionary committee in Versailles. In that latter copy, Ahmed included a preface explaining that the translation had been made by Ruffin, and transcribed in "characters traced by a Muslim hand." He cited the story of a "young Lydian, mute by birth, who suddenly pronounced the name of his father on seeing him tossed onto the funeral pyre." This story of a "miracle of filial piety," derived from Herodotus, seems to suggest an emotional translation from Ahmed's mission to redeem his father's loss to his ideological identification with the Revolution: a sense that he had somehow and very suddenly acquired a voice.[59]

Yet the ground was shifting rapidly. The letter of 19 Frimaire Year 3 (9 December 1794) noting the Committee of Public Safety's intention to place the manuscript "among the curious manuscripts of the National Library" referred to Ahmed consistently as "this foreigner"—a sharp difference from the earlier correspondence that identified him frequently as "this Muslim."[60] The conception of rights as the basis for reaching outward to the Muslim world had already become a "curiosity." Instead, more pragmatic realpolitik was in order.

Both Ruffin and Ahmed understood that a new sign of adhesion was in order after Thermidor. On 24 Frimaire, the commissioner wrote to the new authorities presenting another translation undertaken by Ruffin and transcribed by Ahmed; it would ultimately appear in a printed version. The text was that of the address to the French people after Thermidor, no longer focused on the universal application of the principles of the Revolution, but rather on bringing the Revolution to an end by the elimination of those associated with Robespierre, Saint-Just, and their faction. "Frenchmen!" it began. "In the midst of your triumphs your downfall was being planned. A group of perverse men sought to dig the grave of liberty in the heart of France." The enemies of the French people were no longer the despots and their satellites, but the agents of despotism inside France, who "speak of the rights of the people, while seeking only to destroy them."[61] New arrests were made, accusations of complicity with the "tyrant" Robespierre flew right and left, and Ruffin himself received visits from the local section, as a suspect of association with the former government. Ahmed must have learned from this a deep lesson about the vicissitudes and the hypocrisies of revolutionary transformation. He was to learn further lessons about the new imperial order emerging in the wake of the Revolution, as the revolutionary confrontation between France and Britain transformed into a world struggle over power and territory.

An Agent of the Republic

On 7 September 1796, Ahmed Khan arrived in Bombay and was promptly arrested, searched, interrogated, and imprisoned by the British authorities. Leaving France through the border with Switzerland, it appears he made his way to London, where he discovered his brother Odudeen Khan's deal with the East India Company to buy off the nawab's inheritance with pensions. He remained there two months, requesting funds to return to India and carry his brother's body back to be buried at Dhewar with their father. The suspicions of the company's agents began with Ahmed's arrival in Istanbul in May 1796 after passing via France; the British chargé d'affaires sent a warning letter to the resident at Basra, who wrote to the company in Bombay of "a certain East Indian, a subject of Tippoo Saib's, who lately arrived there from Paris, whither he had formerly accompanied the grand embassy of 1787 [sic] to which he was attached and might be supposed to have outstayed for better reasons than mere personal amusement."[62]

The British official thus conveyed with apparent confidence the suggestion that Ahmed had previously traveled to France with Tipu's ambassadors before the Revolution. This is more than Ahmed had ever suggested to the French. However, there were great gaps in his account of his movements between the death of his father in 1773 and his arrival in France in 1793. The French archives show evidence of a mysterious visitor, Assad-Oullah, who indeed "outstayed" the embassy, remaining in Europe into 1789.[63] The nawab had seven sons, not four, and it may be that the three older sons continued to struggle for their father's inheritance.[64] The departure of the younger sons for Istanbul may have marked a new turn toward a larger network of Muslim support for their struggle against the British.

These are larger questions on which we can only touch lightly here, based on the copious, yet at the same time splintered, record we have of Ahmed Khan as refracted through the archives of imperial powers. We can surmise that the British suspicions of Ahmed Khan were not unfounded, and that he was carrying something suspicious in the box that contained his brother's remains. The British agents asked why he obtained a firman from the Ottoman government instructing their customs officers to leave the box untouched, although it showed clear signs of having been opened and resealed en route. The behavior and comments by Ahmed to a compatriot in Basra led the agents there to suspect he had sent something to Muscat with a ship that sailed shortly before he was picked up by the company.

Ruffin was sent to Istanbul as chargé d'affaires. A letter among his papers makes clear that he and Ahmed Khan were in contact with a Parisian jeweler specializing in "oriental" styles. This correspondence points to the efforts of the Thermidorean regime in bribing the rulers of neutral powers—a kind of "great game" that extended into the Persian Gulf. The jewels for the imam of Muscat were intended to reimburse him for the seizure of a ship, a problem that stood in the way of a closer alliance that could help the French re-establish dominance in India. It is possible that the secret contents of Ahmed's box were these jewels, or the official commission of the ambassador sent to Muscat, given the package he sent there from Basra. It appears that the jewels never reached Muscat, and were accidentally returned to Paris; this may have been due to the interruption of Ahmed's journey, and thus his inability to collect the package he had sent ahead. When he was arrested, Ahmed was carrying several letters in French, Persian, and Arabic, including two from the French consul addressing the question of the ship that had been seized, and instructing its proprietor that "in a few days you will be recompensed in this business."[65]

The decision of the East India Company officials in Bombay was to imprison Ahmed until his name could be cleared. There is no record of when, or indeed whether, he was released. The company considered him a dangerous revolutionary agent at a moment when Islam was becoming the key battleground in the global war of ideas. The events of the two years that followed would have profound effects, not only on the Muslim world, but also on the fate of the Revolution itself.

Something profound changed after Thermidor in the understanding of the role that this Muslim could play in the Revolution. The revolutionary hospitality articulated by Robespierre had become a more instrumental, and even imperial, use of Islam. To observe this shift more closely it is necessary to return to that moment in the middle of 1794 in which the political use of Islam moved into the center of political struggles in France.

9. Robespierre Mahomet

Exterminez, grands dieux, de la terre où nous sommes,
Quiconque avec plaisir répand le sang des hommes.
—Voltaire, *Mahomet*

In the closing months of the year 2 of the French Republic, these lines, along with other caricatures of the Prophet Muhammad, came to play a peculiar role in transforming French politics. On 9 Thermidor (27 July 1794), the National Convention ordered the arrest of Maximilien Robespierre and other members of the Committee of Public Safety. In the confused hours that followed, the initial popular defense of the "champions of the people" holed up in the Hôtel de Ville melted away, leaving a bleeding Robespierre, along with his younger brother and 20 of his associates, to be guillotined the following day.[1] If Thermidor no longer appears the radical break—the salutary end of "the Terror"—that it once did, this does not diminish, but rather magnifies, its importance in the Revolution.[2] Indeed, much of the way in which history came to represent the five years preceding this date—including the notion of "the Terror" itself, as Jean-Clément Martin has argued—was put in place during the months after this night.[3] In thus inventing the Terror, the Thermidoreans also created the first counter-terror. Summary justice, executions, and massacre no longer required even the fig leaf of judicial process.[4] In the rush to condemn the "incorruptible," many epithets abounded—above all those of Cromwell and Catiline, the regicide and the conspirator[5]—but comparisons to Mahomet were more elaborate. Drawing on Voltaire's caricature, they offered not only a monstrous portrait of Robespierre, but a way of recasting the political landscape of the Terror, simplifying a complex factional struggle into guilty

"Omars" and innocent "Séïdes" duped by the machinations of a single man, a false prophet.[6]

Three days earlier, on 6 Thermidor, Benoît Gouly, a colonial deputy from the Île de France (Mauritius), read aloud in the Jacobin Club a letter from Istanbul declaring that the sultan had authorized Muslims to wear revolutionary cockades. The society ordered the letter to be printed in its official newspaper, but the decision was reversed after Robespierre insisted that the letter had insufficient authenticity and the Jacobins "must not expose themselves to a mistake of this kind."[7] At the end of the sitting, Gouly rose again to demand that Robespierre and Couthon explain their allegations of conspiracies against the *patrie* in a special session for the following day. Two days later, that explanation and elaboration of the corruption and conspiracy in the Assembly would provoke the events of 9 Thermidor. After Thermidor, Gouly—himself accused of misdeeds as *représentant en mission* in the Ain— would resurface both as a fervent denouncer of Robespierre and a ferocious supporter of slavery and French colonial expansion.[8] Struggles over the place of Muslims in the Revolution played a key role in the unfolding of the events leading to Thermidor, and representations of Islam served a crucial political function in the crisis that followed.

As Aimé Césaire long ago observed of "le cas Robespierre," the colonies and the racial question, rather than remaining peripheral, went to the very heart of the struggle between "those who wanted to stop the revolution . . . and those who wanted to continue and extend it."[9] Similar questions arose about Muslims, and what part they could play, as the Revolution fought back invasion and counterrevolution and began to expand outward across Europe. Bernard Gainot has noted the four moments in which Robespierre intervened in public debates on the colonies; in the same way, his engagements with the "Muslim question" were few, but also extremely precise.[10] In contrast to other revolutionaries, Robespierre never in his copious speeches and writings invoked Muhammad by name, either for praise or blame; he chose his words meticulously and avoided rhetorical flourishes when speaking about Islam and the Muslim world.[11] In condemning fanatical priests, he made no allusion to Voltaire's *Mahomet,* which was prohibited from performance during his ascendancy, ostensibly because the Prophet was represented as a *chef de parti*—a factionalist conspirator (although the abbé Grégoire later claimed it was because of the play's uncomfortable condemnation of violence). In his *Lettre à d'Alembert* Rousseau judged

Voltaire's play "hardly encouraging for virtue," and it seems that revolutionary authorities of the Year 2 agreed.[12]

As with the colonial question, Robespierre's care with words was an indication not of the relative unimportance of the "Muslim question," but rather of a complex and sensitive problem that had no simple and immediate solution. The same Girondins who had been partisans of the war encouraged a vision of expansionism that sought to "revolutionize" Muslims along with other European peoples. Robespierre by no means rejected the conception that Muslims could participate in the Revolution, but he saw the attempt to recruit them before the internal stabilization of France as a strategy intended to provoke the only remaining neutral powers against the republic.

Henry Laurens has pointed to two schools of revolutionary thought on Islam, one in the line of Rousseau, viewing the Muslim world as naturally egalitarian and closer to the natural origins of humanity, and a more Voltairean view—dominated by ideologues like Volney and taken up by leading Girondins—seeing the ancient "nations" of Greeks, Arabs, and Armenians as an "Oriental Third Estate" oppressed by a Turkish aristocracy and on the brink of revolution. Laurens argued that the Jacobins were, "in this sense also, the heirs of Rousseau."[13]

Recent historians have reappraised Robespierre in a way that removes him from the monster/saint binary, restoring him as one revolutionary figure among many others, someone racked by doubt and contradiction, by illness, fear, and at times by personal vindictiveness, like so many of his revolutionary friends and adversaries.[14] The monstrosity of Robespierre emerges from the uniting of opposite extremes: the supreme, cynical politician and the ideologue driven by unbending utopian principles.[15] It is precisely that impossible duality that was at the center of the figure of "Robespierre Mahomet"—which allowed him to be both hypocrite and fanatic at once. Robespierre's real responses to Muslims give a different picture of the revolutionary leader: a combination of compromise and engagement that combined diplomatic caution with principled commitment, but also at times deficiencies of knowledge, failures of trust and delegation, and tendencies to abstraction. After Thermidor, when papers were seized from his home, they were reported to include swaths of unopened correspondence from the representatives in the Levant.[16]

The figure of Robespierre-Mahomet was not just an expedient trope: it was situated within the larger set of questions around ending or extending the Revolution, at home and abroad. Robespierre sought to restore religious stability in France through a new republican religion that could unite a fractured polity, while advancing only cautiously and defensively beyond France's borders, and showing particular restraint in regard to the Muslim powers that remained favorable to the republic. His Thermidorean opponents tore down these religious and geopolitical projects, sowing religious chaos in France, while pouring revolutionary energies into expansion across Europe and the Mediterranean.

Revolutionizing Muslims?

In his history of the Department of Foreign Affairs during the Revolution, Frédéric Masson observed that "Turkey was, for reasons we don't know, the object of all the solicitude of the Convention." According to the work of Linda and Marsha Frey, the Ottoman diplomatic post was the only one to remain open throughout the revolutionary decade: in 1794, French diplomacy had shrunk to a handful of Swiss and Italian towns, along with Tunis and the United States. Something else emerged under the Convention, both among political elites and in the wider popular culture: a growing conviction that the Muslim world was ripe for some great change, and that the shifts of the Ottoman Empire were crucial to the survival and the universal vocation of the Revolution. What this change would be remained unclear.[17]

In June 1792, the king agreed to recall the French ambassador to the Ottoman Empire, Choiseul-Gouffier, and send a new ambassador, Sémonville, a flamboyant patriot with a reputation for intrigue. Before this could happen, in a letter dated 10 August, Choiseul-Gouffier declared his loyalty to the king's émigré brothers, and notified them that he had sought refuge with the Russian consul. He would spend the following decade at the court of Catherine II.[18] A large number of merchants and officials followed in his wake, leaving the republic's relations with the Ottomans in disarray.

Many of the French inhabitants of Ottoman cities like Istanbul, Smyrna, and Aleppo were fervent supporters of the Revolution, and pursued their own version of revolutionary politics, with mass swearing of revolutionary oaths, attacks on the prerogatives of the influential Catholic orders, and revolutionary festivals to celebrate the events in France.[19] With the dismantling of the Chamber of Commerce in Marseille, which had long governed these communities, hundreds of unlicensed new arrivals joined the older core of merchant families, some settled for centuries in the Levant and intermarried with local Christians.[20] Unemployed sailors stranded in the ports by the British blockade on shipping added to the turbulent atmosphere, carrying out their own ceremonies, destroying royalist symbols, planting liberty trees, and fighting in the streets with Russian sailors and their Greek supporters.[21]

In Paris it was no longer clear how to consider these nominal French citizens residing in the Muslim world. Although they were few in number, the consequences of their behavior could be catastrophic for the republic. The old diplomatic system had been abandoned; as Pascal Firges has recently suggested, this led neither to a new system nor to a continuation of business as usual, but rather to a confusion of elements.[22] The changing factional dominance in Paris produced shifting and contradictory policies. The Convention sent a series of envoys to Istanbul with conflicting instructions, and long silences from their masters in Paris left them to interpret the shifting currents on their own, based on newspapers arriving months after the events they reported. In October 1792, the radical Guffroy—later a fierce enemy of Robespierre and a leading Thermidorean—proposed ominously in the Convention to "stop the sending of customary presents by the king's ambassador . . . to the tyrant of the Turks."[23] This language could only worsen France's position in relation to the Ottoman Empire.

When Sémonville was detained by the Austrians while passing through Bosnia, two other agents were dispatched to Istanbul from Venice and Poland. In key senses they reproduced the factional politics of revolutionary France in the center of the Ottoman world: Étienne-Félix Hénin ensconced himself in the Palais de France, the official residence, and set about forming a Jacobin club among the residents of Istanbul.[24] Meanwhile, another plenipotentiary, Marie-Louis Descorches de Sainte-Croix, took up residence among the French merchants in the suburb of Pera, and sought a more conciliatory approach to seek official recognition from the Ottoman government.[25] By assisting the unemployed sailors stranded in the city, Descorches won the backing of these "sansculottes," who threatened Hénin and accused him of counterrevolution. A furious series of denunciations and counterdenunciations ensued; pamphlets were printed and distributed in Istanbul, and the revolutionary authorities were bombarded with letters promising to reveal conspiracies and foreign plots.[26]

These machinations did not affect only the small merchant society in the Levant; they soon reached Paris. As early as the beginning of 1793, revolutionary politics in Istanbul became a bone of contention between Jacobins and Girondins. On 23 January, just two days after the king's execution, the minister of foreign affairs forwarded a letter from the Ottoman capital informing the National Convention that the French citizens of Istanbul had drawn up a decree of accusation against the ambassador, Choiseul-Gouffier. They declared that they would not communicate with him further, and had elected their own provisional representative. The Marseillais deputy Barbaroux, a key Girondin closely connected to the French communities in the Levant, called for this act of patriotism to be officially recognized by France. Thuriot, an ally of Danton, declared that the action of the French in Istanbul was illegal, and demanded the decision be deferred to the Diplomatic Committee. Carra, another Girondin ally, insisted that "it shows a deep attachment to one's country, and an elevated soul, to dare to commit such an act of sovereignty on the soil of slavery."[27] The Girondin-dominated Assembly voted to approve Barbaroux's proposal.

In his newspaper, *Lettres à ses commettants*, Robespierre declared that the actions of the French in Istanbul constituted a "usurpation of the constituted authority and an infraction of the laws" and gave alarm to the Turkish government, "in forming under its eyes a republican primary assembly, and transplanting the authority of the French constitution to Constantinople. What is certain is that the effect of this step will not be to determine the slaves of the sultan to shrug off suddenly the yoke of their government, but it will have an immediate and infallible effect, which is to provoke that government against us." Was this just "affected patriotism," Robespierre asked, the result of "excessive giddiness"? Or did it betray a more sinister intent "to arm all of the great powers against us at once, and leave us not a single ally?"[28]

At the end of May 1793, an attack on the National Assembly by a large crowd resulted in the expulsion of the Girondins from the Convention. The absence of the opposition made way for dissension among the Jacobins themselves, between the "ultras," who sought the extension of revolutionary action without regard to political consequences, and those who sought increasingly to find ways out of the civil strife, even if that meant slowing the pace of the revolutionary transformation. Robespierre refused to accept either of these courses: he called for a more rigorous application of revolutionary justice to eliminate the enemies of the people, including those whose extremism, he claimed, was a trap set by those who wanted to destroy the republic. This conception of the "enemy"—and, in particular, the "secret enemy" whose actions must be "unmasked"—was a wider feature of responses among both elites and people in the context of external existential threat, and the failing structures of the state in 1792–1793.[29]

On 5 October 1793, the Society of Jacobins in Paris received a letter from the "Popular Club of Constantinople" requesting formal affiliation with the mother society. "The Turks have always been our allies," reported the *Moniteur*. "The imperiousness and malice of our agents turn them against us. The orator drew a picture of the advantages we could gain from the alliance if we managed to attach them to our interests."[30] The affiliation was passed without any hesitation. As Onnik Jamgocyan notes, this picture of overwhelming support for the republic in Istanbul was indeed accurate, and provoked diplomats of other powers and French émigrés to denounce the new regime as "rebels" who sought to spread subversion. An émigré described the new republican envoy, Sémonville, as "a Jacobin coming armed with a torch, to corrupt the religion of Muslims and sow among the people the incendiary principle of a dissolute and unrestrained liberty."[31] The emergence of a Jacobin club inside the Ottoman capital could offer dangerous corroboration for such allegations.

Four days after the affiliation was granted, Tachereau, a close friend of Robespierre's, rose to denounce the club of Istanbul as a ruse to provoke the Ottoman government against France. "Remember, my fellow Jacobins," he declared, "that just a year ago Carra and Brissot proposed the affiliation of a popular society of Manchester in order to give the English despot a pretext to declare more quickly against the republic."[32] At a moment when the *patrie* was in danger, he insisted, the influence of the Jacobins abroad should not be allowed to excite persecution against patriots. The affiliation was hastily revoked. Two days later, the painter Armand-Charles Caraffe, who had himself traveled to Egypt and Turkey just prior to the Revolution, called for the affiliation of the club to be restored. It was astonishing, he declared, that the Jacobins had denied this affiliation, given all the "proofs of civic duty that this society [of Constantinople] has given, the festivals it celebrated on all the great dates of the Revolution." The Turks were well disposed toward the French, and had allowed the "unprecedented" permission to fire cannons in the port on the occasion of the death of Louis XVI. The Turks, he insisted, "are brave, loyal, and although they do not serve liberty, that would not make them any the less sincere in an alliance, if we managed to form one with them."[33]

In response, extending the line drawn by Robespierre, Tachereau suggested that the letter from the Jacobins of Istanbul was a "trap" intended to provoke the Ottomans to join the coalition against France: "It is well known that the Jacobins have sworn to exterminate all despots, " he reasoned. "It would therefore provoke a rupture with the Ottoman Empire to form a society in Constantinople or to correspond with the one said to be established there."[34] The Turks were well disposed toward the republic, he agreed, but the key was to treat them as a "resource" to be exploited, and not as political participants. Another Montagnard speaker, Moenne, went a step further by dismissing the letter as a forgery. Even if it were real, he argued, relations with Muslims must be conducted only through commerce or diplomacy, and not through political involvement: "All other means are insufficient, indeed *they are suspect*."[35] Given the establishment of the "Law of Suspects" a month earlier, allowing arrest and trial on mere suspicion of counterrevolutionary activities, this seemed to place a forbidding warning sign over all attempts to "revolutionize" Muslims, making those who did so into potential enemies of the Revolution.[36]

The former priest François Chabot gave the death blow to the hopes of those who supported the affiliation by accusing the Jacobins in Istanbul of being Girondins in disguise. "The men who compose this club are French, and not Muslims," he asserted, "but it is well known that these French are not sansculottes. They are merchants, and all muscadins; and all the officials are creatures of Roland, Brissot, and Lebrun." These names of Girondin ministers were now tools of political anathematization. "Moreover," he insisted, "religious considerations prevent the Turks from mixing in such establishments."[37]

This insinuation of a fundamental incongruity between Islam and revolutionary ideals did not reflect Robespierre's view. He continued to hold out strong hopes for a decisive shift of the Ottomans toward France, which would require closer engagement between Islam and revolutionary beliefs.

On 27 Brumaire (17 November), Robespierre gave a crucial speech on the situation of the republic in which he made clear his position on relations with the neutral powers. He repeated that the formation of "assemblies" of French in Istanbul "cannot be helpful to our cause, nor to our principles, but is rather intended to upset and provoke the Ottoman court." But he held out hope: "The Turk, necessary enemy of our enemies, the useful and faithful ally of France, neglected by the French government, manipulated by the intrigues of the British cabinet, has maintained up to the present a neutrality more harmful to its own interests than to those of the French Republic." However, he announced more optimistically, "it seems that this empire is ready to awaken."[38]

The subtlety of Robespierre's position demonstrates the false opposition between national self-interest and universal principle. He recommended neither an ideological assault on nor a compromise with Muslim powers that would—as Moenne suggested—exclude Muslims from the purview of the revolutionary transformation. Instead, he argued for a wise restraint, a time-limited, parenthetical realism: "There are two ways to lose everything," he insisted. "One is to do things that are wrong in their nature; the other is to do things that are good in themselves, but to do them badly or at the wrong moment."[39] This is a long way from the unbending "ideology incarnate" of so many versions of Robespierre.[40]

Robespierre went on to blame the Girondins for an aggressive foreign policy that had provoked federalist insurgency and religious counterrevolution, and which now threatened to turn allies and neutral powers against France: "Those who at the end of 1791 wanted to break all the scepters of the world, are the same who, in August 1792, tried to parry the blow that brought down our own tyrant." This was directed equally against those in his own party who sought to shift the focus to external rather than internal enemies. But for Robespierre the difference was about timing rather than underlying principle.

Robespierre declared that the Ottomans were about to "wake": this was a sentiment widely shared among Jacobins of all stripes. But just what the nature of this awakening might be was a matter of political contention. Throughout this period newspapers all over France reported that Muslims were not only sympathetic to the Revolution, but on the verge of joining it. A letter from Izmir in October 1793, printed in the *Journal républicain de Marseille,* declared that the recapture of Toulon had shifted the Ottoman Empire back to strong support of the republic. The sultan, it claimed, had sent a firman to the mullah, instructing him to "take care of the French as you would of my person; consider them as true Muslims, let no harm come to them."[41] A letter to the *Moniteur* reported that the Capudan Pasha had "distributed 2,000 piasters to our crews, and taken his kindness so far as to buy them wine and spirits to enjoy themselves."[42] Given the Islamic prohibition on alcohol, this might appear more than simply an act of generosity.

The *Moniteur* of 3 Frimaire (23 November) reported that the Russian ambassador arriving in the town of Edirne in Thrace had been greeted by angry and silent crowds. The insolent Russians, reported a letter from Istanbul, insulted those wearing tricolor cockades "that the Turks not only permit us to wear, but view with great pleasure."[43] Not only the French, but also all their interpreters—Ottoman subjects—continued to wear this symbol with pride, despite the attacks it provoked from the Russians. In the ensuing confrontations, the local Muslim authorities were compelled to intervene. Two French captains, another letter reported, were attacked by a crowd of Greeks and Russians in the rue de Péra (today Istiklal Street in Istanbul), forcing them to take refuge in a neighboring house: "The janissaries of the French Embassy, having been alerted, now arrived, and . . . a strong patrol protected the path of the two Republican generals through the suburb of Pera."[44]

By early 1794, the *Moniteur* reported "a very rational resistance and new enlightenment" among the Turks.[45] Other letters declared that it was "almost certain" that the Turks would go to war against Russia, and perhaps against Austria.[46] The behavior of the Ottomans toward the French could be considered a "prognostication of the progress that the Ottomans have made in the understanding of European politics," wrote another.[47] The French, another letter confirmed, "never cease to receive from the Turks an ever warmer reception."[48] Not only in Anatolia but in North Africa, this preference appeared undeniable: "The Barbary states show an almost exclusive friendship toward the French republicans; they alone are well treated and favored in the Algerian ports." Six ships loaded with African grain, the letter reported, were under sail "to travel toward the ports of what was formerly known as Provence."[49]

By mid-1794, the anticipation was reaching fever pitch. It was "no longer possible to doubt" that Ottoman aggression against France's enemies would provide urgently needed relief in the war against all of Europe.[50] In the fight against Russia, "the Turks, the most honest [*franc*] people of Europe, will unite bravely with the valiant Poles against their common enemy."[51] Now the Ottomans were preparing their own insurrection, one directed by the sultan himself, who "has a real plan to achieve the independence and restore the dignity of the Ottoman people."[52] By May 1794, the newspaper was certain that the Turks would attack not only Russia but Austria too: "the Court of Vienna will pay dearly for its criminal alliance with the principal enemy of the Turks. It is said that instructions have been given for a campaign beginning in August."[53] The economist Ducher said that a "spark of French liberty" had fallen among neutral powers in Warsaw,

Geneva, and Venice, as Philadelphia prepared its soldiers and sailors. "The Great Turk and the Barbary states are indignant at the hypocrisy of the scoundrel who sends counterfeit bills and daggers into France, armed guards to the pope, and rosaries to Portugal."[54]

Unlike the French, it seemed, the Turks would be led by their religion in attacking Russia: they would not rise up against their own tyrants but against the "irreconcilable enemy of the Crescent."[55] The sultan appeared in this equation not as a tyrant but as a friend of liberty and the representative of a larger Muslim people in revolt against Russian and Austrian expansion: he was reported to spend his time in conversation with French republican officers sent to Istanbul to train the new army corps.[56] If the Turks were still "enslaved by prejudices," *La décade philosophique* declared, they were prejudices that created a greater degree of susceptibility to the "spectacle of virtue and heroism," and needed only an "electric spark" to set in motion the great force of Islam that had once conquered the world, but now "in a better century, for a better cause" would fight for the Revolution. "The Muslims of today," *La décade* declared, "without fanaticism and without barbarity, somewhat behind us in the question of enlightenment, no doubt, by ignorance and not by error, are just as susceptible to a profound and wholehearted regeneration as any other people of Europe."[57] This sense of a great religious regeneration had less to do with the Ottomans—who would frustrate these hopes by maintaining their status quo of cautious multilateral engagement—and more with the shifts taking place in France.

A Revolutionary Religion

On 20 Prairial—8 June 1794—Robespierre marched through Paris at the head of a religious procession. Wearing a sky-blue coat, he strode toward the fantastical scene designed by the painter David, a great heap of earth in the shape of a shaggy hill, honoring "the Mountain"—the group of Jacobins who had "saved" the Revolution. The scene seemed to echo the story of Moses confronting the burning bush on Mount Sinai, a motif already present in the depictions of the Declaration of the Rights of Man and Citizen carved into stone tablets of the law.[58] This very public role, this suggestion of a new kind of individual prominence, even of messianism, was out of character for Robespierre. It encouraged those around him to assert that he was seeking dictatorial power, indeed, that he planned to make himself the head of a new religion. Yet Robespierre saw his purpose as entirely the opposite: to reassure the people of the continuity of the fundamental moral basis of all religions, the belief in a supreme being.[59]

A month earlier, his speech at the Convention had emphasized the centrality of "religious ideas" in the universal vocation of the Revolution. Where in his speech of February 1794 he had called for the exercise of "Terror," now he sought to realize its complement, the cult of Virtue. As danger receded and victory came into sight, the conditions for true "regeneration" seemed in place. "All has changed in the physical order," he declared. "All must change in the moral and political order."[60]

Some historians have seen in this the desire to "nationalize God."[61] Yet when we look closely at Robespierre's speech, it resounds with a different register. The singular word "nation" is never used in the speech, although "patrie" occurs 33 times, and "people" 34 times. In contrast, Robespierre speaks of Man (21 times), humanity (14 times), the world (14 times), the universe (7 times), and the globe (4 times). The words "French" and "France" occur altogether 26 times, and "republic" 21 times. The term "patrie" did not simply refer to the territorial "nation"; "patriots" could equally be Belgians or Italians, or even, on occasion, Muslims. Indeed, in the most sentimental flight of the speech, Robespierre imagined himself in the place of a foreigner, born "in a foreign and distant country," and watching the Revolution from afar, tearfully envying the good fortune of those born in France.

Robespierre condemned those who attempted to "nationalize atheism," taking aim at dechristianizers in his own party, like Cloots, Lequinio, and Fouché, who had preached that there was no God and no existence after death. But Robespierre did not insist that the legislator should stay out of religious questions; he argued that it was necessary to create a new religion of state, broad enough to unite all of the differing religious practices: "Every institution, every doctrine that consoles and lifts up the soul must be welcomed."[62] Robespierre took up Rousseau's conception of a civic rite based on a common foundation that would allow all French people—Catholic, Protestant, Jewish, Muslim—to abandon their theological differences, and unite in a political and moral union without borders.[63]

Robespierre presented his argument less as conviction than as pragmatism. Even if the existence of God and the immortality of the soul were fictions, he suggested, they were necessary fictions that elevated the actions of humanity. Lycurgus, Solon, even Socrates "allowed themselves to mix certain stories with the truth" in order to inspire their fellow citizens.[64] But this was not to make a religion of politics, to substitute materialism for God, as his radical opponents sought to do. Instead, he believed that the existing structures of religion were the most powerful source for combating religious reaction: the Revolution must offer a coherent religious vision that would sponsor virtue and banish vice. "Without constraint, without persecution, all sects will voluntarily mix together in the universal religion of nature."[65] This was a "political religion," not because it sacralized politics, but because its source was in the political requirements of a "good society" rather than in the spiritual traditions of belief. Emotion was key to this construction: it provided the link of feeling that connected this "choice" to a fund of sincerity.

Ultimately, however, the speech suggests the magnitude of the failure to find a solution to the religious problem. Robespierre had always been scrupulously careful to argue for pragmatic political solutions. Here he launched into a doomed attempt to unify opposing beliefs, as Cloots had once attempted to unify opposing factions. While denouncing the dechristianizers, he seemed to sail perilously close to some of their doctrines by deifying nature and identifying it with the Supreme Being. It was unclear from his discourse whether this supremacy was material or supernatural. Moreover, he appeared to believe that all the religions of the world—implicitly including Islam—would cheerfully genuflect to this new truth, without constraint, simply because they would see how useful it was. This political religion was not Robespierre's invention, nor would it die with him; it would plague the revolutionary settlement long after Thermidor and into the century that followed.

The Festival of the Supreme Being was celebrated all over France. In Lyon, a great statue of Hercules was erected in front of the Cathedral of Saint-Jean, now a Temple of Reason. On the stage behind was a great globe, representing the universal nature of the new cult. It was clear that the vocation of this religion was not territorial, a new Gallican church, or a gathering of Christians under the leadership of a new pope. Instead it was global, universal, competing with Christianity and Islam, the two great proselytizing world religions. Many radicals like Filippo Buonarotti were convinced: "At certain moments in world history," he wrote, "extraordinary men appear on the earth, whose genius, virtue, or courage astonishes the world and changes the face of nations: such were Moses, Pythagoras, Lycurgus; such were Jesus and Mahomet; such would Robespierre have been if there were 20 men in the Convention capable of understanding and supporting him."[66]

The Thermidoreans were at pains to suggest that this festival was Robespierre's personal caprice, and had little popular support. Barère, in his memoirs, suggested that people mockingly called the sky-blue figure at the head of this ill-judged procession "the Revolutionary Pope."[67] Joachim Vilate, too, made it seem that the crowd rejected the festival: "Look at that bugger!" he reported someone to have said. "It's not enough to be master, he wants to be God too."[68] This "popular" hostility was largely a fabrication by rivals in the ruling committees, who resented the distance Robespierre appeared to place between himself and the other deputies.[69] As Marisa Linton has shown, the doctrine of political virtue was widely shared, as was Robespierre's belief that it was necessary—to adapt Linton's phrase—to "choose religion" as a necessary source of virtue.[70] Yet just two days after the festival, the Committee of Public Safety pushed through the law of 22 Prairial that ramped up the process of the Revolutionary Tribunals, and permitted only acquittal or death as its outcomes.[71]

But this new religious project also helped rally opposition to Robespierre, months before the speech of 8 Thermidor that frightened many in the Convention. Opponents had already begun to employ tropes associated with Islam. Baudot later reported that many of Robespierre's own Montagnard supporters "were horrified by this ceremony and its pontiff."[72] Lavicomterie wrote that "following the example of Mahomet, who called himself the prophet of the only god, Robespierre pretended to be a wise man inspired by a Supreme Being."[73] Mercier agreed: "He thought he could play the role of Mahomet and give the Supreme Being back all of his rights."[74] It is difficult to extract these events from the coloring they were given after Thermidor, but it is clear that personal, political, and religious motives were all mixed together into a lethal cocktail that was set off by the discovery of an apparently farcical cult.

A little more than a week after Robespierre's appearance at the Festival of the Supreme Being, Marc Vadier, "the king of Voltaireans in the Convention,"[75] delivered a long speech in the National Convention that set out to parody and ridicule Robespierre's vision. He suggested that at that very moment, "perverted men" were conspiring in the shadows to bring disaster to the republic, behind an elderly woman, Catherine Théot, known popularly as the "mother of God."[76] Vadier called her Catherine Théos, thus associating her with the "Supreme Being" and "the immortality of the soul."

At the heart of this alleged conspiracy was not politics, but religion: it was fanaticism, superstition, theocracy. "How else to deceive society, hoodwink reason, while picking the pockets of gullible citizens other than by hypocrisy?" he asked, to general applause. The charlatans sought to dupe their victims "with illusion or terror," creating a god in their image; he repeated the word "terror" three times, associating it unmistakably with this supernatural manipulation. "So, citizens," he said, "this is the theory of priests of every country and every religion; I say every religion, because the Hades of the pagans, the fiery wheel of Ixion, the vulture of Prometheus, the Furies are no less a hell than the fire and brimstone of the Prince of Darkness; the houris of Mahomet have no less attraction than the ineffable happiness and serenity of paradise promised by the pope."[77]

Vadier denounced those who gathered at her house as "a swarm of bigots and dimwits . . . mesmerists, illuminati . . . [a clique] composed of royalists, moneylenders, lunatics, narcissists, muscadins, and counterrevolutionaries of both sexes."[78] His farcical descriptions of the supposed rituals carried out by these adepts, kissing the old woman seven times, "since everything goes by seven in the mystical jargon of oracles and predictions," elicited prolonged outbursts of laughter.[79] Vadier called explicitly upon ridicule as a "weapon." Philarète Chasles, writing in his memoirs of the powerful effects of this "cold and unmoved" irony in the overheated Assembly, called this weaponized satire "the destructive side of the French Revolution."[80] Laughter, as recent studies have suggested, is political: ridicule could be just as powerful and menacing as fear in the atmosphere of these months.[81]

The Convention ordered the publication of Vadier's report, along with the arrest of the "Mother of God" and her followers. Although Vadier made no direct reference to Robespierre in his speech, it was evident that the latter was the target, not just of ridicule, but of an attempt to link him to a counterrevolutionary conspiracy. Vadier accused Robespierre of dismissing the report on Theéot as a "ridiculous farce of mysticism" and of using his influence to prevent the woman and her followers from being tried, fueling allegations of tyranny that would be crucial in the events of Thermidor.[82]

Sénart, one of the officers who infiltrated the group, claimed that when Catherine was arrested, a letter to Robespierre was found in her bed in which "she called him her principal prophet, her beloved minister, and congratulated him on the honors he gave to the Supreme Being, his son."[83] There is no indication that this letter (if it indeed existed) contained any reference to Mahomet. Yet Sénart insisted that the letter addressed to Robespierre "presents him as a new Mahomet who wanted to establish a law dominating

both religion and the constitution, raise a throne on the arms of the illuminati, cement the throne with the blood of victims or nonbelievers, and reign
through these misguided fanatics." How could Robespierre possibly have
played such a foolish and naive role, Sénart asked, unless he was in fact a
manipulative charlatan with eyes on his own interests?[84]

On 8 Thermidor Robespierre declared that the opponents of the
Festival of the Supreme Being who continued to "cast ridicule on everything
related to these ideas" would be punished, along with a vast conspiracy inside
the government itself.[85] This overreach by Robespierre catalyzed his downfall
by alienating his remaining supporters in the Convention. But equally part of
the background to this gesture was the emerging attempt to frame him at the
center of a religious and political conspiracy, using the "Mother of God" as
the instrument. As Michel Eude has observed, the evident political uses of
this affair do not mean that it had no basis: evidence of a new religious practice emerging in the shadows provoked "a real anxiety" among leading
figures.[86] The documents found in the apartments of Catherine Théot became
important in portraying Thermidor as a legal act and not as a coup. Nothing
in them could really suggest that Robespierre was planning to be king, despite
rumors that may have circulated. But the letter calling Robespierre a new
Mahomet, whether forged or otherwise, did important service in suggesting a
conspiracy to raise him as the prophet of a new religion.

The Muslim Thermidor

The figure of Robespierre-Mahomet had, in fact, first been employed by
Girondins. In November 1792, Olympe de Gouges wrote an open letter to the
influential Maximilien. "I am convinced," she wrote, "despite your sudden
modesty, that you console yourself with the frivolous hope of reaching the
level of ancient and modern usurpers. Cromwel[l] caresses your reason and
Mahomet subjugates it; emulating these scoundrels requires no fortune."[87]
The warning here was that ordinary citizens could also become dictators, as a
petition from Nantes insisted: "The tyrant most to be feared is the one who
emerges from the shadows. . . . Mahomet was only a brigand, Tamerlan a
shepherd, Cromwell an obscure citizen."[88] In April 1793, Guadet took the
trope further as the two factions clashed furiously in the Convention. "While
this new Mahomet, in everything but talent, wrapped the victims he wished to
strike in an obscure description, his Omar named them in his paper, and others

took care of targeting them."[89] Here, for the first time, the reference was not to the historical Muhammad but to Voltaire's play: Marat played the role of Omar to Robespierre's Mahomet. These two caricatures of Mahomet—one a figure of theocratic power, the other a figure of Machiavellian intrigue— would be joined together in the hybrid monster of Thermidor.

Joachim Vilate was a former priest who had sworn the constitutional oath in 1792, joined the Jacobin Club, and under the revolutionary name of Sempronius Gracchus served as secretary to several deputies sent out to the provinces, as well as on the jury of the Revolutionary Tribunal.[90] On 3 Thermidor he was arrested by order of the Committee of General Security, and on 9 Thermidor agents of the Paris commune sought unsuccessfully to free him. From prison, he hastened to write and publish an account of his conduct, in a vain attempt to win his freedom. His *Secret Causes of the Revolution of the 9th and 10th Thermidor* placed Mahomet at the symbolic heart of the coup. Vilate essentially rewrote Voltaire's play, to cast himself as a Séide who had recognized the truth and paid a terrible price for revealing his disillusionment: "I had the courage to express my defiance; the Mahomets, the Omars fearing my truthful and babbling tongue, threw me, several days before their unexpected fall, into one of the thousands of bastilles with which they had covered every corner of the republic."[91]

Vilate's "script" was a literal one: he claimed that he had purchased a paper copy of Voltaire's *Mahomet* on the way through the Palais-Royal, carrying it to a meeting with Barère. "Suddenly a powerful idea seemed to rush to his head," Vilate wrote. "He grabbed *Mahomet* from my hand, opened it, and began to declaim in a low and superb voice this tirade of the imposter." Vilate then had Barère declaim a long speech in the character of Omar, declaring the rise of "Arabia" out of the desert, to spread "by the laws, by the arts, and above all by war" across Asia and Africa. "On the debris of this world we will build Arabia. / We need a new religion, we need new chains. / We need a new God for this blind universe."[92]

To illuminate his theme of "fanaticism" in the play, Voltaire had concocted the character of Séide (based vaguely on Zaid ibn Haritha, the Prophet's adopted son), a young man duped by the theatrical Mahomet into killing his own father. The third point of the triangle was Omar, an implacable partisan wielding violence to accomplish his ends. By creating a distinction between innocent dupes and culpable followers—between Séides and Omars— the script of *Mahomet* helped paper over the contradictions of Thermidor: the effective continuation of many of the policies of the committee, and the continuation of the Terror under the sign of retribution for the Terror itself.[93]

Courtois's report on Robespierre's papers distinguished the virtuous Jacobins, taken in by a supernatural cunning, from the "new Omars," who this time had conquered "neither Persia, nor Egypt, nor Libya" but had instead attempted to "make the French of the eighteenth century into a people of barbarians reduced not to the practice but to the reading of the Rights of Man, as the Saracens once did with the science of the Koran."[94] Lanthenas called upon the "Séides of Robespierre" to implement a stricter regime of censorship necessary to the protection of liberty.[95] It was not so easy to sort the Séides from the Omars: the remaining partisans of Robespierre were busy denouncing the Thermidoreans as "new Omars [who] want at any cost to bring back the impious fanaticism of the royalty."[96] Fréron, protesting the massacres carried out in the Midi, identified "several Séides of the Mahomets and Omars of the former Committee of Public Safety" and asked why—even if they were guilty of everything they were charged with—they should be subject to arbitrary assassination.[97] In the criminal procedures against the perpetrators of the mass drownings in Nantes, the nineteen-year-old Lalloué, who had supervised the killings, was described as a "young Séide" whose actions "were a consequence of Robespierre's system."[98]

Joseph Le Bon, accused of terrorism, used the same figure in his defense before the tribunal. A former priest, he had been accused of *modérantisme* at the Revolutionary Tribunal, and on his return to Arras, had sought by every means to demonstrate exceptional severity. The presiding judge declared of Le Bon: "He presents himself as an austere, Stoic philosopher . . . who had learned to master his passions, . . . but then, as another Séide subjugated by the new Mahomet—Maximilien Robespierre, of execrable memory—he silenced this exquisite sensibility that he took from nature, and listened only to the severe voice of duty."[99] The judge asked the jury if this "metaphysical hypothesis" was really convincing. Bombarded by pamphlets that accused Le Bon of being the source, not the victim, of fanaticism—an Omar, not a Séide—the jury sent him to the guillotine.

The district of Beaugency wrote to congratulate the Convention on having "overthrown the new Mahomet."[100] Lequinio, whom Robespierre had saved from denunciations for atheism, joined in the chorus, condemning the new superstition that the new Mahomet was going to establish gradually on the debris of the old.[101]

The caricature of Robespierre-Mahomet was elaborate and drew on a mishmash of Christian anti-Islamic libels, Enlightenment satire, and historical scholarship. One account even claimed that Robespierre had purchased the house of the former princess of Chimay, and would hold rich banquets there with his henchmen, after which "the tyrant would roll on the grass, feigning to be seized with convulsive movements . . . after the manner of Mahomet to impose on the imbeciles and gain more credit in the eyes of the scoundrels."[102] This drew on the old Christian allegation that the revelations of Muhammad were caused by epilepsy.[103] References were also made to the "pigeon" of Muhammad: Christian propagandists had claimed the Prophet trained a bird to peck grains from his ear, to convince gullible onlookers he was receiving divine revelations. Thermidor reanimated the vilifying uses of Islam, and their anxieties around masculinity, that had dominated the pamphlet struggles of 1789, as censorship collapsed and extrajudicial violence was used in revenge against those now blamed for the Terror.[104]

The most elaborate comparison of Robespierre and Mahomet came in Lavicomterie's *Crimes des empereurs turcs*, which set out in a footnote an elaborate "historical comparison" between Robespierre and Mahomet.[105] "Who would have believed," he began, "at the most remarkable epoch for true philosophy and sane politics, in the fifth year of our revolution, we would see arise for a moment a kind of new Mahomet?"[106]

Lavicomterie provided a digest of caricatures: the comparison of petty lawyer and camel driver, both born in obscurity; the appeal to credulous women; the use of force to compel virtue, sword in one hand and Koran in the other; prohibiting all other books as unnecessary; the creation of a "politico-religious code"; the abolition of the freedom of opinion; the destruction of images (in Robespierre's case, supposedly, the bust of Helvetius); announcing "proudly and emphatically that he proposed to bring men back to the simplicity of antique morals of pure deism." Mahomet also served as a way to connect Robespierre to a larger political conspiracy. The Prophet's assumption of political power in Mecca was compared to Robespierre, who "retreated to the Paris town hall to hear himself proclaimed dictator and seal his decrees in blood with a fleur-de-lis stamp."[107]

At the end of this comparison came the curious twist. After all these disparaging caricatures, Lavicomterie declared that Mahomet "was not an ordinary man. Born with genius and even with a certain elevation in his soul, his upward path influenced and dominated. He left after him a long memory and profound traces." Robespierre, in contrast, "was nothing but a pygmy standing on tiptoes to imitate his giant role model." If the Prophet had committed "crimes," it was as a great historical figure, the Lion of the Desert: "Mahomet has his place alongside Moses, Alexander, and Julius Caesar; Robespierre's place is between [the crusading monk] Peter the Hermit and [the poisoner] Desrues."[108] Lavicomterie's book also returned to an outright call to Muslims to revolt against their tyrannical rulers.

The final, most gruesome figure of Robespierre-Mahomet came from Proyart in his *Life and Crimes of Robespierre*, describing Robespierre's journey to the guillotine, his jaw injured and bleeding from a gunshot some imputed to his own hand, others to a violent struggle at his arrest. "Come on, sire," people shouted, "it's your turn now!" After all the other condemned had been executed, Robespierre was brought to the scaffold: "to retain the dressing on his wound, his head had been wrapped in a bandage that formed a kind of turban. This was the only crown that was left to this stage king by his subjects, who had become his executioners." When they ripped it off before pushing him to the block, part of his jaw detached, "and instead of a man, under the bandage could be seen only a hideous monster."[109]

This association of Robespierre with the Prophet of Islam is one of many epithets rained upon him across two centuries, pointing to the difficulties of coming to terms with a man upon whom history has placed so great a burden. Even today, comparisons not only to dictators but to Islamic leaders and militants remain common. As Peter McPhee has suggested, the inexhaustible urge to comparison has endangered evaluation of Robespierre—and consequently of the Revolution itself—with the perils of "reading history backwards."[110] The death of Robespierre also brought to an end his careful policy of restraint in regard to the Muslim world and the return of a much broader policy of expansion under the Directory. In some sense, the post-Thermidoreans came to believe their own rhetoric about Muslims—a strange mixture of universalism and contempt—leading them on a track toward the fatal adventure in Egypt. In this sense, Robespierre's fear of a conspiracy against the republic was not unfounded: the unfettered push to revolutionize Muslims would indeed bring to an end the Revolution to which he had dedicated so much.

10. Bonaparte's Burka

In April 1789, in the town of Auxonne in Burgundy, a 17-year-old Corsican officer signing himself Napoleone di Buonaparte was stationed after his return from a visit to his native island. As the political crisis of the Estates General surged around him, he applied himself closely to the study of Marigny's *History of the Arabs*. From his copious notes on this book he drew an anecdote that he shaped into a short story of his own, entitled *The Prophetic Mask*. This adolescent literary foray centered on the would-be prophet of Khorasan, known as *Burkai*—the veiled one—as Marigny explained, "from the Arabic word *burka*, which means a mask."

In Bonaparte's version, a man named Hakem rises in insurrection against the caliph Mahadi in Baghdad, a prince who, "great, generous, enlightened, magnanimous, watched over the Arab Empire prospering in the bosom of peace."[1] Once renowned for his beauty, Hakem is disfigured by a terrible illness, but disguises his hideous visage with a mask, duping his followers into believing he must wear it to avoid blinding them with the light emanating from his face. Finally cornered in his castle after losses in battle, he uses his oratory to trick his remaining disciples into digging a great pit, claiming that by God's will his enemies will hurl themselves into the trench. When they finish the pit, he poisons them all and burns their bodies in it, then leaps into the flames. When his enemies arrive, there is no sign of his fate, and a legend blossoms of his bodily assumption into heaven. The last line of the story asks the question: *Jusqu'où peut porter la fureur de l'illustration?* (How far can the passion for fame carry us?)[2] The word *illustration* in French has several meanings—example, distinction, divine grace. Here it connected the urge for revolutionary fame and glory to the religious passions of the would-be prophet.

Many historians have remarked on Napoléon's fascination with Islam and the Prophet. They have been slower to remark that this fascination was not his alone, nor was it a romantic urge for the distant and exotic "Orient." Its origins were more practical, more revolutionary, and closer to home.[3] In less than half a decade after 1789, the Revolution had laid waste to the French religious establishment. Thousands of priests had died, fled the country, or abandoned their calling. Churches had been sold, converted to other uses, or dismantled completely, their bells melted down to forge cannons. Traditional Catholicism had been changed forever: pushed out of its inherited role as pillar of the state, it became a kind of dissident minority religion, practiced in the shadows. According to the report of the bishop of Toulouse, well over half of French Catholics continued to reject the Constitutional Church, and of the rest most had abandoned their faith, leaving the official church a depleted and beleaguered entity.[4] Yet no one knew what would take its place. The dream of a rational world without religion proved elusive—what would provide the basis for a republican morality? Robespierre's sponsorship of a deistic, civic, "natural religion" hastened his downfall, but the post-Thermidoreans had no better answer. The constitution of 1795 separated church from state, not as a positive act but as a cost-saving exercise.

In this atmosphere, alternative religious structures like those of Islam became even more present in what Howard Brown has called "the search for stability."[5] André Chénier made this clear in his poem "Byzantium, My Cradle," writing that the "peaceful Muslim" could rest his head each night without fear of denunciation, trial, death. The Koran, he wrote, was "a dam against which the great onslaught of power finds its progress broken." Liberty, he cried, had not left the great city of Islam: "You glide over its minarets!"[6] Chénier's romantic contrast between Islam and the Revolution was inverted by his English fellow poet, Percy Bysshe Shelley, who used "The Revolt of Islam" as a code for the "world revolution." The young Napolione was one of those who looked for models of transformation in the Muslim world, allowing themselves to believe that the shifts taking place under Islam were in some sense conjunctural with those in Europe, and that Muslims themselves were ripe for revolution.

Observers have often stumbled over Bonaparte's complicated relationship to Islam: Edward Said awkwardly described it as "a uniquely benign and selective war."[7] A recent biographer insists that it was no exaggeration for a colonial historian to declare that "no European colonizer ever presented himself to Islam with more toleration and even deference."[8] Some have gone so far as to suggest that he converted to Islam in Egypt, although no evidence exists.[9] As dictator in Egypt, Bonaparte was equally capable of trumpeting the superiority of Islam over Christianity, and tearing down mosques, executing Muslims en masse, and declaring himself to be a Mahdi or a Prophet.[10] The shock of 1798 was once imagined to be that of the arrival of European modernity in a backward Muslim society. It was more the shock of a real Muslim society in collision with an imagined Islam that emerged from the Revolution.

The story of the invasion and occupation of Egypt is too large to be undertaken in full within the scope of this book. Instead, this chapter will explore the strange and overheated atmosphere of the Directory that gave rise to that fatal military adventure, and the great rupture between Islam and the French Revolution that heralded—as Robespierre feared—the end of the Revolution itself.

The Buonaparte family was already shadowed by Islam on their arrival in Corsica: Francesco Buonaparte, nicknamed the "Moor of Sarzana," was among the first in the family to settle on the island in 1529.[11] The head of a Moor is also the key motif of the Corsican flag, reintroduced to the island in the mid-eighteenth century.[12] The word "Moro" in Romance languages is closely connected to racial difference, and this might have referred to his skin color. Until as late as 1778, in southern France as in Spain, tests of "true" aristocracy were based on "purity of blood" (*limpieza de sangre*), requiring proof that noble lineages did not include Jewish or Muslim ancestors.[13] Napolione himself was required to provide proof of nobility stretching back to this "Moor" for his admission to military school at Brienne.[14] Added to the severe poverty in which he found himself, Buonaparte was also in some sense associated with this racial difference, which would later be marshaled against him by his enemies. *The Morning Post* on 1 February 1803 described the First Consul as "an unclassifiable being, half-African, half-European, a Mediterranean mulatto."[15] The nineteenth-century historian Michelet declared that "as Corsica was once peopled by the Semites of Africa, Arabs, Carthaginians, or Moors, Marranos, . . . [Bonaparte] seems to belong to these rather than to the Italians."[16] Florence Gauthier has underlined the connections between Corsica and the other islands under French colonial rule on the other side of the Atlantic.[17] As Jean Defranceschi observed, "Before 30 November 1789, Corsica was not French."[18]

Buonaparte resembled in this sense a colonial *évolué* serving in the army of those he considered his oppressors: in an earlier manuscript, he wrote that the Corsicans "were able, following all the laws of justice, to throw off the Genoese yoke, and they can do the same with the French."[19] He defended Paoli's insurrection, denying the existence of any "divine laws" against just insurrection: even an "ex-eunuch of the seraglio" would revolt, he declared. To the "effeminate moderns" accepting "soft slavery" he contrasted the hero Leonardo of Casanova, who redeems his father in a patriarchal "family romance"—disguising himself as a woman to enter the prison, then taking his father's place. In a later manuscript he violently critiqued the story of Brutus sacrificing his sons for the *patrie*: "This sublime passion that you vaunt is nothing but selfishness . . . vanity that trumps paternal love."[20] This elevation of blood and family over the demands of citizenship is characteristic of Bonaparte throughout his career.

At 16, Buonaparte, unlike his fellow French officers, already subscribed to the revolutionary emotions that would become so dominant in France after 1789: he idolized the Corsican patriots, "enemies of tyrants, of luxury, of vile ambitious flatterers," and blamed the French for corrupting their morals. He wrote of suicidal feelings under the obligation "to praise men that virtue should make me hate. . . . When the *patrie* is no more, a good patriot must die."[21] Buonaparte's patriotism was deeply patriarchal, blood-centered, and anti-French; he searched for new sources that might offer ways of imagining a new destiny for his island, which sat in the middle of the Mediterranean, with connections to Malta, North Africa, and Egypt, as well as to Italy and France. His notebooks in Auxonne are a window into his intellectual world: studies of artillery and cannon, annotations on ancient Greece and Persia, on Raynal's *Histoire philosophique des deux Indes*, on the histories of England, France, Venice, Prussia. Three preoccupations stand out: Corsica, women, and Islam.

The young Buonaparte's summary of Mirabeau's *Des lettres de cachet* began with Montesquieu's faux observation of Louis XIV that "of all the governments in the world, those of Turkey or Persia seemed the most beautiful."[22] In January 1789, he took copious notes on the travels of the Baron de Tott in Turkey and Crimea; here as elsewhere he paused frequently on questions relating to women and marriage. "The Koran, which is the only code in civil, criminal, and moral laws, restricts the Turks to four wives." He interested himself with questions of law and religion: "The sultan is at the same time the successor of the caliphate. His sovereignty is founded on the Koran, and the interpretation of this book is exclusively reserved to the Uléma ['ulama]."[23] He took particular notes on Egypt and the history of the Mamluks, and observed that "Cairo is the entrepôt of Marseille and Madras." In his notes on current events, drawn from pamphlets like *The English Spy*, he drew numerous points related to his focus of interests: Turkey and the Crimea, the mistresses of Louis XV, the Corsican legion, brothels, and aphrodisiacs.[24]

In April 1789, the young officer was placed in command of 100 soldiers dispatched to the town of Seurre, where riots had broken out and local peasants had murdered two Lyonnais merchants who had made large grain purchases in the region. During the weeks he spent there, he read Marigny's *History of the Arabs under the Government of the Caliphs*, and took copious notes on the Prophet Muhammad, who "at the age of 20, was placed with a rich widow, who, after putting him in charge of her camels, married him." Buonaparte was clearly struck by the revenge narrative of a young man whose talents were unrecognized, who fled to escape arrest, and returned at the head of an army to "avenge himself on Mecca." He was impressed by the "valorous Khalid," sword of God, the general who "at the head of 3,000 men, defeated 20,000."[25] Buonaparte expressed his doubts over the assertion that Muhammad could neither read nor write, but appeared more convinced that he had 17 wives. It is striking too that his notes did not present this Islamic history as entirely external to the France in which he was engaged: he mentioned twice the entry of the Saracens into France. It was from this book that he drew the story of "a prophet named Hakem, known as Burkai, meaning 'mask,' because he wore a silver mask."[26] In the midst of the revolutionary upheaval of ideas and violent riots, Buonaparte reimagined revolutionary events clothed in Muslim dress. "Hakem," he wrote, "tall in stature, with a virile and impassioned eloquence, called himself the envoy of God; he preached a pure morality that appealed to the multitude; the equality of ranks and fortunes was the usual text of his sermons."[27]

On 12 June 1789, as the struggle over the Estates General was taking place in Versailles, Buonaparte addressed a letter to Paoli, to solicit his approval for a series of observations on Corsica he hoped to send to Necker. He lamented the "30,000 Frenchmen vomited onto our beaches, drowning the throne of liberty in waves of blood" in the year of his birth, 1769. He described it as a colonial slavery, comparable to that of "the ill-fated Peruvian perishing under the sword of the avid Spaniard."[28] "The French," he wrote in his notes on Mably's *Observations on the History of France*, "vicious and craven, joined the vices of the Gauls to those of the Germans, and were the most hideous people that ever existed."[29] The hatred that Buonaparte poured out against the French in this period is too voluminous to be ignored. It is crucial, however, to see his fascination with Islam through this prism, as a tool in "unthinking" the French domination that he had accepted in the metropole, and not—as some have suggested—as a genuine investment bordering on conversion.[30]

This was the Buonaparte who entered into the Revolution. Witnessing the riots and upheavals of its first months in the provincial town of Auxonne, he wrote of the "sound of the drums, the guns, the blood" as the "populace of this town, reinforced by a horde of foreign brigands" pillaged the customs station and a number of houses.[31] He wrote of the events in Versailles, and celebrated the "good direction" things were taking, believing that the turbulence would pass within a month.

Buonaparte received permission to return to Corsica, an island already racked with political struggles that had preceded the revolutionary shifts of 1789. There he would throw himself into revolutionary activity, perceiving, like many on the island—and others in the Caribbean and the Mascarenes— that the overthrow of the reigning system offered a chance to alter the colonial hierarchy. As in the sugar islands, the "patriot" party increasingly split in two: one that sought local autonomy while receiving the benefits of French support, and another that embraced the universalism of a new regenerated France, and insisted on full integration into the new nation. Buonaparte found himself too French for the Corsicans, just as he had been too Corsican for the French. As a partisan of fuller union with the new France, he became suspect in the eyes of Paoli. He was forced to leave the island with his family in 1793, sailing in a small boat for Toulon, where he distinguished himself among the Jacobin ascendancy that crushed a similar revolt to gain autonomy from Paris. Playing an important military role in the liberation of Toulon, he was caught up in the proscription of Jacobins after Thermidor. His ambitions turned first to the Muslim world: he requested permission to leave for Istanbul in 1794, and even sought to be named as official envoy.

When this permission was refused, he took up the command of the Parisian troops that would place him in a prime position in the repression of popular protest in 1795, even if the famous "whiff of grapeshot" with which he was said to have dispersed the last Parisian popular uprising was apocryphal.[32] Appointed as commander of French forces in Italy, he won stunning victories that brought him fame and fortune. Yet the lure of Islam did not vanish, but apparently grew ever stronger. We should beware of attributing this fascination to Buonaparte alone, however. The Directory was a hothouse in which this strange obsession with Islam and the Koran grew abundantly.

The Republican Koran

The era of the Directory was the scene of a curious religious experimentation. In the wake of the struggle between constitutional and refractory churches, then the struggle over religion itself—a bitter and violent standoff between radical materialism and utilitarian deism—the Directory sought to restore the original "freedom of religion" that the Revolution had ostensibly promoted. The landscape of belief had been scarred by the civil wars of religion, and, as Suzanne Desan's work has demonstrated, instead of a new settlement, the period of the Directory saw strange flowerings of hybrid sects, from local cults combining rationalism with Catholic ritual, to the "theophilanthropy" that emerged as a state-sponsored project.[33] Among these strange blooms, Islam did not wither away, but instead was drawn into the chaos of religious and political debate, not simply as trope, but as precedent, comparison, and an immediately contiguous element of the world in which the settlement of the Revolution would be determined.

On 21 December 1794, the abbé Grégoire announced that the state could not afford to finance or support any religion, but all could be practiced as long as they did not contravene "national sovereignty, liberty, equality, and fraternity." "Once its adherents swear fidelity to the political dogmas," Grégoire declared, "the question of whether an individual is baptized or circumcised, whether he cries Allah or Jehovah, is outside the domain of politics." To disturb "a Jew in his synagogue, a Muslim in his mosque, a Hindu in his temple, would be to violate one of the most perfect of their rights, that of worshipping the Supreme Being in their own way."[34]

Grégoire sought to further normalize France's relationship with the Muslim world. In a speech on education, he deplored the "stale witticisms of ignorance or counterrevolutionary ideas" so common in French responses. "We have continuing relations with the Barbary States, which have on multiple

Figure 19. Jean Duplessi-Bertaux and Pierre-Gabriel Berthault, *Audience of the Directory in Costume, 30 Brumaire Year 4 of the Republic*, 1802. Bibliothèque nationale de France.

occasions given us the resources against famine," he insisted. French trade in the Middle East and India was very important, and at a moment "when the ridiculous system of balance of power in Europe is collapsing," France needed to be in a position to seize the day. Interpreters with a true understanding of Muslim cultures were desperately needed: "If you do not quickly reorganize the Collège de France, you will have no one to maintain correspondence with the beys of Africa, the nawabs of India, and you risk losing the friendship of people whose relationship is extremely precious."[35] The result of this was the establishment of the School of Oriental Languages in 1796.

An image among the series *Tableaux historiques* produced by Jean Duplessi-Bertaux is a case in point. Entitled "An Audience of the Directory in Costume," it is dated to 30 Brumaire of the Year 4 (21 November 1795) (fig. 19). In front of the five directors in their elaborate costumes appears a Muslim ambassador—but here there is no explanation of his presence or purport. Indeed, it is necessary to search the procès-verbaux of the

Directory to find, hidden in a document, the information that on 28 Brumaire, a decision was taken to receive the ambassadors of "neutral powers" in a "simple presentation" and not a solemn ceremony, on the following Décadi, two days later. Thus, what was to be recorded in this image of a historical event was precisely the *absence* of historical events, in an attempt to make it appear that the Directory had stabilized the Revolution and placed it on a normal footing.

In 1797, when the first permanent representative of the Ottoman Empire arrived in Paris, Louis-Sébastien Mercier claimed his arrival "was far from impressive. . . . He hardly made a sensation for more than a week, he turns up everywhere, and everywhere he is viewed with perfect indifference. No one makes a fuss about his turban, or his odd manners, the smaller theaters take turns to invite him to their plays as an added spectacle; no one even bothers to remark on the fact that he was never baptized."[36] Mercier's claim had a political bite, condemning the revolutionary Turkophilia of 1788 as a "very strange moral phenomenon" that led a "great people," lovers of liberty, tolerant and gentle, sociable and joyous, to become infatuated with a "somber and hateful" people of "persecutors and fanatics," enemies of liberty who detested the arts. Mercier's attempt to depoliticize Muslims here was part of a wider attempt at depoliticization by banning political clubs and re-establishing censorship, and it was a fiction that bore little relation to reality.

The royalist review *Paris pendant l'année 1797* used the Muslims of the embassy to lay on heavy sarcasm: "from their childhood, instead of hearing people talk of liberty, equality, unity, indivisibility, and even fraternity, they know only the submission to the orders of a master, perfect resignation, faithfulness to their religion, abstinence, and cleanliness. Thus, as we can see, there is a huge gulf between those who follow the Koran, and those who follow the Declaration of the Rights of Man, the sublime gospel of the French." "Oh!" the newspaper has the ambassador exclaim, "I do not understand any of that pantomime; and my Koran, as obscure as it may be, is a hundred times clearer than what you are trying to teach me. I would prefer to renounce Mahomet altogether than to become a good republican."[37]

"Have you read the Koran?" asked a dialogue in a newspaper of 1797,[38] recoding the predicament of the Year 5 in a supposed "passage of the Koran": "Men! To be happy on this earth, do not assemble anywhere but in your temples, because God makes you quiet there." The prophetic voice was used here to insist upon the need to maintain the prohibition on political clubs. "Do not gather in profane assemblies . . . for you all speak at once, you do not hear one another, and your end will be nigh."[39] Since the Koran dated from the seventh century, the newspaper suggested, "if [Mahomet] outlawed popular societies, and this empire lasted eleven centuries without them, I conclude that they are not useful for the preservation of states."[40]

Again and again, the Koran was invoked in arguments over the constitution. The *Mercure britannique* called Rousseau's *Social Contract* "the Koran of the unnatural chatterers of 1789, the Jacobins of 1790, the Republicans of 1791, and the most atrocious zealots."[41] A letter in a Brussels revolutionary newspaper declared that "this is how superstition does its damage in every part of the globe; everywhere the same ignorance and the same prejudices: the Turk tramples on the Gospel and the Bible, the Christian does the same with the Koran." "Liberty," Lavicomterie wrote in his *Crimes des empereurs turcs*, "so long entombed under the ruins of Greece, will break the Crescent, tear up the Koran, as she has done to the Gospels, and from the top of the minarets of Constantinople, invite Asia and Africa to fraternize with independent Europe." But this liberty no longer appeared so simple after the French experience: he sounded a dire warning to the "half-educated Muslim people," should they "rise up against the long tyranny that oppresses them."[42] At the other end of the cultural spectrum a vaudeville in the *Journal de Paris* declared its "equal contempt" for Jansenists, terrorists, royalists, anarchists, alarmists, apologists, papists, Calvinists, Talmudists, Koranists, and a host of other "ists" that characterized the ideological ferment of France. "When the peace comes at last," it concluded in verse, "everyone will be Deist, even the materialist, Turk, Jew, Greek, or Catholic."[43]

Islam was a common theme in this search for a new religion. "Children of the same God, let us live at least as brothers," declared one writer, calling for a religion with "no dogma, no rite, no liturgy. . . . Neither Moses nor Mahomet *revealed* it, but all wise men have given the precepts and example for it."[44] The *Ami de lois* prayed "to be informed of the morality by which we might once more become the honor and the admiration of Europe and rid ourselves of Catholicism, Mahometanism, Protestantism, and other religions fabricated by the hands of men and presented under a celestial covering. We have requested all good citizens to take up this important work and to each provide a brick to help erect the edifice of theism and philanthropy."[45]

After the coup of 1797, when the Jacobins again took the reins of power, they did exactly this. To reinstitute a civic cult they solicited proposals from the public in answer to the question "What are the most appropriate institutions for the moral foundation of a people?"[46] The answer that emerged was little different from Robespierre's: a simple doctrine of unity and transcendence of God, immortality of the soul, and virtuous behavior on earth.[47]

Theophilanthropy attempted to reverse-engineer virtue by creating a religion that would justify good actions, rather than one that by its revealed truth would dictate morality. In this sense, revolutionaries sought to use the political as the source for the religious, rather than the other way around. The "culte décadaire" would be celebrated every tenth day, explicitly replacing the Sabbath common to all three Abrahamic faiths (although celebrated on different days of the week) with a more appropriately decimal rhythm. But the similarity of this religion to that of Robespierre, and to Mahomet, gave rise to satires. A cartoon of the period reveled in the carnival chaos of the Directory, and its pretensions to a new religion, by creating a hybrid Theophilanthropic Mahomet, who marches on a spinning wheel, marked 18 for the coup of Fructidor, in an endless cycle of coups from Thermidor to Vendémiaire (in fact the true coup d'état would come in Brumaire) (fig. 20). This Mahomet weighs the crown and the liberty bonnet on his scale of tyranny, as the constitution and the sovereignty of the people burn along with the wheat that should feed a hungry populace. This link between subsistence and Islam was only too present in the public mind, since in the context of war at sea, the Muslim world offered a vital lifeline to southern France.

Fraternal Muslims

On 10 Floréal Year 3 (29 April 1795), the Committee of Surveillance of the district of Marseille (which was no longer a city) wrote to the National Convention to announce the defeat of terrorists in their town, and calling for more violence: "Strike off the guilty heads of these abominable conspirators who wanted to turn France into a field covered with corpses."[48] Joseph-Stanislas Rovère, a former Montagnard who now supported the restoration of a constitutional monarchy, read aloud in the National Convention the letter received from the representative on mission in Marseille, sent to suppress the Jacobins and ensure the supply of provisions into southern France.

His colleague Paul Cadroy, who rose to speak next, alluded to the "strong and energetic measures" that had worked to destroy the monster of terrorism and restored the "happy abundance" to which all of the French

Figure 20. *Mahomet-Théophilanthrope*, 1798. Bibliothèque nationale de France.

Republic would soon aspire. "You will learn with pleasure," he declared, "that the Barbary States wish to be friends to France, and useful ones: they are increasing the arrivals of grain; they wish for the success of the French Revolution as much or more by loyalty, and by agreement with the principles of a sacred morality, as by interest." As proof, he produced a letter from his pocket and announced that it was addressed to him "by Mohamed Dyghis, Turk, ally of the bey of Tunis, a man precious by his sentiments and his attachment to the French nation."[49]

"I swear to you by our holy Prophet, Citizen Representative," the letter began, "that my expressions of affection toward you are not motivated by commercial interests. They are a homage for the good things I have witnessed you doing here. . . . I love the justice that you love, I worship the principles of humanity that you consistently profess. Your good deeds have elevated my soul, and that alone makes us brothers in our hearts. No matter where I first drew breath, or the religion in which I was born, we are brothers. Indeed, we are more than brothers when every moral precept is shared by two thinking beings. Conserve your friendship for me, it is very precious. You will have in me, for all my days, the most devoted friend in the middle of Barbary, which is much less barbarous than people think."[50]

This is perhaps the most remarkable expression by any Muslim of support for revolutionary principles. Doubtless it served a convenient purpose in helping to justify the conduct of Cadroy and his colleagues that would later be called into serious question, given his complicity in the massacre of Jacobins incarcerated in Fort Saint-Jean.[51] Importation of wheat, oil, and other staples from North Africa was vital to the survival of the republic, and the letter offered practical promises of "lots of shipments that I have convinced several of my friends to expedite" from Tunis and other ports. Nonetheless, the letter declared, "I speak in this sense as a Frenchman, because I have a French soul and sentiments. . . . I am awaiting a letter from my bey. I expect to come to Paris as soon as I receive it."[52] This expression of ideological—and affective—alignment went far beyond the cautious expressions of other Muslims.

We can see the mirror reflection of this new sense of the Muslim role in French life in one of a series of sketches depicting the Boyer-Fonfrède family by François-André Vincent. The scenes of their daily life in Toulon speak to Suzanne Desan's observations on the centrality of patriarchal domesticity in the reconstruction of the republic under the Directory: a nursing mother embraces her infant, a child gives alms to an elderly beggar, a father gives his son a lesson in plowing. The final image, however, shifts the action to the port of Marseille, as the son, grown to manhood, negotiates with Muslim merchants (fig. 21). At the center of the scene is not the young man, but the turbaned merchant, furrowing his brow as he writes with a quill on a folio, while one of his companions gestures toward the ship (but also—by coincidence?— toward Fort Saint-Jean, scene of the massacre of Jacobins months earlier). The family, the hearth and home, even the hometown are absent, and adult-hood is conceived on a larger economic, religious, and political canvas. The Muslims are depicted as literate, peaceful, punctilious, conceived in solid, classical standing forms, like Roman figures. The young Frenchman is placed in a kind of tutelary position, seated, emphasizing the continuity with the

Figure 21. François-André Vincent, *Merchants on the Quais at the Port of Marseille*, 1795. Musée de la Marine, Marseille. Photo SCALA, Florence.

earlier images of education. Here, however, it is the Muslims who serve as guides and interlocutors. This image differs from the traditional port paintings that showed colorful, beturbaned Muslims among the bustling crowds: its focus is less the port than commerce itself as a kind of transnational public sphere.

This trade with the Muslim world was crucial not only for connection but for survival. Buchot, in the Ministry of External Affairs, wrote to the Committee of Public Safety soon after Thermidor, declaring that on the evidence of the assistance provided by the bey of Tunis "we may conclude that the despots of Africa are worth more than the despots of Europe."[53] In March 1794, a merchant called Vianis wrote to the newly restored revolutionary authorities in Commune Affranchie (Lyon) to offer to procure grains: "I cannot obtain rice," he wrote, "but I can get *couscous*, which is a kind of pasta good for making soup."[54] There is no indication whether couscous was in fact imported during the Revolution, but other forms of grain were certainly sent in large quantities.

In June 1794, the Committee of Public Safety dispatched a letter to Hammuda Bey, omitting the conventional deferential forms of address and using the familiar "tu" mandated by revolutionary equality, and omitting the customary forms of praise. Unable to present the letter in person, because of restrictions on movement due to plague in the region, the consul sent the letter in its original form: it was returned with a demand for translation into Arabic or Turkish as was customary, but not before the letter had been roughly translated by the bey's Italian physician. The bey was initially "very infuriated by the suppression of these titles," but the consul reported that "I recalled to him that our constitution, which I had read to him and which he had admired, being founded on reason, the republic must logically adopt its language, and I read to him your own expressions, 'so that its sentiments should be purer, its friendship more constant, and its promises more sacred.' On these conditions, he replied, 'I will be the warmest friend of France.' "[55]

Buchot declared that the bey's acceptance was a triumph for reason against "oriental prejudices."[56] The bey demanded only that the republic release "38 of my subjects seized on French territory, and who have been languishing for three years in Sardinian chains," along with the restitution of Tunisian cargoes seized and sold in Corsica.[57] Along with the alteration of forms of address, the French Republic was also at pains to insist on the erasure of its Christian religious character. The French envoy Herculais decided to close the chapel in the *fondouk* where the French lived, sell its contents, and turn it into a room for the consulate. The consul opposed this and claimed that even the Muslims would be outraged. Herculais wrote that instead "the bey said that he observed with pleasure that the French were becoming closer to the Muslims, and manifested his low estimation of the Jews and the Christians."[58] This language appeared to imply a growing distinction between "Christians" and "French," which the bey (or at least Herculais) interpreted not only as greater friendliness, but as a real religious convergence between French deists and Muslims.

This sense of rapprochement between French and Muslims opened a path for North Africans to articulate their connections to the values and ideas of the Revolution. Sidi Mustapha Khoja, one of the key advisers of the bey, was well known to be "well-disposed for the French," and Herculais reported that he was working to procure for this minister "the works of [the naturalist] Buffon that he has long desired," explaining that "the efforts we have made to collect the engravings and have the work bound were the cause of the delay."[59] The interpreter Venture de Paradis wrote that it was "rare to see, I do not say in despotic lands, but even among the most civilized peoples, a man more wise, more regular in his morals, more disinterested, and more equitable than Mustapha Cogea," and noted both his close awareness of events in Europe and his fluency in Arabic, Turkish, and Italian.[60] At the same time, when the French government demanded the expulsion of the former consul Devoize, his secretary, and an émigré, "Sidi Mustapha strongly opposed it, fearing after his disloyal insinuations that his throat would be slit if he returned to France."[61] The bey—like the dey of Algiers—appeared to be willing to extend hospitality to those fleeing retribution, despite his support of the French.

Like Dyghis, other Tunisian merchants traveled to Paris in this period: citizen Guys, the agent of external relations in Marseille, wrote to announce the arrival of "Moulla Mahmet Aga and Sidi Ahmed Selby."[62] Mohamed Dyghis himself is identifiable as Muhammad al-Daghīs, more commonly written as D'Ghies, a merchant from Tripoli who traded in Tunis, and was well known to travelers across the period. In a letter to the Committee of Public Safety on 29 Thermidor, Cadroy mentioned "the importance of the friendship of the Tunisians, and Mohamed Dyghis, who had been here for six months, well-considered in his country, a friend of the French and worthy to be so."[63] D'Ghies's son Hassuna—a significant reformer who would work with Jeremy Bentham—later described his father's "ten years travelling in Europe."[64] It is difficult to date or reconstruct these travels, which may have been undertaken in shorter periods over the course of the elder D'Ghies's career. The *Gazette de France* mentioned various instances of envoys from Tripoli: in London in 1765, Stockholm in 1772, Holland in 1774. In July 1797, Friedrich Hornemann, the African explorer, traveled from London to Paris, and met with "a Turk of distinction (a native of Tripoly), then resident at Paris."[65] This may well have been D'Ghies; it can be seen how difficult it is to determine these movements in a period when records were kept only where conflicts arose.

Muhammad D'Ghies's statement comes to us only at thirdhand, read aloud in the assembly from Cadroy's letter. It nonetheless bears a number of similarities with the language of Ahmed Khan. In both cases, the expression of ideological alignment was made *through* the conventional forms of

Islam—here swearing by the Prophet, a popular practice rejected by strict Muslims and by Wahhabis in particular—and the revolutionary ideals mentioned were those most aligned to Islam. The letter does not mention liberty or equality, but focuses instead on justice, humanity, and fraternity. The third of these values, the only one to bear a direct connection to the explicit values of the Revolution, receives the deepest expression of emotional connection. Fraternity (*ikhwa'*) was a value already present in Islam, which had from the outset rejected other forms of clan and tribal loyalties (*'asabiyya*) in order to insist upon the brotherhood/sisterhood between all Muslims. In the *Surah Al-Hujurat*, the Koran declares, "Indeed all the believers are brothers, so make settlement between your brothers, and fear Allah that you may receive mercy."

Religious fraternity was not necessarily isomorphic with political fraternity, which had taken on particular complexions in the context of revolutionary consciousness. Three decades later, Rifa'a al-Tahtawi, a Muslim intellectual living in Paris during the 1830 revolution, would explain to his readers the meaning of "liberty " to the French: "That which they call freedom and which they crave is what we call 'justice' and 'equity,' inasmuch as 'rule by freedom' means establishing equality in justice and laws so that the ruler cannot oppress any human being."[66] We can compare D'Ghies's statement with Albert Hourani's conclusion that Tahtawi's ideas about society and the state were "neither a mere restatement of a traditional view nor a simple reflection of the ideas he had learnt in Paris," but he reconceived these ideas "within the tradition of Islamic thought" and with reference to the example of the Prophet and his companions, and even gave them "a new and significant development."[67] A first step was taken here, one that would bear fruit in the work of D'Ghies's son Hassuna, who would follow his father in seeking both to adapt and to challenge European ideas about North Africa.[68] The events of 1798, however, would transform this new openness into violent confrontation.

The Rupture with Islam

In 1797, the French Revolution had gained much ground in the Muslim world, winning a gradual circle of interest and engagement, as French citizens celebrated the constitutional place that Muslims could occupy, should they choose to settle in France as some had already begun to do. Just two years later, France was at war with Islam, Muslims along with other subjects of Muslim powers were expelled from France, and the sultan declared a jihad against the French as enemies of God. This was by no means an inevitable outcome: indeed, it ran entirely counter to the current that had brought French citizens and Muslims closer together over the preceding decade. It helped bring to power factions in the Muslim world who denied that Muslims had ever subscribed to any of the ideals of the Revolution, and it compelled those who did to conceal their sympathies, or to imagine different ways of achieving them.

The invasion of Egypt, a majority Muslim country and province of a neutral power that had consistently refused to join with France's enemies, was the fatal betrayal that effectively ended the French Revolution. Was it intentional or accidental? Perhaps that is the wrong question. Such decisions are the result of multiple voices speaking for different interests, sometimes sincerely and sometimes with rank hypocrisy. The coup of Fructidor 1797 brought to power the Thermidorean shape-shifter Barras, the inveterate Jew-hating Rewbell, and the theophilanthropic Reveillère-Lépeaux. Alongside them were the generals, seizing increasing power for themselves, and above all, General Bonaparte.

Yet behind the curtain moved the long shadow of the bishop and politician Talleyrand, promoted to foreign minister in the coup of 1797. It was Talleyrand who recognized in Bonaparte the useful figure that could end the Revolution. Picking up loose claims made by a disgruntled former consul from Egypt, Talleyrand began to militate actively for an invasion.[69] He had already presented an official address promoting the acquisition of new colonies, and on 25 Pluviôse he made a long report to the Directory on a plan for the conquest of Egypt. It would be "the complement of everything beautiful, great, and useful that the French Revolution has presented to an astonished world," Talleyrand declared. "This people [the Egyptians] abhors its tyrants . . . they will bless the French who deliver them." In what can only have been a conscious falsehood, he insisted that the conquest would be easy, and that there would be no resistance. French forces would move through Suez to the Red Sea and onward to India, where they would join Tipu Sultan to defeat the British. Military knowledge would not be required, he declared astonishingly; all that would be needed was to "ensure that the French respect the prejudices of an ignorant people. The points on which they must not be disturbed are religion and women." As a result of this simple mask of pro-Islamic sentiment, "the people will greet us with joy." On his return from Egypt, Bonaparte dug out the document and left a series of furious annotations: "This is false," "What folly!" and "To the madhouse."[70] Yet in 1797, Bonaparte, the product of a revolutionary education and his own fascination with Islam, was chafing at the bit to embark upon this absurd and disastrous course, and readily believed Talleyrand's fabrications. With him, he took the fate of the Revolution itself.

After the death of the new ambassador to the Ottoman Empire, Aubert-Dubayet, Talleyrand assured Bonaparte that he would himself travel to Istanbul to ensure Ottoman support for the invasion, which would serve them by punishing the Mamluk beys of Egypt for their mismanagement of the country. Talleyrand never moved a toe in the direction of Turkey. Whether this was due to shifting circumstances or intentional deception has not been conclusively determined.[71] Instead it was Pierre Ruffin—the interpreter who had accompanied Ishak Bey in 1789 and Ahmed Khan in 1794, now acting consul in Istanbul—who was thrown into the prison of the Seven Towers.

Sometime after Thermidor, Buonaparte changed his name—along with his allegiances—to become Napoléon Bonaparte, the French general who would embark from Toulon with 400 ships and some 50,000 men. Of the three years of the occupation that followed, he would remain in Egypt for only one, before turning tail and sailing back to France on rumors of an impending coup. Biographers have seen in the Egyptian experience a transformation of the republican officer into the dictatorial emperor who would rule most of Europe in the fifteen years that followed.[72] Later, he would claim his attempts to win Muslim support were mere tactics, a canny recognition of the usefulness of religion in governing the credulous.[73] Yet there are many indications that his naivete was real, and that, at least in part, he believed his own propaganda. If, like others, he believed that Muslims were awaiting the moment to rise in insurrection, he seems not to have imagined that they might rise to defend their society and their religion against the invading "atheists."

It is a terrible irony that it was Bonaparte's successor, Kléber—a true republican, who detested the invasion he had been ordered to join, and who sought new alliances to ensure an effective exit—who paid the ultimate price for Bonaparte's unwise speculation on Islam, as the first French leader to be assassinated by a Muslim. But the greatest casualty of this mistaken adventure was the fragile convergence between Europe and a Muslim world in the throes of modernization, convincing many Muslims that liberty, equality, and fraternity were no more than chimeras to be quickly abandoned for an embrace of the strong, the cynical, the self-serving. In this moment, empire was reborn, and the dreams of universal citizenship were crushed—but they could not be extinguished forever. In spite of the "granite masses" that Bonaparte would build, his expert manipulation of the mask of propaganda, his cynical and cunning ministers and charade of democratic plebiscites, his empire fell at last, and the monarchies and empires that followed ceded again and again to a revolutionary project that was not forgotten. This book has been dedicated to the proposition that this project was, in some way, a much bigger one than the French Revolution. It was a human project in which many diverse people could share, with no ultimate barrier for Muslims, for Jews, for Hindus, or for Buddhists; no barrier to color, gender, or religion; a project that remains unfinished, and a struggle that continues today.

Epilogue

1799

"As soon as you receive the present order," the commissioner of the executive directory in the central administration of the Seine-et-Oise instructed his municipal subordinates in January 1799, "you will conduct the most precise investigations in the areas assigned to your surveillance in order to locate all Muslims, subjects of the sultan, and communicate as quickly as possible a list that details their names, the commune in which they live, their profession or trade, the businesses they deal with, and lastly an account of their property and estates throughout the republic."[1] In the wake of the invasion of Egypt and the jihad declared against France, the Directory had issued a series of warrants against Muslims and North Africans in every department of France. Muslims like Ishak Bey and Ahmed Khan who had been living in the Seine-et-Oise had long ago departed, and it appears no others were located around Versailles, which had reverted to a small provincial town.

The commissioner of the Seine-et-Marne, however, signaled a Muslim living in the rural canton of Chaumes-sur-Brie, near Melun: "Michel Fertali, subject of the Ottoman Porte," who had been taken prisoner during the siege of Landrecies in Belgium in 1794. However, this Muslim, the commissioner added, "has made the declaration necessary to enjoy the rights of a French citizen, after the law prescribed by the constitution."[2] Fertali is thus the first recorded Muslim citizen of the French Republic. It is telling that his case comes to light only as a result of the abrogation of the principles upon which such citizenship was based. The order made clear that the provisions applied only to Muslims, and did not include Ottoman Jews, Greeks, or Armenians, "with whom the republic has good relations." A few weeks later, a new decree ordered the arrest of all North Africans. Four Muslim Tunisian merchants—Sidi Osman Aga, Sidi Muhammad ben Ibrahim, Sidi Kadi ben Ibrahim, and Sidi Muhammed ben Mustapha—along with their servants, were arrested in Lyon and held until August, when they were given passports to leave France. A report to the chief of police made evident the shift that had taken place: "if the finest law of nature and the respect for humanity is the desire of every republican soul, the preservation and the glory of the *patrie* is also the incommutable duty of the leaders of the state."[3] Even before the return of Napoléon Bonaparte and the coup d'état that he helped direct, the primacy of national glory was already casting its shadow over the universalist ambitions of the Revolution.

But the mobilization of the republic to register and arrest Muslims from the Vendée to the Var, which gave rise to no more than a handful of identifications, also suggests just how amplified the Muslim presence had become in the revolutionary mind. Just two years later, hundreds of Egyptians and Syrians would arrive in Marseille with the army evacuating Egypt: for the first time, a considerable number of Muslims would settle permanently in France. Yet their presence would be almost invisible. The history we have traced in this book can help us understand why. The prominence of Muslims was indissociably linked to the universal vocation of the Revolution and its vision of human citizenship and equality across the globe. With the establishment of Napoléon's dictatorship, such questions no longer applied. Bonaparte would restore the centrality of the Catholic Church, place religious minorities back into distinct categories, and re-establish a hierarchy of privileges stretching from a new imperial aristocracy to a restored category of the slave denuded of all rights. The question of whether Muslims could be citizens, was, therefore, moot, since *no* French subject was a citizen, and would not be so again for half a century. By the time citizenship was ultimately and haltingly restored, the imperial legacy had taken such hold that Muslims would be denied citizenship for another century.

We must conclude, therefore, that the question of Muslim citizenship and the role of Islam in the republic arose out of the Revolution itself: it did not arise belatedly as a result of colonial and postcolonial Muslim migration to the metropole. Moreover, the results of that consideration can tell us much about the Revolution and its principles. The citizenship of Muslims was not only a contingent possibility but a necessary condition for liberty, equality, and fraternity to be universal principles rather than merely national ones. At the same time, as the case of Fertali suggests, at the heart of the Revolution, until the rupture of its principles in 1798, the Muslim path to citizenship had become a routine process, greeted with the *indifference* proper to a society of equals, leaving few traces, and for this reason we cannot know with any exactitude how many individuals followed this path.

Yet if the French Revolution opened a space for Muslim participation, it also slammed that door shut in ways that have left long-standing legacies. The failure of universal equality in its application to Muslims was in part the result of the politicization of Islam itself during the Revolution. Even as older patterns of religious anathema fell away, and with them certain fixed conceptions about despotism and fanaticism, new uses of Islam emerged that distorted the revolutionary conception of the Muslim citizen. At its most hopeful, the Revolution accommodated Muslims with an active hospitality that asked for participation, but did not demand an impossible assimilation or renunciation of faith. At its nadir, the category of Muslim was deployed in disingenuous ways to stave off the equality that threatened entrenched privilege, or was emptied of content and weaponized in factional struggles over religion and equality. Whether in the struggle to retain patriarchal control, the attempt to exclude Jews from citizenship, the violent conflicts over the clergy, or the clashes over race and slavery, Muslims emerged as rhetorical counters in ways utterly disproportionate to their presence in France. Yet Muslims *were* present, and the impact of that presence could itself be intensified by its discursive amplification.

It is only this process that can help us explain the logic that took revolutionary France into an utterly illogical war with the Ottoman Empire in 1798, invading the territory of a neutral power for no conceivable gain. That decision was the last "use" of Islam in the Revolution—to bring the Revolution to an end. Yet it did not mean that the Revolution was "over," and it will not be so until these questions that it opened are finally resolved. What kind of republic can make equal citizens of men and women, Muslims, Christians, Jews, believers and nonbelievers, people of all colors, creeds, and convictions? Much of the "republican" culture that has claimed to answer this question in the recent past is a result of the illiberal regimes of the nineteenth century, built on colonial racial hierarchies, masculine prerogative, and class division. In this sense, the revolution—not the white, male, and French Revolution, but a more diverse revolution that reflects the plural history of the real France today—has never ceased to be relevant, and never ceased to be fought.

In 1799, the chief Muslim resistance to British expansion in India also came to an end, with the death of Tipu Sultan, a different kind of "Muslim citizen." In 1797, a French corsair named François Ripaud found his ship forced into the port of Mangalore; he was taken to the court of Tipu Sultan at Srirangapatna and interrogated about the political situation in France. Described by British officials as a "violent republican," Ripaud claimed to be second-in-command of the French colony of Île de France (Réunion), dispatched on official mission to Tipu's court, and he exaggerated the strength of French forces in the Indian Ocean. In fact it was precisely due to the absence of a defensive fleet that the governor had been compelled to make use of the assistance of corsairs like Ripaud. Tipu's advisers counseled against trusting Ripaud, but they were ignored. Most strikingly, the documents seized and published by the British demonstrated that Ripaud had sought rapidly to establish a revolutionary political culture among the French of Mysore, the 60 or so engineers and artisans recruited before the Revolution, who had remained largely isolated from the changes in France. The British seized upon this evidence of a "Jacobin" conversion taking place in India, in order to identify Indian resistance with the hated revolutionary France born in the context of the war. But, as Jean Boutier observes, nowhere was the word "Jacobin" used by the French citizens in the club: its framing and vocabulary were entirely republican.[4] The oath swore "to support the Republican Constitution, to defend it, and my country, with all my strength and with all my powers; to submit to the laws decreed by the Convention, and to those of equality which we shall frame, or to die in arms at my post, in the defence of the sacred right of a citizen, to live free, or perish."[5] They elaborated a code of discipline and punishments for insubordination, burned the white Bourbon flag, and raised the tricolor. In the ceremony, Ripaud called on them to "swear hatred to all kings, except Tippoo Sultaun the Victorious, the ally of the French Republic. War against tyrants; and love to our country, and that of citizen Tippoo."[6] The flag they were burning stood for the monarchy, Christianity, and the English, he declared: "the army of the Vendée was that of Jesus, the white flag, the Fleur de Lys in one hand and a dagger in the other."[7] One document was written by an "Ahmud Khan," who occupied the function of *malik at-tujjar*, or minister of commerce; there is no indication whether this might have been the same Ahmed Khan who traveled to France. His observations to

Tipu contained warnings about Ripaud, and counseled him to send letters to the French to determine the real character of the corsair's credentials.[8] Within a year, the question would be moot. On 20 September 1798, in the wake of the French invasion of Egypt, the sultan and caliph of the Ottoman Empire wrote to Tipu: "It is notorious, that the French, bent upon the overthrow of all Sects and Religions, have invented a new doctrine, under the name of Liberty." Insisting that the French aim was the extinction of Islam, he called on Tipu to "assist your brother Muslims in this general cause of Religion" and reject all alliance with the French.[9]

On 4 May 1799, Tipu's body was discovered under the corpses of slain soldiers at the gate of his palace; betrayed by agents inside his own palace, he died fighting at the now famous "Water Gate." Taking the claims of cooperation with the French as their pretext, the company had, as so often before, gained the assistance of local rivals and internal traitors to divide and destroy. This ignominious slaughter made the British into the preeminent power in India: as one Englishman crowed, "The Empire of the East is at our feet."[10] The British came to believe that there remained no "Mohammedan" resistance left in India; historians have suggested that Tipu's death in fact helped transform him into a martyr in the defense of Islam.[11] The legacies of Tipu's struggle can be traced into the Vellore Mutiny of 1806 and onward to the great uprising of 1857, along networks that have yet to be fully explored.

The French Revolution was conceived from the outset on a global scale, as a universal transformation that would change the world as much as France itself. The Muslim world was crucial to France's fortunes and even to the subsistence of French men and women. When the very survival of the republic was threatened in 1793 and 1794, the Ottoman Empire and the North African city-states were the only major powers to remain neutral and even friendly to France. Yet revolutionaries were divided about what this meant: some believed that Muslim societies were naturally more amenable to the new order, while others hoped for parallel uprising in the Muslim world against rulers they perceived as tyrants and despots. The decision to invade Egypt was a lamentable (if not a deliberate) confusion of these two principles. While declaring themselves the liberators of Egypt from the tyranny of the Mamluks, the French seemed to believe they would be welcomed both by the Egyptians and the Ottoman sultan. For the first time, during these years, France ruled over millions of Muslims. The hypothetical conception of the Muslim citizen that the Revolution had generated could have become a reality. In the event,

Bonaparte forged a new system that erased not simply the Muslim citizen, but citizenship itself, in a Napoleonic system that in many ways borrowed elements of Ottoman rule: a segmentary society focused on an ideologically legitimated "great sultan"—as Bonaparte himself was known in Egypt.

The Revolution foundered not only on the political ambitions of Bonaparte, but also on the difficulties of rethinking religion, the most ancient structure for stabilizing social relations. A world without religion proved impossible. There was no smooth step toward secularism: the passions of religious devotion and visceral anticlericalism raged violently against one another, as deputies and citizens alike struggled to find some compromise. In this context, new perceptions and understandings of Islam that had emerged over the late eighteenth century were infused with political valency. Bonaparte once again was a figure who embodied the intellectual investment in Islam, conflating it with a radically simplified version of Rousseau's deism. Theirs was an Islam without religion—stripped of "superstition" and tradition, and reduced to a radical core claim of the oneness of God. It is curious to find in this an echo of the claims of the Wahhabi "revolution" in Arabia and its hostility to *shirk*, or idolatry, and *bida'*, or religious innovation. Bonaparte would indeed send a mission (equally futile) to the Saudis to seek an alliance in 1810. Many of those fighting the French in Egypt were followers of Wahhabism who had taken up the call to jihad: they were hardly likely a decade later to join his imperial project. It remains for scholars to determine what role these events played in the development of the movement that is at the origin of radical *salafist* versions of Islam today.

Muslims themselves were not simply ciphers in that shift. Their presence in a France on the brink of revolution was in itself the index of interconnected changes and challenges in the Muslim world of the Middle East and North Africa. These Muslims, though only a few individuals, were frequently ventriloquized in revolutionary pamphlets to remind readers of the French monarchy's failure to provide support to key Muslim allies, and in their counterrevolutionary equivalents as figures of a more stable patriarchal rule. Sentimental conceptions of the Muslim as a just father and generous brother coexisted with satirical conceptions that recycled older anti-Muslim tropes. In a more general sense, we can see in this politicization a form of "desacralization" of the category of Muslim, no longer conceived in theological terms of belief and heresy, of truth and error, but rather in terms of customs, social structure, and practices.

In December of 1789, the "Muslim citizen" became a real possibility through the admission of non-Catholics to eligibility for active citizenship. For the first time, in Marseille during this period, we can detect the engagement of local Muslims in the political affairs of a French city. Their engagement was as Muslims, and not as citizens; their role was made possible by their simultaneous residence in France and ties to the polities of North Africa. These were nonetheless the first Muslims to play such a role in France, a role that was welcomed by revolutionary authorities.

The early optimism of a world where barriers of faith would fall, and universal fraternity take their place, collapsed in the face of the great religious civil war provoked by the clerical oath. Throughout 1791 and 1792, the clergy and intransigent Catholics took up the potential citizenship of Jews and Muslims as emblematic of the blasphemous nature of the new regime. They asserted repeatedly an elaborate and increasingly absurd series of allegations about the role of Muslims in the state, which blossomed into a landscape of Muslim voters, Muslim bishops, minarets on the horizon, and imams swearing oaths to the constitution. In response, revolutionaries did not seek to deny the potential participation of Muslims, but insisted upon its theoretical legality, or took it up as proof of the need to create a religiously plural constitution.

The entanglement of Muslims in revolutionary politics was not, however, merely rhetorical. The subsistence crisis that had helped drive the uprisings of 1789 was aggravated when France entered war against neighboring states. Southern France, and even Paris, was dependent upon the supplemental supplies of grain coming from outside France, and peaceful relations with North African states were essential to that flow. Algiers was emerging as the major power in the Maghreb at the same moment that France became a republic; after early contentions, a remarkable confluence of interest and ideology seemed to offer new hopes for the connection between the two states. A new dey, Hassan Pacha, was well versed in European politics, and became closely engaged with events in France, offering generous support from his own treasury to ensure the continued supply of grain, creating debts that successive French regimes would leave unpaid, and leading to the French invasion and colonization of Algeria.

The suppression of the counterrevolution by late 1793 did not resolve the Revolution's religious problem. The profound anticlerical hatred provoked by the violence in the countryside undermined all manifestations of Catholicism and even Christianity itself. Many revolutionaries who had once sought a return to a gentler, simpler "primitive church" now rejected all forms of organized religion. Yet there was no consensus on what should take its place. A number of representatives in the provinces began dismantling religious establishments and creating temples of Truth, Reason, and Nature, calling upon Catholics, Protestants, Jews, and—on occasion—Muslims to renounce their superstition and celebrate nature alone. In Paris, this was viewed with alarm at a moment when the Revolution seemed in the balance. Robespierre in particular opposed the "nationalization of atheism" even as he proposed a dechristianized cult of the Supreme Being, a civic religion open to all.

The arrival of an Indian Muslim in Paris at the height of these struggles served as a test case for this politics. Ahmed Khan was ostensibly traveling from Istanbul to London with his brother to seek redress for the East India Company's usurpation of his family's rights, but found himself confined for many months in Lyon when his brother fell ill. After the death of his brother, Ahmed arrived in Paris at the height of the period known as "the Terror," a moment racked by fears of conspiracy and violence that has been identified with a rise of nationalism and xenophobia, yet he was greeted with open arms. The hospitality offered by revolutionary authorities was not simply passive: it was an active negotiation that both recognized difference and remained "indifferent" to it. Ahmed Khan himself actively embraced this opportunity, undertaking to translate the Declaration of the Rights of Man and Citizen into Persian.

Ahmed's story is not just a footnote. It can help us to see another dimension of this period that has become known as "the Terror." It touched in some way even the most prominent revolutionary figure of this moment, Robespierre. In his responses to the wider Muslim world, we can see how Robespierre combined pragmatism and principle, recognizing the need to cooperate with neutral Muslim regimes while refusing to exclude Muslims from the universal principles he espoused. Yet these contradictions were not so easily reconciled in a rabidly factionalized political situation. His decision to lend direct support to the re-establishment of religious principles at the Festival of the Supreme Being led to accusations that he was attempting to found a new religion with himself as prophet. In the wake of Thermidor, and his precipitous fall from power, the figure of Mahomet, drawn from Voltaire's satirical play, was used to condemn Robespierre's supposed "fanaticism," and at the same time to declare him a cunning impostor with a superhuman gift for duping the credulous. At the same time, these comparisons often ended by praising the historical figure of Muhammad, declared a great man and a model of the kind of politico-religious legislator France lacked.

The religious politics that followed Thermidor were confused: the Koran emerged as a recurring theme in the search for a durable pact to resolve France's religious problems. The Directory, beneficiary of a victorious political situation, looked outward with renewed energy to globalize the Revolution—a return of earlier beliefs, but now in the form of a realpolitik of conquest and occupation. The fascination with Islam of a young Corsican officer who had abandoned his fierce anti-French commitments to embrace the Revolution was in this sense quite characteristic of wider conceptions of Islam during these years. Buonaparte dreamed of the Muslim world as a way out of the tangled complications of revolutionary France under the Directory: he requested in 1795 to be sent to Istanbul as an artillery officer to train the Ottoman army. Instead, in the wake of a series of stunning victories in Italy that made him the most renowned general in France, his fevered imaginings about Islam led him to take up the disastrous plan advocated by Talleyrand of an attack on British power through Egypt. The project of bringing the republic to Egypt soon became a precarious and increasingly violent act of occupation.

Yet when the French declared that they were Muslims in 1798, it was not a lie but a half-believed fiction. A decade of revolutionary engagements with Islam had convinced many that "dechristianization"—from the Temples of Reason and the Festival of the Supreme Being to the invasion of Rome—had brought the French closer to Islam, conceived as a rational, civic religion. This conception was as false in practice as the former theological caricatures by the Catholic Church. As internecine violence increased, universalism became even more crucial as a driving force of the Revolution. Yet there was not just one universalism but many. Inherent in the very naming of Catholicism was a powerful claim to universality: like Islam it offered no limitation upon conversion and projected millennial visions of universal faith. It is no coincidence that Tocqueville should have compared the Revolution itself to Islam in the way that it "flooded the earth with its soldiers, apostles, and martyrs."[12] But Tocqueville himself was a product of an imperial age, one that had ceased to see in Muslims potential citizens, and reascribed them as colonial subjects.

This is not to suggest the logics of the French Revolution were imperial. It is instead to insist that the Revolution was a complex and conflictual engagement of many strands that played out into the history that followed. It would take France until 1848 to offer men universal suffrage and to abolish slavery in all colonies, and until 1944 to offer women and Muslims the right to vote. Muslim women gained the vote only in 1958. Yet in all of these cases—and even in that of the anticolonial resistance against French imperialism—those fighting for rights saw their struggles reflected in the Revolution. They were right to do so. In the political creativity generated by a crisis that was much larger than France alone, yet found its most intense point of convergence in that unexpected place, possibilities emerged that had never been imagined, and which have not ceased to inspire and to challenge, and sometimes to frighten. The great studies of the French Revolution have almost always understood it as an event in world-historical terms, whether as a model for other revolutions or as the epicenter of a world transformation. They have been more reticent to investigate the place of the world *in* the unfolding of the French Revolution itself. It is for this reason that this book has focused on France, rather than on Europe, the Atlantic, the colonies, or the world. That larger consideration must await another, more ambitious work.

The most surprising thing about the Revolution is that the radical possibilities it unleashed reach beyond its historical moment and offer us ways of thinking about the present. Revolutionaries believed that a Muslim need not abandon Islam or be forced to adopt French ways of thinking and being in order to be a citizen. Muslims showed that ideas of liberty, equality, and fraternity are not anathema to Islam and Muslim traditions, although they might well threaten existing structures of power and authority. These are vital principles for the task of living together in complex modern societies, where the diversity imagined by many during the French Revolution has become a reality. They are also crucial in demonstrating that the Revolution was much more than just a French, European, or Atlantic experience: it was perhaps the first political event whose ramifications were truly global, stretching from Europe and the Americas into Asia and Africa.

"If you should penetrate the campus of an American Ivy League college," W. E. B. du Bois wrote in 1961, "and challenging a Senior, ask what, in his opinion, was the influence of Africa on the French Revolution, he would answer in surprise if not pity, 'None.' " Du Bois imagined the withering scorn of the professor of historiography who, while admitting through gritted teeth that African slavery might after all have existed on the same planet as the "greatest Revolution of Europe," could confidently declare that there could be in this link "nothing causal, nothing of real importance, since

Africans have no history."[13] If the patronizing dismissal of slavery's importance in the origins, processes, and outcomes of the French Revolution has been set aside by decades of scholarship, this shift has been restricted largely to the Caribbean. To ask today what was the influence of Africa, of Asia, of Islam on the French Revolution is still to evoke the same surprise, and, on some occasions at least, the same scorn.

This book has investigated the French Revolution as a lived experience, and also as a living one. I have not sought here simply to put Muslims back into the French Revolution, but to explore what happens when we choose to see it in some sense through their eyes. My aim has been to restore those lost and neglected voices, and to shift in some way the sense of whose Revolution this was. I believe—as so many revolutionaries of the 1790s believed—that this Revolution belongs in complex ways to everyone, no matter where they first drew breath, or the religion into which they were born, to borrow the words of Muhammad D'Ghies in 1795. I have sought on every possible occasion to avoid speculation, even—or especially—where the crucial records are absent, to build cautiously from the evidence I collected, to subject that evidence to critical questioning, and to allow it to interrogate me in return. The Revolution that emerged for me in this process is not simply one in which Muslims are no longer absent: it is no longer quite the same Revolution.

Notes

Introduction

1. Commissioner of Seine-et-Marne to minister of police, 23 Ventôse Year 7, Archives nationales, Paris (henceforth AN), F7 7415.

2. A number of Google Ngrams, although unreliable in any absolute sense, do confirm this trend for the percentage of published works in which different terms appear over the period 1775–1800. Combined use of the two words "Musulmans" and "Mahométans," plural and singular, peaks in 1790 and falls away in 1792–1794, to rise again from 1795. "Turcs," by comparison, peaks in 1787 before falling in a similar way toward 1794.

3. Carla Hesse, *Publishing and Cultural Politics in Revolutionary Paris, 1789–1810* (Berkeley: University of California Press, 1991), 134.

4. In comparison to the overall total, according to the Google Ngram, of less than 0.002 percent.

5. These calculations refer only to "Musulmans," "Mahométans," and "Turcs" and do not include other expressions used to describe Muslims, Islam, Muhammad, the turban, etc. They include only the period to the end of 1793 for which the *AP* is digitized, and are indicative only.

6. See Abdullah Saeed, "Muslims under Non-Muslim Rule: Evolution of a Discourse," in Anthony Reid and Michael Gilsenan (eds), *Islamic Legitimacy in a Plural Asia* (London: Routledge, 2007), 14–27.

7. See Jocelyne Dakhlia and Bernard Vincent (eds), *Les Musulmans dans l'histoire de l'Europe:* vol. 1, *Une intégration invisible* (Paris: Albin Michel, 2011). For Muslims in early modern Britain, see Nabil Matar, *Turks, Moors, and Englishmen in the Age of Discovery* (New York: Columbia University Press, 1999) and *Islam in Britain: 1558–1685* (Cambridge: Cambridge University Press, 1998).

8. For the most negative interpretation, see Arthur Hertzberg, *The French Enlightenment and the Jews* (New York: Columbia University Press, 1968).

9. Ronald Schechter, *Obstinate Hebrews: Representations of Jews in France, 1715–1815* (Berkeley: University of California Press, 2003).

10. Simon Schwarzfuchs, *Du Juif à l'israélite: Histoire d'une mutation 1770–1870* (Paris: Fayard, 1989); David Feuerwerker, *L'émancipation des Juifs en France, de l'ancien régime à la fin du second empire* (Paris: Albin Michel, 1976).

11. Maurice Samuels, *The Right to Difference: French Universalism and the Jews* (Chicago: University of Chicago Press, 2016), 14.

12. Jacques Revel, "Juifs et citoyens: Les incertitudes de la Révolution française," in Diogo Ramada Curto et al. (eds), *From Florence to the Mediterranean and Beyond: Essays in Honour of Antony Molho* (Florence: Olschki, 2009), 531–544.

13. Schechter, *Obstinate Hebrews*, 36.

14. This reconsideration is in progress: see, for example, Ali Yaycioglu, *Partners of the Empire: The Crisis of the Ottoman Order in the Age of Revolutions* (Palo Alto: Stanford University Press, 2016); Paul E. Lovejoy, *Jihad in West Africa during the Age of Revolutions* (Athens: Ohio University Press, 2016).

15. Lynn Hunt, "The French Revolution in Global Context," in David Armitage and Sanjay Subrahmanyam (eds), *The Age of Revolutions in Global Contexts, c. 1760–1840* (Basingstoke: Palgrave Macmillan, 2010), 20–36.

16. David A. Bell, "Questioning the Global Turn: The Case of the French Revolution," *French Historical Studies* 37.1 (2014): 1–24. The highly publicized *Histoire mondiale de la France*, ed. Patrick Boucheron et al. (Paris: Seuil, 2017), a refreshing step forward, nonetheless largely circumscribes the "global" history of the Revolution in the Atlantic, as historians have done since the 1950s.

17. Michel-Rolph Trouillot, *Silencing the Past: Power and the Production of History* (Boston: Beacon Press, 1995), 26–27.

18. Joan Scott, "Gender: A Useful Category of Historical Analysis," *American Historical Review* 91.5 (1986): 1055.

19. Dominique Godineau, *The Women of Paris and Their French Revolution*, trans. Katherine Streip (Berkeley: University of California Press, 1998); Olwen Hufton, *Women and the Limits of Citizenship in the French Revolution* (Toronto: University of Toronto Press, 1999); Joan B. Landes, *Women and the Public Sphere in the Age of the French Revolution* (Ithaca: Cornell University Press, 1988); Suzanne Desan, *The Family on Trial in Revolutionary France* (Berkeley: University of California Press, 2004).

20. Sara E. Melzer and Leslie W. Rabine (eds), *Rebel Daughters: Women and the French Revolution* (Oxford: Oxford University Press, 1992); Serge Aberdam,

"Deux occasions de participation féminine en 1793: Le vote sur la constitution et le partage des biens communaux," *Annales historiques de la Révolution française* 339 (2005): 17–34. I thank Peter McPhee for providing the latter reference, and a student in my undergraduate class The French Revolution in Global Context for pointing it out, in McPhee, *Liberty or Death: The French Revolution* (New Haven, CT: Yale University Press, 2016), 207.

21. Lynn Hunt, "The Many Bodies of Marie Antoinette: Political Pornography and the Problem of the Feminine in the French Revolution" in Lynn Hunt (ed), *Eroticism and the Body Politic* (Baltimore: Johns Hopkins University Press, 1991), 108–130; Antoine de Baecque, *The Body Politic: Corporeal Metaphor in Revolutionary France, 1770–1800*, trans. Charlotte Mandell (Stanford: Stanford University Press, 1997).

22. For discussion of Muslim women in Europe in the early modern period, see Jocelyne Dakhlia, "Musulmans en France et en Grande Bretagne à l'époque moderne: Exemplaires et invisibles," in Dakhlia and Vincent (eds), *Les Musulmans dans l'histoire de l'Europe*, 471–522.

23. Mehammed Amadeus Mack, *Sexagon: Muslims, France, and the Sexualization of National Culture* (New York: Fordham University Press, 2017); Todd Shepard, *Sex, France and Arab Men, 1962–1979* (Chicago: University of Chicago Press, 2018).

24. *Archives parlementaires de 1787 à 1860: Recueil complet des débats législatifs et politiques des Chambres françaises, imprimé par ordre du Corps législatif*, 1st series, ed. Jérôme Mavidal and Émile Laurent (Paris: P. Dupont/CNRS, 1867–1990) (henceforth *AP*), 30 October 1793 (78:49). See Godineau, *Women of Paris*, 279.

25. Pierre H. Boulle, *Race et esclavage dans la France de l'Ancien Régime* (Paris: Perrin, 2007); Sue Peabody, *"There Are No Slaves in France": The Political Culture of Race and Slavery in the Ancien Régime* (Oxford: Oxford University Press, 1996).

26. Erick Noël, "Les Indiens en France au XVIIIe siècle," in J. Weber (ed), *Les relations entre la France et l'Inde de 1673 à nos jours* (Paris: Les Indes Savantes, 2002), 203–219.

27. Erick Noël, *Être noir en France au XVIIIe siècle* (Paris: Tallandier, 2006); Lise Schreier, "Zamore 'the African' and the Haunting of France's Collective Consciousness," *Nineteenth-Century Contexts* 38.2 (2016): 123–139.

28. I have chosen not to include these converted individuals as Muslims, despite the intrinsic interest of their stories, which deserve their own full investigation.

29. An analogous "de-negroification of enslaved African Muslims" occurred in colonial America, as Kambiz Ghanea-Bassiri has shown in *A History of Islam in America: From the New World to the New World Order* (Cambridge: Cambridge University Press, 2010), 18–27.

30. It is suggested that "Boukman" was in fact "bookman," a reference to his knowledge of the Koran. Sylviane A. Diouf, *Servants of Allah: African Muslims Enslaved in the Americas* (New York: NYU Press, 1998), 152.

31. Terry Rey, *The Priest and the Prophetess: Abbé Ouvière, Romaine Rivière, and the Revolutionary Atlantic World* (Oxford: Oxford University Press, 2017), 52.

32. *AP*, 29 September 1793 (75:330). "Ils portent deux drapeaux, dont l'un blanc, l'autre tricolore, ayant en haut une fleur de lys. . . . Sur cet autre drapeau blanc etaient des éloges de leur chef et une prière à Mahomet."

33. *Gazette nationale; ou, Le Moniteur universel* (henceforth *Moniteur*), 12 Floréal Year 2 (1 May 1795).

34. See Ian Coller, "African Liberalism in the Age of Empire? Hassuna D'Ghies and Liberal Constitutionalism in North Africa," *Modern Intellectual History* 12 (2015): 1–25.

35. Ilham Khuri-Makdisi, *The Eastern Mediterranean and the Making of Global Radicalism, 1860–1914* (Berkeley: University of California Press, 2010), 80–82; Elbaki Hermassi, "The French Revolution and the Arab World," in Joseph Klaits and Michael H. Haltzel (eds), *The Global Ramifications of the French Revolution* (Cambridge: Cambridge University Press, 1994), 139.

Prologue

1. See Suraiya Faroqhi, *The Ottoman Empire and the World around It* (London: I.B. Tauris, 2007), 211.

2. Mohammed Arkoun (ed), *Histoire de l'islam et des musulmans en France du Moyen Âge à nos jours* (Paris: Albin Michel, 2006).

3. Lucette Valensi, *Ces étrangers familiers: Musulmans en Europe, XVIe–XVIIIe siècles* (Paris: Payot, 2012).

4. Marshall G. S. Hodgson, "The Role of Islam in World History," *International Journal of Middle East Studies* 1.2 (1970): 99.

5. Cemil Aydin, *The Idea of the Muslim World: A Global Intellectual History* (Cambridge, MA: Harvard University Press, 2017); Seema Alavi, *Muslim Cosmopolitanism in the Age of Empire* (Cambridge, MA: Harvard University Press, 2015).

6. Jonathan Israel, *Enlightenment Contested: Philosophy, Modernity and the Emancipation of Man, 1670–1752* (Oxford: Oxford University Press, 2006), 616.

7. This runs in contrast to the argument by Alexander Bevilacqua in *The Arabic Republic of Letters: Islam and the European Enlightenment* (Cambridge, MA: Harvard University Press, 2018) that a more careful attention to precision in naming Islam represented a major change of attitude: Jaucourt, the article's author, was certainly demonstrating his erudition, but he describes Muhammad conventionally, as an "imposter" drawing on the ignorance of his people, in a way very similar to Voltaire. Rebecca Joubin has estimated the number of articles dealing with Islam and Arabs at 2,313 (4 percent of the total entries): "Islam and Arabs through the Eyes of the *Encyclopédie:* The 'Other' as a Case of French Cultural Criticism," *International Journal of Middle East Studies* 32.2 (May 2000): 198.

8. Hamid Dabashi, *Persophilia: Persian Culture on the Global Scene* (Cambridge, MA: Harvard University Press, 2015).

9. Edward Said, *Orientalism* (New York: Random House, 1978).

10. See Ian Coller, "Rousseau's Turban: Entangled Encounters of Europe and Islam in the Age of Enlightenment," *Historical Reflections/Réflexions Historiques* 40.2 (2014): 56–77.

11. François-Marie Arouet de Voltaire, *Oeuvres complètes* (Paris: Garnier frères, 1877), 11:221. See also Djavad Hadidi, *Voltaire et l'Islam* (Paris: Publications orientalistes de France, 1974); Faruk Bilici, "L'Islam en France sous l'Ancien Régime et la Révolution: Attraction et répulsion," *Rives nord-méditerranéennes* 14 (2003): 17–37.

12. Alain Grosrichard, *Structure du serail: La fiction du despotisme asiatique dans l'Occident classique* (Paris: Éd. du seuil, 1979), translated as *The Sultan's Court: European Fantasies of the East,* trans. Liz Heron (London: Verso, 1998), 3.

13. Thomas Kaiser, "The Evil Empire? The Debate on Turkish Despotism in Eighteenth-Century French Political Culture," *Journal of Modern History* 72.1 (2000): 6–34.

14. Mouradgea would leave France in 1791 and become a key member of the Jacobin club in Istanbul that became so controversial in Paris during 1793. See chap. 9 in this book.

15. Mouradgea d'Ohsson, *Tableau général de l'empire othoman* (Paris: Imprimerie de Monsieur, 1787), 1:xxxiii. See Elisabeth A. Fraser, *Mediterranean Encounters: Artists between Europe and the Ottoman Empire, 1774–1839*

(University Park: Penn State University Press, 2017), chap. 3 for a useful discussion.

16. *Monthly Review* 80 (1789).

17. The "curé rouge" Cournand joined the Jacobin club and militated for the marriage of priests; he was notable also for his passionate defense of the rights of free people of color in the National Assembly, and his proto-socialist ideas on the radical redistribution of property. See Antoine de Cournand, *Requête présentée à nosseigneurs de l'Assemblée nationale en faveur des gens de couleur de l'île de Saint-Domingue* (n.p., [1790]); Maurice Dommanget and Michel Vovelle, *Enragés et curés rouges en 1793: Jacques Roux, Pierre Dolivier* (Paris: Spartacus, 1993), 26.

18. Julia Clancy Smith, *Mediterraneans: North Africa and Europe in an Age of Migration, c. 1800–1900* (Berkeley: University of California Press, 2011).

19. Regis Bertrand, "Les cimetières des 'esclaves turcs' des arsenaux de Marseille et de Toulon au XVIIIe siècle," *Revue des mondes musulmans et de la Méditerranée* 99–100 (2002): 205–217.

20. Jean-Baptiste-Bernard Grosson, *Almanach historique de Marseille* (Marseille: Jean Mossy, 1777), 214.

21. Archives municipales, Marseille (henceforth Arch. Mun. Marseille), DD 138, 27 April 1782.

22. Ministre des Affaires Etrangères to Consul d'Alger, 15 December 1783, Archives diplomatiques (henceforth AMAE) (Nantes), CC Alger A 11.

23. Arch. Mun. Marseille FF 192.

24. Chambre de Commerce de Marseille (henceforth CCM) to Consul d'Alger, 30 June 1785, AMAE (Nantes), CC Alger A 13.

25. CCM to Consul d'Alger, 25 June 1787, AMAE (Nantes), CC Alger A 17.

26. Surintendant de Santé de Marseille to Maréchal de Castries, 13 June 1787, AMAE (Nantes), CC Alger A 15.

27. Written variously as Mohammed Techeliby or Celebi; Xavier Yacono, *Un siècle de franc-maçonnerie algérienne (1785–1884)* (Paris: Maisonneuve et Larose, 1969), 15.

28. Pierre-Yves Beaurepaire, "Le cosmopolitisme maçonnique," *Cahiers de la Méditerranée* 67 (2003): 33–50.

29. Kenneth B. Loiselle, *Brotherly Love: Freemasonry and Male Friendship in Enlightenment France* (Ithaca: Cornell University Press, 2014), 174; Xavier Yacono, "La Franc-Maçonnerie française et les algériens musulmans (1787–1962)," *Anales de Historia Contemporánea* 6 (1987): 103–125.

30. Michel Taillefer, "Une loge maçonnique toulousaine à la veille de la Révolution: Les 'Coeurs réunis' (1774–1789)," *Annales du Midi: Revue archéologique, historique et philologique de la France méridionale* 87.122 (1975): 218. Taillefer notes foreign Masons from the lodges of both Tunis and Algiers.

31. Xavier Yacono, "Les débuts de la franc-maçonnerie à Alger (1830–1852)," *Revue Africaine* 103 (1959): 59.

32. AMAE CCC Alger 32, 28 January 1793.

33. Jacques de Cauna, "L'odyssée d'un esclave musulman: Du Sénégal à Versailles en passant par Tobago," *Revue de la Société haïtienne d'histoire et de géographie* 46 (1990): 59–63.

2. Paris Turned Turk

1. *L'esprit des journaux, francais et etrangers*, May 1788.

2. See Keith Baker, "Revolution," in Colin Lucas (ed), *The French Revolution and the Creation of Modern Political Culture:* vol. 2, *The Political Culture of the French Revolution* (Oxford: Pergamon Press, 1988), 41–62.

3. *L'esprit des journaux, francais et etrangers*, May 1788.

4. [Louis Brion de la Tour], *Du partage de la peau de l'ours; ou, lettres à l'auteur du Rêve politique sur le partage de l'empire ottoman, et à l'auteur des Considérations sur la guerre actuelle des turcs* (Cussac, 1788), 3.

5. *Journal politique; ou, Gazette des gazettes*, July 1788, 1st fortnight.

6. Kemal Karpat calls it "the starting point of the new relations between Istanbul and the periphery" in *The Politicization of Islam: Reconstructing Identity, State, Faith, and Community in the Late Ottoman State* (Oxford: Oxford University Press, 2001), 49.

7. See Thomas E. Kaiser, "The Diplomatic Origins of the French Revolution," in David Andress (ed), *The Oxford Handbook of the French Revolution* (Oxford: Oxford University Press, 2015), 109–127. A similar argument is made by Bailey Stone in *Reinterpreting the French Revolution: A Global-Historical Perspective* (Cambridge: Cambridge University Press, 2002).

8. Thomas E. Kaiser, "From the Austrian Committee to the Foreign Plot: Marie-Antoinette, Austrophobia, and the Terror," *French Historical Studies* 26.4 (2003): 579–617.

9. S.-P. Hardy, "Mes loisirs; ou, Journal d'evenemens tels qu'ils parviennent à ma connoissance," 1764–1789, vol. 7, 1787–1788, folio 403.

10. See Jeremy D. Popkin, *News and Politics in the Age of Revolution: Jean Luzac's "Gazette de Leyde"* (Ithaca: Cornell University Press, 2016). The issue of 15 April 1788 lamented the difficulties of communication with Constantinople

during the war, and declared much of the news produced in Paris to be inaccurate, but it still printed a letter received by sea dated 22 February, less than
two months earlier.

11. Adolphe Mathurin de Lescure (ed), *Correspondance secrète inédite sur Louis XVI, Marie-Antoinette, la cour et la ville de 1777 à 1792 publiée d'après des MSS de la bibliothèque impériale de Saint-Pétersbourg* (Paris: H. Plon, 1866), 241.

12. Peyssonel would become a key influence in foreign affairs in the early months of the new regime. Jeremy J. Whiteman, *Reform, Revolution and French Global Policy, 1787–1791* (Aldershot: Ashgate, 2003), 110–113.

13. Charles de Peyssonel, *Examen du livre intitulé Considérations sur la guerre actuelle des Turcs* (Amsterdam, 1788), 2.

14. *Les révolutions de France et de Brabant,* no. 11, Jan.–Feb. 1790.

15. Charles Walton, "La liberté de la presse selon les cahiers de doléances de 1789," *Revue d'histoire moderne et contemporaine* 53.1 (2006): 63–87.

16. Raymond Birn, "The Pamphlet Press and the Estates General of 1789," *Studies on Voltaire and the Eighteenth Century* 287 (1991): 59.

17. Antoine de Baecque, *The Body Politic: Corporeal Metaphor in Revolutionary France, 1770–1800,* trans. Charlotte Mandell (Stanford: Stanford University Press, 1997), 16.

18. *Ah! Ah! Conférence sur les affaires du temps, entre un royaliste et un parlementaire* (London, 1788), 3.

19. Jean-Louis Carra, *Essai particulier de politique, dans lequel on propose un partage de la Turquie européenne* (1777), in *L'orateur des États generaux pour 1789* (n.p., 1789), 22. Carra later became a deputy and was executed with the Girondins in 1793.

20. [Louis-Antoine Caraccioli], *Anecdotes piquantes relatives aux États généraux* (n.p., 1789).

21. AMAE (La Courneuve), Contrôle des étrangers au XVIIIe siècle, 1771–1791, 67, 25 January 1788.

22. Albert Merle, "La pêche sur les côtes orientales d'Afrique," *Bulletin de la Société de géographie commerciale de Bordeaux* 2 (1879): 350–356.

23. AMAE (La Courneuve), Contrôle des étrangers au XVIIIe siècle, 1771–1791, 69, 4 July 1788.

24. Elizabeth Craven, *A Journey through the Crimea to Constantinople: In a Series of Letters from the Right Honourable Elizabeth Lady Craven, to His Serene Highness the Margrave of Brandebourg, Anspach, and Bareith* (London: G.G.J. and J. Robinson, 1789), 279. This formulation for expressing hostility to

foreigners was very common in England according to other travelers: "Tout ce qui est étranger est Français, et le mot d'amitié, *chien*, ne manque jamais de s'y joindre." John Taylor and Louis Marie Joseph Ohier de Grandpré, *Voyage dans l'Inde, au travers du grand désert, par Alep, Antioche et Bassora, exécuté par le major Taylor . . .* (Paris: Dentu, 1801), 152.

25. Aysel Yıldız points out how difficult it is to map those struggles, partly in the absence of sources that can help us unpack the elite rivalries of the period: *Crisis and Rebellion in the Ottoman Empire: The Downfall of a Sultan in the Age of Revolution* (London: I. B. Tauris, 2017). See also Kemal Beydilli, "Şehzâde Elçisi Safiyesultanzâde İshak Bey," *İslam Araştırmaları Dergisi* 3 (1999): 73–81.

26. AMAE (La Courneuve), MD Turquie 8 (doc 27), "Notions particulières sur Ishac Bey," 1781.

27. *Correspondance secrète, politique et littéraire; ou, Mémoires pour servir à l'histoire de la république des lettres,* 30 April 1783.

28. *Correspondance secrète, politique et littéraire; ou, Mémoires pour servir à l'histoire de la république des lettres,* 14 December 1776.

29. Thomas Hope, *Anastasius; or, Memoirs of a Greek, Written at the Close of the Eighteenth Century* (London: John Murray, 1820), 2:383.

30. AMAE (La Courneuve) MD Turquie 8 (doc 27), "Notions particulières sur Ishac Bey," 1781.

31. *Correspondance secrète, politique et littéraire; ou, Mémoires pour servir à l'histoire des cours, des sociétès et de la littérature en France, depuis la mort de Louis XV* (Paris: J. Adamson, 1788), 292–293.

32. In contrast to Bernard Lewis's statement that it was "clearly due to European influence and example." Bernard Lewis, "Watan," *Journal of Contemporary History* 26.3–4 (1991): 526.

33. See *Journal historique et politique de Genève,* 30 October 1784.

34. See Caroline Finkel, *Osman's Dream: The History of the Ottoman Empire* (New York: Basic Books, 2007), 381–382; Guy Lemarchand, "Éléments de la crise de l'Empire ottoman sous Sélim III (1789–1807)," *Annales historiques de la Révolution française* 329 (2002): 141–159.

35. In the Caucasus, a "new prophet" called Sheikh Mansour rose up against Russian rule: the *Mercure de France* reported at length a harangue by this "reformer of the Koran according to the principles of natural law" (*réformateur de l'Alcoran d'après les principes de la Loi Naturelle*) (10 June 1786). See Anna Zelkina, *In Quest for God and Freedom: The Sufi Response to the Russian Advance in the North Caucasus* (New York: NYU Press, 2000). This perception of an Islam in the throes of transformation would be taken up later in the Revolution.

36. Alan W. Fisher, *The Russian Annexation of the Crimea, 1772–1783* (Cambridge: Cambridge University Press, 1970), 137–159.

37. Hennin correspondence, Bibliothèque de l'Académie. My thanks to the librarian for kindly providing me with these letters.

38. Betül Başaran, *Selim III, Social Control and Policing in Istanbul at the End of the Eighteenth Century: Between Crisis and Order* (Leiden: Brill, 2014), 73–75.

39. Salih Munir Pacha, "Louis XVI et le Sultan Selim III," *Revue d'histoire diplomatique* 26 (1912): 528. For the Turkish text, see Enver Ziya Karal, *Selim III'ün Hat-tı hümayunları: Nizam-ı cedit, 1789–1807* (Ankara: Türk tarih kurumu basımevi, 1946).

40. A small handwritten song from a family entertainment among the Lafayette papers reveals Ishak's intimacy with the Tessé family. Cornell University Library, Lafayette Papers 4611/133.

41. Archives Nationales d'Outre Mer (ANOM), Aix-en-Provence, COL E 9.

42. Ghulam Husain Khan Tabatabai, *Siyar-al Muta'akhkhirin* (Calcutta, 1834), 3:335.

43. Antoine François Bertrand de Molleville, *Mémoires secrets pour servir à l'histoire de la dernière année du règne de Louis XVI, roi de France* (London: Strahan and Cadell, 1797), 3:32.

44. A. L. de Breuil, *La France il y a trente ans: Ouvrage contenant des grandes vérités historiques sur les hommes de ce temps-là* (Paris: Lerouge, 1822), 22. For questions of race in French India, see Adrian Carton, *Mixed-Race and Modernity in Colonial India: Changing Concepts of Hybridity across Empires* (New York: Routledge, 2012).

45. Louise-Élisabeth Vigée-LeBrun, *Souvenirs de madame Louise-Élisabeth Vigée-LeBrun* (Paris: H. Fournier, 1835), 60.

46. Kate Brittlebank, *Tipu Sultan's Search for Legitimacy: Islam and Kingship in a Hindu Domain* (Delhi: Oxford University Press, 1997), 79, 139–140.

47. The portrait is discussed by Kate Marsh in *India in the French Imagination: Peripheral Voices, 1754–1815* (London: Routledge, 2015), 53–56.

48. Lynn Hunt, *The Family Romance of the French Revolution* (Berkeley: University of California Press, 1992).

49. De Baecque, *Body Politic*, 13.

50. *La nouvelle épiphanie; ou, La liberté adorée des mages* (n.p., c. 1789). Frank Bowman considers such parallels between the Christ story and the Revolution to be purely formal, lacking an "effort to give the Revolution a religious meaning." Frank Paul Bowman, *Le Christ romantique* (Geneva: Librairie Droz, 1973), 61. Yet the associations between the aristocracy and Herod, the

October Days and the flight to Egypt do suggest how conceptions of religious violence emerged in these symbolic readings, as the next chapter will suggest.

51. In particular the *amabilité,* or "charm," that structured social relations. See Antoine Lilti, *The World of the Salons: Sociability and Worldliness in Eighteenth-Century Paris* (New York: Oxford University Press, 2015), 80.

52. John Shovlin observes the gendered aspects of the critique of luxury, notably the effeminization of men, in *The Political Economy of Virtue: Luxury, Patriotism, and the Origins of the French Revolution* (Ithaca: Cornell University Press, 2007), 30.

53. *Lettres de l'un des ambassadeurs de Typoo-Saïb où il est beaucoup parlé des affaires du royaume de Gogo [i.e. France], avec l'aventure de Gigy, prince du sang des rois de cet empire, etc.,* 1789, p. 3.

54. Louis-Antoine Caraccioli, *Lettres d'un Indien à Paris, à son ami Glazir, sur les moeurs françoises, et sur les bizarreries du tems* (Amsterdam [Paris?]: Briand, 1789), 1:3.

55. This image, presented to the National Assembly in May 1790, and displayed to the public for subscription to purchase copies, "doit être considéré comme un monument numismatique, gravé à la gloire de la nation, pour conserver l'époque et la mémoire de la conquête de la liberté, en retracer les principaux événements et la part glorieuse qu'y ont eue la capitale et les provinces du royaume." *Moniteur,* 6 June 1790.

56. Voltaire, in one of his satirical sallies to impress the Russian czarina Catherine II, made a connection between the French form of arbitrary detention and the Islamic fatwa (pronounced "fetva" in Turkish): "Fetfa! ce mot arabe est bien dur à l'oreille; On ne le trouve point chez Racine & Corneille; Du Dieu de l'harmonie il fait frémir l'archet. On l'exprime en Français par *lettres de cachet.*" Voltaire, *Épîtres, satires, contes, odes et pièces fugitives du poëte philosophe* (1771), 1.

57. William H. Sewell Jr., "Historical Events as Transformations of Structures: Inventing Revolution at the Bastille," *Theory and Society* 25.6 (1996): 847–848.

58. *Lettre turque, relative aux circonstances* (n.p., 1789).

59. "From the very beginning, the violence which made the Revolution possible in the first place created exactly the brutal distinctions between Patriots and Enemies, Citizens and Aristocrats, within which there could be no human shades of gray." Simon Schama, *Citizens: A Chronicle of the French Revolution* (New York: Random House, 1989), 436.

60. *Lettre du Grand Turc au Roi de France* ([Paris]: Chez Volland, [1789]).

61. *Les Parisiens au Grand Turc* (Paris: Imprimerie de Knapen fils, 1789), 1.

62. Lynn Hunt, "Hercules and the Radical Image in the French Revolution," *Representations* 2 (1983): 105.

63. *Les Parisiens au Grand Turc.*

64. *Lettre du Muphty de Constantinople, à Monsieur l'Abbé Mauri* (Au sérail [Paris]: Imprimerie de la Sultane favorite, 1789).

65. Maury (recast as Umaïr) features in another pamphlet, *Le dernier cri du monstre, conte indien du 6 août 1789* (n.p., 1789). See de Baecque, *Body Politic*, 158–159.

66. *Lettre du Muphty de Constantinople.*

2. *The Turban and the Axe*

1. *Mémoires secrets pour servir à l'histoire de la république des lettres en France,* 1789, 149.

2. *Mémoires secrets*, 149. The only official record from the register of evidence at the Châtelet uses the name Achmet Bender, so this is the version I will use.

3. Arch. Mun. Marseille, FF 192, 18 April 1785.

4. Daniel Ligou, "Les protestants français a la veille de la Révolution," in Pierre Léon Féral (ed), *La France pré-révolutionnaire* (Paris: Publisud, 1991), 125–135.

5. Cit. David Garrioch, *The Huguenots of Paris and the Coming of Religious Freedom, 1685–1789* (Cambridge: Cambridge University Press, 2014), 210.

6. Burdette Crawford Poland, *French Protestantism and the French Revolution: Church and State, Thought and Religion, 1685–1815* (Princeton, NJ: Princeton University Press, 1957), 80–88.

7. Louis Mazoyer, "L'application de l'Édit de 1787 dans le Midi de la France," *Bulletin de la Société de l'histoire du protestantisme français* 174 (1925): 170.

8. Patrick Cabanel, *Juifs et protestants en France: Les affinités électives, XVIe–XXIe siècle* (Paris: Fayard, 2004), 59–73.

9. David Feuerwerker, *L'émancipation des Juifs en France, de l'ancien régime à la fin du second empire* (Paris: Albin Michel, 1976); Zosa Szajkowski, "The Case of the Counterfeit Receipts in Alsace, 1777–1789," in *Jews and the French Revolutions of 1789, 1830 and 1848* (New York: KTAV Publishing House, 1970), 202–219.

10. Chrétien-Guillaume de Lamoignon de Malesherbes, *Second mémoire sur le mariage des protestans* (London, 1787), 95.

11. Mazoyer, "L'application de l'Édit de 1787 dans le Midi."

12. See Eva Guillorel, *La complainte et la plainte: Chansons, justice et culture dans la Bretagne (XVIe au XVIIIe siècles)* (Rennes: Presses universitaires de Rennes, 2010).

13. "Chrétiens, dans la mémoire / Placez-vous bien ce fait / L'action la plus noire / Commise par Achmet."

14. Jules Declève, "Les complaintes célèbres," *Mémoires et publications de la Société des sciences, des arts et des lettres du Hainaut*, 5th series, 9 (1897): 305.

15. *Portrait d'Ali Mustapha, né à Candie en 1734, en buste, de profil dirigé à gauche dans une bordure ronde* [1787], Bibliothèque nationale de France.

16. Michel Foucault, *Discipline and Punish: The Birth of the Prison*, trans. Alan Sheridan (New York: Vintage, 1977), 261–262.

17. "Le Coche d'Auxerre," *Almanach statistique de Sens et du Département de l'Yonne*, (Sens, 1857), 16.

18. Nicolas-Edmé Rétif de la Bretonne, *Les nuits de Paris; ou, Le spectateur-nocturne*, ed. Henri Bachelin (Paris: Livre Club du Libraire, 1960), 132–133.

19. The name "Bedeer" turned into "Bender," possibly because of the Ottoman fortress of that name, which had been prominent in news about the war in the East.

20. This account is similar to the one provided by a resident of Sens, kept in the library of Auxerre, and reprinted later in a local almanac. Details added in that version include the suggestion that Achmet spoke English and Italian but not French. See *Almanach statistique de Sens et du Département de l'Yonne* (Sens: Ch. Duchemin, 1861), 17–21.

21. *Mémoires secrets*, 149–150.

22. *The Annual Register; or, A View of the History, Politics and Literature, for the Year 1787* (1789).

23. François-Marie Mayeur de Saint Paul, *Tableau du nouveau Palais-Royal* (Paris: Maradan, 1788), 101.

24. Jean-Joseph Mounier, *Appel au tribunal de l'opinion publique* (Geneva, 1790), 95; Albert Mathiez, "Étude critique sur les journées des 5 et 6 octobre 1789," *Revue historique* 67 (1898): 253.

25. *Révolutions de Versailles et de Paris, dédiées aux dames françoises* 1, October 1789; *Procédure criminelle instruite au Châtelet de Paris sur la dénonciation des faits arrivés à Versailles dans la journée du 6 octobre 1789* (Paris: Baudouin, 1790), 211; Jean-Joseph Mounier, *Exposé de ma conduite dans l'Assemblée Nationale et motifs de mon retour en Dauphiné* (Paris: Cuchet, 1789), 62; Laura Mason, *Singing the French Revolution: Popular Culture and Politics, 1787–1799* (Ithaca: Cornell University Press, 1996), 45–46.

26. AN, Y13319 B.

27. David Garrioch, "The Everyday Lives of Parisian Women and the October Days of 1789," *Social History* 24.3 (1999): 231–249. See also Micah Alpaugh,

"The Politics of Escalation in French Revolutionary Protest: Political Demonstrations, Non-violence and Violence in the *Grandes Journées* of 1789," *French History* 23.3 (2009): 336–359; and Haïm Burstin, *Révolutionnaires: Pour une anthropologie politique de la Révolution française* (Paris: Vendémiaire, 2013), 270–281.

28. François Dominique de Reynaud de Montlosier, *Mémoires de M. le Comte de Montlosier, sur la Revolution française* (Paris: Dufey, 1830), 1:289.

29. The sequence of events is disputed: none of the testimonies in the Châtelet inquiry mentioned this event. Mathiez reported it from the account of Batiffol, but others suggested it was invented. Louis Batiffol, *Les journées des 5 et 6 octobre 1789 à Versailles* (Paris: Vve E. Aubert, 1891), 59; Mathiez, "Étude critique sur les journées des 5 et 6 octobre," *Revue historique* 69 (1900): 48.

30. Louis-Sébastien Mercier, *Le nouveau Paris* (Paris: Fuchs, C. Pougens & C. F. Cramer, 1797), 3:71–72.

31. Michel Foucault, *"Society Must Be Defended": Lectures at the Collège de France, 1975–1976,* trans. David Macey (New York: Picador, 2003), 196.

32. Foucault, *"Society Must Be Defended,"* 240.

33. Germaine de Staël, *Considérations sur la Révolution française* (Paris: Delaunay, 1818), 1:333. See also Timothy Tackett, *Becoming a Revolutionary: The Deputies of the French National Assembly and the Emergence of a Revolutionary Culture, 1789–1790* (Princeton, NJ: Princeton University Press, 1996), 199.

34. Micah Alpaugh, *Non-violence and the French Revolution: Political Demonstrations in Paris, 1787–1795* (Cambridge: Cambridge University Press, 2015), 32–33. This was not, however, an "annual" procession, but a singular event in 1785, for the reasons that follow.

35. Gillian Weiss, *Captives and Corsairs: France and Slavery in the Early Modern Mediterranean* (Stanford: Stanford University Press, 2011), 110.

36. *Trouvaille, signé le Parisien, témoin occulaire [sic] des journées des 5 et 6 oct.* (n.p., c. 1790).

37. Jean-Paul Rabaut Saint-Étienne, *Précis de l'histoire de la Révolution française* (Paris: Servier, 1827), 226.

38. *Le patriote français,* 9 October 1789.

39. *Moniteur,* 17 April 1790.

40. *Courier français,* 16 April 1790.

41. Mohamed el Mansour, *Morocco in the Reign of Mawlay Sulayman* (Wisbech, Cambridgeshire: Middle East & North African Studies Press, 1990).

42. Khalifa Chater, *Dépendance et mutations précoloniales: La régence de Tunis de 1815 à 1857* (Tunis: Faculté des sciences humaines et sociales de Tunis, 1984).

43. Daniel Panzac, *La caravane maritime: Européens et marchands ottomans en Méditerranée (1680–1830)* (Paris: CNRS Éditions, 2004), 153.

44. The British consul in Algiers also spread rumors of a possible invasion by Morocco with French and Spanish support. AN, AE, B I 143/29.

45. AN, AE, B I 143/29, 28 May 1789.

46. Honoré-Gabriel de Riquetti Mirabeau, *Avis au peuple marseillais* ([Marseille], 1789).

47. Mirabeau, *Avis au peuple marseillais*.

48. Léon Biollay, *Un épisode de l'approvisionnement de Paris en 1789* (Paris: Paul Dupont, 1878), 60.

49. Ministre de la Marine to Consul d'Alger, 3 October 1789, AMAE (Nantes), CC Alger A 16.

50. The collection of correspondence by Eugène Plantet shows no communication between 11 August 1788 and 6 December 1789. Plantet (ed), *Correspondence des deys d'Alger, avec la cour de France, 1579–1833* (Paris: F. Alcan, 1889), 2:388.

51. AN, AE, B I 143/29.

52. Extrait d'une lettre écrite à MM de la Chambre de commerce de Marseille par M. du Rocher, consul général de la France à Salé, 11 August 1789, AN, AE, B I 143/29.

53. *AP*, 4 July 1789 (8:191).

54. *Correspondance littéraire secrete, francais et entrangers*, 11 July 1789.

55. *L'esprit des journaux, francais et etrangers*, December 1789.

56. *Quès-à-co? ou, Histoire des troubles et révolutions modernes de Marseille* ([Paris]: Cailleau fils, 1789).

57. AMAE (Nantes), CC Alger A 16.

58. Chambre de Commerce de Marseille to Consul d'Alger, 25 May 1789, AMAE (Nantes), CC Alger A 17.

59. Ministre des Affaires Etrangères au Consul d'Alger, 3 October 1790, AMAE (Nantes), CC Alger A 17.

60. Mémoire des Officiers de l'Amirauté de Toulon, n.d., AN, AE B III 144.

61. Plantet, *Correspondance des deys d'Alger*, 2:396.

62. Claude Muller notes that in 1794 "dans le Haut-Rhin, on s'en prend à la fois à la barbe des capucins, des juifs et des anabaptistes." See "Religion et révolution en Alsace," *Annales historiques de la Révolution française* 337 (2004): 76.

63. AN, AE B III 144.

64. AMAE (Nantes), CC Alger A 17.

65. See Christian Windler, *La diplomatie comme experience de l'autre: Consuls français au Maghreb (1700–1840)* (Geneva: Droz, 2002), 98–99; Daniel Panzac, *The Barbary Corsairs: The End of a Legend, 1800–1820*, trans. Victoria Hobson (Leiden: Brill, 2005), 234–237; Morton Rosenstock, "The House of Bacri and Busnach: A Chapter from Algeria's Commercial History," *Jewish Social Studies* 14.4 (1952): 343–364.

66. Maurice Herbette, *Une ambassade turque sous le directoire* (Paris: Perrin, 1902), 24–25.

67. See Mathiez, "Étude critique sur les journées des 5 et 6 octobre," 48.

68. See Julia V. Douthwaite, *The Frankenstein of 1790 and Other Lost Chapters from Revolutionary France* (Chicago: University of Chicago Press, 2012), chap. 1; [Antoine-François-Claude Ferrand], *Lettre au roi par un françois royaliste* (Paris, 1790), 48.

69. Sylvie Steinberg, *La confusion des sexes: Le travestissement de la Renaissance à la Révolution* (Paris: Fayard, 2001) notes how much more frequent the phenomenon of women cross-dressing as men was in this period.

70. *Journal politique-national* 12, 1789.

71. For the analysis of these questions of gender as performance, see Judith Butler, *Gender Trouble: Feminism and the Subversion of Identity* (London: Routledge, 1990).

72. [J. Harvant], *Dialogue entre Ibrahim Pacha et un municipal* (Constantinople [Paris], 1790).

73. "Nous voulons être heureux." [Harvant], *Dialogue*.

74. Louis-Philippe de Ségur, *Mémoires; ou, Souvenirs et anecdotes* (Brussels: Lacrosse, 1825), 2:76.

75. François-Charles-Hugues-Laurent Pouqueville, *Voyage en Morée, à Constantinople, en Albanie et dans plusieurs autres parties de l'empire othoman, pendant les années 1798, 1799, 1800 et 1801* (Paris: Gabon, 1805), 166–172.

76. Baptistin Poujoulat, *Histoire de Constantinople comprenant le bas-empire et l'empire ottoman* (Paris: Amyot, 1853), 428.

77. Antoine Laurent Castellan, *Lettres sur la Gréce, l'Hellespont et Constantinople, faisant suite aux lettres sur la Morée* (Paris: H. Agasse, 1811), 85.

78. Castellan, *Lettres sur la Gréce, l'Hellespont et Constantinople*, 74, 84.

79. For recent reassessments, see Carter Vaughn Findley, *Turkey, Islam, Nationalism, and Modernity: A History, 1789–2007* (New Haven, CT: Yale University Press, 2010); Frederick F. Anscombe, *State, Faith, and Nation in Ottoman and Post-Ottoman Lands* (Cambridge: Cambridge University Press, 2014).

80. Thomas Walsh, *Journal of the late campaign in Egypt: including descriptions of that country, and of Gibraltar, Minorca, Malta, Marmorice, and Macri; with an appendix; containing official papers and documents* (London, 1803), 147.

81. Henri Grégoire, *Histoire des sectes religieuses, qui, depuis le commencement du siècle dernier jusqu'à l'époque actuelle, sont nées, se sont modifiées, se sont éteintes dans les quatre parties du Monde* (Paris: Potey, 1814), 424.

82. Robert Thomas Wilson, *History of the British Expedition to Egypt* (London: Egerton, 1803), 330.

3. The Rights of Muslims

1. Timothy Tackett, *Becoming a Revolutionary: The Deputies of the French National Assembly and the Emergence of a Revolutionary Culture (1789–1790)*, (University Park: Penn State University Press, 2006), 65–74.

2. See Marisa Linton, "Citizenship and Religious Toleration in France," in Ole Peter Grell and Roy Porter (eds), *Toleration in Enlightenment Europe* (Cambridge: Cambridge University Press, 2000), 157–174.

3. A recent book by Rita Hermon-Belot has investigated the plurality of religions in the Revolution and the foundations of *laïcité*, while suggesting that revolutionaries lacked any notion of "pluralism." In contrast, I argue that pluralism and its contestation were precisely at the heart of this violent struggle over religion. Hermon-Belot, *Aux sources de l'idée laïque: Révolution et pluralité religieuse* (Paris: Odile Jacob, 2015). See Mayanthi L. Fernando, *The Republic Unsettled: Muslim French and the Contradictions of Secularism* (Durham, NC: Duke University Press, 2014).

4. *AP*, 24 December 1789 (10:780).

5. *AP*, 1 August 1789 (8:321).

6. Georg Jellinek, *The Declaration of the Rights of Man and of Citizens: A Contribution to Modern Constitutional History* (New York: Holt, 1901).

7. *Moniteur*, 1 August 1789.

8. Adrien Cyprien Duquesnoy, *Journal d'Adrien Duquesnoy, député de Bar-le-Duc*, ed. Robert Crèvecoeur (Paris: Picard, 1894), 1:311.

9. *AP*, 1 August 1789 (8:320).

10. Asia was traditionally indicated through the symbolism of Islam: "On peut observer que toutes les religions ont pris naissance en Asie, mais la musulmane y est la seule dominante; c'est ce qu'indique la mosquée qu'on aperçoit dans le fond du tableau." Hubert François Gravelot, Charles Nicolas Cochin, and Charles Étienne Gaucher, *Iconologie par figures; ou, Traité complet des allégories, emblêmes &c. . . . .* (Paris: Le Pan, 1791), 1:37–38.

11. Marcel Gauchet, *La Révolution des droits de l'homme* (Paris: Gallimard, 1989), x.

12. *AP*, 3 August 1789 (8:335).

13. See Michael P. Fitzsimmons, *The Night the Old Regime Ended: August 4, 1789, and the French Revolution* (University Park: Penn State Press, 2010).

14. Adrien Cyprien Duquesnoy, *Opinion de M. Duquesnoy sur les projets de Déclaration de droits* (Versailles: Baudouin, 1789), 2–3.

15. *AP*, 19 August 1789 (8:459).

16. Antoine de Baecque, Wolfgang Schmale, and Michel Vovelle (eds), *L'an 1 des droits de l'homme* (Paris: Presses du CNRS, 1988), 164.

17. Tackett, *Becoming a Revolutionary*, 50–54.

18. *AP*, 22 August 1789 (8:472).

19. *AP*, 22 August 1789 (8:473).

20. *AP*, 22 August 1789 (8:473).

21. Philippe-Joseph-Benjamin Buchez and Prosper Charles Roux, *Histoire parlementaire de la révolution française; ou, Journal des assemblées nationales, depuis 1789 jusqu'en 1815* (Paris: Paulin, 1834), 2:324.

22. *AP*, 22 August 1789 (8:473).

23. *AP*, 23 August 1789 (8:475).

24. *AP*, 23 August 1789 (8:476).

25. See Claude Langlois, "Religion, culte ou opinion religieuse: La politique des révolutionnaires," *Revue française de sociologie* 30.3–4 (1989): 471–496.

26. AP, 23 August 1789 (8:476).

27. AP, 23 August 1789 (8:476).

28. AP, 23 August 1789 (8:477).

29. The published text of Castellane's speech presented his riposte differently, suggesting that these apostates were hardly obliged to convert: they would not "deliver themselves to an inevitable ridicule: and without adopting the Muslim religion, for example, they could quite happily live like the Muslims." Boniface Louis André Castellane, *Opinion de M. le comte de Castellane, du 23, sur sa Motion de la veille* (Versailles: Baudouin, 1789), 4.

30. *Moniteur*, 23–26 August 1789.

31. *AP*, 23 August 1789 (8:480).

32. *AP*, 23 August 1789 (8:479).

33. *Moniteur*, 23–26 August 1789.

34. Jean-Paul Rabaut de Saint-Étienne, *Opinion de M. Rabaut de Saint-Étienne, sur la motion suivante de le Comte de Castellane: Nul homme ne peut être inquieté pour ses opinions, ni troublé dans l'exercice de sa religion* (Versailles: Baudoin, 1789), 8.

35. *AP*, 23 August 1789 (8:480).

36. *AP*, 22 August 1789 (8:477).

37. Castellane, *Opinion*, 7.

38. *Courrier de Provence* 12, 22–23 August 1789.

39. *Pétition des juifs établis en France, adressée à l'Assemblée nationale, le 28 janvier 1790, sur l'ajournement du 24 décembre 1789* (Paris: Prault, 1790).

40. Feuerwerker, *Émancipation des Juifs en France*, 388.

41. X. Yacono, "Les débuts de la franc-maçonnerie à Alger (1830–1852)," *Revue africaine* 103 (1959): 59.

42. A romantic Masonic novel of 1779 imagines such an Algerian, Zamey, being received into the order: [Sain de Manévieux], *Le porte-feuille lyonnois; ou, Bigarrures provinciales, trouvées par un Q . . . ni cuirassé, ni mitré, mais botté* (Minorca [Lyon]: Aux dépens du Gouvernement, 1779), 164.

43. Archives Municipales, Marseille, DD 138.

44. Archives Municipales, Marseille, DD 138.

45. Archives Municipales, Marseille, DD 138.

46. For the admission of actors, see Paul Friedland, *Political Actors: Representative Bodies and Theatricality in the Age of the French Revolution* (Ithaca: Cornell University Press, 2002), 219–224; for the exclusion and admission of executioners, see Friedland, *Seeing Justice Done: The Age of Spectacular Capital Punishment in France* (Oxford: Oxford University Press, 2012), esp. 224–226.

47. *Journal de Paris*, 11 April 1789.

48. *Journal de Paris*, 24 May 1789.

49. *Le danger de la liberté des nègres [par un bon citoyen]* (1790), 4–5.

50. *Danger de la liberté des nègres*, 6.

51. *Lettre adressée à M. Grégoire, curé d'Emberménil, député de Nancy, par les députés de la nation juive portugaise, de Bordeaux* [signed Furtado-Lainé, Azevedo, David Gradis, et al.] (Paris: Baudouin, 1789).

52. *Lettre adressée à M. Grégoire*.

53. Stanislas Marie Adelaïde Clermont-Tonnerre, *Opinion de M. le comte Stanislas de Clermont-Tonnerre, député de Paris: le 23 décembre 1789* (Paris: Baudouin, 1789).

54. *AP*, 21 December 1789 (10:711).

55. *AP*, 22 December 1789 (10:714).

56. Clermont-Tonnerre, *Opinion*.

57. Maurice Samuels, *The Right to Difference: French Universalism and the Jews* (Chicago: University of Chicago Press, 2016).

58. *AP*, 23 December 1789 (10:736–737).

59. *AP*, 23 December 1789 (10:757).

60. AP, 24 December 1789 (10:780).

61. See Jean-Daniel Piquet, *L'émancipation des noirs dans la révolution française: 1789–1795* (Paris: Karthala, 2002), 121–122.

62. *AP*, 24 December 1789 (10:779).

63. The consequences of the breakdown of existing reciprocality for French subjects in Ottoman cities proved extremely complex; see Christian Windler, *La diplomatie comme experience de l'autre: Consuls français au Maghreb (1700–1840)* (Geneva: Droz, 2002).

64. Hermon-Belot, *Aux sources de l'idée laïque*, xx.

65. Robert Badinter, *Libres et égaux . . . : L'émancipation des Juifs sous la Révolution française, 1789–1791* (Paris: Fayard, 1989), chap. 5, n. 58.

66. Ronald Schechter, *Obstinate Hebrews: Representations of Jews in France, 1715–1815* (Berkeley: University of California Press, 2003), 160.

67. This was the basis of the *droit d'aubaine* that offered foreigners limited rights in France dependent on the treatment of French subjects in their own state. See Peter Sahlins, *Unnaturally French: Foreign Citizens in the Old Regime and After* (Ithaca: Cornell University Press, 2004).

68. Bernard Gainot, "Métropole/colonies," in Yves Bénot and Marcel Dorigny (eds), *Rétablissement de l'esclavage dans les colonies françaises: Aux origines de Haïti* (Paris: Maisonneuve et Larose, 2003), 13–28.

69. *Courrier de Lyon* 51, 30 December 1789.

70. *AP*, 27 September 1791 (31:372).

71. Maurice Samuels, *The Right to Difference: French Universalism and the Jews* (Chicago: University of Chicago Press, 2016), 30.

4. *The Turbans of Liberty*

1. The classical interpretation is that by Albert Mathiez in *La Révolution et les étrangers: Cosmopolitisme et défense nationale* (Paris: La Renaissance du livre, 1918), 52–57; see also Sophie Wahnich, *L'impossible citoyen: L'étranger dans le discours de la Révolution française* (Paris: Albin Michel, 1997), 185–200.

2. Sophie Wahnich, "L'étranger, paradoxe de l'universel: Analyse du discours politique révolutionnaire sur l'étranger de la Fédération à Thermidor" (doctoral thesis, Université de Paris 1, 1994), 1:163.

3. Jean Philippe Guy Le Gentil, marquis de Paroy, *Mémoires du Comte de Paroy: Souvenirs d'un défenseur de la famille royale pendant la révolution (1789–1797)* (Paris: E. Plon, Nourrit, 1895), 182.

4. *Journal général de l'Europe*, 26 June 1790.

5. Adolphe Thiers, *Histoire de la Révolution française* (Paris: Lebeau-Ouwerx, 1828), 1:92.

6. Robert Darnton, *The Kiss of Lamourette: Reflections in Cultural History* (New York: Norton, 1990). Timothy Tackett has written extensively about revolutionary emotions in *The Coming of the Terror in the French Revolution* (Cambridge, MA: Harvard University Press, 2015).

7. William Doyle, *Aristocracy and Its Enemies in the Age of Revolution* (Oxford: Oxford University Press, 2009), 3–7.

8. Rafe Blaufarb, *The French Army, 1750–1820: Careers, Talent, Merit* (Manchester: Manchester University Press, 2002), 60–61.

9. *Courrier français*, 20 June 1790.

10. Paroy, *Mémoires du Comte de Paroy,* 184. The last line suggests the ongoing association of these revolutionary actions as an Orleanist plot.

11. Jean-Baptiste [Anacharsis] Cloots, *Discours prononcé à la barre de l'Assemblée nationale par M. de Cloots, du Val-de-Grâce* (1790), in *Écrits révolutionnaires, 1790–1794,* ed. Michèle Duval (Paris: Éditions Champ libre, 1979), 28–29.

12. *Collection générale des décrets rendus par l'Assemblée Nationale* (Paris: Baudouin, imprimeur de l'Assemblée nationale, 1789), 2:323.

13. *Procès verbale* AN C/1/7; *Mercure de France,* 1790, 307.

14. *L'espion de la Révolution française* 1 (1790), 165.

15. *Les Révolutions de France et de Brabant* 4 (1790), 612.

16. *Almanach littéraire; ou, Étrennes d'Apollon pour l'Année 1791.*

17. *AP,* 19 June 1790 (16:373).

18. Petition, AN C/42/378; Journal de M. Sillery, AN KK 645 fol. 696; John Goldworth Alger, *Paris in 1789–94: Farewell letters of victims of the guillotine* (London: George Allen, 1902), 68–69.

19. Jules Lair and Emile Legrand (eds), *Lettres de Constantin Stamaty à Panagiotis Kodrikas* (Paris: Maisonneuve, 1872), 8.

20. The classic "postsocial" account of the aristocracy is Guy Chaussinand-Nogaret, *La noblesse au XVIIIe siècle: De la féodalité aux lumières* (Paris: Éditions Complexe, 2000); for recent re-assessments, see Jay M. Smith, *Nobility Reimagined: The Patriotic Nation in Eighteenth-Century France* (Ithaca: Cornell University Press, 2005). For scandals in the late ancien régime, often involving individuals passing themselves off as noble, see Sarah Maza, *Private Lives and Public Affairs: The Causes Célèbres of Prerevolutionary France* (Berkeley: University of California Press, 1993).

21. Vincent Denis, *Une histoire de l'identité: France, 1715–1815* (Paris: Champ Vallon, 2008).

22. Michel-Rolph Trouillot, "An Unthinkable History: The Haitian Revolution as a Non-event," in *Silencing the Past: Power and the Production of History* (Boston: Beacon Press, 1995), 73.

23. Edmond Géraud, *Journal d'un étudiant pendant la révolution, 1789–1793* (Paris: C. Lévy, 1890), 101.

24. Richard Taws, *The Politics of the Provisional: Art and Ephemera in Revolutionary France* (University Park: Penn State University Press, 2013), 141.

25. [L. A. de Caraccioli], *La petite Lutèce devenue grande fille* (Paris: Cuchet, Libraire, 1790), 2:267–269.

26. Philippe Bourdin, *Des lieux, des mots, les révolutionnaires: Le Puy-de-Dôme entre 1789 et 1799* (Clermont-Ferrand: Presses universitaires Blaise Pascal, 1995), 39.

27. Charles Lenient, *La comédie en France au XVIIIe siècle* (Paris: Hachette, 1888), 2:413.

28. *Le guide national* (Paris: Imprimerie de la liberté, 1790), 6.

29. *Lettre à un censeur royal sur la liberté de la presse* (Paris: Chez Volland, 1789), 5.

30. "Ah! ça ira! ça ira! ça ira! / L'Almanach Gerard partout se lira; / Le musulman, dès qu'il l'apercevra, / Pour l'acheter, son Alkoran vendra." *Étrennes à tous les tyrans et aristocrates de l'univers: Pour le premier jour de l'an 3me de la liberté; par M.G.***, Patriote de la Savoie* (Paris: Imprimerie du Patriote françois). The almanac was later replaced by "Le code français" in the lyric. See Michel Biard, "L'almanach du Père Gérard: Un exemple de diffusion des idées jacobines," *Annales historiques de la Révolution française* 238.1 (1990): 19–29.

31. Louis Damade, *Histoire chantée de la première République, 1789 à 1799: Chants patriotiques, révolutionnaires et populaires* (Paris: Paul Schmidt, 1892), 176, 191.

32. *Liste des membres de l'Assemblée Nationale qui ont donné leurs voix pour ou contre les assignats* (n.p., 1790), 8–9.

33. *Les actes des apôtres* 134 (1790).

34. *Correspondance patriotique*, 1791.

35. *Gazette de Paris*, 23 June 1790.

36. *Gazette de Paris*, 23 June 1790.

37. *Mercure de France*, 11 September 1790.

38. Cloots, "Éclaircissements sur la députation du 19 juin 1790" (1790), in *Écrits révolutionnaires*, 30–31.

39. *La députation étrangere au Champ de Mars: Aux confédérés français* (1791).

40. The rehabilitation of Cloots as a "visionary" began with Georges Avenel's hagiographic and often inaccurate biography, *Anacharsis Cloots: L'orateur du*

genre humain (Paris: Librairie Internationale, 1865). Jean Jaurès wrote admiringly of him, followed by more critical, yet still fundamentally heroic, versions from Mathiez and Soboul. See also Madeleine Rebérioux, "Anacharsis Cloots: The Other Citizen of the World," in Georges Kantin and Douglas A. Cooper (eds), *Thomas Paine, Citizen of the World* (Paris: Créaphis Éditions, 1990), 31–41.

41. The most useful biography is François Labbé, *Anacharsis Cloots, le Prussien francophile: Un philosophe au service de la Révolution française et universelle* (Paris: L'Harmattan, 2000). See also Roland Mortier, *Anacharsis Cloots; ou, l'utopie foudroyée* (Paris: Stock, 1995); Selma Stern, *Anacharsis Cloots, der Redner des Menschengeschlechts* (Berlin, 1914).

42. Robert Darnton, *The Literary Underground of the Old Regime* (Cambridge, MA: Harvard University Press, 1982); Simon Burrows, "Grub Street Revolutionaries: Marginal Writers at the Enlightenment's Periphery?" in Richard Butterwick, Simon Davies, and Gabriel Sánchez Espinosa (eds), *Peripheries of the Enlightenment* (Oxford: Voltaire Foundation, 2008), 145–162.

43. Daniel Roche, *France in the Enlightenment* (Cambridge, MA: Harvard University Press, 1998).

44. See Ulrich L. Lehner, *The Catholic Enlightenment: The Forgotten History of a Global Movement* (Oxford: Oxford University Press, 2016), 22–25.

45. Jean-Baptiste [Anacharsis] Cloots, *La certitude des preuves du Mahométisme; ou, Réfutation de l'examen critique des apologistes de la religion mahométane* (London, 1780), 82.

46. For example, Marmontel, Raynal, and Chamfort. Alan Kors, *D'Holbach's Coterie* (Princeton, NJ: Princeton University Press, 2008).

47. Jean-Baptiste [Anacharsis] Cloots, *Voeux d'un Gallophile* (Amsterdam, 1786), 23.

48. Cloots, *Voeux d'un Gallophile*, 24–25, 54.

49. See Philip Mansel, *Constantinople: City of the World's Desire, 1453–1924* (Harmondsworth: Penguin, 1997), 183–184; Richard Price, *The Correspondence of Richard Price: February 1786–February 1791*, ed. Bernard Peach (Durham, NC: Duke University Press, 1983), 3:258–259.

50. *Les révolutions de France et de Brabant* 43 (1790).

51. Cloots, "Anacharsis à Paris; ou, Lettre de Jean-Baptiste Cloots, à un prince d'Allemagne" (1790), in *Écrits révolutionnaires*, 81.

52. Henri Baulig, "Anacharsis Cloots, journaliste et théoricien (1789–1792)," *La Révolution française* 41 (1901): 316.

53. *La Bouche de fer* 5.

54. Jean-Jacques Barthélemy, *Voyage du jeune Anacharsis en Grèce* (Paris, 1788).

55. See Peter McPhee on revolutionary names in *Living the French Revolution, 1789–1799* (Houndmills: Palgrave Macmillan, 2006), 149–153.

56. Cloots, "L'Orateur du genre-humain; ou, Dépêche du Prussien Cloots au Prussien Hertzberg" (1791), in *Écrits révolutionnaires*, 102; see also Charles Gliozzo, "The Philosophes and Religion: Intellectual Origins of the Dechristianization Movement in the French Revolution," *Church History* 40.3 (1971): 273–283.

57. *Gens de couleur* was a term with a specific legal sense, meaning Caribbeans of mixed heritage, and opposed to the *créoles* or white *résidents*; it grouped together both free people of color and manumitted former slaves. See Malick Ghachem, *The Old Regime and the Haitian Revolution* (Cambridge: Cambridge University Press, 2012), 13–14; Jennifer Palmer, *Intimate Bonds: Family and Slavery in the French Atlantic* (Philadelphia: University of Pennsylvania Press, 2016).

58. See John D. Garrigus, "Opportunist or Patriot? Julien Raimond (1744–1801) and the Haitian Revolution," *Slavery and Abolition* 28.1 (2007): 1–21.

59. Antoine François Bertrand de Molleville, *Histoire de la Révolution de France pendant les dernières années du règne de Louis XVI* (Paris, 1801–1803), 7:181.

60. Letter of the "citoyens de couleur et nègres libres," *Moniteur*, 12 June 1791.

61. *Le patriote français*, 16 June 1791.

62. *Le patriote français*, 18 June 1791.

63. Marisa Linton, "Fatal Friendships: The Politics of Jacobin Friendship," *French Historical Studies* 31.1 (2008): 51–76.

64. Albert Mathiez, *La Révolution et les étrangers: Cosmopolitisme et défense nationale* (Paris: La Renaissance du livre, 1918), 54.

65. *Mercure de France*, 26 June 1790.

66. Bertrand de Molleville, *Histoire de la Révolution de France*, 7:181.

67. *Journal des débats et des décrets* 316 (19 June 1790); *AP*, 19 June 1790 (16:373).

68. *AP*, 19 June 1790 (16:373).

69. François-Alphonse Aulard (ed), *La société des Jacobins: Recueil de documents pour l'histoire du club des Jacobins de Paris* (Paris: Jouaust-Noblet-Quantin, 1889–1897), 1:42.

70. See Muhsin Mahdi, *The Thousand and One Nights* (Leiden: Brill, 1995).

71. Georges Décote (ed), *Correspondance de Jacques Cazotte: Édition critique* (Paris: Klincksieck, 1982), 100–101.

72. Décote, *Correspondance de Jacques Cazotte*, 143. For a fuller account of Chawich, see Ian Coller, "Citizen Chawich: Arabs, Islam and Rights in the French Revolution," *French History and Civilization* 5 (2014): 42–52.

73. Cloots, "L'Orateur du genre humain," 159–160.

74. "Lettres patentes en forme d'édit, qui permettent à une partie de la famille de Cyriac Cazadour Chammas, né à Diarbekir en Mésopotamie, naturalisé François, de s'établir dans tel endroit du Royaume qu'elle avisera," BNF F-23627 (268). Peter Sahlins calls this "the first legally documented instance of 'family reunification' in France." *Unnaturally French: Foreign Citizens in the Old Regime and After* (Ithaca: Cornell University Press, 2004), 147.

75. *Chronique de Paris*, 14 September 1790.

76. Aulard, *La société des Jacobins*, 2:415.

77. *Journal des Clubs ou Sociétés patriotiques* 26 (6–12 May 1791).

5. *The Constitutional Mosque*

1. Timothy Tackett, *Religion, Revolution, and Regional Culture in Eighteenth-Century France: The Ecclesiastical Oath of 1791* (Princeton, NJ: Princeton University Press, 1986), 4.

2. Tackett, *Religion, Revolution, and Regional Culture*, 282.

3. *AP*, 7 May 1791 (25:652).

4. A deputy also recalled Couturier crying out during the debate on whether the new constitutional bishops could be ordained in their own churches, "I move that it should be in the mosques and synagogues!"

5. Léon Kahn, *Les Juifs de Paris pendant la révolution* (Paris: Paul Ollendorff, 1898), 51.

6. *L'ami du roi, des François, de l'ordre et sur-tout de la vérité* 336, 20 April 1791.

7. Sylvain Codet, *Opinion motivée de M. Codet, député de l'Isle et vilaine à l'Assemblée Nationale* (Paris: Imprimerie nationale, 1791), 2.

8. *AP*, 21 October 1791 (34:330–331).

9. *Journal de la cour et de la ville*, 4 December 1791.

10. *Les sabats jacobites* 48 (1791). My translation.

11. *Le naviget-anticyras; ou, Le système sans principe, l'édifice sans fondement élevé sur le sable . . .*, (1789), 30.

12. *Le naviget-anticyras*, 211, 98.

13. *Remercimens du Parlement à l'Assemblée nationale* (n.p., 1790), 4.

14. *Remercimens du Parlement à l'Assemblée nationale*, 35.

15. *Remercimens du Parlement à l'Assemblée nationale*, 36.

16. Isaac Jean Joseph Cassius, *Sermon patriotique prêché dans l'Église de S. Germain-des-Prés, le dimanche de quasimodo, 11 avril 1790* (Paris: Le Clère, 1790).

17. François-Philippe Mésenguy, *Exposition de la doctrine chrétienne; ou, Instructions sur les principales vérités de la religion* (Utrecht: Aux dépens de la Compagnie, 1744), liii.

18. Cassius, *Sermon patriotique*.

19. *AP*, 12 April 1790 (12:702).

20. *AP*, 13 February 1790 (11:589).

21. *Lettre de M.***, député à l'Assemblée nationale, à M.***, sur la conduite du clergé dans l'Assemblée nationale; ou, Histoire fidèle des décrets de l'Assemblée, relativement aux biens ecclésiastiques et à la religion* (Paris, 1791), 47.

22. *AP*, 13 April 1790 (12:716).

23. *AP*, 13 April 1790 (12:717).

24. *AP*, 13 April 1790 (12:719–720).

25. Recent historians have pointed to Mirabeau's uses of the classical past in this manner. See Robert Blackman, "Did Cicero Swear the Tennis Court Oath?," *French History* 28.4 (2014): 471–497.

26. Augustin Barruel (ed), *Collection ecclésiastique; ou, Recueil complet des ouvrages faits depuis l'ouverture des États-généraux* (Paris: Crapart, 1791), 1:464.

27. *Journal des états généraux, convoqués par Louis XVI, le 27 avril 1789*, 17 August 1790.

28. *Moniteur*, 2 June 1790. This line does not appear in the *Archives Parlementaires*. The phrase "changer la religion," however, was used repeatedly throughout late 1789 and 1790 by Garat, Maury, Cazalès, and others: see *AP* 9:519, 9:610, 11:589, 15:553, and 21: 29. By November 1790, the abbé Maury was openly contesting what he declared to be the Assembly's attempts to change the state's religion and abolish Christianity: "Vous auriez besoin de l'autorisation la plus spéciale pour changer la religion de l'État" (*AP* 21:91).

29. *L'ami du roi*, 30 November 1790.

30. François Guillaume Jean Stanislas Andrieux, *Épitre au pape* (Paris: Fiévée, 1791).

31. See Dale Van Kley, "The Ancien Régime, Catholic Europe, and the Revolution's Religious Schism," in Peter McPhee (ed), *A Companion to the French Revolution* (Oxford: Wiley-Blackwell, 2012), 123–144.

32. *Acta in consistorio secreto a sanctissimo domino nostro Pio Papa Sexto, habito die XXVI, mensis septembris MDCCXCI in Palatio Apostolico Quirinali* (Rome: Camerae Apostolicae, 1791). A French translation was reported in *Gazette*

universelle; ou, Papier-nouvelles de tous les pays et de tous les jours, 21 October 1791.

33. Emmanuel Henri Louis Alexandre de Launay d'Antraigues, *Dénonciation aux français catholiques, des moyens employés par l'Assemblée nationale pour détruire en France la religion catholique* (London: Edwart Pall-Mall, 1791), 204.

34. D'Antraigues, *Dénonciation*, 203.

35. A royalist newspaper published a text purporting to be a lost Menippean satire: "Qui n'aime point ouïr prêcher, Greg[oire] . . . Gou[pil] . . . Fau[chet]. . . . Qui né salue jusqu'à terre Mi[rabeau] . . . Tar[get] . . . Rob[espierre]. . . . . C'est un maheustre et un frelu / Pire qu'un turc ou mamelu." "Extrait dé la satyre ménippée, édition de Ratisbonne, 1732," *Les actes des apôtres* 129 (July 1790). By 1791, in a satirical take on the deposition of Voltaire's remains in the Panthéon, the *Journal de la Cour et de la Ville* (4 June 1791) described the leading revolutionaries as dressed in costumes from Voltaire's plays: the Bishop of Autun (Talleyrand) was Mahomet, and Desmoulins Séïde.

36. "Extrait du *Journal ecclésiastique*, juillet 1790; ou, Réponse à l'opinion de M. Treilhard, sur le rapport du Comité ecclesiastique, concernant l'organisation du clergé," in Barruel, *Collection ecclésiastique*, 2:318.

37. *Réflexions sommaires sur le serment civique* (n.p., 1790), 12.

38. *Réflexions sommaires sur le serment civique*, 15.

39. Quarre de Monay, *Declaration de L'eglise Cathedrale d'Autun* (Autun: Dejussieu, 1790).

40. *Lettre pastorale de M. l'Archevêque d'Auch* (1790).

41. See André Latreille, *L'Église catholique et la Révolution française* (Paris: Hachette, 1946); Nigel Aston, *Religion and Revolution in France, 1780–1804* (Washington, DC: Catholic University of America Press, 2000).

42. *Rapport fait à l'Assemblée nationale, au nom du Comité ecclésiastique, par M. Martineau, député de la ville de Paris, sur la Constitution du clergé. Imprimé par ordre de l'Assemblée nationale* (Paris: Impr. nationale, 1790), 31.

43. *AP*, 21 April 1790 (13:167).

44. *AP*, 30 May 1790 (15:253).

45. Tackett, *Religion, Revolution, and Regional Culture*, 308–312.

46. *Moniteur*, 17 May 1791.

47. *Gazette universelle*, 21 May 1791.

48. *Gazette universelle*, 21 May 1791.

49. *Courier de l'Europe*, 11 October 1791.

50. *L'ami du roi* 73, 1790.

51. Condorcet: "À Constantinople même le despotisme militaire des sultans a été forcé de plier devant le crédit des interprètes privilégiés des loix de l'alcoran." "Sur l'instruction publique," *Bibliothèque de l'homme public*, 1791, 7. Maury insisted that the Turks "n'ont pas d'autres loix civiles que leur code religieux." *Assemblée Nationale permanente; ou, Journal logographique*, 17 January 1791.

52. *Journal de la cour et de la ville*, 20 January 1792.

53. *Mercure de France* 53 (31 December 1791).

54. Bernard Lambert, *Le préservatif contre le schisme, convaincu de graves erreurs* (Paris: Desaint, 1791), 124.

55. *Gros-Jean qui remontre à son curé, et les doutes d'un villageois résolus par son pasteur: Suivis du parallèle de la persécution de Julien l'Apostat avec la persécution de l'Eglise de France des années 362–363 et 1790–1791* (Paris: Chez Lallemand, 1792). The curé of Saint-Laurent was Charles-Alexandre de Moy, author of *Accord de la religion et des cultes chez une nation libre* (Paris: Au presbytère de Saint-Laurent, an IV de la liberté [1792]).

56. Sigismond Lacroix (ed), *Actes de la commune de Paris pendant la Révolution*, series 2 (Paris: L. Cerf, 1894), 8:669.

57. *L'ami de la religion et de la patrie, adresse à MM. les électeurs du département de la Seine Inférieure* (Paris: Crapart, 1791).

58. *Journal de la cour et de la ville*, 29 November 1791.

59. *Moniteur*, 18 October 1791.

60. *Moniteur*, 22 October 1791.

61. *Le cri de l'humanité; ou, L'ami des vieillards* [1791].

62. *La feuille villageoise*, 6 January 1791.

63. *Journal de Paris*, 22 January 1791.

64. *AP*, 21 October 1791 (34:333).

65. *AP*, 21 October 1791 (34:333).

66. *AP*, 21 October 1791 (34:339).

67. *AP*, 26 October 1791 (34:417).

68. *AP*, 26 October 1791 (34:417).

69. *AP*, 27 March 1792 (40:517).

70. *Moniteur*, 21 June 1792.

71. *AP*, 16 November 1792 (40:517). This is a perfect example of the ways in which conservatives helped fuel the very shift they opposed. They reported François's words as saying, "Religion is nothing but a pretext, abused by the enemies of the constitution" rather than "Religion is used by the enemies of the constitution as a pretext."

72. *AP*, 16 November 1791 (35:97).

73. *AP*, 16 November 1791 (35:99).

74. Antoine-Adrien Lamourette, *Instruction pastorale de M. l'évêque du département de Rhône et Loire* (Lyon: Impr. d'Amable Le Roy, 1791), 17.

75. Antoine-Adrien Lamourette, *Les délices de la religion; ou, Le pouvoir des Évangiles pour nous rendre heureux* (Paris: Merigot jeune, 1789), 14.

76. On Fauchet, see Gary Kates, *The Cercle Social, the Girondins, and the French Revolution* (Princeton, NJ: Princeton University Press, 1985); for a brief mention of his views on Islam, see Jonathan Israel, *Revolutionary Ideas: An Intellectual History of the French Revolution from the Rights of Man to Robespierre* (Princeton, NJ: Princeton University Press, 2014), 138–139.

77. Claude Fauchet, *De la religion nationale* (Paris: Bailly, 1789), 14–16.

78. Robert Darnton, *The Kiss of Lamourette: Reflections in Cultural History* (New York: Norton, 1990), 17–19; Caroline Chopelin-Blanc, "Le 'baiser Lamourette' (7 juillet 1792)," *Annales historiques de la révolution française* 355 (2009): 73–100.

6. The Muslim Republic

1. Mathieu Blanc-Gilli, *Réveil d'alarme d'un député de Marseille, aux bons citoyens de Paris* (Paris: Imprimerie de Crapart, 1792), 5–6.

2. Jean-Gabriel Peltier, *Dernier tableau de Paris; ou, Récit historique de la révolution du 10 août 1792, . . .* (London: Chez l'auteur, 1793), 143. Another writer, some years later, went even further: "More than two hundred brigands—Genoese, Italians, Poles, Piedmontese, Maltese, Moors, Barbaresques, and others—taken from the bagnio in Marseille, had already been transported to Paris along with cannons by Charles Barbaroux." Pierre Anne Louis de Maton de La Varenne, *Histoire particulière des événemens qui ont eu lieu en France pendant les mois de juin . . . 1792* (Paris, 1806), 58.

3. Thomas Bailey, *A Diplomatic History of the American People*, 6th ed. (New York: Appleton-Century-Crofts, 1958), 65. It is worth noting that this sentence did not appear in the previous edition (1955), and likely has much to do with changing US engagements with the Middle East in the context of the Suez Crisis and the Algerian War.

4. *Moniteur*, 18 June 1793.

5. Francis D. Cogliano, *Emperor of Liberty: Thomas Jefferson's Foreign Policy* (New Haven, CT: Yale University Press, 2014), 104.

6. *Moniteur*, 18 June 1793.

7. See Jamil M. Abun-Nasr, *A History of the Maghrib in the Islamic Period* (Cambridge: Cambridge University Press, 1987), 164–165; Lucette Valensi,

On the Eve of Colonialism: North Africa before the French Conquest, 1790–1830 (New York: Africana, 1977), 74–75.

8. Dalenda Larguèche, "The Mahalla: The Origins of Beylical Sovereignty in Ottoman Tunisia during the Early Modern Period," in Julia Clancy-Smith (ed), *North Africa, Islam and the Mediterranean World: From the Almoravids to the Algerian War* (London: Frank Cass, 2001) 163–64; Mohamed Oualdi, "Mamluks in Ottoman Tunisia: A Category Connecting State and Social Forces," *International Journal of Middle East Studies* 48.3 (2016): 473–490.

9. See Ernest Watbled, "Pachas, Pachas-Deys," *Revue africaine* 17 (1873): 438–443.

10. Ahmad Tawfīq Madanī, *Harb al-thalāthimi'at sanah bayna al-Jazā'ir wa-Isbāniyā, 1492–1792* (Algiers: Al-Mu'assassah al-Watanaīyah lil-Kitāb, 1984), 7. It is worth noting that in Arabic, no distinction is made between Algiers and Algeria—both are rendered as *al-Jazā'ir*, and Algiers is generally referred to as *al-āsima* (the capital).

11. Tal Shuval, *La ville d'Alger vers la fin du XVIIIe siècle: Population et cadre urbain* (Paris: CNRS Éditions, 2013), 163–171.

12. Jean-Jacques Rousseau, *Émile et Sophie; ou, Les solitaires: Ouvrage posthume de M. J.-J. Rousseau* (Geneva: Société Typographique, 1781), 101–102.

13. Jean-Louis-Marie Poiret, *Voyage en Barbarie; ou, Lettres écrites de l'ancienne Numidie pendant les années 1785 et 1786* (Paris: J. B. F. Née de la Rochelle, 1789), 1:208.

14. H. D. de Grammont, *Histoire d'Alger sous la domination turque, 1515–1830* (Paris: E. Leroux, 1887), 307–308.

15. Ann Thomson, *Barbary and Enlightenment: European Attitudes towards the Maghreb in the 18th Century* (Leiden: Brill, 1987), 114.

16. Charles de Secondat Montesquieu, *Considerations sur les causes de la grandeur des Romains et de leur decadence* (Amsterdam: Chez J. Desbordes, 1734). See also Derek Beales, "Philosophical Kingship and Enlightened Despotism," in Mark Goldie and Robert Wokler (eds), *The Cambridge History of Eighteenth-Century Political Thought* (Cambridge: Cambridge University Press, 2006), 495–524.

17. Edward Gibbon, *The Decline and Fall of the Roman Empire: AD 180–AD 395* (repr., New York: Modern Library, 1983), 2:166.

18. *Journal de Paris*, 6 November 1792.

19. Pierre-Victor Malouet, *Lettre de M. Malouet à M. de Lally-Tolendal* (Paris, 1792), 8.

20. Edmund Burke, *Revolutionary Writings: Reflections on the Revolution in France and the First Letter on a Regicide Peace* (Cambridge: Cambridge University Press, 2014), 327–328.

21. CCM to Vallière AMAE (Nantes), Consulat d'Alger 18 (1791), 31 June 1791.

22. Weiss, *Captives and Corsairs*, 119–120.

23. Aulard, *La société des Jacobins*, 3:595, 598; *Annales patriotiques et littéraires*, 24 April 1792.

24. AN, AE B I 144, 30, 28 July 1791.

25. See Tackett, *Coming of the Terror*, 34–35.

26. Abun-Nasr, *History of the Maghrib*, 195–196.

27. See Pierre Péan, *Main basse sur Alger: Enquête sur un pillage, Juillet 1830* (Paris: Plon, 2004).

28. *Mercure universel*, 18 August 1791.

29. AN, AE B I 144, 30, 15 July 1791.

30. Plantet, *Correspondance des deys d'Alger*, 2:407.

31. See Richard Herr, *The Eighteenth-Century Revolution in Spain* (Princeton, NJ: Princeton University Press, 1958), 239–268.

32. Ismet Terki Hassaine, "Oran au XVIIIe siècle: Du désarroi à la clairvoyance politique de l'Espagne," *Insaniyat: Revue algérienne d'anthropologie et de sciences sociales* 23–24 (2004): 197–222.

33. AN, AE B I 144, 30, 13 September 1791.

34. Edmond de Goncourt and Jules de Goncourt, *L'art du dix-huitième siècle: Watteau, Chardin, Boucher, Latour, Greuze, Les Saint-Aubin* (Paris: Rapilly, 1873), 246.

35. See the discussion of images of Egyptians at the Palais-Royal in the Napoleonic period in my *Arab France: Islam and the Making of Modern Europe, 1798–1831* (Berkeley: University of California Press, 2010).

36. AMAE (Nantes), Consulat d'Alger 18 (1791).

37. AMAE (Nantes), Consulat d'Alger 18 (1791), Conseil d'état, 3 April 1791.

38. Alexandre Tuetey, *Répertoire général des sources manuscrites de l'histoire de Paris pendant la révolution française:* vol. 5, *Assemblée legislative* (Paris: Imprimerie nouvelle, 1900), 421–422.

39. Sophie Wahnich, *In Defence of the Terror: Liberty or Death in the French Revolution*, trans. David Fernbach (London: Verso, 2012), 61.

40. Arch. Mun. Marseille, 2 I 173 Étrangers 1793.

41. *Journal politique des empires*, 14 November 1791.

42. *Révolutions de Paris*, 29 October–5 November 1791.

43. *Journal politique; ou, Gazette des gazettes*, 20 November 1791.

44. *Journal politique des empires*, 14 November 1791.

45. *AP*, 4 November 1791 (34:627).

46. *AP*, 4 November 1791 (34:628).

47. *Révolutions de Paris*, 17–24 December 1791.

48. Addressing this question in a speech at the Jacobin Club, Brissot used a comparison with Muslim societies to insist that no individual could be placed above the law, even the king. The ancient Egyptians, he declared, to avoid the dangers of monarchy, put a rock on the throne and treated it as a monarch. Similarly, he added, "The sheiks placed [on the throne] the Koran and a sword, and lived as republicans." Aulard, *La société des Jacobins*, 2:611.

49. *AP*, 2 November 1791 (34:593).

50. *La rocambole; ou, Journal des honnêtes gens*, 10 November 1791.

51. *Journal de la cour et de la ville*, 1 November 1791.

52. *Journal général de l'Europe*, 14 November 1791.

53. *Journal général de l'Europe*, 14 November 1791.

54. *Journal de la cour et de la ville*, 9 January 1792.

55. *Journal politique; ou, Gazette des gazettes*, 10 December 1791.

56. *AP*, 4 November 1791 (34:627).

57. Pascal Even, "Un épisode des relations de la France avec la régence d'Alger, au début de la Révolution: La mission du capitaine Doumergues en 1791," *Revue d'histoire diplomatique* 98 (1984): 50–70.

58. Nabil Matar, " 'Abdallah ibn 'Aisha and the French Court, 1699–1701: An Ambassador without Diplomacy," *French History* 29.1 (2015): 62–75.

59. Sanjay Subrahmanyam, *Courtly Encounters: Translating Courtliness and Violence in Early Modern Eurasia* (Cambridge, MA: Harvard University Press, 2012), 1–30.

60. Marisa Linton, "Fatal Friendships: The Politics of Jacobin Friendship," *French Historical Studies* 31.1 (2008): 51–76.

61. Antoine François Bertrand de Molleville, *Mémoires secrets pour servir à l'histoire de la dernière année du règne de Louis XVI, roi de France* (London: Strahan and Cadell, 1797), 2:31.

62. *AP*, 29 May 1792 (44:287).

63. *AP*, 29 May 1792 (44:287).

64. *AP*, 31 May 1792 (44:391).

65. *Moniteur*, 29 August 1792; Plantet, *Correspondance des deys d'Alger*, 2:428.

66. *Moniteur*, 29 August 1792.

67. Aulard, *La société des Jacobins*, 7 December 1792 (4:552).

68. Édouard Olivier, *La France avant et pendant la révolution: Les classes, les droits féodaux, les services publics* (Paris: Guillaumin, 1889), 553.

69. *Moniteur*, 23 November 1793.

70. AMAE (Nantes), Consulat d'Alger A 19 (1792).

71. *Moniteur*, 5 June 1793.

72. Marisa Linton, *Choosing Terror: Virtue, Friendship, and Authenticity in the French Revolution* (Oxford: Oxford University Press, 2015).

73. Text and translation in Tayeb Chenntouf, "La Révolution française: L'évènement vue d'Algérie," in Hédia Khadar (ed) *La Révolution française et le monde arabo-musulman* (Tunis: Éditions de la Mediterranée, 1989), 61–70.

74. Giuseppe Gorani, *Lettres aux français* (London, 1794), 1:22.

75. *Gazette des cours de l'Europe: Le royaliste, ami de l'humanité*, 19 September 1791.

76. See Ian Coller, "The Revolutionary Mediterranean," in Peter McPhee (ed), *A Companion to the French Revolution* (Oxford: Wiley-Blackwell, 2012), 419–434.

77. See Nile Green, *Sufism: A Global History* (Chichester, West Sussex: John Wiley & Sons, 2012), 169–176.

78. Abun-Nasr, *History of the Maghrib in the Islamic Period*, 163.

79. H. D. de Grammont, *Histoire d'Alger sous la domination turque (1515–1830)* (E. Leroux, 1887), 349.

80. Plantet, *Correspondance des deys d'Alger*, 440.

81. Meifrund's letters form part of the corpus used by Timothy Tackett; see *Becoming a Revolutionary*, 155.

82. A.-Jacques Parès, *Un toulonnais à Alger au XVIIIe siècle: Meifrund (Pierre-Joseph), 1723–1814* (Paris: Rieder, 1931), 48–49.

83. Plantet, *Correspondance des deys d'Alger*, 446.

84. Plantet, *Correspondance des deys d'Alger*, 447.

7. Islam in the Temple of Reason

1. Joseph-Marie Lequinio, *Du bonheur . . . prononcé dans le Temple de la Vérité de Rochefort, le deuxième décadi de brumaire, l'an II de la République* (Angoulême: P. Broquisse, 1793). For a description of Lequinio's ideas on happiness, see Darrin M. McMahon, *Happiness: A History* (New York: Grove Press, 2006), 253–264.

2. For these festivals, see Mona Ozouf, *Festivals and the French Revolution* (Cambridge, MA: Harvard University Press, 1991), 97–102.

3. Joseph-Marie Lequinio, *Des fêtes nationales* (Paris: Imprimerie nationale, 1795).

4. Bernard Plongeron, *Histoire du christianisme* (Paris: Desclée, 1997), 365.

5. Like Aulard, Vovelle treats the "cult of Reason" and the "cult of the Supreme Being" as interchangeable. Michel Vovelle, *1793, la révolution contre l'église* (Brussels: Complexes, 1988), 15.

6. Michaël Culoma, *La religion civile de Rousseau à Robespierre* (Paris: Harmattan, 2010), 150–151. Jonathan Smyth demonstrated the breadth of the movement effectively in his *Robespierre and the Festival of the Supreme Being: The Search for a Republican Morality* (Manchester: Manchester University Press, 2016).

7. Fauchet had insisted that "La Parole est à nous": Claude Fauchet, *Sermon sur l'accord de la religion et de la liberté, prononcé dans la Métropole de Paris, le 4 février 1791* (Paris: Imprimerie du Cercle Social, 1791), 22.

8. Jean-Jacques Rousseau, *Oeuvres complètes* (Paris: Gallimard, 1959–1969), 4:619.

9. Marie Jean Antoine Nicolas Caritat de Condorcet, *Esquisse d'un tableau historique des progrès de l'esprit humain* (Paris: Chez Agasse, 1795), 165.

10. Louis Thomas Hébert Lavicomterie de Saint Samson, *Les crimes des empereurs turcs, depuis Osman I, jusqu'à Selim IV* (Paris: Bureau des Revolutions de Paris, 1795), viii.

11. Review of Elias Abeschi, *État actuel de l'empire Ottoman*, in the *Mercure de France*, 30 March 1793. The Catholic thinker Lamennais would sum up this thought equally inaccurately 50 years later: "Apart from the matter of rites, the Muslim is hardly different from a deist." Félicité Robert de Lamennais, *Du catholicisme dans ses rapports avec la societe politique*: *Questions politiques et philosophiques* (Paris: Pagnerre, 1844), 352.

12. *Feuille du salut public*, Tridi de la 2e décade de pluviôse an 2e (1 February 1794). These suggestions can be found in *Gazette des Pays Bas*, 26 January 1794: "Cet aventurier nie la prétendue mission de Mahomet, ses révélations, l'origine céleste du Coran, la nécessité des mosquées publiques, & en général le service divin. Son père, vieillard de 90 ans, est le véritable créateur de cette nouvelle doctrine, qu'il a dirigé en code, & introduite dans sa famille; il l'a propagée ensuite dans toute sa tribu, qui par-là s'est augmentée au point de former un peuple nombreux." The *Moniteur* called this movement more soberly a "nouvelle secte" led by a "réformateur ambitieux de la religion de Mahomet." *Moniteur*, 2 Germinal Year 2 (22 March 1794). The *Journal général de la guerre* gave a more detailed background report, noting that the anxious Ottomans had expelled many people who could not establish four decades of residence in the city. *Journal général de la guerre*, 24 April 1794.

13. Giovanni Bonacina, *The Wahhabis Seen through European Eyes (1772–1830)* (Leiden: Brill, 2015).

14. Constantin-François Volney, *Voyage en Syrie et en Égypte pendant les années 1783, 1784 et 1785* (Paris: Desenne, 1787), 1:383. These are also the closing words (in a note) of the first volume.

15. Volney, *Voyage en Syrie et en Égypte*, 1:381.

16. Guillaume-Antoine Olivier, *Voyage dans l'empire Othoman, l'Egypte et la Perse, fait par ordre du gouvernement pendant les six premières années de la République* (Paris: Henri Agasse, 1801–1807), 2:441.

17. Pascal Firges, *French Revolutionaries in the Ottoman Empire: Political Culture, Diplomacy, and the Limits of Universal Revolution, 1792–1798* (Oxford: Oxford University Press, 2017), 138.

18. Jean-Marie Chassaignon, *Les nudités; ou, Les crimes du peuple* (1792), 36.

19. Jean-Baptiste [Anacharsis] Cloots, *La république universelle; ou, Adresse aux tyrannicides* (Paris: Chez les Marchands de Nouveautés, 1792), 182. The word was previously used only once that I can trace, in reflexive form in a 1619 pamphlet defending the church: "Le Pape aimerait mieux se déchristianiser que se depapizer." Anthoine Fusi, *Le franc-archer de la vraye Eglise, contre les abus et énormités de la fausse* (Paris: Aux despens de l'autheur, 1619).

20. Dale K. Van Kley, *The Religious Origins of the French Revolution: From Calvin to the Civil Constitution, 1560–1791* (New Haven, CT: Yale University Press, 1996), 367.

21. Suzanne Desan, *Reclaiming the Sacred: Lay Religion and Popular Politics in Revolutionary France* (Ithaca: Cornell University Press, 1990), 77.

22. Dan Edelstein, *The Terror of Natural Right: Republicanism, the Cult of Nature, and the French Revolution* (Chicago: University of Chicago Press, 2009), 21.

23. Leon Lévy-Schneider, *Le conventionnel Jeanbon Saint-André: Membre du Comité de salut public, organisateur de la marine de la terreur, 1749–1813* (Paris: F. Alcan, 1901), 1:614.

24. Charles-Alexandre de Moy, *Accord de la religion et des cultes chez une nation libre* (Paris: Au presbytère de Saint-Laurent, an IV de la liberté [1792]), 2–3.

25. Moy, *Accord de la religion et des cultes*, 18.

26. *Le patriote français* 1203 (1792).

27. M. Albert Babeau, *Histoire de Troyes pendant la Révolution* (Paris: Dumoulin, 1874), 2:38.

28. "Réclamation adressée aux évêques de France, par des curés de Paris, contre l'institution canonique, accordée par M. Gobel, évêque métropolitain de Paris, à un prêtre marié, élu à une cure de son diocèse" (June 1793), in

Annales de la religion; ou, Mémoires pour servir a l'histoire du dix-huitième siècle (Paris: Imprimerie-Librairie Chrétienne, 1803), 27:294.

29. Antoine-Joseph Thorillon, *Idées ou bases d'une nouvelle declaration des droits de l'homme* (Paris: Chez les marchands de Nouveautés, 1793), 16.

30. Thorillon, *Idées ou bases d'une nouvelle declaration*, 16, 19.

31. François-Xavier Lanthenas, *Déclaration des devoirs de l'homme, des principes et maximes de la morale universelle, proposée par F. Lanthenas . . .* (Paris: Imprimerie Nationale, 1793), 30.

32. Albert Mathiez, *Robespierre et la déchristianisation* (Le Puy: Imprimerie Peyriller, Rouchon & Gamon, 1909), 53.

33. François-Alphonse Aulard, *Le culte de la raison et le culte de l'être suprême (1793–1794): Essai historique* (Paris: Alcan, 1904), 70.

34. Victor Pierre Dubarat and Pierre Haristoy, *Études historiques et religieuses du diocèse de Bayonne, comprenant les anciens diocèses de Bayonne, Lescar, Oloron, etc.* (Pau: Vignancour, 1893), 200.

35. Dubarat and Haristoy, *Études historiques et religieuses*, 201.

36. Ozouf, *Festivals and the French Revolution*, 103.

37. Sébastien Lacroix, *La religion naturelle, la seule qui convient à des républicains* (Marseille, [1793]).

38. *AP*, 3 October 1793 (75:503).

39. See Edward J. Woell, *Small-Town Martyrs and Murderers: Religious Revolution and Counterrevolution in Western France, 1774–1914* (Milwaukee: Marquette University Press, 2006).

40. Donald Sutherland notes 34 fatal attacks on priests in the provinces in the months prior to the September massacres. Donald M. G. Sutherland, *The French Revolution and Empire: The Quest for a Civic Order* (Malden, MA: Blackwell, 2008), 140.

41. Nicolas-Edmé Rétif de la Bretonne, *Les nuits de Paris; ou, Le spectateur-nocturne*, ed. Henri Bachelin (Paris: Livre Club du Libraire, 1960), 231–232.

42. Rétif de la Bretonne, *Les nuits de Paris*, 227.

43. Jean-Jacques Cart, *Lettres de Jean-Jacques Cart à Bernard Demuralt, trésorier du pays de Vaud, sur le droit public de ce pays, et sur les événemens actuels* (Paris: Chez les Directeurs de l'Imprimerie du Cercle Social, 1793), 55.

44. "Le Musulman, dès qu'il l'apercevra, / Pour l'acheter, son Alkoran vendra." *Étrennes à tous les tyrans et aristocrates de l'univers: Pour le premier jour de l'an 3me de la liberté; par M.G. ***, Patriote de la Savoie* (Paris: Imprimerie du Patriote françois, 1791).

45. Louis Damade, *Histoire chantée de la première République, 1789 à 1799: Chants patriotiques, révolutionnaires et populaires* (Paris: Paul Schmidt, 1892), 176.

46. Damade, *Histoire chantée*, 191.

47. [Le citoyen P.B.T.], *L'origine des trois religions revolutionnaires, des Jacobins, des chretiens, et des mahometans* ([Paris]: Chez les marchands de nouveautés, Year 2 [1793–1794]).

48. [Le citoyen P.B.T.], *L'origine des trois religions revolutionnaires*.

49. *AP,* 20 January 1792 (37:528).

50. *AP,* 27 Brumaire Year 2/17 November 1793 (79:371).

51. *AP,* 27 Brumaire, Year 2/17 November 1793 (79:371).

52. AN, F17 Instruction Publique 1006.

53. Georges Duval, *Souvenirs de la terreur de 1788 à 1793* (Paris: Werdet, 1842), 121.

54. Marc Belissa, *Fraternité universelle et intérêt national, 1713–1795: Les cosmo-politiques du droit des gens* (Paris: Éditions Kimé, 1998); Alexander Bevilacqua, "Conceiving the Republic of Mankind: The Political Thought of Anacharsis Cloots," *History of European Ideas* 38.4 (2012): 550–569.

55. Jean-Baptiste [Anacharsis] Cloots, *La republique universelle; ou, Adresse aux tyrannicides* (Paris: Chez les Marchands de Nouveautés, 1792), 12.

56. On Chandernagor, see Adrian Carton, *Mixed-Race and Modernity in Colonial India: Changing Concepts of Hybridity across Empires* (Abingdon: Routledge, 2012), 45–62.

57. Cloots, *La republique universelle,* 20–21.

58. Cloots, *La republique universelle,* 22.

59. Cloots, *La republique universelle,* 27.

60. Cloots, *La republique universelle,* 73.

61. Cloots, *La republique universelle,* 154.

62. Suzanne Desan, "Foreigners, Cosmopolitanism, and French Revolutionary Universalism," in Suzanne Desan, Lynn Hunt, and William Max Nelson (eds), *The French Revolution in Global Perspective* (Ithaca: Cornell University Press, 2013), 86–100.

63. See Tackett, *Coming of the Terror,* 192–216; Brian Singer, "Violence in the French Revolution: Forms of Ingestion/Forms of Expulsion," in Ferenc Fehér (ed), *The French Revolution and the Birth of Modernity* (Berkeley: University of California Press, 1990), 150–173.

64. Jean-Baptiste [Anacharsis] Cloots, "Un mot d'Anacharsis Cloots sur les conférences secrètes entre quelques membres de la convention" (1793), in *Écrits révolutionnaires, 1790–1794,* ed. Michèle Duval (Paris: Éditions Champ libre, 1979), 471.

65. "La fièvre révolutionnaire est une terrible maladie!" Nicolas Ruault wrote in a letter to his brother. Cloots, "si doux, si honnête, si généreux, est devenu terrible; il faut l'écouter et ne pas le contredire. Ce serait peine perdue d'entreprendre de le guérir de sa furie." Nicolas Ruault, Brice Ruault, and Anne Vassal, *Gazette d'un Parisien sous la Révolution: Lettres à son frère, 1783–1796* (Paris: Perrin, 1976), 325. I am grateful to Tim Tackett for these references.

66. *AP*, 9 September 1792 (49:500).

67. See Sophie Wahnich, "La notion d'étranger, paradoxe de l'universel dans le discours révolutionnaire (1789–1794)," in *Langages de la Révolution (1770–1815): Actes du 4ème Colloque international de lexicologie politique* (Paris: ENS Éditions, 1995), 503–512.

68. *AP*, 26 April 1793 (63:397).

69. *AP*, 26 April 1793 (63:397).

70. *AP*, 26 April 1793 (63:398).

71. See Richard Clay, *Iconoclasm in Revolutionary Paris: The Transformation of Signs* (Oxford: Voltaire Foundation, 2012); Simone Bernard-Griffiths, Marie-Claude Chemin, and Jean Ehrard (eds), *Révolution française et "vandalisme révolutionnaire": Actes du colloque international de Clermont-Ferrand, 15–17 décembre 1988* (Paris: Universitas, 1992).

72. Aulard, *Le culte de la raison*, 41.

73. Aulard, *Le culte de la raison*, 41–42; Albert Soboul, *La 1re république, 1792–1804: Naissance et mort* (Paris: Calmann-Lévy, 1968), 85–86.

74. *AP*, 7 November 1793 (78:552).

75. Michel Vovelle, *Religion et révolution: La déchristianisation de l'an II* (Paris: Hachette, 1976).

76. Maximilien Robespierre, *Oeuvres de Maximilien Robespierre:* vol. 10, *Discours* (Paris: Presses Universitaires de France, 1967), 196.

77. Joseph-Marie Lequinio, *Les préjugés détruits* . . . (Paris: Imprimerie Nationale, 1792), 258.

78. Joseph-Marie Lequinio, *Adresse populaire aux habitants des campagnes, par J.-M. Lequinio, lue à la Société des Amis de la constitution séante au Collége de Bourges, et imprimée par son ordre, 4 décembre 1791* (Bourges: Manceron, 1791).

79. Lequinio, *Les préjugés détruits*, 206–208, 205.

80. Lequinio, *Les préjugés détruits*, 154, 311.

81. Lequinio, *Les préjugés détruits*, 19, 16, 156.

82. Lequinio, *Du bonheur.*

83. *Moniteur*, 7 December 1793.

84. Cited in Charles-Louis Chassin, *La Vendée patriote, 1793–1800* (Mayenne: J. Floch, 1894), 548.

85. François-Alphonse Aulard (ed), *Recueil des actes du Comité de salut public avec la correspondance officielle des représentants en mission et le registre du Conseil exécutif provisoire* (Paris: Impr. Nationale, 1889–1910), 10:341.

86. Claudy Valin, *Lequinio: La loi et le salut publique* (Rennes: Presses Universitaires de Rennes, 2014), 234.

87. Alexandre Lambert, *Discours de morale, prononcé le 2e décadi, 20 frimaire, l'an 2e de la République une et indivisible, au temple de la vérité, ci-devant l'église des bénédictins, à Angély-Boutonne, ci-devant St. Jean d'Angély* ([Rochefort], [1794]).

88. Valin, *Lequinio*, 238–239; Szajkowski, *Jews and the French Revolutions of 1789, 1830 and 1848*, 411.

89. Robespierre, *Oeuvres*, 10:450.

90. Robespierre, *Oeuvres*, 10:468.

91. Joseph-Marie Lequinio de Kerblay, *La guerre de la Vendée et des Chouans* (Paris: Pougin, 1794), 187–188.

92. Louis-François de Bausset, *Exposé des principes sur le serment de liberté et d'égalité et sur la déclaration exigée des ministres du culte, par la loi du 7 vendémiaire, an IV* (Paris, 1795), 33.

8. *The Muslim Jacobins*

1. "Considérant que la nation française honore le malheur": AMAE (La Courneuve), MD Asie 20, f. 106. My emphasis.

2. "Nous honorons le malheur": Maximilien Robespierre, *Oeuvres de Maximilien Robespierre*: vol. 10, *Discours* (Paris: Presses Universitaires de France, 1967), 461. My emphasis.

3. Ahmed Khan's journey was described by the Indian historian Aniruddha Ray in "Revolutionary France, 1793–94: Experience of an Indian Prince," *History* 4.1 (2001): 30–37.

4. For one example, see Fatih Yeşil, "Looking at the French Revolution through Ottoman Eyes: Ebubekir Ratib Efendi's Observations," *Bulletin of the School of Oriental and African Studies* 70.2 (2007): 283–304. The chief observer usually cited to demonstrate the rejection of the Revolution is Ahmad Cevdet Pasha (1822–1895), who described the Revolution as "frengi," or syphilis, but Cevdet was a later historian. See Bernard Lewis, *The Emergence of Modern Turkey* (London: Oxford University Press, 1961), 53–65; Wajda Sendesni, *Regard de l'historiographie ottomane sur la Révolution française et l'expédition d'Égypte* (Istanbul: Les Éditions Isis, 2003); Serif Mardin, "The Influence of the French Revolution on the Ottoman Empire," *International Social Science Journal* 44.1 (1989): 17–32. For a longer discussion, see Ian

Coller, "The French Revolution and the Islamic World of the Middle East and North Africa," in Alan Forrest and Matthias Middell (eds), *The Routledge Companion to the French Revolution in World History* (London: Routledge, 2015), 117–134.

5. Adrian Carton, "Shades of Fraternity: Creolization and the Making of Citizenship in French India, 1790–1792," *French Historical Studies* 31.4 (Fall 2008): 583; and *Mixed-Race and Modernity in Colonial India: Changing Concepts of Hybridity across Empires* (Abingdon: Routledge, 2012); see also Kate Marsh, *India in the French Imagination: Peripheral Voices, 1754–1815* (London: Routledge, 2015).

6. C. A. Bayly, *Recovering Liberties: Indian Thought in the Age of Liberalism and Empire* (Cambridge: Cambridge University Press, 2012).

7. See S. Maqbul Ahmad, *A History of the Nawābs of Broach: Based on the Persian Manuscript, Majmū'a-e-Dānish* (Delhi: Dept. of Persian, University of Delhi, 1985).

8. G. J. Bryant, *The Emergence of British Power in India, 1600–1784: A Grand Strategic Interpretation* (Woodbridge: Boydell & Brewer, 2013), 267–271.

9. Nicholas B. Dirks, *The Scandal of Empire: India and the Creation of Imperial Britain* (Cambridge, MA: Harvard University Press, 2006).

10. AMAE (La Courneuve), MD Asie 20, f. 101.

11. Paul R. Hanson, *The Jacobin Republic under Fire: The Federalist Revolt in the French Revolution* (University Park: Pennsylvania State University Press, 2010).

12. See Jean René Suratteau, "Lyon," in Albert Soboul et al. (eds), *Dictionnaire historique de la Révolution française* (Paris: Presses Universitaires de France, 1989).

13. Michel Biard, *1793: Le siège de Lyon; Entre mythes et réalités* (Clermont-Ferrand: Lemme, 2013); W. D. Edmonds, *Jacobinism and the Revolt of Lyon, 1789–1793* (Oxford: Clarendon Press, 1990).

14. Salomon de La Chapelle, *Histoire des tribunaux révolutionnaires de Lyon et de Feurs établis en 1793 par les représentants du peuple et liste des contre-révolutionnaires mis à mort* (Lyon, 1879), 123.

15. P. Mansfield, "The Management of Terror in Montagnard Lyon: Year II," *European History Quarterly* 20.4 (1990): 465–496; Chantal Thomas, "Terror in Lyon," *SubStance* 27.2 (1998): 33–42.

16. Jacques Guilhaumou, *Marseille républicaine (1791–1793)* (Paris: Presses de la Fondation Nationale des Sciences Politiques, 1992), 229; Paul Gaffarel, "Marseille sans nom (Nivôse-Pluviôse An II)," *La Revolution française* 60 (1911): 193–215.

17. AMAE (La Courneuve), MD Asie 20, 19 Brumaire Year 2 (9 November 1793).

18. AMAE (La Courneuve), MD Asie 20, 19 Brumaire Year 2 (9 November 1793).

19. AMAE (La Courneuve), MD Asie 20, 19 Brumaire Year 2 (9 November 1793).

20. AMAE (La Courneuve), MD Asie 20, 18 Frimaire Year 2 (8 December 1793).

21. Jean-Yves Guiomar, "Histoire et significations de la 'Grande Nation' (août 1797–automne 1799): Problèmes d'interprétation," in Jacques Bernet, Jean-Pierre Jessenne, and Hervé Leuwers (eds), *Du directoire au consulat:* vol. 1, *Le lien politique local dans la Grande Nation* (Villeneuve d'Ascq: ANRT, Lille 3, 1999), 317–328; for a different reading, see Henry Laurens, "Bonaparte, l'Orient et la 'Grande Nation,' " *Annales historiques de la Révolution française* 273.1 (1988): 289–301.

22. *Procès-verbaux des séances des corps municipaux de la ville de Lyon* (Lyon: Impr. Nouvelle lyonnaise, 1899–1907), 5:96.

23. AMAE (La Courneuve), MD Asie 20, 6 Floréal, Year 2 (21 April 1794).

24. Sophie Wahnich, *L'impossible citoyen: L'étranger dans le discours de la Révolution française* (Paris: Albin Michel, 1997); Sophie Wahnich, "Hospitalité," in *Dictionnaire des usages socio-politiques (1770–1815): Notions pratiques* (Paris: ENS Éditions, 1999), 34.

25. Sanjay Subrahmanyam, *Courtly Encounters: Translating Courtliness and Violence in Early Modern Eurasia* (Cambridge, MA: Harvard University Press, 2012), 29.

26. Michael H. Fisher, *Counterflows to Colonialism: Indian Travellers and Settlers in Britain, 1600–1857* (Delhi: Orient Blackswan, 2006), 97–100.

27. AMAE (La Courneuve), MD Asie 20, 24 Floréal Year 2.

28. AMAE (La Courneuve), MD Asie 20, Rapport, 26 Floréal Year 2.

29. AMAE (La Courneuve), MD Asie 20, 29 Floréal Year 2.

30. Jacques Derrida, "The Principle of Hospitality," *Parallax* 11.1 (2005): 6–9.

31. AMAE (La Courneuve), MD Asie 20, 29 Floréal Year 2.

32. AMAE (La Courneuve), MD Asie 20, 25 Floréal Year 2.

33. Juan R. I. Cole, "Invisible Occidentalism: Eighteenth-Century Indo-Persian Constructions of the West," *Iranian Studies* 25.3–4 (1992): 10; Kaveh Yazdani, *India, Modernity and the Great Divergence: Mysore and Gujarat (17th to 19th c.)* (Leiden: Brill, 2017), 79.

34. AMAE (La Courneuve), MD Asie 20, 12 Prairial Year 2.

35. AMAE (La Courneuve), MD Asie 20, 16 Messidor Year 2.

36. Albert Mathiez, *La Révolution et les étrangers: Cosmopolitisme et défense nationale* (Paris: La Renaissance du livre, 1918), 1; Wahnich, *L'impossible citoyen.*

37. Michael Rapport, *Nationality and Citizenship in Revolutionary France: The Treatment of Foreigners, 1789–1799* (London: Clarendon Press, 2000), 131–132.

38. Perhaps the most famous account is Simon Schama, *Citizens: A Chronicle of the French Revolution* (New York: Random House, 1989). Others who identified the Terror with the whole Revolution include Norman Hampson, *Prelude to Terror: The Constituent Assembly and the Failure of Consensus, 1789–1791* (London: Basil Blackwell, 1988). Patrice Gueniffey has argued that the Terror should be traced back at least to the laws against émigrés in 1791. Other historians, such as Jean-Clément Martin and Michel Biard, have questioned the very notion of a "Terror."

39. Suzanne Desan, "Foreigners, Cosmopolitanism, and French Revolutionary Universalism," in Suzanne Desan, Lynn Hunt, and William Max Nelson (eds), *The French Revolution in Global Perspective* (Ithaca: Cornell University Press, 2013), 86–100 (89).

40. *AP*, 24 August 1792 (48:688).

41. Peter Sahlins, *Unnaturally French: Foreign Citizens in the Old Regime and After* (Ithaca: Cornell University Press, 2004), 275–276.

42. *Journal des débats et de la correspondance de la Société des Jacobins*, 21 October 1792.

43. *Journal des débats et de la correspondance de la Société des Jacobins*, 21 October 1792.

44. Joseph Behenam (abbé), *Discours prononcé dans l'église de Saint-Jacques et des Saints-Innocents, le dimanche 16 janvier 1791, à la prestation du serment des ecclésiastiques, en présence de la députation du Conseil général de la commune* (n.p., 1791).

45. [Antoine-François-Claude Ferrand], *Tableau de la conduite de l'Assemblée prétendue nationale*, part 2 (Paris, 1790), 5.

46. Aulard, *La société des Jacobins*, 2:415.

47. Aulard, *La société des Jacobins*, 2:577.

48. AMAE (La Courneuve), Dossiers Personnel 1er Série, vol. 16, 20 June 1793.

49. AMAE (La Courneuve), Dossiers Personnel 1er Série, vol. 16, 13 August 1793.

50. AMAE (La Courneuve), Dossiers Personnel 1er Série, vol. 16, 21 Pluviôse Year 2 (9 February 1794).

51. AMAE (La Courneuve), Dossiers Personnel 1er Série, vol. 16, 5 Ventôse Year 2 (23 February 1794).

52. AMAE (La Courneuve), Dossiers Personnel 1er Série, vol. 16, Rapport, n.d. [1795].

53. AMAE (La Courneuve), MD Asie 20, 30 Messidor Year 2 (18 July 1794).

54. Jacques Godechot leaves open the question of the translation of the declaration beyond Europe and North America: "Reste à savoir aussi quand elle a été connue de l'Afrique, de l'Asie, du monde musulman." Godechot,

"L'expansion de la declaration des droits de l'homme de 1789 dans le monde," *Annales historiques de la Révolution française* 232 (1978): 213. J.-P. Allinne discussed only Europe: "La déclaration des Droits de l'Homme et les aspirations libérales en Europe: Le témoignage de la presse," *Annales historiques de la Révolution française* 262.1 (1985): 426–446.

55. In the Ruffin papers in the Archives of the Ministry of Foreign Affairs are several guides to French grammar in Persian, and transcriptions in Ahmed's hand of fables by La Fontaine. AMAE (Nantes), 166 PO B 95.

56. A century later, in 1888, the Persian intellectual Mirza Yusuf Khan Mustashar al-Dawlah "grafted the 17 principles of the French *Declaration of the Rights of Man and Citizen* into Islamic legal culture," according to Mohamad Tavakoli-Targhi, *Refashioning Iran: Orientalism, Occidentalism and Historiography* (Houndmills, Basingstoke: Palgrave, 2001), 136. Tavakoli-Targhi considers this "not a passive imitation of the French code, but its creative relocation within a different textual and political universe."

57. AMAE (La Courneuve), MD Asie 20, 26 Thermidor Year 2 (13 August 1794).

58. AMAE (La Courneuve), MD Asie 20, 1 Fructidor Year 2 (18 August 1794).

59. Archives départementales Yvelines, 1L 412.

60. AMAE (La Courneuve), MD Asie 20, 19 Frimaire Year 3 (9 December 1794).

61. Full text in *Moniteur*, 12 October 1794. For the printed Arabic pamphlet (which features Ruffin's name but not Ahmed's), see Robert Darnton and Daniel Roche (eds), *Revolution in Print: The Press in France, 1775–1800* (Berkeley: University of California Press, 1989), fig. 11.

62. British Library, India Office IOR/F/4/35/898.

63. See chap. 1.

64. Mānekshāh Sorābshāh Commissariat, *A History of Gujarat: The Maratha Period, 1758 A.D. to 1818 A.D.* (Ahmedabad: Gujarat Vidya Sabha, 1980), 717.

65. British Library, India Office IOR/F/4/35/898.

9. Robespierre Mahomet

1. Colin Jones, "The Overthrow of Maximilien Robespierre and the 'Indifference' of the People," *American Historical Review* 119.3 (2014): 689–713.

2. Laura Mason, "The Thermidorian Reaction," in Peter McPhee (ed), *A Companion to the French Revolution* (Oxford: Wiley-Blackwell, 2012), 313–327.

3. Jean-Clément Martin shows that while "terror" was a popular demand for dealing with enemies and traitors in September 1793, it was never made "the order of the day" as legend would have it, nor invested with the meaning

later attributed to it. Martin, *Violence et Révolution: Essai sur la naissance d'un mythe national* (Paris: Seuil, 2006), 189. See also Annie Jourdan, "La journée du 5 septembre 1793: La terreur a-t-elle été à l'ordre du jour?," in Michel Biard and Hervé Leuwers (eds), *Visages de la Terreur: L'exception politique de l'an II* (Paris: Armand Colin, 2014), 45–60.

4. Mette Harder, "A Second Terror: The Purges of French Revolutionary Legislators after Thermidor," *French Historical Studies* 38.1 (2015): 33–60.

5. Roger Barny counts 14 comparisons to Catiline and 13 to Cromwell in the period 13 to 25 Thermidor. These figures were also further entangled: Barny describes a 1790 play entitled *Cromvelet* as a "flat imitation of Voltaire's *Mahomet*." Roger Barny, "L'image de Cromwell dans la Révolution française," *Dix-huitième siècle* 25.1 (1993): 391. Bronislaw Baczko notes how frequently the comparison was inverted to suggest Robespierre was not worthy even to be compared to these historical figures. Baczko, *Ending the Terror: The French Revolution after Robespierre*, trans. Michael Petheram (Cambridge: Cambridge University Press, 1994), 44.

6. On this question of political transition and the conception of "common victimhood," see Robert Meister, "Forgiving and Forgetting: Lincoln and the Politics of National Recovery," in Carla Hesse and Robert Post (eds), *Human Rights in Political Transitions: Gettysburg to Bosnia* (New York: Zone Books, 1999), 135–176.

7. Robespierre, *Oeuvres*, 10:537.

8. Claude Wanquet, "Un Jacobin esclavagiste, Benoît Gouly," *Annales historiques de la Révolution française* 293–294 (1993): 445–468.

9. Aimé Césaire, *Toussaint-Louverture: La Révolution française et le problème colonial* (Paris: Présence Africaine, 1961), 110; Florence Gauthier, "La Révolution française et le problème colonial: Le cas Robespierre," *Annales historiques de la Révolution française* 288.1 (1992): 169–192.

10. Bernard Gainot, "Robespierre et la question coloniale," in Michel Biard and Philippe Bourdin (eds), *Robespierre: Portraits croisés* (Paris: Armand Colin, 2012), 79–94.

11. For Robespierre's suspicion of the impact of rhetorical language and desire for "transparency," see Sophia A. Rosenfeld, *A Revolution in Language: The Problem of Signs in Late Eighteenth-Century France* (Stanford: Stanford University Press, 2003), 168–170.

12. A. F. A. Vivien, *Études administratives* (Paris: Guillaumin, 1845), 445; Henri Grégoire, *Troisième rapport sur le vandalisme* (Paris: Imprimerie nationale des lois, 1794), 2; Jean-Jacques Rousseau, *Lettre à d'Alembert* (Paris:

Garnier-Flammarion, 1967), 81; see also Roger Barny, "Robespierre et les lumières," in Jean-Pierre Jessenne et al. (eds), *Robespierre: De la Nation artésienne à la République et aux Nations* (Lille: Publications de l'Institut de recherches historiques du Septentrion, 1994), 45–60.

13. Henry Laurens, "La Révolution française et l'Islam," *Revue du monde musulman et de la Méditerranée* 52.1 (1989): 30.

14. Peter McPhee, *Robespierre: A Revolutionary Life* (New Haven, CT: Yale University Press, 2012); Michel Biard and Philippe Bourdin (eds), *Robespierre: Portraits croisés* (Paris: Armand Colin, 2012); Marisa Linton, *Choosing Terror: Virtue, Friendship, and Authenticity in the French Revolution* (Oxford: Oxford University Press, 2015); Jean-Clément Martin, *Robespierre* (Paris: Perrin, 2016).

15. Mona Ozouf gives a résumé of these opposing interpretations in *Festivals and the French Revolution* (Cambridge, MA: Harvard University Press, 1991), 107–108.

16. E. B. Courtois, *Rapport fait au nom de la commission chargée de l'examen des papiers trouvés chez Robespierre et ses complices* (Paris: Imprimerie Nationale des Lois, 1795), 98–99.

17. Frédéric Masson, *Le Département des affaires étrangères pendant la révolution, 1787–1804* (Paris: Société d'éditions littéraires et artistiques, 1903), 267; Linda and Marsha Frey, *"Proven Patriots": The French Diplomatic Corps, 1789–1799* (St Andrews: St Andrews Studies in French History and Culture, 2011), 144–150.

18. Léonce Pingaud, *Choiseul-Gouffier: La France en Orient sous Louis XVI* (Paris: Alphonse Picard, 1887), 239–256.

19. See Édouard de Marcère, *Une ambassade à Constantinople: La politique orientale de la Révolution française* (Paris: F. Alcan, 1927); Amaury Faivre d'Arcier, *Les oubliés de la liberté: Négociants, consuls et missionnaires français au Levant pendant la Révolution, 1784–1798* (Brussels: Peter Lang, 2007); Pascal Firges, *French Revolutionaries in the Ottoman Empire: Political Culture, Diplomacy, and the Limits of Universal Revolution, 1792–1798* (Oxford: Oxford University Press, 2017).

20. Octave Teissier, *La chambre de commerce de Marseille: Son origine—sa mission* (Marseille: Barlatier et Barthelet, 1892), 325–336.

21. Firges, *French Revolutionaries in the Ottoman Empire*, 178–190. For a description of sailors' mutinies in the Mediterranean, see William S. Cormack, *Revolution and Political Conflict in the French Navy, 1789–1794* (Cambridge: Cambridge University Press, 2002), 163–169.

22. Firges, *French Revolutionaries in the Ottoman Empire*.

23. *Moniteur*, 15 October 1792. On Guffroy, see Linton, *Choosing Terror*, 259n; J. M. Thompson, *Robespierre: From the Death of Louis XVI to the Death of Robespierre* (New York: H. Fertig, 1968), 231–232.

24. On Hénin, see Frédéric Hitzel, "Étienne-Félix Hénin: Un Jacobin à Constantinople," *Anatolia moderna* 1 (1991): 35–46.

25. On Descorches, see Rachida Tlili Sellaouti, "The Republic and the Muslim World: For a Regenerated Mediterranean System," in Alan Forrest and Matthias Middell (eds), *The Routledge Companion to the French Revolution in World History* (London: Routledge, 2015), 97–116.

26. See Gerard Groc, "Propagande révolutionnaire et presse française à Constantinople à la fin du XVIIIe siècle," in Daniel Panzac (ed), *Histoire économique et sociale de l'Empire ottoman et de la Turquie* (Paris: Peeters, 1995), 795–812.

27. *AP*, 23 January 1793 (57:633).

28. Maximilien Robespierre, *Oeuvres de Maximilien Robespierre:* vol. 5, *Les journaux*, ed. Gustave Laurent (Paris: Impr. Louis-Jean, 1961), 300. On the newspaper, see Hervé Leuwers, *Robespierre* (Paris: Fayard, 2014), chap. 5.

29. See Marisa Linton, "Friends, Enemies, and the Role of the Individual," in McPhee (ed), *A Companion to the French Revolution*, 263–303; Timothy Tackett, "Conspiracy Obsession in a Time of Revolution: French Elites and the Origins of the Terror, 1789–1792," *American Historical Review* 105.3 (2000): 691–713.

30. *Moniteur*, 9 October 1793.

31. Onnik Jamgocyan, "La Révolution française vue et vécue de Constantinople (1789–1795)," *Annales historiques de la Révolution française* 282 (1990): 462.

32. Aulard, *La société des Jacobins*, 9 October 1793 (5:451).

33. *Moniteur*, 15 October 1793.

34. *Moniteur*, 15 October 1793.

35. *Moniteur*, 15 October 1793. My emphasis.

36. J. L. Matharan discusses the notion of "suspect" in "Suspects/soupçon/suspicion: La designation des ennemis (été 1793–an III)," in *Dictionnaire des usages socio-politiques* (Paris: ENS Éditions, 1999), 4:167–185; Jacques Guilhaumou, "Fragments of a Discourse of Denunciation (1789–1794)," in Keith M. Baker (ed), *The French Revolution and the Creation of Modern Political Culture:* vol. 4, *The Terror* (Oxford: Pergamon Press, 1994), 139–156.

37. *Moniteur*, 15 October 1793.

38. Maximilien Robespierre, *Oeuvres de Maximilien Robespierre:* vol. 10, *Discours* (Paris: Presses Universitaires de France, 1967), 174.

39. Robespierre, *Oeuvres*, 10:172–173.

40. Patrice Gueniffey, "Robespierre," in François Furet and Mona Ozouf (eds), *A Critical Dictionary of the French Revolution*, trans. Arthur Goldhammer (Cambridge, MA: Harvard University Press, 1989), 299.

41. *Journal républicain de Marseille*, 17 January 1794.

42. *Moniteur*, 25 November 1793. There are dozens of similar statements in the *Moniteur* at this time; the following represent only a selection.

43. *Moniteur*, 23 November 1793.

44. *Moniteur*, 23 November 1793.

45. "Une résistance raisonnée et des lumières nouvelles": *Moniteur*, 2 Germinal Year 2 (22 March 1794).

46. *Moniteur*, 26 March 1794.

47. *Moniteur*, 10 April 1794.

48. *Moniteur*, 28 April 1794.

49. *Moniteur*, 7 May 1794.

50. *Moniteur*, 21 April 1794.

51. *Moniteur*, 7 May 1794.

52. *Moniteur*, 11 June 1794.

53. *Moniteur*, 20 May 1794.

54. *Moniteur*, 16 June 1794.

55. *Moniteur*, 1 July 1794.

56. *Moniteur*, 19 June 1794. See Tuncay Zorlu, *Innovation and Empire in Turkey: Sultan Selim III and the Modernisation of the Ottoman Navy* (London: I. B. Tauris, 2011).

57. *La décade philosophique*, 29 May 1794.

58. Jonathan P. Ribner, *Broken Tablets: The Cult of the Law in French Art from David to Delacroix* (Berkeley: University of California Press, 1993).

59. Mona Ozouf concluded that the festival was a hollow pretense of social unity based on a "huge lie": *Festivals and the French Revolution*, 106–118. Jonathan Smyth has argued that it was neither a piece of political theater nor the expression of devout religious sentiment, but an attempt to launch a new republican morality: Jonathan Smyth, *Robespierre and the Festival of the Supreme Being: The Search for a Republican Morality* (Manchester: Manchester University Press, 2016).

60. *Moniteur*, 8 May 1794.

61. Frank Tallett, "Robespierre and Religion," in Colin Haydon and William Doyle (eds), *Robespierre* (Cambridge: Cambridge University Press, 2006), 102.

62. Robespierre, *Oeuvres*, 10:451.

63. See Michaël Culoma, *La religion civile de Rousseau à Robespierre* (Paris: Harmattan, 2010).

64. Robespierre, *Oeuvres,* 10:453.

65. Robespierre, *Oeuvres,* 10:457.

66. Filippo Buonarotti, "Observations sur Maximilien Robespierre," reprinted in *La fraternité: Journal mensuel* 2 (1842): 88.

67. Bertrand Barère, *Mémoires* (Paris: Labitte, 1842), 2:202.

68. Joachim Vilate, *Les mystères de la Mère de Dieu, dévoilés: Troisième volume des causes secrètes de la Révolution du 9 au 10 thermidor* (Paris, 1795), 64.

69. Émilie Cadio, "Le Comité de sûreté générale (1792–1795)," *La Révolution française* 3 (2012), http://lrf.revues.org/676.

70. Marisa Linton, *Choosing Terror: Virtue, Friendship, and Authenticity in the French Revolution* (Oxford: Oxford University Press, 2015).

71. The Law of Prairial is the subject of a long-standing debate that it is not directly in the interest of this book to engage. It has been seen as both a betrayal and a mirror image of the festival it followed so closely; as the inevitable expression of a fixed Jacobin ideology; as a response to threats of assassination, war, and counterrevolution; or as an attempt to end terror with terror. It may well have had aspects of all of these. See Dan Edelstein, "The Law of 22 Prairial: Introduction," *Telos* 141 (2007): 82–91.

72. Marc-Antoine Baudot, *Notes historiques sur la Convention nationale, le Directoire, l'Empire et l'exil des votants* (Paris: L. Cerf, 1893), 5.

73. Louis Thomas Hébert Lavicomterie de Saint Samson, *Les crimes des empereurs turcs, depuis Osman I, jusqu'à Selim IV,* (Paris: Bureau des Revolutions de Paris, 1795), x.

74. Louis-Sébastien Mercier, *Le nouveau Paris* (Paris: Fuchs, C. Pougens & C. F. Cramer, 1797), 4:146–147.

75. Philarète Chasles, *Oeuvres* (Paris: G. Charpentier, 1876), 1:47. For Vadier, see Gilles Dussert, *Vadier: Le grand inquisiteur, 1736–1828* (Paris: Impr. nationale, 1989).

76. Marc Vadier, *Rapport et projet de décret, présentés à la Convention Nationale, au nom des comités de sûreté générale et de salut public* (Paris: Imprimerie Nationale, 1794), 2. See Albert Mathiez, "Robespierre et le procès de Catherine Théot," *Annales historiques de la Révolution française* 6 (1929): 392–339; Clarke Garrett, "Popular Piety in the French Revolution: Catherine Théot," *Catholic Historical Review* 60.2 (1974): 215–232.

77. *Moniteur,* 29 Prairial Year 2 (17 June 1794).

78. Vadier, *Rapport,* 3.

79. Vadier, *Rapport,* 4.

80. Chasles, *Oeuvres,* 1:49.

81. Pierra Serna (ed), *La politique du rire: Satires, caricatures et blasphèmes XVIe–XXIe siècle* (Ceyzérieu: Champ Vallon, 2015).

82. *Moniteur*, 11 Thermidor Year 2 (29 July 1794).

83. Gabriel-Jérôme Sénart, *Mémoires de Sénart secrétaire du comité de sureté générale; ou, Révélations puisées dans les cartons des comités de salut public et de sureté générale* (Paris: Baudouin, 1824), 182.

84. Sénart, *Mémoires de Sénart*, 186.

85. Robespierre, *Oeuvres*, 10:578–580; René Levasseur, *Mémoires de Levasseur de la Sarthe* (Paris: Baudouin, 1830), 134.

86. Michel Eude, "Points de vue sur l'affaire Catherine Théot," *Annales historiques de la Révolution française* 41 (1969): 607.

87. Olympe de Gouges, *Réponse à la justification de Maximilien Robespierre, adressée à Jérôme Pétion* (n.p., 1792), 6.

88. *Les Nantais à tous les départements de la République (proclamation)* (Halles de la Grenette [Lyon]: Impr. d'Aimé Vatar-Delaroche, 1793), 3.

89. *AP*, 12 April 1793 (41:637).

90. Maurice Favone, *Dans le sillage de Maximilien Robespierre: Joachim Vilate* (Paris: Marcel Rivière, 1938).

91. Joachim Vilate, *Causes secrètes de la Révolution du 9 au 10 thermidor* (n.p., 1794), 4.

92. Vilate, *Causes secretes*, 10.

93. See Howard Brown and Judith Miller, "New Paths from the Terror to the Empire: A Historiographical Introduction," in Howard Brown and Judith Miller (eds), *Taking Liberties: Problems of a New Order from the French Revolution to Napoleon* (Manchester: Manchester University Press, 2002), 1–19.

94. E. B. Courtois, *Rapport fait au nom de la commission chargée de l'examen des papiers trouvés chez Robespierre et ses complices* (Paris: Imprimerie Nationale des Lois, 1795), 70.

95. François-Xavier Lanthenas, *Mesures de salut public contre les obstacles intérieurs à l'établissement de la République* (Paris: Chez l'auteur et chez les marchands de nouveauté, 1794), 8.

96. F. V. Aigoin, *Discours prononcé par F. V. Aigoin, dans la séance des Jacobins du 5 vendémiaire, l'an trois de la République française* (Paris: Impr. des Sans-Culottes, 1794), 3–4.

97. Louis-Marie-Stanislas Fréron, *Mémoire historique sur la réaction royale et sur les massacres du Midi* (Paris: Marchant, 1795), 25.

98. *Procès criminel des membres du Comité révolutionnaire de Nantes et du ci-devant Représentant du peuple Carrier, instruit par le Tribunal révolutionnaire* (Paris:

La Citoyenne Toubon, 1794), 65–66. Lalloué apparently also claimed to be Robespierre's nephew: *Moniteur*, 14 Frimaire Year 3 (4 December 1794).

99. Edmond Lecesne, *Arras sous la Révolution* (Arras: Sueur-Charruey, 1883), 3:201. See Ronen Steinberg, "Terror on Trial: Accountability, Transitional Justice, and the Affaire Le Bon in Thermidorian France," *French Historical Studies* 39.3 (2016): 419–444.

100. Marcel David, *Fraternité et Révolution française, 1789–1799* (Paris: Aubier, 1987), 203.

101. Joseph-Marie Lequinio de Kerblay, *La guerre de la Vendée et des chouans* (Paris: Pougin, 1794), 188.

102. *Vies secrètes et politiques de Couthon, Saint-Just, Robespierre jeune, complices du tyran Robespierre, et assassins de la République* (Paris: Prévost, 1794), cited in Baczko, *Ending the Terror*, 13.

103. John V. Tolam, "European Accounts of Muhammad's Life," in Jonathan E. Brockopp (ed), *The Cambridge Companion to Muhammad* (Cambridge: Cambridge University Press, 2010), 237.

104. Several of the pamphlets denouncing the remaining Jacobins in obviously phallic terms as "Robespierre's tail" used epigraphs from Voltaire's play: Jean Claude Hippolyte Méhée de la Touche, *La queue de Robespierre* (Paris: Imprimerie de Rougyff, 1794); *Le secret des Jacobins* (Imprimerie de Guffroi, 1794); Joseph Chardon, *Les crimes des Jacobins à Lyon, depuis 1792, jusqu'au 9 thermidor, an 2* (Lyon: Chez les Marchands de Nouveautés, 1801). For a brilliant discussion of these metaphors, see Antoine de Baecque, *Glory and Terror: Seven Deaths under the French Revolution*, trans. Charlotte Mandell (London: Routledge, 2003), 160–174.

105. Lavicomterie de Saint Samson, *Les crimes des empereurs turcs*, x.

106. Lavicomterie de Saint Samson, *Les crimes des empereurs turcs*, ix.

107. Lavicomterie de Saint Samson, *Les crimes des empereurs turcs*, xii.

108. Lavicomterie de Saint Samson, *Les crimes des empereurs turcs*, xiii.

109. Liévin-Bonaventure Proyart, *La vie et les crimes de Robespierre, surnommé le tyran: Depuis sa naissance jusqu'à sa mort; Ouvrage dédié à ceux qui commandent et à ceux qui obéissent* (Augsburg: Chez Tous les Libraires, 1795), 313.

110. Peter McPhee, *Robespierre: A Revolutionary Life* (New Haven, CT: Yale University Press, 2012), xvi.

10. Bonaparte's Burka

1. Napoléon Bonaparte, *Napoléon inconnu: Papiers inédits (1786–1793)*, ed. Frédéric Masson and Guido Biagi (Paris: P. Ollendorff, 1895), 2:17. See

Andrew Martin, "The Mask of the Prophet: Napoleon, Borges, Verne," *Comparative Literature* 40.4 (1988): 318–334.

2. Bonaparte, *Napoléon inconnu*, 2:19. Patrice Gueniffey parses the meaning of this story rather prosaically as "the fascination with the end of a figure who chooses, by means of a final deception, to live in men's memories rather than to continue an earthly existence without glory": *Bonaparte 1769–1802*, trans. Steven Rendall (Cambridge, MA: Harvard University Press, 2015), 393.

3. See Juan Cole's chapter on "Ali Bonaparte" in *Napoleon's Egypt: Invading the Middle East* (Houndmills: Palgrave Macmillan, 2007), 123–142.

4. Martyn Lyons, *France under the Directory* (Cambridge: Cambridge University Press, 1975), 110.

5. Howard Brown, "The Search for Stability," in Howard Brown and Judith Miller (eds), *Taking Liberties: Problems of a New Order from the French Revolution to Napoleon* (Manchester: Manchester University Press, 2002), 20–50.

6. "Voilà donc une digue où la toute-puissance / Voit briser le torrent de ses vastes progrès! / Liberté qui nous fuis, tu ne fuis point Byzance; / Tu planes sur ses minarets!" André Chénier, *Oeuvres complètes* (Paris: Gallimard, 1958), 183.

7. Edward Said, *Orientalism* (New York: Random House, 1978), 82.

8. Gueniffey, *Bonaparte*, 438, citing François Charles-Roux, *Bonaparte, gouverneur d'Égypte* (Paris: Plon, 1936), 76.

9. See Christian Cherfils, *Bonaparte et l'Islam d'après les documents français et arabes* (Paris: A. Pedone, 1914); Ahmed Youssef, *Bonaparte et Mahomet: Le conquérant conquis* (Monaco: Rocher, 2003).

10. Cole, *Napoleon's Egypt*, 217–218.

11. Mentioned in Gueniffey, *Bonaparte*, 19. Gueniffey identifies Giovanni (Francesco's father) as the first to settle in Corsica, but Jean Defranceschi suggested to the contrary that "personne ne peut dire aujourd'hui à quel moment précis les ancêtres de Napoléon s'installèrent en Corse." Jean Defranceschi, *La jeunesse de Napoléon: Les dessous de l'histoire* (Paris: Lettrage, 2001), 46.

12. This head has a contested genealogy, which may suggest either a head severed in battle or a claim of "Saracen" lineage.

13. A decree of 1778 declared that "il ne soit fait aucune distinction entre les familles nobles de notre pays de Provence, sous prétexte de descendance ou alliance avec des juifs, sarrasins, mahométans, et autres infidèles; et qu'en conséquence nos sujets nobles dudit pays soient admis, sans distinction, dans nos ordres, chapitres, corps et communautés nobles." See Jocelyne Dakhlia, "Musulmans en France et en Grande-Bretagne à l'époque moderne: Exemplaires et invisibles," in Jocelyne Dakhlia and Bernard Vincent (eds), *Les*

Musulmans dans l'histoire de l'Europe: vol. 1, *Une intégration invisible* (Paris: Albin Michel, 2011), 471–522.

14. Michel Vergé-Franceschi, *Napoléon, une enfance corse* (Paris: Larousse, 2009), 154.

15. Frank McLynn, *Napoleon: A Biography* (London: Jonathan Cape, 1997), 265.

16. "Comme la Corse fut autrefois peuplée par les Sémites d'Afrique, Arabes, Carthaginois ou Maures, Maranes, disent les Espagnols, il semble appartenir à ceux-ci plus qu'aux Italiens." Jules Michelet, *Histoire du XIXe siècle* (Paris: Michel Lévy, 1875), 3:421.

17. Florence Gauthier, *Triomphe et mort de la révolution des droits de l'homme et du citoyen: 1789–1795–1802* (Paris: Syllepse, 2014), 189–196, 337–338. Gauthier points out the "préjugés tenaces, qui refusent d'admetter aujourd'hui, que la Corse alors conquise, fut une colonie": "La Révolution française et le problème colonial: Le cas Robespierre," *Annales historiques de la Révolution française* 288.1 (1992): 170.

18. Jean Defranceschi, *La Corse française: 30 novembre 1789–15 juin 1794* (Paris: Société des études robespierristes, 1980), 9.

19. Bonaparte, *Napoléon inconnu,* 1:144.

20. Bonaparte, *Napoléon inconnu,* 1:186.

21. Bonaparte, *Napoléon inconnu,* 1:146.

22. Bonaparte, *Napoléon inconnu,* 1:441.

23. Bonaparte, *Napoléon inconnu,* 1:435.

24. Bonaparte, *Napoléon inconnu,* 1:457–458.

25. Bonaparte, *Napoléon inconnu,* 2:2.

26. Bonaparte, *Napoléon inconnu,* 1:441.

27. Bonaparte, *Napoléon inconnu,* 2:17. This was his own invention: Marigny claimed the sect believed only in metempsychosis.

28. Bonaparte, *Napoléon inconnu,* 2:64.

29. Bonaparte, *Napoléon inconnu,* 2:34–35.

30. For example, Khalid Sheldrake, who "took pride in European converts to Islam, including Napoleon Bonaparte's alleged conversion": see Umar Ryad, "Salafiyya, Ahmadiyya, and European Converts to Islam in the Interwar Period," in Umar Ryad et al. (eds), *Muslims in Interwar Europe: A Transcultural Historical Perspective* (Leiden: Brill, 2016), 70. See also Cole, *Napoleon's Egypt,* 128–129.

31. Ernest d'Hauterive, "Lettres de jeunesse de Bonaparte (1789–1792)," *Revue des deux mondes,* 15 December 1931, 767–794.

32. Alpaugh, *Non-violence and the French Revolution,* 201–203.

33. Suzanne Desan, *Reclaiming the Sacred: Lay Religion and Popular Politics in Revolutionary France* (Ithaca: Cornell University Press, 1990).

34. *Moniteur*, 3 Nivôse Year 3 (23 December 1794).

35. Henri Grégoire, *Rapport sur les encouragements, récompenses et pensions à accorder aux savants, aux gens de lettres et aux artistes* (Paris: Imprimerie Nationale, 1794).

36. Louis-Sébastien Mercier, *Le nouveau Paris* (Paris: Fuchs, C. Pougens & C. F. Cramer, 1797), 6:234–235.

37. *Paris pendant l'année 1797*, 15 June 1797.

38. *Semaines critiques; ou, Gestes de l'an cinq*, 3:13. The title may be understood as "Critical Weekly" or "Critical Weeks." This dialogue is addressed to the author as "Semainier," or "Weekly writer."

39. *Semaines critiques*, 3:16.

40. *Semaines critiques*, 3:17.

41. *Mercure britannique*, 10 March 1799.

42. *Le républicain du nord*, 26 June 1796; Lavicomterie de Saint Samson, *Les crimes des empereurs turcs*, 598.

43. *Journal de Paris*, 23 May 1795.

44. Cited in Albert Mathiez, *La théophilanthropie et le culte décadaire, 1796–1801: Essai sur l'histoire religieuse de la Révolution* (Paris: Félix Alcan, 1904), 73–74.

45. Cited in Mathiez, *La théophilanthropie et le culte décadaire*, 74.

46. E. Gachon, *Histoire de la théophilanthropie* (Paris: Cherbuliez, 1870), 12.

47. Mathiez, *La théophilanthropie et le culte décadaire*; Jean-Pierre Chantin, "Les adeptes de la théophilanthropie," *Rives nord-méditerranéennes* 14 (2003): 63–73.

48. *Moniteur*, 12 Floréal Year 3 (1 May 1795).

49. *Moniteur*, 12 Floréal Year 3 (1 May 1795).

50. *Moniteur*, 12 Floréal Year 3 (1 May 1795).

51. Stephen Clay, "Le massacre du fort Saint-Jean: Un épisode de la Terreur blanche à Marseille," in Michel Vovelle (ed), *Le tournant de l'an III: Réaction et terreur blanche dans la France révolutionnaire* (Paris: Éd. CTHS, 1997), 579–583.

52. *Moniteur*, 12 Floréal Year 3 (1 May 1795).

53. AN CCC Tunis 32 (1793), 13 Messidor Year 2.

54. AN AF III 74.

55. Devoize to Minister of External Relations, 12 Prairial Year 2, AN, CCC Tunis 32 (1793). In Istanbul, the new envoy, Verninac de St. Maur, insisted he should be addressed as "Citizen"; the grand vizier refused, but Mouradgea

d'Ohsson, now officially in the service of France, encouraged the vizier to address the envoy in customary fashion, while instructing the Ottoman dragoman to translate it as "citoyen." However, Verninac claimed that the grand vizier pronounced it in French, and that the word "has since spread, and the Turkish language is surprised to find itself enriched with this expression." Letter from Verninac to Delacroix, cited in Adrien Fleury, *Soldats ambassadeurs sous le Directoire, an IV et VIII* (Paris: Plon-Nourrit, 1906), 1:34.

56. Eugène Plantet, *Correspondance des beys de Tunis et des consuls de France avec la cour: 1577–1830* (Paris: F. Alcan, 1899), 238.

57. AN, CCC Tunis 32 (1793).

58. Extract of a report on the church of the fondouck in Tunis by Cit[izen] Herculais, AN, AF III 74.

59. AN, CCC Tunis 33 (1793–1795).

60. Jean Michel Venture de Paradis, *Tunis et Alger au XVIIIe siècle*, ed. Joseph Cuoq (Paris: Sindbad, 1983), 81–82.

61. Extract of a letter from citizen Herculais in Algiers, 27 Messidor Year 4, AN, AF III 74.

62. Extract of a letter from citizen Guys, agent of external relations in Marseille, 21 Floréal Year 4, AN, AF III 74.

63. AN, CCC Tunis 33 (1793–1795).

64. Hassuna D'Ghies, "A Letter Addressed to James Scarlett" [1822], British Library.

65. Friedrich Hornemann et al., *The Journal of Frederick Horneman's Travels: From Cairo to Mourzouk, the Capital of the Kingdom of Fezzan, in Africa* (London: G. and W. Nicol, 1802), xix.

66. Rifā'ah Rāfi' al-Ṭahṭāwī and Daniel L. Newman, *An Imam in Paris: Account of a Stay in France by an Egyptian Cleric (1826–1831)* (London: Saqi, 2004), 206.

67. Albert Hourani, *Arabic Thought in the Liberal Age, 1798–1939* (London: Oxford University Press, 1962), 73.

68. See Ian Coller, "African Liberalism in the Age of Empire? Hassuna D'Ghies and Liberal Constitutionalism in North Africa," *Modern Intellectual History* 12 (2015): 1–25.

69. See Ian Coller, "Egypt in the French Revolution," in Desan, Hunt, and Nelson (eds). *French Revolution in Global Perspective*, 115–131.

70. "Cela est feaux [sic]. . . . Quelle folie! . . . Aux petites maisons." Cited in Clément de la Jonquière, *L'expédition d'Égypte, 1798–1801* (Paris: H. Charles-Lavauzelle, 1899–1907), 1:167.

71. Carl Ludwig Lokke, "Pourquoi Talleyrand ne fut pas envoyé a Constanti-nople," *Annales historiques de la Révolution française* 56 (1933): 153–159.

72. Philip Dwyer, *Napoleon: The Path to Power 1769–1799* (New Haven, CT: Yale University Press, 2008).

73. Michael Broers observes that Napoleon's later comments "overestimated his tolerance of what he considered backward and obscurantist"; he soon turned on an Islam that "did not match the vision he had acquired of it from Voltaire." If this credits Voltaire too particularly, it demonstrates the shock of collision between an imagined and a real Islam. Michael Broers, *Napoleon: Soldier of Destiny* (New York: Pegasus Books, 2015), 347.

Epilogue: 1799

1. Archives départementales Yvelines, 1L 428.

2. Letter from commissaire du pouvoir executif près l'Administration du Départment de Seine-et-Marne, to minister of police, 23 Ventôse Year 7, AN, F7 7415.

3. AN, F7 7415, AF IV 1687. The worst treatment was reserved for 18 Algerian Jews who had settled in Marseille, and were thrown into the dungeons of the Fort Saint-Nicolas, and they remained there six months later, despite the release of the French in Algiers.

4. Jean Boutier, "Les 'lettres de créances' du corsaire Ripaud: Un 'club jacobin' à Srirangapatnam (Inde), mai–juin 1797," *Les Indes savantes* (2005), halshs-00007971.

5. *Official Documents, Relative to the Negotiations Carried On by Tippoo Sultaun, with the French Nation, and Other Foreign States, for Purposes Hostile to the British Nation* ([London]: Honorable Company's Press, 1799), 180.

6. *Official Documents, Relative to the Negotiations Carried On by Tippoo Sultaun,* 192.

7. *Official Documents, Relative to the Negotiations Carried On by Tippoo Sultaun,* 189–190.

8. *Official Documents, Relative to the Negotiations Carried On by Tippoo Sultaun,* 18.

9. Richard Wellesley, *The Despatches, Minutes, and Correspondence of the Marquess of Wellesley, K. G., during His Administration in India,* ed. Montgomery Martin (London: J. Murray, 1836), 1:416.

10. Thomas Cockburn (1799), quoted in Peter Auber, *Rise and Progress of the British Power in India* (London: W. H. Allen, 1837), 2:192.

11. Kate Brittlebank, "Islamic Responses to the Fall of Srirangapattana and the Death of Tipu Sultan (1799)," *South Asia: Journal of South Asian Studies* 22 (1999): 79–86.

12. Alexis de Tocqueville, *The Old Regime and the Revolution*, trans. Alan S. Kahan (Chicago: University of Chicago Press, 1998), 101.

13. W. E. B. du Bois, "Africa and the French Revolution," *Freedomways* 1 (1961): 136.

Bibliography

Archives

Archives nationales (AN), Paris

AE B I Correspondance consulaire

AE B III Consulats: mémoires et documents

AF II Conseil exécutif provisoire et Convention: Comité de salut public (1789–1792)

AF III Directoire exécutif (an IV–an VIII)

AF IV Secrétairerie d'État impériale (an VIII–1815)

Correspondance consulaire et commerciale (CCC) Alep

Correspondance consulaire et commerciale (CCC) Alger

Correspondance consulaire et commerciale (CCC) Constantinople

Correspondance consulaire et commerciale (CCC) Seyde

Correspondance consulaire et commerciale (CCC) Smyrne

Correspondance consulaire et commerciale (CCC) Tripoli de Barbarie

Correspondance consulaire et commerciale (CCC) Tripoli de Syrie

Correspondance consulaire et commerciale (CCC) Tunis

F7 Police Générale

F17 Instruction Publique

Y Châtelet de Paris et prévôté d'Ile-de-France

Archives nationales d'Outre Mer (Aix-en-Provence)

COL E 9

Archives diplomatiques (AMAE) (Nantes)

Consulat d'Alger

Correspondance consulaire (CC) Alger

166 PO B 95 Papiers Ruffin

Archives diplomatiques (AMAE) (La Courneuve)

Contrôle des étrangers au XVIIIe siècle, 1771–1791

CP Turquie

Dossiers Personnel 1er Série

MD Afrique

MD Algérie

MD Asie 20

MD Turquie

Archives départementales, Yvelines

1L 428 Musulmans 1799

Archives municipales, Marseille

2 I 173 Étrangers 1793

DD 55 Cimetière des Turcs et forçats

DD 138 Cimetières

FF 192 Police générale. Étrangers, passeports, 1498–1785

British Library, London

India Office IOR/F/4/35/898

Cornell University Library, Ithaca, NY

Lafayette Papers

Newspapers

Les actes des apôtres

L'ami du roi

L'ami du roi, des François, de l'ordre et sur-tout de la vérité

Annales patriotiques et littéraires

L'année littéraire; ou, Suite des lettres sur quelques écrits

The Annual Register; or, a View of the History, Politics and Literature, for the Year 1787

Assemblée nationale permanente; ou, Journal logographique

Bibliothèque de l'homme public

La bouche de fer

Chronique de Paris

La chronique du mois; ou, Les cahiers patriotiques

Correspondance littéraire secrete

Correspondance patriotique

Correspondance secrète, politique et littéraire

Courier de l'Europe

Courier français

Courrier de Lyon

Courrier de Provence

La décade philosophique

L'espion de la Révolution française

L'esprit des journaux, francais et etrangers

Feuille du salut public

La feuille villageoise

La fraternité: Journal mensuel

Gazette de Paris

Gazette des cours de l'Europe: Le royaliste, ami de l'humanité

Gazette des Pays Bas

Gazette nationale; ou, Le moniteur universel

Gazette universelle; ou, Papier-nouvelles de tous les pays et de tous les jours

Journal de la cour et de la ville

Journal de l'Assemblée nationale; ou, Journal logographique

Journal de l'instruction publique

Journal de Paris

Journal des clubs ou sociétés patriotiques

Journal des débats et de la correspondance de la Société des Jacobins

Journal des débats et des décrets

Journal des états généraux, convoqués par Louis XVI, le 27 avril 1789

Journal général de la guerre

Journal général de l'Europe

Journal historique et politique de Genève

Journal politique des empires

Journal politique-national

Journal politique; ou, Gazette des gazettes

Journal républicain de Marseille

Mémoires secrets pour servir à l'histoire de la république des lettres en France

Mercure britannique

Mercure de France

Mercure universel

Monthly Review

Paris pendant l'année 1797

Le patriote français

Le républicain du nord

Les révolutions de France et de Brabant

Révolutions de Paris

Révolutions de Versailles et de Paris, dédiées aux dames françoises

La rocambole; ou, Journal des honnêtes gens

Les sabats jacobites

Semaines critiques; ou, Gestes de l'an cinq

Unpublished Primary Sources

Hardy, S.-P. "Mes loisirs; ou, Journal d'evenemens tels qu'ils parviennent à ma connoissance." 1764–1789. Vol. 7, 1787–1788. Bibliothèque nationale de France.

Hennin correspondence, Bibliothèque de l'Académie, Paris.

Published Primary Sources

Abū Tālib Khān, Mirza. *The Travels of Mirza Abu Taleb Khan in Asia, Africa, and Europe during the Years 1799, 1800, 1801, 1802, and 1803.* Trans. Charles Stewart. London: R. Watts, 1814. 2v.

Acta in consistorio secreto a sanctissimo domino nostro Pio Papa Sexto. Rome: Camerae Apostolicae, 1791.

Ah! Ah! Conférence sur les affaires du temps, entre un royaliste et un parlementaire. London, 1788.

Aigoin, F. V. *Discours prononcé par F. V. Aigoin, dans la séance des Jacobins du 5 vendémiaire, l'an trois de la République française.* Paris: Impr. des Sans-Culottes, 1794.

Almanach littéraire; ou, Étrennes d'Apollon pour l'année 1791.

Almanach statistique de Sens et du Département de l'Yonne. Sens, 1857.

L'ami de la religion et de la patrie, adresse à MM. les électeurs du département de la Seine Inférieure. Paris: Crapart, 1791.

Andrieux, François Guillaume Jean Stanislas. *Épitre au pape.* Paris: Fiévée, 1791.

Annales de la religion; ou, Mémoires pour servir a l'histoire du dix-huitième siècle. Paris: Imprimerie-Librairie Chrétienne, 1803.

Archives parlementaires de 1787 à 1860: Recueil complet des débats législatifs et politiques des Chambres françaises, imprimé par ordre du Corps législatif. 1st series. Ed. Jérôme Mavidal and Émile Laurent. Paris: P. Dupont/CNRS, 1867–1990. 96v.

Aulard, François-Alphonse (ed). *Recueil des actes du Comité de salut public avec la correspondance officielle des représentants en mission et le registre du Conseil exécutif provisoire.* Paris: Impr. nationale, 1889–1910. 19v.

Aulard, François-Alphonse (ed). *La société des Jacobins: Recueil de documents pour l'histoire du Club des Jacobins de Paris.* Paris: Jouaust-Noblet-Quantin, 1889–1897. 6v.

Barère, Bertrand. *Mémoires.* Paris: Labitte, 1842–1844. 4v.

Barruel, Augustin. *Collection ecclésiastique; ou, Recueil complet des ouvrages faits depuis l'ouverture des États-généraux.* Paris: Crapart, 1791–1793. 14v.

Barthélemy, Jean-Jacques. *Voyage du jeune Anacharsis en Grèce.* Paris, 1788.

Baudot, Marc-Antoine. *Notes historiques sur la Convention nationale, le Directoire, l'Empire et l'exil des votants.* Paris: L. Cerf, 1893.

Behenam, Joseph. *Discours prononcé dans l'église de Saint-Jacques et des Saints-Innocents, le dimanche 16 janvier 1791, à la prestation du serment des ecclésiastiques, en présence de la députation du Conseil général de la commune.* N.p., 1791.

Bertrand de Molleville, Antoine François. *Histoire de la Révolution de France pendant les dernières années du règne de Louis XVI.* Paris, 1801–1803. 14v.

Bertrand de Molleville, Antoine François. *Mémoires secrets pour servir à l'histoire de la dernière année du règne de Louis XVI, roi de France.* London: Strahan and Cadell, 1797. 3v.

Blanc-Gilli, Mathieu. *Réveil d'alarme d'un député de Marseille, aux bons citoyens de Paris.* Paris: Imprimerie de Crapart, 1792.

Boissy D'Anglas, François Antoine de. *Essai sur les fêtes nationales, suivi de quelques idées sur les arts et sur la nécessité de les encourager, adressé à la convention nationale.* Paris: Imprimerie Polyglotte, 1793.

Bonaparte, Napoléon. *Napoléon inconnu: Papiers inédits (1786–1793).* Ed. Frédéric Masson and Guido Biagi. Paris: P. Ollendorff, 1895. 2v.

Boullier, Isidore. *Mémoires ecclésiastiques concernant la ville de Laval et ses environs, diocèse du Mans, pendant la révolution de 1789 à 1802.* Laval: H. Godbert, 1846.

[Brion de la Tour, Louis]. *Du partage de la peau de l'ours; ou, lettres à l'auteur du Rêve politique sur le partage de l'empire ottoman, et à l'auteur des Considérations sur la guerre actuelle des turcs.* Paris: Cussac, 1788.

Buchez, Philippe-Joseph-Benjamin, and Prosper Charles Roux. *Histoire parlementaire de la révolution française; ou, Journal des assemblées nationales, depuis 1789 jusqu'en 1815.* Paris: Paulin, 1834–1838. 40v.

Burke, Edmund. *Revolutionary Writings: Reflections on the Revolution in France and the First Letter on a Regicide Peace.* Cambridge: Cambridge University Press, 2014.

[Caraccioli, Louis-Antoine]. *Anecdotes piquantes relatives aux États généraux.* N.p., 1789.

Caraccioli, Louis-Antoine. *Lettres d'un Indien à Paris, à son ami Glazir, sur les moeurs françoises, et sur les bizarreries du tems.* Amsterdam [Paris?]: Briand, 1789. 2v.

[Caraccioli, Louis-Antoine]. *La petite Lutèce devenue grande fille.* Paris: Chez Cuchet, Libraire, 1790. 2v.

Carnot, Hippolyte Lazare. *Mémoires sur Carnot par son fils.* Paris: Pagnerre, 1863.

Carra, Jean-Louis. *L'orateur des États généraux pour 1789.* N.p., 1789.

Cart, Jean-Jacques. *Lettres de Jean-Jacques Cart à Bernard Demuralt, trésorier du pays de Vaud, sur le droit public de ce pays, et sur les événemens actuels.* Paris: Chez les Directeurs de l'Imprimerie du Cercle Social, 1793.

Cassius, Isaac Jean Joseph. *Sermon patriotique prêché dans l'Église de S. Germain-des-Prés, le dimanche de quasimodo, 11 avril 1790.* Paris: Le Clère, 1790.

Castellan, Antoine Laurent. *Lettres sur la Grece, l'Hellespont et Constantinople, faisant suite aux lettres sur la morée.* Paris: H. Agasse, 1811.

Castellane, Boniface Louis André. *Opinion de M. le comte de Castellane, du 23, sur sa motion de la veille.* Versailles: Baudouin, 1789.

Chardon, Joseph. *Les crimes des Jacobins à Lyon, depuis 1792, jusqu'au 9 thermidor, an 2.* Lyon: Chez les Marchands de Nouveautés, 1801.

Chasles, Philarète. *Oeuvres.* Paris: G. Charpentier, 1876. 2v.

Chassaignon, Jean-Marie. *Les nudités; ou, Les crimes du peuple.* N.p., 1792.

Chénier, André. *Oeuvres complètes.* Paris: Gallimard, 1958.

Chénier, Louis de. *Révolutions de l'Empire ottoman.* Paris, 1789.

Clermont-Tonnerre, Stanislas Marie Adelaïde. *Opinion de M. le comte Stanislas de Clermont-Tonnerre, député de Paris: le 23 décembre 1789.* Paris: Baudouin, 1789.

Cloots, Jean-Baptiste [Anacharsis]. *La certitude des preuves du Mahométisme; ou, Réfutation de l'examen critique des apologistes de la religion mahométane.* London, 1780.

Cloots, Jean-Baptiste [Anacharsis]. *Écrits révolutionnaires, 1790–1794.* Ed. Michèle Duval. Paris: Éditions Champ libre, 1979.

Cloots, Jean-Baptiste [Anacharsis]. *Oeuvres.* Preface by Albert Soboul. Munich: Kraus Reprint, 1980. 3v.

Cloots, Jean-Baptiste [Anacharsis]. *La republique universelle; ou, Adresse aux tyrannicides.* Paris: Chez les Marchands de Nouveautés, 1792.

Cloots, Jean-Baptiste [Anacharsis]. *Voeux d'un Gallophile.* Amsterdam, 1786.

Codet, Sylvain. *Opinion motivée de M. Codet, député de l'Isle et vilaine à l'Assemblée nationale.* Paris: Imprimerie nationale, 1791.

Collection générale des décrets rendus par l'Assemblée nationale. Paris: Baudouin, imprimeur de l'Assemblée nationale, 1789–1791. 16v.

Condorcet, Marie Jean Antoine Nicolas Caritat de. *Esquisse d'un tableau historique des progrès de l'esprit humain*. Paris: Chez Agasse, 1795.

Conversation de l'ambassadeur de Tippoo-Saib, avec son interprète. N.p., 1788.

Cournand, Antoine de. *Requête présentée à nosseigneurs de l'Assemblée nationale en faveur des gens de couleur de l'île de Saint-Domingue*. N.p., [1790].

Courtois, E. B. *Rapport fait au nom de la commission chargée de l'examen des papiers trouvés chez Robespierre et ses complices*. Paris: Imprimerie Nationale des Lois, 1795.

Craven, Elizabeth. *A Journey through the Crimea to Constantinople, in a Series of Letters from the Right Honourable Elizabeth Lady Craven, to His Serene Highness the Margrave of Brandebourg, Anspach, and Bareith*. London: G. G. J. and J. Robinson, 1789.

Le cri de l'humanité; ou, L'ami des vieillards. N.p., [1791].

Damade, Louis. *Histoire chantée de la première république, 1789 à 1799: Chants patriotiques, révolutionnaires et populaires*. Paris: Paul Schmidt, 1892.

Le danger de la liberté des nègres [par un bon citoyen]. N.p., 1790.

d'Antraigues, Emmanuel Henri Louis Alexandre de Launay. *Dénonciation aux français catholiques, des moyens employés par l'Assemblée nationale pour détruire en France la religion catholique*. London: Edwart Pall-Mall, 1791.

d'Arnery, Claude Gaspard Barbat Du Closel. *Vues sur l'intolérance et le rapport essentiel qu'ont toutes les sectes ou religions avec les religions chrétienne et naturelle*. N.p., 1788.

de Baecque, Antoine, Wolfgang Schmale, and Michel Vovelle (eds). *L'an 1 des droits de l'homme*. Paris: Presses du CNRS, 1988.

de Bausset, Louis-François. *Exposé des principes sur le serment de liberté et d'égalité et sur la déclaration exigée des ministres du culte, par la loi du 7 vendémiaire, an IV*. Paris, 1795.

de Breuil, A. L. *La France il y a trente ans: Ouvrage contenant des grandes vérités historiques sur les hommes de ce temps-là*. Paris: Lerouge, 1822.

Décote, Georges (ed). *Correspondance de Jacques Cazotte: Édition critique*. Paris: Klincksieck, 1982.

de Gouges, Olympe. *Réponse à la justification de Maximilien Robespierre, adressée à Jérôme Pétion*. N.p., 1792.

de La Chapelle, Salomon. *Histoire des tribunaux révolutionnaires de Lyon et de Feurs établis en 1793 par les représentants du peuple et liste des contre-révolutionnaires mis à mort*. Lyon, 1879.

de La Porte, Arnaud. *Plan d'une constitution libre et heureuse*. Leipzig: J. G. Dyck, 1793.

de La Varenne, Pierre Anne Louis de Maton. *Histoire particulière des événements qui ont eu lieu en France pendant les mois de juin . . . 1792*. Paris, 1806.

de Monay, Quarre. *Declaration de L'eglise Cathedrale d'Autun*. Autun: Dejussieu, 1790.

Denham, Dixon. *Narrative of Travels and Discoveries in Northern and Central Africa in the Years 1822, 1823 and 1824*. London: John Murray, 1826.

La députation étrangère au Champ de Mars: aux confédérés français. N.p., [1791].

Le dernier cri du monstre, conte indien du 6 août 1789. N.p., 1789.

Desmoulins, Camille. *Jean Pierre Brissot Démasqué*. Paris, 1792.

D'Ghies, Hassuna. "A Letter Addressed to James Scarlett." [1822]. British Library.

d'Hupay, Victor. *Alcoran républicain; ou, Institutions fondamentales du gouvernement populaire ou légitime*. [Aix-en-Provence]: Generalif, maison patriarcale et champêtre, an IIIe [1795].

Dillon, Arthur. *Progrès de la Révolution française en Angleterre*. Paris: Gattey, 1792.

d'Ohsson, Mouradgea. *Tableau général de l'Empire othoman, divisé en deux parties, dont l'une comprend la législation mahométane, l'autre, l'histoire de l'Empire othoman*. Paris: Imprimerie de Monsieur [Firmin Didot], 1787–1820. 3v.

Duquesnoy, Adrien Cyprien. *Journal d'Adrien Duquesnoy, député de Bar-le-Duc*. Ed. Robert Crèvecoeur. Paris: Picard, 1894. 2v.

Duquesnoy, Adrien Cyprien. *Opinion de M. Duquesnoy sur les projets de Déclaration de droits*. Versailles: Baudouin, 1789.

Duval, Georges. *Souvenirs de la terreur de 1788 à 1793*. Paris: Werdet, 1842.

*Étrennes à tous les tyrans et aristocrates de l'univers: Pour le premier jour de l'an 3me de la liberté, par M.G.***, Patriote de la Savoie*. Paris: Imprimerie du Patriote françois, 1791.

Extrait du "Moniteur universel": Générosité du roi de l'Inde. Marseille: F. Brebion, 1790.

Fauchet, Claude. *De la religion nationale*. Paris: Bailly, 1789.

Fauchet, Claude. *Sermon sur l'accord de la religion et de la liberté, prononcé dans la métropole de Paris, le 4 février 1791*. Paris: Imprimerie du Cercle Social, 1791.

[Ferrand, Antoine-François-Claude]. *Lettre au roi par un françois royaliste*. Paris, 1790.

[Ferrand, Antoine-François-Claude]. *Tableau de la conduite de l'Assemblée prétendue nationale*. Part 2. Paris, 1790.

Les forfaits du 6 octobre; ou, Examen approfondi du Rapport de la procédure du Châtelet sur les faits des 5 et 6 octobre 1789: Fait à l'Assemblée nationale par M. Charles Chabroud. N.p., 1790.

Fréron, Louis-Marie-Stanislas. *Mémoire historique sur la réaction royale et sur les massacres du Midi*. Paris: Marchant, 1795.

Fusi, Anthoine. *Le franc-archer de la vraye Eglise, contre les abus et enormités de la fausse*. Paris: Aux despens de l'autheur, 1619.

Gorani, Giuseppe. *Lettres aux français*. London, 1794. 3v.

Gorani, Giuseppe. *Mémoires secrets et critiques des cours, des gouvernemens, et des moeurs des principaux états de l'Italie*. London, 1794.

Gravelot, Hubert François, Charles Nicolas Cochin, and Charles Étienne Gaucher. *Iconologie par figures; ou, Traité complet des allégories, emblêmes &c*. Paris: Le Pan, 1791. 4v.

Grégoire, Henri. *Histoire des sectes religieuses, qui, depuis le commencement du siècle dernier jusqu'à l'époque actuelle, sont nées, se sont modifiées, se sont éteintes dans les quatre parties du Monde*. Paris: Potey, 1814.

Grégoire, Henri. *Rapport sur les encouragements, récompenses et pensions à accorder aux savants, aux gens de lettres et aux artistes*. Paris: Imprimerie Nationale, 1794.

Grégoire, Henri. *Troisième rapport sur le vandalisme*. Paris: Imprimerie nationale des lois, 1794.

Gros-Jean qui remontre à son curé, et les doutes d'un villageois résolus par son pasteur: Suivis du parallèle de la persécution de Julien l'Apostat avec la persécution de l'Eglise de France des années 362–363 et 1790–1791. Paris: Chez Lallemand, 1792.

Grosson, Jean-Baptiste-Bernard. *Almanach historique de Marseille*. Marseille: Jean Mossy, 1777.

Le guide national. Imprimerie de la liberté, 1790.

Hamilton, Alexander. *A New Account of the East Indies*. London: C. Hitch, 1744.

[Harvant, J.]. *Dialogue entre Ibrahim Pacha et un municipal*. Constantinople [Paris], 1790.

Hénin de Cuvillers, Étienne-Félix. *Sommaire de la correspondance d'Étienne-Félix Hénin, chargé d'affaires de la république française à Constantinople, pendant les première, seconde et troisième années de la république*. Paris: Impr. du dépôt des lois, 1795.

Hope, Thomas. *Anastasius; or, Memoirs of a Greek, Written at the Close of the Eighteenth Century*. London: John Murray, 1820. 3v.

Hornemann, Friedrich, et al. *The Journal of Frederick Horneman's Travels: From Cairo to Mourzouk, the Capital of the Kingdom of Fezzan, in Africa*. London: G. and W. Nicol, 1802.

Idée générale de la Turquie et des Turcs, pour servir à l'intelligence des opérations de la guerre actuelle. Paris: Leroy, 1788.

Jones, William. *Asiatic Researches; or, Transactions of the Society Instituted in Bengal for Inquiring into the History and Antiquities, the Arts, Sciences and Literature of Asia*. Calcutta: Cantopher, 1788.

Lacroix, Sébastien. *La religion naturelle, la seule qui convient à des républicains*. Marseille, [1793].

Lacroix, Sigismond (ed). *Actes de la commune de Paris pendant la Révolution*. Series 2. Paris: L. Cerf, 1894. 8v.

Lair, Jules, and Emile Legrand (eds). *Lettres de Constantin Stamaty à Panagiotis Kodrikas*. Paris: Maisonneuve, 1872.

Lambert, Alexandre. *Discours de morale, prononcé le 2e décadi, 20 frimaire, l'an 2e de la République une et indivisible, au temple de la Vérité, ci-devant l'église des bénédictins, à Angély-Boutonne, ci-devant St. Jean d'Angély*. [Rochefort], [1794].

Lambert, Bernard. *Le préservatif contre le schisme, convaincu de graves erreurs*. Paris: Desaint, 1791.

Lamennais, Félicité Robert de. *Du catholicisme dans ses rapports avec la société politique: Questions politiques et philosophiques*. Paris: Pagnerre, 1844.

Lamourette, Antoine-Adrien. *Les délices de la religion; ou, Le pouvoir des évangiles pour nous rendre heureux*. Paris: Merigot jeune, 1789.

Lamourette, Antoine-Adrien. *Instruction pastorale de M. l'évêque du département de Rhône et Loire*. Lyon: Impr. d'Amable Le Roy, 1791.

Lanthenas, François-Xavier. *Déclaration des devoirs de l'homme, des principes et maximes de la morale universelle, proposée par F. Lanthenas*. Paris: Imprimerie Nationale, 1793.

Lanthenas, François-Xavier. *Mesures de salut public contre les obstacles intérieurs à l'établissement de la République*. Paris: Chez l'auteur et chez les marchands de nouveauté, 1794.

Lavicomterie de Saint Samson, Louis Thomas Hébert. *Les crimes des empereurs turcs, depuis Osman I, jusqu'à Selim IV*. Paris: Bureau des Revolutions de Paris, 1795.

Lefebvre de Villebrune, Jean-Baptiste. *Pacte fait entre Mahomet et les Chrétiens de toutes les sectes, par lequel il leur accorde la liberté de leur culte et maintient leurs propriétés et leurs hiérarchies.* Paris: [Imprimerie Nationale?], 1797.

Lequinio, Joseph-Marie. *Adresse populaire aux habitants des campagnes, par J.-M. Lequinio, lue à la Société des Amis de la constitution séante au Collége de Bourges, et imprimée par son ordre, 4 décembre 1791.* Bourges: Manceron, 1791.

Lequinio, Joseph-Marie. *Des fêtes nationales.* Paris: Imprimerie nationale, 1795.

Lequinio, Joseph-Marie. *Du bonheur, par Lequinio, prononcé dans le Temple de la Vérité de Rochefort, le deuxième décadi de brumaire, l'an II de la République.* Angoulême: P. Broquisse, 1793.

Lequinio, Joseph-Marie. *Les préjugés détruits.* Paris: Imprimerie Nationale, 1792.

Lequinio de Kerblay, Joseph-Marie. *La guerre de la Vendée et des Chouans.* Paris: Pougin, 1794.

Lescure, Adolphe Mathurin de (ed). *Correspondance secrète inédite sur Louis XVI, Marie-Antoinette, la cour et la ville de 1777 à 1792 publiée d'après des MSS de la bibliothèque impériale de Saint-Pétersbourg.* Paris: H. Plon, 1866.

Lettre adressée à M. Grégoire, curé d'Emberménil, député de Nancy, par les députés de la nation juive portugaise, de Bordeaux [signed: Furtado-Lainé, Azevedo, David Gradis, et al.]. Paris: Baudouin, 1789.

Lettre amicale du roi des Indes (Tipoo-Say) au roi de France. Paris: C. Volland, [1788].

Lettre à un censeur royal sur la liberté de la presse. Paris: Chez Volland, 1789.

*Lettre de M.***, député à l'Assemblée nationale, à M.***, sur la conduite du clergé dans l'Assemblée nationale; ou, Histoire fidèle des décrets de l'Assemblée, relativement aux biens ecclésiastiques et à la religion.* Paris, 1791.

Lettre de Rallier, membre du Conseil des Anciens, au citoyen Grégoire, membre du Conseil des Cinq-cents. Paris: Desenne, Year 4 [1795–1796].

Lettre du Grand Turc au Roi de France. [Paris]: Chez Volland, [1789].

Lettre du Muphty de Constantinople, à Monsieur l'Abbé Mauri. Au sérail [Paris]: Imprimerie de la Sultane favorite, 1789.

Lettre pastorale de M. l'Archevêque d'Auch. N.p., 1790.

Lettres de l'un des ambassadeurs de Typoo-Saïb où il est beaucoup parlé des affaires du royaume de Gogo [i.e., France], *avec l'aventure de Gigy, prince du sang des rois de cet empire, etc.* N.p., 1789.

Lettre turque, relative aux circonstances. N.p., 1789.

Levasseur, René. *Mémoires de Levasseur de la Sarthe.* Paris: Baudouin, 1830.

Liste des membres de l'Assemblée nationale qui ont donné leurs voix pour ou contre les assignats. N.p., 1790.

Malesherbes, Chrétien-Guillaume de Lamoignon de. *Second mémoire sur le mariage des protestans*. London, 1787.

Malouet, Pierre-Victor. *Lettre de M. Malouet à M. de Lally-Tolendal*. Paris, 1792.

[Manévieux, Sain de]. *Le porte-feuille lyonnois; ou, Bigarrures provinciales, trouvées par un Q. . . ni cuirassé, ni mitré, mais botté*. Minorca [Lyon]: Aux dépens du Gouvernement, 1779.

Marigny, François Augier de. *Histoire des Arabes sous le gouvernement des Califes*. Paris: Vve Estienne-Desaint-Saillant, 1750.

Mayeur de Saint Paul, François-Marie. *Tableau du nouveau Palais-Royal*. Paris: Maradan, 1788.

Méhée de la Touche, Jean Claude Hippolyte. *La queue de Robespierre*. Paris: Imprimerie de Rougyff, 1794.

Mercier, Louis-Sébastien. *Le nouveau Paris*. Paris: Fuchs, C. Pougens & C. F. Cramer, 1797. 6v.

Mésenguy, François-Philippe. *Exposition de la doctrine chrétienne; ou, Instructions sur les principales vérités de la religion*. Utrecht: Aux dépens de la Compagnie, 1744.

Michelet, Jules. *Histoire du XIXe siècle*. Paris: Michel Lévy, 1875. 3v.

Mirabeau, Honoré-Gabriel de Riquetti. *Avis au peuple marseillais*. [Marseille], 1789.

Montesquieu, Charles de Secondat. *Considerations sur les causes de la grandeur des Romains et de leur decadence*. Amsterdam: Chez J. Desbordes, 1734.

Montlosier, François Dominique de Reynaud de. *Mémoires de M. le Comte de Montlosier, sur la Revolution française*. Paris: Dufey, 1830. 2v.

Mounier, Jean-Joseph. *Appel au tribunal de l'opinion publique*. Geneva, 1790.

Mounier, Jean-Joseph. *Exposé de ma conduite dans l'Assemblée nationale et motifs de mon retour en Dauphiné*. Paris: Cuchet, 1789.

Moy, Charles-Alexandre de. *Accord de la religion et des cultes chez une nation libre*. Paris: Au presbytère de Saint-Laurent, an IV de la liberté [1792].

Les Nantais à tous les départements de la République (proclamation). Halles de la Grenette [Lyon]: Impr. d'Aimé Vatar-Delaroche, 1793.

Le naviget-anticyras; ou, Le système sans principe, l'édifice sans fondement élevé sur le sable. N.p., 1789.

Necker, Jacques. *Du pouvoir exécutif dans les grands états*. N.p., 1792.

La nouvelle épiphanie; ou, La liberté adorée des mages. N.p., c. 1789.

Official Documents, Relative to the Negotiations Carried On by Tippoo Sultaun, with the French Nation, and Other Foreign States, for Purposes Hostile to the British Nation. [London]: Honorable Company's Press, 1799.

Olivier, Guillaume-Antoine. *Voyage dans l'empire Othoman, l'Egypte et la Perse, fait par ordre du gouvernement pendant les six premières années de la République*. Paris: Henri Agasse, 1801–1807. 6v.

Les Parisiens au grand turc. Paris: Imprimerie de Knapen fils, 1789.

Paroy, Jean Philippe Guy Le Gentil, marquis de. *Mémoires du Comte de Paroy: Souvenirs d'un défenseur de la famille royale pendant la révolution (1789–1797)*. Paris: E. Plon, Nourrit, 1895.

[P.B.T., Le citoyen]. *L'origine des trois religions revolutionnaires, des Jacobins, des chretiens, et des mahometans*. [Paris]: Chez les marchands de nouveautés, Year 2 [1793–1794].

Peltier, Jean-Gabriel. *Dernier tableau de Paris; ou, Récit historique de la révolution du 10 août 1792*. London: Chez l'auteur, 1793.

Le Petit Catéchisme Français. N.p., 1789.

Pétition des juifs établis en France, adressée à l'Assemblée nationale, le 28 janvier 1790, sur l'ajournement du 24 décembre 1789. Paris: Prault, 1790.

Peyssonel, Charles de. *Examen du livre intitulé Considérations sur la guerre actuelle des Turcs*. Amsterdam, 1788.

Plantet, Eugène (ed). *Correspondance des beys de Tunis et des consuls de France avec la cour: 1577–1830*. Paris: F. Alcan, 1899.

Plantet, Eugène (ed). *Correspondance des deys d'Alger, avec la cour de France, 1579–1833*. Paris: F. Alcan, 1889. 2v.

Poiret, Jean-Louis-Marie. *Voyage en Barbarie; ou, Lettres écrites de l'ancienne Numidie pendant les années 1785 et 1786*. Paris: J. B. F. Née de la Rochelle, 1789. 2v.

Pons, Z. *Mémoires pour servir à l'histoire de la ville de Toulon, en 1793*. Paris: C. J. Trouvé, 1825.

Pouqueville, François-Charles-Hugues-Laurent. *Voyage en Morée, à Constantinople, en Albanie et dans plusieurs autres parties de l'empire othoman, pendant les années 1798, 1799, 1800 et 1801*. Paris: Gabon, 1805.

Price, Richard. *The Correspondence of Richard Price: February 1786–February 1791*. Ed. Bernard Peach. Durham, NC: Duke University Press, 1983. 3v.

Procédure criminelle instruite au Châtelet de Paris sur la dénonciation des faits arrivés à Versailles dans la journée du 6 octobre 1789. Paris: Baudouin, 1790.

Procès criminel des membres du Comité révolutionnaire de Nantes et du ci-devant Représentant du peuple Carrier, instruit par le Tribunal révolutionnaire. Paris: La Citoyenne Toubon, 1794.

Procès-verbaux des séances des corps municipaux de la ville de Lyon. Lyon: Impr. nouvelle lyonnaise, 1899–1907. 6v.

Procès-verbaux du Comité d'instruction publique de la Convention nationale. Paris: Imprimerie Nationale, 1891–1958. 8v.

Proyart, Liévin-Bonaventure. *La vie et les crimes de Robespierre, surnommé le tyran: Depuis sa naissance jusqu'à sa mort; Ouvrage dédié à ceux qui commandent et à ceux qui obéissent.* Augsburg: Chez Tous les Libraires, 1795.

Quès-à-co? ou, Histoire des troubles et révolutions modernes de Marseille. [Paris]: Cailleau fils, 1789.

Rabaut de Saint-Étienne, Jean-Paul. *Opinion de M. Rabaut de Saint-Étienne, sur la motion suivante de le Comte de Castellane: Nul homme ne peut être inquieté pour ses opinions, ni troublé dans l'exercice de sa religion.* Versailles: Baudoin, 1789.

Rabaut de Saint-Étienne, Jean-Paul. *Précis de l'histoire de la Révolution française.* Paris: Servier, 1827.

Rapport fait à l'Assemblée nationale, au nom du Comité ecclésiastique, par M. Martineau, député de la ville de Paris, sur la Constitution du clergé: Imprimé par ordre de l'Assemblée nationale. Paris: Impr. nationale, 1790.

Réflexions sommaires sur le serment civique. N.p., 1790.

Remercimens du Parlement a l'Assemblée nationale. N.p., 1790.

Rétif de la Bretonne, Nicolas-Edmé. *Les nuits de Paris; ou, Le spectateur-nocturne.* Ed. Henri Bachelin. Paris: Livre Club du Libraire, 1960.

Robespierre, Maximilien. *Oeuvres de Maximilien Robespierre:* vol. 5, *Les journaux.* Ed. Gustave Laurent. Paris: Impr. Louis-Jean, 1961.

Robespierre, Maximilien. *Oeuvres de Maximilien Robespierre:* vol. 10, *Discours.* Paris: Presses Universitaires de France, 1967.

Roland, Manon. *Lettres de Madame Roland.* Ed. Claude Perroud. Paris: Imprimerie Nationale, 1902.

Rousseau, Jean-Jacques. *Émile et Sophie; ou, Les solitaires: Ouvrage posthume de M. J.-J. Rousseau.* Geneva: Société Typographique, 1781.

Rousseau, Jean-Jacques. *Oeuvres complètes.* Paris: Gallimard. 1959–1969. 4v.

Saʻdī. *Essai historique sur la législation de la Perse, précédé de la traduction complette du Jardin des roses de Sady.* Trans. Abbé Gaudin. Paris: Le Jay fils, 1789.

Saint-Just, Louis-Antoine. *Oeuvres complètes.* Ed. Charles Vellay. Paris: Charpentier et Fasquelle, 1908.

Sanson, Charles-Henri. *La Révolution française vue par son bourreau: Journal.* Paris: Éditions de l'Instant, 1988.

Le secret des Jacobins. Paris: Imprimerie de Guffroi, 1794.

Ségur, Louis-Philippe de. *Mémoires; ou, Souvenirs et anecdotes.* Brussels: Lacrosse, 1825. 3v.

Sénart, Gabriel-Jérôme. *Mémoires de Sénart secrétaire du comité de sureté générale; ou, Révélations puisées dans les cartons des comités de salut public et de sureté générale*. Paris: Baudouin, 1824.

Shaw, Thomas. *Travels; or, Observations Relating to Several Parts of Barbary and the Levant, Illustrated with Cuts*. 2nd ed. London: A. Millar, 1757.

Sieyès, Emmanuel-Joseph. *Qu'est-ce que le tiers-état?* N.p., 1789.

Staël, Germaine de. *Considérations sur la Révolution française*. Paris: Delaunay, 1818.

Tabatabai, Ghulam Husain Khan. *Siyar-al Muta'akhkhirin*. Calcutta, 1834. 8v.

al-Tahtawi, Rifa'ah Rafi', and Daniel L. Newman. *An Imam in Paris: Account of a Stay in France by an Egyptian Cleric (1826–1831)*. London: Saqi, 2004.

Taylor, John, and Louis Marie Joseph Ohier de Grandpré. *Voyage dans l'Inde, au travers du grand désert, par Alep, Antioche et Bassora, exécuté par le major Taylor . . .* Paris: Chez Genets ainé, 1803.

Thiers, Adolphe. *Histoire de la Révolution française*. Paris: Lebeau-Ouwerx, 1828. 10v.

Thorillon, Antoine-Joseph. *Idées ou bases d'une nouvelle declaration des droits de l'homme*. Paris: Chez les marchands de Nouveautés, 1793.

Tocqueville, Alexis de. *Oeuvres*. Ed. André Jardin. Gallimard, 2004.

Toderini, Giambattista. *De la littérature des Turcs*. Trans. Antoine de Cournand. Paris: Poinçot, 1789.

Trouvaille, signé le Parisien, témoin occulaire [sic] des journées des 5 et 6 oct. N.p., c. 1790.

Tuetey, Alexandre. *Répertoire général des sources manuscrites de l'histoire de Paris pendant la révolution française: Assemblée legislative*. Paris: Imprimerie nouvelle, 1900.

Vadier, Marc. *Rapport et projet de décret, présentés à la Convention Nationale, au nom des comités de sûreté générale et de salut public*. Paris: Imprimerie Nationale, 1794.

Venture de Paradis, Jean Michel. *Tunis et Alger au XVIIIe siècle*. Ed. Joseph Cuoq. Paris: Sindbad, 1983.

Vies secrètes et politiques de Couthon, Saint-Just, Robespierre jeune, complices du tyran Robespierre, et assassins de la République. Paris: Prévost, 1794.

Vigée-LeBrun, Louise-Élisabeth. *Souvenirs de madame Louise-Élisabeth Vigée-LeBrun*. Paris: H. Fournier, 1835.

Vilate, Joachim. *Les mystères de la Mère de Dieu, dévoilés: Troisième volume des causes secrètes de la Révolution du 9 au 10 thermidor*. Paris, 1795.

Volney, Constantin-François. *Voyage en Syrie et en Égypte pendant les années 1783, 1784 et 1785*. Paris: Desenne, 1787. 2v.

Voltaire, François-Marie Arouet de. *Épîtres, satires, contes, odes et pièces fugitives du poëte philosophe*. London, 1771.

Voltaire, François-Marie Arouet de. *Oeuvres complètes*. Paris: Garnier frères, 1877. 52v.

Walsh, Thomas. *Journal of the late campaign in Egypt, including descriptions of that country, and of Gibraltar, Minorca, Malta, Marmorice, and Macri; with an appendix; containing official papers and documents*. London: Luke Hansard 1803.

Wellesley, Richard. *The Despatches, Minutes, and Correspondence of the Marquess of Wellesley, K. G. during his administration in India*. Ed. Montgomery Martin. London: J. Murray, 1836. 5v.

Wilson, Robert Thomas. *History of the British Expedition to Egypt*. London: Egerton, 1803.

Secondary Sources

Aberdam, Serge. "Deux occasions de participation féminine en 1793: Le vote sur la constitution et le partage des biens communaux." *Annales historiques de la Révolution française* 339 (2005): 17–34.

Aberdam, Serge, et al. (eds). *Voter, élire pendant la Révolution française 1789–1799: Guide pour la recherché*. Paris: CTHS, 2006.

Abun-Nasr, Jamil M. *A History of the Maghrib in the Islamic Period*. Cambridge: Cambridge University Press, 1987.

Ado, Anatoli. *Paysans en Révolution: Terre, pouvoir et jacquerie, 1789–1794*. Paris: Société des études robespierristes, 2012.

Ahmad, S. Maqbul. *A History of the Nawābs of Broach: Based on the Persian Manuscript, Majmū'a-e-Dānish*. Delhi: Dept. of Persian, University of Delhi, 1985.

Aksan, Virginia. *Ottoman Wars, 1700–1870: An Empire Besieged*. London: Routledge, 2014.

Alavi, Seema. *Muslim Cosmopolitanism in the Age of Empire*. Cambridge, MA: Harvard University Press, 2015.

Alger, John Goldworth. *Paris in 1789–94: Farewell letters of victims of the guillotine*. London: George Allen, 1902.

Allinne, Jean-Pierre. "La déclaration des Droits de l'Homme et les aspirations libérales en Europe: Le témoignage de la presse." *Annales historiques de la Révolution française* 262.1 (1985): 426–446.

Alpaugh, Micah. *Non-violence and the French Revolution: Political Demonstrations in Paris, 1787–1795*. Cambridge: Cambridge University Press, 2015.

Alpaugh, Micah. "The Politics of Escalation in French Revolutionary Protest: Political Demonstrations, Non-violence and Violence in the *Grandes Journées* of 1789." *French History* 23.3 (2009): 336–359.

Andress, David (ed). *Experiencing the French Revolution.* Oxford: SVEC, 2013.

Andress, David (ed). *The Oxford Handbook of the French Revolution.* Oxford: Oxford University Press, 2015.

Anscombe, Frederick F. *State, Faith, and Nation in Ottoman and Post-Ottoman Lands.* Cambridge: Cambridge University Press, 2014.

Arkoun, Mohammed (ed). *Histoire de l'Islam et des musulmans en France du Moyen Âge à nos jours.* Paris: Albin Michel, 2006.

Armitage, David, and Sanjay Subrahmanyam (eds). *The Age of Revolutions in Global Contexts, c. 1760–1840.* Basingstoke: Palgrave Macmillan, 2010.

Aston, Nigel. *Religion and Revolution in France, 1780–1804.* Washington, DC: Catholic University of America Press, 2000.

Auber, Peter. *Rise and Progress of the British Power in India.* London: W. H. Allen, 1837. 2v.

Aulard, François-Alphonse. *Le culte de la raison et le culte de l'être suprême, 1793–1794: Essai historique.* Paris: Alcan, 1892.

Aulard, François-Alphonse. *Paris pendant la réaction thermidorienne et sous le Directoire: Du 21 ventôse an V au 2 thermidor an VI, 11 mars 1797–20 juillet 1798.* Paris: L. Cerf, 1900.

Avenel, Georges. *Anacharsis Cloots: L'orateur du genre humain.* Paris: Librairie Internationale, 1865.

Aydin, Cemil. *The Idea of the Muslim World: A Global Intellectual History.* Cambridge, MA: Harvard University Press, 2017.

Babeau, Albert. *Histoire de Troyes pendant la Révolution.* Paris: Dumoulin, 1874. 2v.

Baczko, Bronislaw. *Ending the Terror: The French Revolution after Robespierre.* Trans. Michael Petheram. Cambridge: Cambridge University Press, 1994.

Baczko, Bronisław. *Utopian Lights: The Evolution of the Idea of Social Progress.* New York: Paragon House, 1989.

Badinter, Robert. *Libres et égaux . . . : L'émancipation des Juifs sous la Révolution française, 1789–1791.* Paris: Fayard, 1989.

Bailey, Thomas. *A Diplomatic History of the American People.* 6th ed. New York: Appleton-Century-Crofts, 1958.

Baker, Keith. *Inventing the French Revolution: Essays on French Political Culture in the Eighteenth Century.* Cambridge: Cambridge University Press, 1990.

Baker, Keith. "Revolution." In Colin Lucas (ed), *The French Revolution and the Creation of Modern Political Culture:* vol. 2, *The Political Culture of the French Revolution.* Oxford: Pergamon Press, 1988. 41–62.

Baker, Keith, and Dan Edelstein (eds). *Scripting Revolution: A Historical Approach to the Comparative Study of Revolutions*. Stanford: Stanford University Press, 2015.

Barny, Roger. "L'image de Cromwell dans la Révolution française." *Dix-huitième siècle* 25.1 (1993): 387–397.

Başaran, Betül. *Selim III, Social Control and Policing in Istanbul at the End of the Eighteenth Century: Between Crisis and Order*. Leiden: Brill, 2014.

Batiffol, Louis. *Les journées des 5 et 6 octobre 1789 à Versailles*. Paris: Vve. E. Aubert, 1891.

Baulig, Henri. "Anacharsis Cloots, journaliste et théoricien (1789–1792)." *La Révolution française* 41 (1901): 311–355.

Bayly, C. A. *Recovering Liberties: Indian Thought in the Age of Liberalism and Empire*. Cambridge: Cambridge University Press, 2012.

Bayly, Christopher. *The Birth of the Modern World: 1780–1914*. London: Black-well Wiley, 2004.

Bayly, Christopher. "The 'Revolutionary Age' in the Wider World." In Richard Bessel, Nicholas Guyatt, and Jane Rendall (eds), *War, Empire and Slavery, 1770–1830*. Houndmills: Palgrave Macmillan, 2010. 21–43.

Beales, Derek. "Philosophical Kingship and Enlightened Despotism." In Mark Goldie and Robert Wokler (eds), *The Cambridge History of Eighteenth-Century Political Thought*. Cambridge: Cambridge University Press, 2006. 495–524.

Beaurepaire, Pierre-Yves. "Le cosmopolitisme maçonnique." *Cahiers de la Méditerranée* 67 (2003): 33–50.

Belissa, Marc. *Fraternité universelle et intérêt national, 1713–1795: Les cosmopolitiques du droit des gens*. Paris: Éditions Kimé, 1998.

Belissa, Marc, and Yannick Bosc. *Robespierre: La fabrication d'un mythe*. Paris: Ellipses, 2013.

Bell, David A. "Questioning the Global Turn: The Case of the French Revolution." *French Historical Studies* 37.1 (2014): 1–24.

Bellance, Hurard. *La police des Noirs en Amérique (Martinique, Guadeloupe, Guyane, Saint-Dominique) et en France aux XVIIe et XVIIIe siècles*. Paris: Ibis rouge, 2011.

Bély, Lucien (ed). *Turcs et turqueries: XVIe–XVIIIe siècles*. Paris: PU Paris-Sorbonne, 2009.

Bénot, Yves, and Marcel Dorigny (eds). *Rétablissement de l'esclavage dans les colonies françaises, 1802*. Paris: Maisonneuve et Larose, 2003.

Bernard-Griffiths, Simone, Marie-Claude Chemin, and Jean Ehrard (eds). *Révolution française et "vandalisme révolutionnaire": Actes du Colloque*

International de Clermont-Ferrand, 15–17 décembre 1988. Paris: Universitas, 1992.

Bertrand, Regis. "Les cimetières des 'esclaves turcs' des arsenaux de Marseille et de Toulon au XVIIIe siècle." *Revue des mondes musulmans et de la Méditerranée* 99–100 (2002): 205–217.

Bevilacqua, Alexander. *The Arabic Republic of Letters: Islam and the European Enlightenment*. Cambridge, MA: Harvard University Press, 2018.

Bevilacqua, Alexander. "Conceiving the Republic of Mankind: The Political Thought of Anacharsis Cloots." *History of European Ideas* 38.4 (2012): 550–569.

Beydilli, Kemal. "Şehzâde Elçisi Safiyesultanzâde İshak Bey." *İslam Araştırmaları Dergisi* 3 (1999): 73–81.

Bianchi, Serge. *La Révolution et la première république au village: Pouvoirs, votes et politisation dans les campagnes de l'Île-de-France 1787–1800*. Paris: Éditions du CTHS, 2003.

Biard, Michel. "L'almanach du Père Gérard: Un exemple de diffusion des idées jacobines." *Annales historiques de la Révolution française* 238.1 (1990): 19–29.

Biard, Michel. *La liberté ou la mort: Mourir en député 1792–1795*. Paris: Tallandier, 2015.

Biard, Michel. *Missionnaires de la République: Les représentants du peuple en mission, 1793–1795*. Paris: CTHS, 2002.

Biard, Michel. *1793: Le siège de Lyon; Entre mythes et réalités*. Clermont-Ferrand: Lemme, 2013.

Biard, Michel. "Types de conflits, formes de politisation et historiographie de la Révolution française." In Laurent Bourquin and Philippe Hamon (eds), *La politisation: Conflits et construction du politique depuis le Moyen Âge*. Paris: PUF, 2010. 53–66.

Biard, Michel, and Philippe Bourdin (eds). *Robespierre: Portraits croisés*. Paris: Armand Colin, 2012.

Bilici, Faruk. "L'Islam en France sous l'ancien régime et la Révolution: Attraction et répulsion." *Rives nord-méditerranéennes* 14 (2003): 17–37.

Biollay, Léon. *Un épisode de l'approvisionnement de Paris en 1789*. Paris: Paul Dupont, 1878.

Birn, Raymond. "The Pamphlet Press and the Estates General of 1789." *Studies on Voltaire and the Eighteenth Century* 287 (1991): 56–59.

Blackman, Robert. "Did Cicero Swear the Tennis Court Oath?" *French History* 28.4 (2014): 471–497.

Blanc, Olivier. *Les espions de la Révolution et de l'empire*. Paris: Perrin, 1995.

Blaufarb, Rafe. *The French Army, 1750–1820: Careers, Talent, Merit*. Manchester: Manchester University Press, 2002.

Blaufarb, Rafe. *The Great Demarcation: The French Revolution and the Invention of Modern Property*. Oxford: Oxford University Press, 2016.

Bonacina, Giovanni. *The Wahhabis Seen through European Eyes, 1772–1830*. Leiden: Brill, 2015.

Boucheron, Patrick, et al. (eds). *Histoire mondiale de la France*. Paris: Seuil, 2017.

Boulle, Pierre H. *Race et esclavage dans la France de l'ancien régime*. Paris: Perrin, 2007.

Bourdin, Philippe. *Des lieux, des mots, les révolutionnaires: Le Puy-de-Dôme entre 1789 et 1799*. Clermont-Ferrand: Presses universitaires Blaise Pascal, 1995.

Boutier, Jean. "Les 'lettres de créances' du corsaire Ripaud: Un 'club jacobin' à Srirangapatnam (Inde), mai–juin 1797." *Les Indes savantes* (2005), halshs-00007971.

Bowman, Frank Paul. *Le Christ romantique*. Geneva: Librairie Droz, 1973.

Brittlebank, Kate. "Islamic Responses to the Fall of Srirangapattana and the Death of Tipu Sultan (1799)." *South Asia: Journal of South Asian Studies* 22 (1999): 79–86.

Brittlebank, Kate. *Tipu Sultan's Search for Legitimacy: Islam and Kingship in a Hindu Domain*. Delhi: Oxford University Press, 1997.

Broers, Michael. *The Napoleonic Mediterranean: Enlightenment, Revolution and Empire*. London: I.B.Tauris, 2017.

Broers, Michael. *Napoleon: Soldier of Destiny*. New York: Pegasus Books, 2015.

Brown, Howard G. *Ending the French Revolution: Violence, Justice, and Repression from the Terror to Napoleon*. Charlottesville: University of Virginia Press, 2006.

Brown, Howard, and Judith Miller (eds). *Taking Liberties: Problems of a New Order from the French Revolution to Napoleon*. Manchester: Manchester University Press, 2002.

Bryant, G. J. *The Emergence of British Power in India, 1600–1784: A Grand Strategic Interpretation*. Woodbridge: Boydell & Brewer, 2013.

Buck-Morss, Susan. "Hegel and Haiti." *Critical Inquiry* 26.4 (2000): 821–865.

Burrows, Simon. "Grub Street Revolutionaries: Marginal Writers at the Enlightenment's Periphery?" In Richard Butterwick, Simon Davies, and Gabriel Sánchez Espinosa (eds), *Peripheries of the Enlightenment*. Oxford: Voltaire Foundation, 2008. 145–162.

Burstin, Haïm. *Révolutionnaires: Pour une anthropologie politique de la Révolution française*. Paris: Vendémiaire, 2013.

Butler, Judith. *Gender Trouble: Feminism and the Subversion of Identity*. London: Routledge, 1990.

Cabanel, Patrick. *Juifs et protestants en France: Les affinités électives, XVIe–XXIe siècle*. Paris: Fayard, 2004.

Cadio, Émilie. "Le Comité de sûreté générale (1792–1795)." *La Révolution française* 3 (2012), http://lrf.revues.org/676.

Carton, Adrian. *Mixed-Race and Modernity in Colonial India: Changing Concepts of Hybridity across Empires*. Abingdon: Routledge, 2012.

Carton, Adrian. "Shades of Fraternity: Creolization and the Making of Citizenship in French India, 1790–1792." *French Historical Studies* 31.4 (Fall 2008): 581–607.

Césaire, Aimé. *Toussaint-Louverture: La Révolution française et le problème colonial*. Paris: Présence Africaine, 1961.

Chakrabarty, Dipesh. *Provincializing Europe: Postcolonial Thought and Historical Difference*. Princeton, NJ: Princeton University Press, 2000.

Chantin, Jean-Pierre. "Les adeptes de la théophilanthropie." *Rives nord-méditerranéennes* 14 (2003): 63–73.

Charles-Roux, François. *Bonaparte, gouverneur d'Égypte*. Paris: Plon, 1936.

Charles-Roux, François. "Les travaux d'Herculais; ou, Une extraordinaire mission en Barbarie." *Revue de l'histoire des colonies françaises* 20 (1927): 321–368.

Chartier, Roger. *The Cultural Origins of the French Revolution*. Trans. Lydia Cochrane. Durham, NC: Duke University Press, 1991.

Chassin, Charles-Louis. *La Vendée patriote, 1793–1800*. Mayenne: J. Floch, 1894.

Chater, Khalifa. *Dépendance et mutations précoloniales: La régence de Tunis de 1815 à 1857*. Tunis: Faculté des sciences humaines et sociales de Tunis, 1984.

Chaussinand-Nogaret, Guy. *La noblesse au XVIIIe siècle: De la féodalité aux lumières*. Paris: Éditions Complexe, 2000.

Cheney, Paul. *Revolutionary Commerce: Globalization and the French Monarchy*. Cambridge, MA: Harvard University Press, 2010.

Chenntouf, Tayeb. "La Révolution française: L'évènement vue d'Algérie." In Hédia Khadhar (ed), *La Révolution française et le monde arabo-musulman*. Tunis: Alif-Les Éditions de la Mediterranée, 1991. 61–70.

Cherfils, Christian. *Bonaparte et l'Islam d'après les documents français et arabes*. Paris: A. Pedone, 1914.

Chopelin-Blanc, Caroline. "Le 'baiser Lamourette' (7 juillet 1792)." *Annales historiques de la Révolution française* 355 (2009): 73–100.

Clancy Smith, Julia. *Mediterraneans: North Africa and Europe in an Age of Migration, c. 1800–1900*. Berkeley: University of California Press, 2011.

Clarence Smith, William G., and David Eltis. "White Servitude." In David Eltis et al. (eds), *Cambridge World History of Slavery*: vol. 3, *1420–1804*. Cambridge: Cambridge University Press, 2011. 132–159.

Clay, Richard. *Iconoclasm in Revolutionary Paris: The Transformation of Signs*. Oxford: Voltaire Foundation, 2012.

Clay, Stephen. "Le massacre du fort Saint-Jean: Un épisode de la Terreur blanche à Marseille." In Michel Vovelle (ed), *Le tournant de l'an III: Réaction et terreur blanche dans la France révolutionnaire*. Paris: Éd. CTHS, 1997. 579–583.

Cogliano, Francis D. *Emperor of Liberty: Thomas Jefferson's Foreign Policy*. New Haven, CT: Yale University Press, 2014.

Cohen, William B. *The French Encounter with Africans: White Response to Blacks, 1530–1880*. Bloomington: Indiana University Press, 2009.

Cole, Juan R. I. "Invisible Occidentalism: Eighteenth-Century Indo-Persian Constructions of the West." *Iranian Studies* 25.3–4 (1992): 3–16.

Cole, Juan. *Napoleon's Egypt: Invading the Middle East*. Houndmills: Palgrave Macmillan, 2007.

Coller, Ian. "African Liberalism in the Age of Empire? Hassuna D'Ghies and Liberal Constitutionalism in North Africa." *Modern Intellectual History* 12 (2015): 1–25.

Coller, Ian. *Arab France: Islam and the Making of Modern Europe, 1798–1831*. Berkeley: University of California Press, 2010.

Coller, Ian. "Barbary and Revolution: France and North Africa in the Revolutionary Era." In Patricia Lorcin and Todd Shepard (eds), *French Mediterraneans: Transnational and Imperial Histories*. Lincoln: University of Nebraska Press, 2016. 97–116.

Coller, Ian. "Citizen Chawich: Arabs, Islam and Rights in the French Revolution." *French History and Civilization* 5 (2014): 42–52.

Coller, Ian. "The French Revolution and the Islamic World of the Middle East and North Africa." In Alan Forrest and Matthias Middell (eds), *The Routledge Companion to the French Revolution in World History*. London: Routledge, 2015. 117–134.

Coller, Ian. "The Revolutionary Mediterranean." In Peter McPhee (ed), *A Companion to the French Revolution*. Oxford: Wiley-Blackwell, 2012. 419–434.

Coller, Ian. "Rousseau's Turban: Entangled Encounters of Europe and Islam in the Age of Enlightenment." *Historical Reflections/Réflexions Historiques* 40.2 (2014): 56–77.

Cooper, Frederick. "From Imperial Inclusion to Republican Exclusion? France's Ambiguous Postwar Trajectory." In Charles Tshimanga, Ch. Didier Gondola, and Peter J. Bloom (eds), *Frenchness and the African Diaspora: Identity and Uprising in Contemporary France*. Bloomington: Indiana University Press, 2009. 91–119.

Cormack, William S. *Revolution and Political Conflict in the French Navy, 1789–1794*. Cambridge: Cambridge University Press, 2002.

Cousin, Bernard, Monique Cubells, and René Moulinas. *La pique et la croix: Histoire religieuse de la Révolution française*. Paris: Centurion, 1989.

Culoma, Michaël. *La religion civile de Rousseau à Robespierre*. Paris: Harmattan, 2010.

Dabashi, Hamid. *Persophilia: Persian Culture on the Global Scene*. Cambridge, MA: Harvard University Press, 2015.

Dakhlia, Jocelyne. *Lingua franca: Histoire d'une langue metisse*. Arles: Actes Sud, 2008.

Dakhlia, Jocelyne, and Bernard Vincent (eds). *Les Musulmans dans l'histoire de l'Europe:* vol. 1, *Une intégration invisible*. Paris: Albin Michel, 2011.

Darnton, Robert. *The Kiss of Lamourette: Reflections in Cultural History*. New York: Norton, 1990.

Darnton, Robert. *The Literary Underground of the Old Regime*. Cambridge, MA: Harvard University Press, 1982.

Darnton, Robert, and Daniel Roche (eds). *Revolution in Print: The Press in France, 1775–1800*. Berkeley: University of California Press, 1989.

David, Marcel. *Fraternité et Révolution française, 1789–1799*. Paris: Aubier, 1987.

Davidson, Denise Z. *France after Revolution: Urban Life, Gender, and the New Social Order*. Cambridge, MA: Harvard University Press, 2007.

Davis, Robert C. *Christian Slaves, Muslim Masters: White Slavery in the Mediterranean, the Barbary Coast and Italy, 1500–1800*. Houndmills: Palgrave Macmillan, 2003.

de Baecque, Antoine. *The Body Politic: Corporeal Metaphor in Revolutionary France, 1770–1800*. Trans. Charlotte Mandell. Stanford: Stanford University Press, 1997.

de Baecque, Antoine. *Glory and Terror: Seven Deaths under the French Revolution*. Trans. Charlotte Mandell. London: Routledge, 2003.

de Baecque, Antoine, Wolfgang Schmale, and Michel Vovelle (eds). *L'an 1 des droits de l'homme*. Paris: Presses CNRS, 1988.

de Cauna, Jacques. "L'odyssée d'un esclave musulman: Du Sénégal à Versailles en passant par Tobago." *Revue de la Société haïtienne d'histoire et de géographie* 46 (1990): 59–63.

Declève, Jules. "Les complaintes célèbres." *Mémoires et publications de la Société des sciences, des arts et des lettres du Hainaut.* 5th series. 9 (1897): 203–509.

Defranceschi, Jean. *La Corse française: 30 novembre 1789–15 juin 1794.* Paris: Société des études robespierristes, 1980.

Defranceschi, Jean. *La jeunesse de Napoléon: Les dessous de l'histoire.* Paris: Lettrage, 2001.

Dehérain, Henri. *Orientalistes et antiquaires: La vie de Pierre Ruffin, orientaliste et diplomate, 1742–1824.* Paris: P. Geuthner, 1929.

Delon, Michel. "La Saint-Barthélémy et la Terreur chez Mme de Staël et les historiens de la Révolution au XIXème siècle." *Romantisme* 11.31 (1981): 49–62.

de Marcère, Édouard. *Une ambassade à Constantinople: La politique orientale de la Révolution française.* Paris: F. Alcan, 1927. 2v.

Denis, Vincent. *Une histoire de l'identité: France, 1715–1815.* Paris: Champ Vallon, 2008.

Derrida, Jacques. "The Principle of Hospitality." *Parallax* 11.1 (2005): 6–9.

Desan, Suzanne. *The Family on Trial in Revolutionary France.* Berkeley: University of California Press, 2004.

Desan, Suzanne. "The French Revolution and Religion, 1795–1815." In *The Cambridge History of Christianity:* vol. 7, Stewart J. Brown and Timothy Tackett (eds), *Enlightenment, Reawakening and Revolution, 1660–1815.* Cambridge: Cambridge University Press, 2006. 556–574.

Desan, Suzanne. *Reclaiming the Sacred: Lay Religion and Popular Politics in Revolutionary France.* Ithaca: Cornell University Press, 1990.

Desan, Suzanne, Lynn Hunt, and William Max Nelson (eds). *The French Revolution in Global Perspective.* Ithaca: Cornell University Press, 2013.

Desmet-Gregoire, Hélène. *Le divan magique: L'Orient turc en France au XVIIIe siècle.* Paris: L'Harmattan, 1994.

de Villiers du Terrage, Marc. *Les 5 et 6 octobre 1789: Reine Audu, les legendes des journées d'octobre.* Paris: E.-Paul frères, 1917.

d'Hauterive, Ernest. "Lettres de jeunesse de Bonaparte (1789–1792)." *Revue des deux mondes,* 15 December 1931, 767–794.

Dimmock, Matthew. *Mythologies of the Prophet Muhammad in Early Modern English Culture.* Cambridge: Cambridge University Press, 2013.

Diouf, Sylviane A. *Servants of Allah: African Muslims Enslaved in the Americas.* New York: NYU Press, 1998.

Dirks, Nicholas B. *The Scandal of Empire: India and the Creation of Imperial Britain.* Cambridge, MA: Harvard University Press, 2006.

Dommanget, Maurice, and Michel Vovelle. *Enragés et curés rouges en 1793: Jacques Roux, Pierre Dolivier*. Paris: Spartacus, 1993.

Dorigny, Marcel, and Rachida Tlili Sellaouti (eds). *Droit des gens et relations entre les peuples dans l'espace méditerranéen autour de la Révolution française*. Paris: SER, 2006.

Douthwaite, Julia. *The Frankenstein of 1790 and Other Lost Chapters from Revolutionary France*. Chicago: University of Chicago Press, 2012.

Doyle, William. *Aristocracy and Its Enemies in the Age of Revolution*. Oxford: Oxford University Press, 2009.

Dubarat, Victor Pierre, and Pierre Haristoy. *Études historiques et religieuses du diocèse de Bayonne, comprenant les anciens diocèses de Bayonne, Lescar, Oloron, etc.* Pau: Vignancour, 1893.

Dubois, Laurent. *A Colony of Citizens: Revolution and Slave Emancipation in the French Caribbean, 1787–1804*. Chapel Hill: University of North Carolina Press, 2004.

du Bois, W. E. B. "Africa and the French Revolution." *Freedomways* 1 (1961): 136–151.

Dufrenoy, Marie-Louise. *L'Orient Romanesque en France 1704–1789*. Montreal: Beauchemin, 1946. 3v.

Dussert, Gilles. *Vadier: Le grand inquisiteur, 1736–1828*. Paris: Impr. nationale, 1989.

Dwyer, Philip. *Napoleon: The Path to Power, 1769–1799*. New Haven, CT: Yale University Press, 2008.

Échinard, Pierre. "Pour une histoire de l'établissement juif à Marseille au XVIIIe siècle." In Jean A. Gili and Ralph Schor (eds), *Hommes, idées, journaux: Mélanges en l'honneur de Pierre Guiral*. Paris: Publications de la Sorbonne, 1988.

Edelstein, Dan. "The Law of 22 Prairial: Introduction." *Telos* 141 (2007): 82–91.

Edelstein, Dan. *The Terror of Natural Right: Republicanism, the Cult of Nature, and the French Revolution*. Chicago: University of Chicago Press, 2009.

Edmonds, W. D. *Jacobinism and the Revolt of Lyon, 1789–1793*. Oxford: Clarendon Press, 1990.

Elmarsafy, Ziad. *The Enlightenment Qur'an: The Politics of Translation and the Construction of Islam*. London: Oneworld Publications, 2014.

Engerand, Fernand. *Ange Pitou, agent royaliste et chanteur des rues, 1767–1846*. Paris: Ernest Leroux, 1899.

Eude, Michel. "Points de vue sur l'affaire Catherine Théot." *Annales historiques de la Révolution française* 41 (1969): 606–629.

Even, Pascal. "Un épisode des relations de la France avec la régence d'Alger, au début de la Révolution: La mission du capitaine Doumergues en 1791." *Revue d'histoire diplomatique* 98 (1984): 50–70.

Faivre d'Arcier, Amaury. *Les oubliés de la liberté: Négociants, consuls et missionnaires français au Levant pendant la Révolution, 1784–1798*. Brussels: Peter Lang, 2007.

Faroqhi, Suraiya. *The Ottoman Empire and the World around It*. London: I.B. Tauris, 2007.

Favone, Maurice. *Dans le sillage de Maximilien Robespierre: Joachim Vilate*. Paris: Marcel Rivière, 1938.

Fernando, Mayanthi L. *The Republic Unsettled: Muslim French and the Contradictions of Secularism*. Durham, NC: Duke University Press, 2014.

Feuerwerker, David. *L'émancipation des Juifs en France, de l'ancien régime à la fin du second empire*. Paris: Albin Michel, 1976.

Findley, Carter Vaughn. *Turkey, Islam, Nationalism, and Modernity: A History, 1789–2007*. New Haven, CT: Yale University Press, 2010.

Finkel, Caroline. *Osman's Dream: The History of the Ottoman Empire*. New York: Basic Books, 2007.

Firges, Pascal. *French Revolutionaries in the Ottoman Empire: Political Culture, Diplomacy, and the Limits of Universal Revolution, 1792–1798*. Oxford: Oxford University Press, 2017.

Fisher, Alan W. *The Russian Annexation of the Crimea, 1772–1783*. Cambridge: Cambridge University Press, 1970.

Fisher, Michael H. *Counterflows to Colonialism: Indian Travellers and Settlers in Britain, 1600–1857*. Delhi: Orient Blackswan, 2006.

Fitzsimmons, Michael P. *The Night the Old Regime Ended: August 4, 1789, and the French Revolution*. University Park: Penn State University Press, 2010.

Fleury, Adrien. *Soldats ambassadeurs sous le Directoire, an IV – an VIII*. Paris: Plon-Nourrit, 1906.

Forrest, Alan, and Matthias Middell (eds). *The Routledge Companion to the French Revolution in World History*. London: Routledge, 2015.

Foucault, Michel. *Discipline and Punish: The Birth of the Prison*. Trans. Alan Sheridan. New York: Vintage, 1977.

Foucault, Michel. *Security, Territory, Population: Lectures at the Collège de France, 1977–78*. Houndmills: Palgrave Macmillan, 2009.

Foucault, Michel. *"Society Must Be Defended": Lectures at the Collège de France, 1975–1976*. Trans. David Macey. New York: Picador, 2003.

Fraser, Elisabeth A. *Mediterranean Encounters: Artists between Europe and the Ottoman Empire, 1774–1839*. University Park: Penn State University Press, 2017.

Frey, Linda and Marsha. *"Proven Patriots": The French Diplomatic Corps, 1789–1799.* St Andrews: St Andrews Studies in French History and Culture, 2011.

Friedland, Paul. *Political Actors: Representative Bodies and Theatricality in the Age of the French Revolution.* Ithaca: Cornell University Press, 2002.

Friedland, Paul. *Seeing Justice Done: The Age of Spectacular Capital Punishment in France.* Oxford: Oxford University Press, 2012.

Fruchtman, Jack. *Thomas Paine and the Religion of Nature.* Baltimore: Johns Hopkins University Press, 1993.

Furet, François. *Interpreting the French Revolution.* Cambridge: Cambridge University Press, 1981.

Gachon, E. *Histoire de la théophilanthropie.* Paris: Cherbuliez, 1870.

Gaffarel, Paul. "Marseille sans nom (Nivôse-Pluviôse An II)." *La Revolution française* 60 (1911): 193–215.

Gainot, Bernard. "Métropole/colonies." In Yves Bénot and Marcel Dorigny (eds), *Rétablissement de l'esclavage dans les colonies françaises: Aux origines de Haïti.* Paris: Maisonneuve et Larose, 2003. 13–28.

Garrett, Clarke. "Popular Piety in the French Revolution: Catherine Théot." *Catholic Historical Review* 60.2 (1974): 215–232.

Garrigus, John D. "Opportunist or Patriot? Julien Raimond (1744–1801) and the Haitian Revolution." *Slavery and Abolition* 28.1 (2007): 1–21.

Garrioch, David. "The Everyday Lives of Parisian Women and the October Days of 1789." *Social History* 24.3 (1999): 231–249.

Garrioch, David. *The Huguenots of Paris and the Coming of Religious Freedom, 1685–1789.* Cambridge: Cambridge University Press, 2014.

Gauchet, Marcel. *La Révolution des droits de l'homme.* Paris: Gallimard, 1989.

Gauthier, Florence. *L'aristocratie de l'épiderme: Le combat de la Société des citoyens de couleur 1789–1791.* Paris: CNRS Éditions, 2007.

Gauthier, Florence. "La Révolution française et le problème colonial: Le cas Robespierre." *Annales historiques de la Révolution française* 288.1 (1992): 169–192.

Gauthier, Florence. *Triomphe et mort de la révolution des droits de l'homme et du citoyen: 1789–1795–1802.* Paris: Syllepse, 2014.

Géraud, Edmond. *Journal d'un étudiant pendant la révolution, 1789–1793.* Paris: C. Lévy, 1890.

Ghachem, Malick. *The Old Regime and the Haitian Revolution.* Cambridge: Cambridge University Press, 2012.

Ghanea-Bassiri, Kambiz. *A History of Islam in America: From the New World to the New World Order.* Cambridge: Cambridge University Press, 2010.

Gibbon, Edward. *The Decline and Fall of the Roman Empire: AD 180–AD 395.* Reprint, New York: Modern Library, 1983. 3v.

Gilroy, Paul. *The Black Atlantic: Modernity and Double Consciousness*. Cambridge, MA: Harvard University Press, 1993.

Gliozzo, Charles. "The Philosophes and Religion: Intellectual Origins of the Dechristianization Movement in the French Revolution." *Church History* 40.3 (1971): 273–283.

Godechot, Jacques. "L'expansion de la declaration des droits de l'homme de 1789 dans le monde." *Annales historiques de la Révolution française* 232 (1978): 201–213.

Godineau, Dominique. *The Women of Paris and Their French Revolution*. Trans. Katherine Streip. Berkeley: University of California Press, 1998.

Goncourt, Edmond de, and Jules de Goncourt. *L'art du dix-huitième siècle: Watteau, Chardin, Boucher, Latour, Greuze, Les Saint-Aubin*. Paris: Rapilly, 1873.

Grammont, H. D. de. *Histoire d'Alger sous la domination turque (1515–1830)*. Paris: E. Leroux, 1887.

Grandsaignes, R. de. "Enquête sur les bulletins de Dropmore." *Annales historiques de la Révolution française* 29.148 (1957): 214–237.

Green, Nile. *Sufism: A Global History*. Chichester, West Sussex: John Wiley & Sons, 2012.

Griffiths, Robert Howell. *Le centre perdu: Malouet et les "monarchiens" dans la Révolution française*. Grenoble: Presses universitaires de Grenoble, 1988.

Groc, Gérard. "Les premiers contacts de l'Empire ottoman avec le message de la Révolution française (1789–1798)." *Cahiers d'Études sur la Méditerranée Orientale et le monde Turco-Iranien* 12 (1991): 20–45.

Groc, Gérard. "Propagande révolutionnaire et presse française à Constantinople à la fin du XVIIIe siècle." In Daniel Panzac (ed), *Histoire économique et sociale de l'Empire ottoman et de la Turquie*. Paris: Peeters, 1995. 795–812.

Grosrichard, Alain. *Structure du serail: La fiction du despotisme asiatique dans l'Occident classique*. Paris: Éd. du Seuil, 1979, translated as *The Sultan's Court: European Fantasies of the East*, trans. Liz Heron. London: Verso, 1998.

Gueniffey, Patrice. *Bonaparte, 1769–1802*. Trans. Steven Rendall. Cambridge, MA: Harvard University Press, 2015.

Gueniffey, Patrice. "Robespierre." In François Furet and Mona Ozouf (eds), *A Critical Dictionary of the French Revolution*. Trans. Arthur Goldhammer. Cambridge, MA: Harvard University Press, 1989. 299–312.

Guilhaumou, Jacques. "Fragments of a Discourse of Denunciation (1789–1794)." In Keith M. Baker (ed), *The French Revolution and the Creation of Modern Political Culture: vol. 4, The Terror*. Oxford: Pergamon Press, 1994. 139–156.

Guilhaumou, Jacques. *Marseille républicaine (1791–1793)*. Paris: Presses de la Fondation Nationale des Sciences Politiques, 1992.

Guillorel, Eva. *La complainte et la plainte: Chansons, justice et culture dans la Bretagne (XVIe au XVIIIe siècles)*. Rennes: Presses universitaires de Rennes, 2010.

Guiomar, Jean-Yves. "Histoire et significations de la 'Grande Nation' (août 1797–automne 1799): Problèmes d'interprétation." In Jacques Bernet, Jean-Pierre Jessenne, and Hervé Leuwers (eds), *Du directoire au consulat:* vol. 1, *Le lien politique local dans la Grande Nation*. Villeneuve d'Ascq: ANRT, Lille 3, 1999. 317–328.

Gunny, Ahmad. *Prophet Muhammad in French and English Literature, 1650 to the Present*. Leicestershire: Kube, 2015.

Hadidi, Djavad. *Voltaire et l'Islam*. Paris: Publications orientalistes de France, 1974.

Hampson, Norman. *Prelude to Terror: The Constituent Assembly and the Failure of Consensus, 1789–1791*. London: Basil Blackwell, 1988.

Hanson, Paul R. *The Jacobin Republic under Fire: The Federalist Revolt in the French Revolution*. University Park: Pennsylvania State University Press, 2010.

Harder, Mette. "A Second Terror: The Purges of French Revolutionary Legislators after Thermidor." *French Historical Studies* 38.1 (2015): 33–60.

Harvey, David. *The French Enlightenment and Its Others: The Mandarin, the Savage, and the Invention of the Human Sciences*. Houndmills: Palgrave Macmillan, 2012.

Hassaine, Ismet Terki. "Oran au XVIIIe siècle: Du désarroi à la clairvoyance politique de l'Espagne." *Insaniyat: Revue algérienne d'anthropologie et de sciences sociales* 23–24 (2004): 197–222.

Herbert, Robert L. *David, Voltaire, Brutus and the French Revolution: An Essay in Art and Politics*. New York: Viking Press, 1972.

Herbette, Maurice. *Une ambassade turque sous le directoire*. Paris: Perrin, 1902.

Hermassi, Elbaki. "The French Revolution and the Arab World." In Joseph Klaits and Michael Haltzel (eds), *The Global Ramifications of the French Revolution*. Cambridge: Cambridge University Press, 1994. 127–139.

Hermon-Belot, Rita. *Aux sources de l'idée laïque: Révolution et pluralité religieuse*. Paris: Odile Jacob, 2015.

Hermon-Belot, Rita. "Religion et révolution: Rencontres interdisciplinaires et interrogations du present." In Jean-Clément Martin (ed), *La Révolution à l'Oeuvre: Perspectives actuelles dans l'histoire de la Révolution française*. Rennes: Presses universitaires de Rennes, 2005. 193–203.

Herr, Richard. *The Eighteenth-Century Revolution in Spain*. Princeton, NJ: Princeton University Press, 1958.

Hertzberg, Arthur. *The French Enlightenment and the Jews*. New York: Columbia University Press, 1968.

Hess, Andrew C. *The Forgotten Frontier: A History of the Sixteenth-Century Ibero-African Frontier*. Chicago: University of Chicago Press, 1978.

Hesse, Carla. *The Other Enlightenment: How French Women Became Modern*. Princeton, NJ: Princeton University Press, 2003.

Hesse, Carla. *Publishing and Cultural Politics in Revolutionary Paris, 1789–1810*. Berkeley: University of California Press, 1991.

Hildenfinger, P. *Documents sur les Juifs à Paris au XVIIIe siècle: Actes d'inhumation et scellés*. Paris: E. Champion, 1913.

Hitzel, Frédéric. "Étienne-Félix Hénin: Un Jacobin à Constantinople." *Anatolia moderna* 1 (1991): 35–46.

Hobsbawm, Eric. *The Age of Revolution, 1789–1848*. London: Weidenfeld & Nicolson, 1962.

Hodgson, Marshall G. S. "The Role of Islam in World History." *International Journal of Middle East Studies* 1.2 (1970): 99–123.

Hodgson, Marshall G. S. *The Venture of Islam:* vol. 3, *The Gunpower Empires and Modern Times*. Chicago: University of Chicago Press, 1975.

Hourani, Albert. *Arabic Thought in the Liberal Age, 1798–1939*. London: Oxford University Press, 1962.

Hufton, Olwen. *Women and the Limits of Citizenship in the French Revolution*. Toronto: University of Toronto Press, 1999.

Hunt, Lynn. *The Family Romance of the French Revolution*. Berkeley: University of California Press, 1992.

Hunt, Lynn. "The French Revolution in Global Context." In David Armitage and Sanjay Subrahmanyam (eds), *The Age of Revolutions in Global Contexts, c. 1760–1840*. Basingstoke: Palgrave Macmillan, 2010. 20–36.

Hunt, Lynn. "Hercules and the Radical Image in the French Revolution." *Representations* 2 (1983): 95–117.

Hunt, Lynn. *Inventing Human Rights: A History*. New York: W. W. Norton, 2008.

Hunt, Lynn. "The Many Bodies of Marie Antoinette: Political Pornography and the Problem of the Feminine in the French Revolution." In Lynn Hunt (ed), *Eroticism and the Body Politic*. Baltimore: Johns Hopkins University Press, 1991. 108–130.

Hunt, Lynn. *Politics, Culture, and Class in the French Revolution.* Berkeley: University of California Press, 1984.

Hunt, Lynn. "The Sacred and the French Revolution." In Jeffrey C. Alexander (ed), *Durkheimian Sociology: Cultural Studies.* Cambridge: Cambridge University Press, 1990. 25–43.

Hunt, Lynn, and Margaret Jacob (eds). *Bernard Picart and the First Global Vision of Religion.* Los Angeles: Getty Research Institute, 2010.

Hunt, Lynn, and Margaret Jacob. *The Book That Changed Europe: Picart and Bernard's Religious Ceremonies of the World.* Cambridge, MA: Belknap Press of Harvard University Press, 2010.

Innes, Joanna, and Mark Philp (eds), *Re-imagining Democracy in the Age of Revolutions: America, France, Britain, Ireland, 1750–1850.* Oxford: Oxford University Press, 2013.

Israel, Jonathan. *Enlightenment Contested: Philosophy, Modernity and the Emancipation of Man, 1670–1752.* Oxford: Oxford University Press, 2006.

Israel, Jonathan. *Revolutionary Ideas: An Intellectual History of the French Revolution from the Rights of Man to Robespierre.* Princeton, NJ: Princeton University Press, 2014.

James, C. L. R. *The Black Jacobins: Toussaint L'Ouverture and the San Domingo Revolution.* 2nd ed. New York: Vintage Books, 1989.

Jameson, Fredric. *Postmodernism; or, The Cultural Logic of Late Capitalism.* Durham, NC: Duke University Press, 1991.

Jamgocyan, Onnik. "La Révolution française vue et vécue de Constantinople (1789–1795)." *Annales historiques de la Révolution française* 282 (1990): 462–469.

Jellinek, Georg. *The Declaration of the Rights of Man and of Citizens: A Contribution to Modern Constitutional History.* New York: Holt, 1901.

Jessenne, Jean-Pierre, et al. (eds). *Robespierre: De la nation artésienne à la république et aux nations.* Lille: Publications de l'Institut de recherches historiques du Septentrion, 1994.

Jones, Colin. "The Overthrow of Maximilien Robespierre and the 'Indifference' of the People." *American Historical Review* 119.3 (2014): 689–713.

Jonquière, Clément de la. *L'expédition d'Égypte, 1798–1801.* Paris: H. Charles-Lavauzelle, 1899–1907. 5v.

Joubin, Rebecca. "Islam and Arabs through the Eyes of the *Encyclopédie:* The 'Other' as a Case of French Cultural Criticism." *International Journal of Middle East Studies* 32.2 (May 2000): 197–217.

Jourdan, Annie. "La journée du 5 septembre 1793: La terreur a-t-elle été à l'ordre du jour?" In Michel Biard and Hervé Leuwers (eds), *Visages de la Terreur: L'exception politique de l'an II*. Paris: Armand Colin, 2014. 45–60.

Kahn, Léon. *Les Juifs de Paris pendant la révolution*. Paris: Paul Ollendorff, 1898.

Kaiser, Thomas. "The Evil Empire? The Debate on Turkish Despotism in Eighteenth-Century French Political Culture." *Journal of Modern History* 72.1 (2000): 6–34.

Kaiser, Thomas E. "From the Austrian Committee to the Foreign Plot: Marie-Antoinette, Austrophobia, and the Terror." *French Historical Studies* 26.4 (2003): 579–617.

Kaiser, Thomas, and Dale Van Kley (eds). *From Deficit to Deluge: The Origins of the French Revolution*. Stanford: Stanford University Press, 2011.

Kaiser, Wolfgang. *Le commerce des captifs*. Rome: École française de Rome, 2008.

Karal, Enver Ziya. *Selim III'ün Hat-tı hümayunları: Niẓam-ı cedit, 1789–1807*. Ankara: Türk tarih kurumu basımevi, 1946.

Karpat, Kemal. *The Politiciẓation of Islam: Reconstructing Identity, State, Faith, and Community in the Late Ottoman State*. Oxford: Oxford University Press, 2001.

Kates, Gary. *The Cercle Social, the Girondins, and the French Revolution*. Princeton, NJ: Princeton University Press, 1985.

Keddie, Nikki R. "The French Revolution and the Middle East." In Joseph Klaits and Michael Haltzel (eds), *Global Ramifications of the French Revolution*. Cambridge: Cambridge University Press, 1994. 140–157.

Khadhar, Hédia (ed). *La Révolution française et le monde arabo-musulman*. Tunis: Alif-Les Éditions de la Méditerranée, 1991.

Khan, Gulfishan. *Indian Muslim Perceptions of the West during the Eighteenth Century*. Karachi: Oxford University Press, 1998.

Khuri-Makdisi, Ilham. *The Eastern Mediterranean and the Making of Global Radicalism, 1860–1914*. Berkeley: University of California Press, 2010.

Kors, Alan. *D'Holbach's Coterie*. Princeton, NJ: Princeton University Press, 2008.

Kwass, Michael. *Contraband: Louis Mandrin and the Making of a Global Underground*. Cambridge, MA: Harvard University Press, 2014.

Labbé, François. *Anacharsis Cloots, le Prussien francophile: Un philosophe au service de la Révolution française et universelle*. Paris: L'Harmattan, 2000.

Laffetay, Vérité J. *Histoire de diocèse de Bayeux, XVIIIe et XIXe siècle*. Bayeux: H. Grobon et O. Payan, 1877.

Lamb, Robert. *Thomas Paine and the Idea of Human Rights*. Cambridge: Cambridge University Press, 2015.

Landes, Joan B. *Women and the Public Sphere in the Age of the French Revolution*. Ithaca: Cornell University Press, 1988.

Langlois, Claude. "Religion, culte ou opinion religieuse: La politique des révolutionnaires." *Revue française de sociologie* 30.3–4 (1989): 471–496.

Larguèche, Dalenda. "The Mahalla: The Origins of Beylical Sovereignty in Ottoman Tunisia during the Early Modern Period." In Julia Clancy-Smith (ed), *North Africa, Islam and the Mediterranean World: From the Almoravids to the Algerian War*. London: Frank Cass, 2001. 163–179.

Latreille, André. *L'Église catholique et la Révolution française*. Paris: Hachette, 1946.

Laurens, Henry. *Aux sources de l'orientalisme: La bibliothèque orientale de Barthélemi d'Herbelot*. Paris: G. P. Maisonneuve et Larose, 1978.

Laurens, Henry. "Bonaparte, l'orient et la 'Grande Nation.' " *Annales historiques de la Révolution française* 273.1 (1988): 289–301.

Laurens, Henry. *L'expédition d'Egypte (1798–1801)*. Paris: A. Colin, 1989.

Laurens, Henry. *Orientales:* vol. 1. *Autour de l'expédition d'Égypte*. Paris: CNRS, 2004.

Laurens, Henry. *Les origines intellectuelles de l'expédition d'Égypte: L'orientalisme islamisant en France (1698–1798)*. Istanbul: Isis, 1987.

Laurens, Henry. "La Révolution française et l'Islam." *Revue du monde musulman et de la Méditerranée* 52.1 (1989): 29–34.

Laurens, Henry, Gilles Veinstein, and John Tolan. *L'Europe et l'Islam: Quinze siècles d'histoire*. Paris: Odile Jacob, 2009.

Lecesne, Edmond. *Arras sous la Révolution*. Arras: Sueur-Charruey, 1883. 3v.

Lefebvre, Georges. *The French Revolution*. Trans. Elizabeth Moss Evanson. New York: Columbia University Press, 1962.

Lehner, Ulrich L. *The Catholic Enlightenment: The Forgotten History of a Global Movement*. Oxford: Oxford University Press, 2016.

Lemarchand, Guy. "Éléments de la crise de l'Empire ottoman sous Sélim III (1789–1807)." *Annales historiques de la Révolution française* 329 (2002): 141–159.

Lenient, Charles. *La comédie en France au XVIIIe siècle*. Paris: Hachette, 1888. 2v.

Leuwers, Hervé. *Robespierre*. Paris: Fayard, 2014.

Lévy-Schneider, Leon. *Le conventionnel Jeanbon Saint-André: Membre du Comité de salut public, organisateur de la marine de la Terreur, 1749–1813*. Paris: F. Alcan, 1901. 2v.

Lewis, Bernard. *The Emergence of Modern Turkey*. London: Oxford University Press, 1961.

Lewis, Bernard. "The Impact of the French Revolution on Turkey: Some Notes on the Transmission of Ideas." *Journal of World History* 1 (1953): 105–125.

Lewis, Bernard. "Watan." *Journal of Contemporary History* 26.3–4 (1991): 523–533.

Ligou, Daniel. "Les protestants français a la veille de la Révolution." In Pierre Léon Féral (ed), *La France pré-révolutionnaire*. Paris: Publisud, 1991. 125–135.

Lilti, Antoine. *The World of the Salons: Sociability and Worldliness in Eighteenth-Century Paris*. New York: Oxford University Press, 2015.

Linebaugh, Peter, and Marcus Rediker. *The Many-Headed Hydra: Sailors, Slaves, Commoners, and the Hidden History of the Revolutionary Atlantic*. London: Verso, 2000.

Linton, Marisa. *Choosing Terror: Virtue, Friendship, and Authenticity in the French Revolution*. Oxford: Oxford University Press, 2015.

Linton, Marisa. "Citizenship and Religious Toleration in France." In Ole Peter Grell and Roy Porter (eds), *Toleration in Enlightenment Europe*. Cambridge: Cambridge University Press, 2000. 157–174.

Linton, Marisa. "Fatal Friendships: The Politics of Jacobin Friendship." *French Historical Studies* 31.1 (2008): 51–76.

Loiselle, Kenneth B. *Brotherly Love: Freemasonry and Male Friendship in Enlightenment France*. Ithaca: Cornell University Press, 2014.

Lokke, Carl Ludwig. "Pourquoi Talleyrand ne fut pas envoyé a Constantinople." *Annales historiques de la Révolution française* 56 (1933): 153–159.

Lovejoy, Paul E. *Jihad in West Africa during the Age of Revolutions*. Athens: Ohio University Press, 2016.

Lucas, Colin. "Revolutionary Violence, the People, and the Terror." In Keith Michael Baker (ed), *The French Revolution and the Creation of Modern Political Culture:* vol. 4, *The Terror*. Oxford: Pergamon Press, 1994. 57–79.

Lydon, Ghislaine. *On Trans-Saharan Trails: Islamic Law, Trade Networks, and Cross-Cultural Exchange in Nineteenth-Century Western Africa*. Cambridge: Cambridge University Press, 2009.

Lyons, Martyn. *France under the Directory*. Cambridge: Cambridge University Press, 1975.

Mack, Mehammed Amadeus. *Sexagon: Muslims, France, and the Sexualization of National Culture*. New York: Fordham University Press, 2017.

Madanī, Ahmad Tawfīq. *Harb al-thalāthimi'at sanah bayna al-Jazā'ir wa-Isbāniyā, 1492–1792*. Algiers: al-Mu'assassah al-Watanaīyah lil-Kitāb, 1984.

Mahdi, Muhsin. *The Thousand and One Nights*. Leiden: Brill, 1995.

Maire, Catherine. *De la cause de Dieu à la cause de la nation: Le jansénisme au XVIIIe siècle*. Paris: Gallimard, 1998.

Mānekshāh Sorābshāh Commissariat. *A History of Gujarat: The Maratha Period, 1758 A.D. to 1818 A.D.* Ahmedabad: Gujarat Vidya Sabha, 1980.

Mansel, Philip. *Constantinople: City of the World's Desire, 1453–1924*. Harmondsworth: Penguin, 1997.

Mansfield, P. "The Management of Terror in Montagnard Lyon: Year II." *European History Quarterly* 20.4 (1990): 465–496.

Mansour, Mohamed el. *Morocco in the Reign of Mawlay Sulayman*. Wisbech, Cambridgeshire: Middle East & North African Studies Press, 1990.

Marcel, Jean Joseph, and Louis Frank. *Histoire de Tunis, précédée d'une description de cette régence*. Paris: Firmin Didot Frères. 1851.

Mardin, Serif. "The Influence of the French Revolution on the Ottoman Empire." *International Social Science Journal* 44.1 (1989): 17–32.

Marsh, Kate. *India in the French Imagination: Peripheral Voices, 1754–1815*. London: Routledge, 2015.

Martin, Andrew. "The Mask of the Prophet: Napoleon, Borges, Verne." *Comparative Literature* 40.4 (1988): 318–334.

Martin, Jean-Clément. *La révolte brisée: Femmes dans la Révolution française et l'empire*. Paris: Armand Colin, 2008.

Martin, Jean-Clément. *Robespierre*. Paris: Perrin, 2016.

Martin, Jean-Clément. *Violence et révolution: Essai sur la naissance d'un mythe national*. Paris: Seuil, 2006.

Martin, Meredith. "Tipu Sultan's Ambassadors at Saint-Cloud: Indomania and Anglophobia in Pre-Revolutionary Paris." *West 86th: A Journal of Decorative Arts, Design History, and Material Culture* 21.1 (2014): 37–68.

Mason, Laura. *Singing the French Revolution: Popular Culture and Politics, 1787–1799*. Ithaca: Cornell University Press, 1996.

Masson, Frédéric. *Le Département des affaires étrangères pendant la révolution, 1787–1804*. Paris: Société d'éditions littéraires et artistiques, 1903.

Matar, Nabil. " 'Abdallah ibn 'Aisha and the French Court, 1699–1701: An Ambassador without Diplomacy." *French History* 29.1 (2015): 62–75.

Matar, Nabil. *Islam in Britain: 1558–1685*. Cambridge: Cambridge University Press, 1998.

Matar, Nabil. *Turks, Moors, and Englishmen in the Age of Discovery*. New York: Columbia University Press, 1999.

Matharan, J. L. "Suspects/soupçon/suspicion: La designation des ennemis (été 1793–an III)." In *Dictionnaire des usages socio-politiques*. Paris: ENS Éditions, 1999. 4:167–185.

Mathiez, Albert. "Étude critique sur les journées des 5 et 6 octobre 1789." *Revue historique* 67 (1898): 241–281; 68 (1899): 258–294; 69 (1900): 41–66.

Mathiez, Albert. "Un faux rapport de Saint-Just." *Annales revolutionnaires* 8 (1916): 599–611.

Mathiez, Albert. *Les origines des cultes révolutionnaires, 1789–1792*. Paris: Société Nouvelle de Librairie et d'Édition, 1904.

Mathiez, Albert. *La Réaction thermidorienne*. Geneva: Slatkine Reprints, 1975.

Mathiez, Albert. *La Révolution et les étrangers: Cosmopolitisme et défense nationale*. Paris: La Renaissance du livre, 1918.

Mathiez, Albert. *Robespierre et la déchristianisation*. Le Puy: Imprimerie Peyriller, Rouchon & Gamon, 1909.

Mathiez, Albert. "Robespierre et le procès de Catherine Théot." *Annales historiques de la Révolution française* 6 (1929): 392–339.

Mathiez, Albert. *La théophilanthropie et le culte décadaire, 1796–1801: Essai sur l'histoire religieuse de la Révolution*. Paris: Félix Alcan, 1904.

Maza, Sarah. *Private Lives and Public Affairs: The Causes Célèbres of Prerevolutionary France*. Berkeley: University of California Press, 1993.

Mazoyer, Louis. "L'application de l'Édit de 1787 dans le Midi de la France." *Bulletin de la Société de l'histoire du protestantisme français* 174 (1925): 149–176.

McCabe, Ina Baghdiantz. *Orientalism in Early Modern France: Eurasian Trade, Exoticism and the Ancien Regime*. Oxford: Berg, 2008.

McLynn, Frank. *Napoleon: A Biography*. London: Jonathan Cape, 1997.

McMahon, Darrin M. *Happiness: A History*. New York: Grove Press, 2006.

McPhee, Peter (ed). *A Companion to the French Revolution*. Oxford: Wiley-Blackwell, 2012.

McPhee, Peter. *Liberty or Death: The French Revolution*. New Haven, CT: Yale University Press, 2016.

McPhee, Peter. *Living the French Revolution, 1789–1799*. Houndmills: Palgrave Macmillan, 2006.

McPhee, Peter. *Robespierre: A Revolutionary Life*. New Haven, CT: Yale University Press, 2012.

Meister, Robert. "Forgiving and Forgetting: Lincoln and the Politics of National Recovery." In Carla Hesse and Robert Post (eds), *Human Rights in Political Transitions: Gettysburg to Bosnia*. New York: Zone Books, 1999. 135–176.

Melzer, Sara E., and Kathryn Norberg. *From the Royal to the Republican Body: Incorporating the Political in Seventeenth- and Eighteenth-Century France.* Berkeley: University of California Press, 1998.

Melzer, Sara E., and Leslie W. Rabine (eds). *Rebel Daughters: Women and the French Revolution.* Oxford: Oxford University Press, 1992.

Merle, Albert. "La pêche sur les côtes orientales d'Afrique." *Bulletin de la Société de géographie commerciale de Bordeaux* 2 (1879): 350–356.

Merrick, Jeffrey. *The Desacralization of the French Monarchy in the Eighteenth Century.* Baton Rouge: Louisiana State University Press, 1990.

Missak, H. "Une princesse ottomane au XVIIIe siècle." *Revue de Paris* 13 (1906): 355–370.

Mornet, Daniel. *Les origines intellectuelles de la Révolution française.* Paris: Armand Colin, 1933.

Mortier, Roland. *Anacharsis Cloots; ou, L'utopie foudroyée.* Paris: Stock, 1995.

Moulin, Annie. *Peasantry and Society in France since 1789.* Cambridge: Cambridge University Press, 1991.

Muller, Claude. "Religion et révolution en Alsace." *Annales historiques de la Révolution française* 337 (2004): 63–83.

Munir Pacha, Salih. "Louis XVI et le Sultan Sélim III." *Revue d'histoire diplomatique* 26 (1912): 516–548.

Nelson, Eric. *The Hebrew Republic: Jewish Sources and the Transformation of European Political Thought.* Cambridge, MA: Harvard University Press, 2010.

Noël, Erick. *Être noir en France au XVIIIe siècle.* Paris: Tallandier, 2006.

Noël, Erick. "Les Indiens en France au XVIIIe siècle." In J. Weber (ed), *Les relations entre la France et l'Inde de 1673 à nos jours.* Paris: Les Indes Savantes, 2002. 203–219.

Olivier, Édouard. *La France avant et pendant la révolution: Les classes, les droits féodaux, les services publics.* Paris: Guillaumin, 1889.

Oualdi, Mohamed. *Esclaves et maîtres: Les Mamelouks des beys de Tunis du XVIIe siècle aux années 1880.* Paris: Publications de la Sorbonne, 2011.

Oualdi, Mohamed. "Mamluks in Ottoman Tunisia: A Category Connecting State and Social Forces." *International Journal of Middle East Studies* 48.3 (2016): 473–490.

Ozouf, Mona. *Festivals and the French Revolution.* Cambridge, MA: Harvard University Press, 1991.

Palmer, Jennifer. *Intimate Bonds: Family and Slavery in the French Atlantic.* Philadelphia: University of Pennsylvania Press, 2016.

Palmer, R. R. *The Age of the Democratic Revolution*. Princeton, NJ: Princeton University Press, 1959. 2v.

Palmer, R. R. *Twelve Who Ruled: The Year of the Terror in the French Revolution*. Princeton, NJ: Princeton University Press, 2005.

Panzac, Daniel. *The Barbary Corsairs: The End of a Legend, 1800–1820*. Trans. Victoria Hobson. Leiden: Brill, 2005.

Panzac, Daniel. *La caravane maritime: Européens et marchands ottomans en Méditerranée (1680–1830)*. Paris: CNRS Éditions, 2004.

Panzac, Daniel. "International and Domestic Maritime Trade in the Ottoman Empire during the 18th Century." *International Journal of Middle East Studies* 24.2 (1992): 189–206.

Panzac, Daniel (ed). "Les Arabes, les Turcs et la Révolution française." Special issue, *Revue du monde musulman et de la Méditerranée* 52–53 (1989).

Parès, A.-Jacques. *Un toulonnais à Alger au XVIIIe siècle: Meifrund (Pierre-Joseph), 1723–1814*. Paris: Rieder, 1931.

Peabody, Sue. *"There Are No Slaves in France": The Political Culture of Race and Slavery in the Ancien Régime*. Oxford: Oxford University Press, 1996.

Péan, Pierre. *Main basse sur Alger: Enquête sur un pillage, Juillet 1830*. Paris: Plon, 2004.

Pellegrin, Nicole. "Les femmes et le don patriotique: Les offrandes d'artistes de septembre 1789." In Marie-France Brive (ed), *Les femmes et la Révolution française*. Toulouse: Presses Universitaires du Mirail, 1990. 11:361–380.

Pingaud, Léonce. *Choiseul-Gouffier: La France en orient sous Louis XVI*. Paris: Alphonse Picard, 1887.

Piquet, Jean-Daniel. *L'émancipation des noirs dans la révolution française: 1789–1795*. Paris: Karthala, 2002.

Plongeron, Bernard. *Conscience religieuse en Révolution: Regards sur l'historiographie religieuse de la Revolution française*. Paris: A. et J. Picard, 1969.

Plongeron, Bernard. *Histoire du christianisme*. Paris: Desclée, 1997.

Poland, Burdette Crawford. *French Protestantism and the French Revolution: Church and State, Thought and Religion, 1685–1815*. Princeton, NJ: Princeton University Press, 1957.

Popkin, Jeremy D. *News and Politics in the Age of Revolution: Jean Luzac's "Gazette de Leyde."* Ithaca: Cornell University Press, 2016.

Popkin, Jeremy D. *Revolutionary News: The Press in France, 1789–1799*. Durham, NC: Duke University Press, 1990.

Popkin, Jeremy D. *You Are All Free: The Haitian Revolution and the Abolition of Slavery*. New York: Cambridge University Press, 2010.

Poujoulat, Baptistin. *Histoire de Constantinople comprenant le bas-empire et l'empire ottoman.* Paris: Amyot, 1853.

Rapport, Michael. " 'Complaints Lost in the Wind': French India and the Crisis of the Absolute Monarchy; A Global Dimension?" In Julian Swann and Joel Felix (eds), *The Crisis of the Absolute Monarchy: From Old Regime to the French Revolution.* Oxford: Oxford University Press, 2013. 223–243.

Rapport, Michael. *Nationality and Citizenship in Revolutionary France: The Treatment of Foreigners, 1789–1799.* London: Clarendon Press, 2000.

Ray, Aniruddha. "Revolutionary France, 1793–94: Experience of an Indian Prince." *History* 4.1 (2001): 30–37.

Rebérioux, Madeleine. "Anacharsis Cloots: The Other Citizen of the World." In Georges Kantin and Douglas A. Cooper (eds), *Thomas Paine, Citizen of the World.* Paris: Créaphis Éditions, 1990. 31–41.

Régent, Frédéric. *Esclavage, métissage, liberté: La Révolution française en Guadeloupe (1789–1802).* Paris: Grasset, 2004.

Régent, Frédéric, Jean-François Niort, and Pierre Serna (eds). *Les colonies, la Révolution française, la loi.* Rennes: Presses universitaires de Rennes, 2014.

Reinhard, Marcel R. *Le grand carnot.* Paris: Hachette, 1952.

Renard, Michel. "Aperçu sur l'histoire de l'Islam à Marseille, 1813–1962: Pratiques religieuses et encadrement des Nords-Africains." *Outre-mers* 90.340–341 (2003): 269–296.

Revel, Jacques (ed). *Jeux d'échelles: La micro-analyse à l'expérience.* Paris: Gallimard, 1996.

Revel, Jacques. "Juifs et citoyens: Les incertitudes de la Révolution française." In Diogo Ramada Curto et al. (eds), *From Florence to the Mediterranean and Beyond: Essays in Honour of Antony Molho.* Florence: Olschki, 2009. 531–544.

Rey, Terry. *The Priest and the Prophetess: Abbé Ouvière, Romaine Rivière, and the Revolutionary Atlantic World.* Oxford: Oxford University Press, 2017

Ribner, Jonathan P. *Broken Tablets: The Cult of the Law in French Art from David to Delacroix.* Berkeley: University of California Press, 1993.

Roche, Daniel. *France in the Enlightenment.* Cambridge, MA: Harvard University Press, 1998.

Rosenfeld, Sophia A. *A Revolution in Language: The Problem of Signs in Late Eighteenth-Century France.* Stanford: Stanford University Press, 2003.

Rosenstock, Morton. "The House of Bacri and Busnach: A Chapter from Algeria's Commercial History." *Jewish Social Studies* 14.4 (1952): 343–364.

Rousseau, Alphonse. *Annales tunisiennes; ou, Aperçu historique sur la régence de Tunis.* Algiers: Bastide, 1864.

Rubiés, Joan-Pau. "Oriental Despotism and European Orientalism: Botero to Montesquieu." *Journal of Early Modern History* 9 (2005): 109–180.

Rudé, George. *The Crowd in the French Revolution*. Oxford: Clarendon Press, 1959.

Ruiz, Alain. "Un regard sur le jacobinisme allemand: Idéologie et activités de certains de ses représentants notoires en France pendant la Révolution." In François Furet and Mona Ozouf (eds), *The Transformation of Political Culture, 1789–1848*. Oxford: Pergamon Press, 1989. 253–272.

Ryad, Umar. "Salafiyya, Ahmadiyya, and European Converts to Islam in the Interwar Period." In Umar Ryad et al. (eds), *Muslims in Interwar Europe: A Transcultural Historical Perspective*. Leiden: Brill, 2016. 47–87.

Saeed, Abdullah. "Muslims under Non-Muslim Rule: Evolution of a Discourse." In Anthony Reid and Michael Gilsenan (eds), *Islamic Legitimacy in a Plural Asia*. London: Routledge, 2007. 14–27.

Sahlins, Peter. "Fictions of a Catholic France: The Naturalization of Foreigners, 1685–1787." *Representations* 47 (1994): 85–110.

Sahlins, Peter. *Unnaturally French: Foreign Citizens in the Old Regime and After*. Ithaca: Cornell University Press, 2004.

Sahlins, Peter, and Jean-François Dubost. *Et si on faisait payer les étrangers? Louis XIV, les immigrés, et quelques autres*. Paris: Éditions Flammarion, 1999.

Said, Edward. *Orientalism*. New York: Random House, 1978.

Samuels, Maurice. *The Right to Difference: French Universalism and the Jews*. Chicago: University of Chicago Press, 2016.

Schama, Simon. *Citizens: A Chronicle of the French Revolution*. New York: Random House, 1989.

Schechter, Ronald. *Obstinate Hebrews: Representations of Jews in France, 1715–1815*. Berkeley: University of California Press, 2003.

Schreier, Lise. "Zamore 'the African' and the Haunting of France's Collective Consciousness." *Nineteenth-Century Contexts* 38.2 (2016): 123–139.

Schwarzfuchs, Simon. *Du Juif à l'israélite: Histoire d'une mutation, 1770–1870*. Paris: Fayard, 1989.

Scott, Hamish. *The Birth of a Great Power System: 1740–1815*. London: Routledge, 2014.

Scott, Joan. "Gender: A Useful Category of Historical Analysis." *American Historical Review* 91.5 (1986): 1053–1075.

Sendesni, Wajda. *Regard de l'historiographie ottomane sur la Révolution française et l'expédition d'Égypte*. Istanbul: Les Éditions Isis, 2003.

Serna, Pierra (ed). *La politique du rire: Satires, caricatures et blasphèmes XVIe–XXIe siècle*. Ceyzérieu: Champ Vallon, 2015.

Sewell, William H., Jr. "Historical Events as Transformations of Structures: Inventing Revolution at the Bastille." *Theory and Society* 25.6 (1996): 841–881.

Shadid, Wasif, and Sjoerd van Koningsfeld. "Loyalty to a Non-Muslim Government: An Analysis of Islamic Normative Discussions and the Views of Some Contemporary Islamicists." In W. A. R. Shadid and P. S. van Koningsveld (eds), *Political Participation and Identities of Muslims in Non-Muslim States*. Kampen: Kok Pharos, 1996. 84–114.

Shapiro, Barry M. *Traumatic Politics: The Deputies and the King in the Early French Revolution*. University Park: Penn State University Press, 2010.

Shepard, Todd. *Sex, France and Arab Men, 1962–1979*. Chicago: University of Chicago Press, 2018.

Shovlin, John. *The Political Economy of Virtue: Luxury, Patriotism, and the Origins of the French Revolution*. Ithaca: Cornell University Press, 2007.

Shuval, Tal. *La ville d'Alger vers la fin du XVIIIe siècle: Population et cadre urbain*. Paris: CNRS Éditions, 2013.

Singer, Brian. "Violence in the French Revolution: Forms of Ingestion/Forms of Expulsion." In Ferenc Fehér (ed), *The French Revolution and the Birth of Modernity*. Berkeley: University of California Press, 1990. 150–173.

Smith, Jay M. *Nobility Reimagined: The Patriotic Nation in Eighteenth-Century France*. Ithaca: Cornell University Press, 2005.

Smyth, Jonathan. *Robespierre and the Festival of the Supreme Being: The Search for a Republican Morality*. Manchester: Manchester University Press, 2016.

Soboul, Albert. *La 1re république, 1792–1804: Naissance et mort*. Paris: Calmann-Lévy, 1968.

Spang, Rebecca L. *Stuff and Money in the Time of the French Revolution*. Cambridge, MA: Harvard University Press, 2015.

Spieler, Miranda. *Empire and Underworld: Captivity in French Guiana*. Cambridge, MA: Harvard University Press, 2012.

Spieler, Miranda. "The Legal Structure of Colonial Rule during the French Revolution." *William and Mary Quarterly* 66.2 (2009): 365–408.

Steinberg, Ronen. "Terror on Trial: Accountability, Transitional Justice, and the Affaire Le Bon in Thermidorian France." *French Historical Studies* 39.3 (2016): 419–444.

Steinberg, Sylvie. *La confusion des sexes: Le travestissement de la Renaissance à la Révolution*. Paris: Fayard, 2001.

Stern, Selma. *Anacharsis Cloots, der Redner des Menschengeschlechts*. Berlin, 1914.

Stone, Bailey. *Reinterpreting the French Revolution: A Global-Historical Perspective*. Cambridge: Cambridge University Press, 2002.

Subrahmanyam, Sanjay. *Courtly Encounters: Translating Courtliness and Violence in Early Modern Eurasia*. Cambridge, MA: Harvard University Press, 2012.

Suratteau, Jean René. "Lyon." In Albert Soboul et al. (eds), *Dictionnaire historique de la Révolution française*. Paris: Presses Universitaires de France, 1989.

Sutcliffe, Adam. *Judaism and Enlightenment*. Cambridge: Cambridge University Press, 2005.

Sutherland, Donald M. G. *The French Revolution and Empire: The Quest for a Civic Order*. Malden, MA: Blackwell, 2008.

Sutherland, Donald M. G. "Justice and Murder: Massacres in the Provinces, Versailles, Meaux and Reims in 1792." *Past and Present* 222.1 (2014): 129–162.

Sutherland, Donald M. G. *Murder in Aubagne: Lynching, Law, and Justice during the French Revolution*. New York: Cambridge University Press, 2009.

Szajkowski, Zosa. *Jews and the French Revolutions of 1789, 1830 and 1848*. New York: KTAV Publishing House, 1970.

Tackett, Timothy. *Becoming a Revolutionary: The Deputies of the French National Assembly and the Emergence of a Revolutionary Culture, 1789–1790*. 1996. Reprint, University Park: Penn State University Press, 2006.

Tackett, Timothy. *The Coming of the Terror in the French Revolution*. Cambridge, MA: Harvard University Press, 2015.

Tackett, Timothy. "Conspiracy Obsession in a Time of Revolution: French Elites and the Origins of the Terror, 1789–1792." *American Historical Review* 105.3 (2000): 691–713.

Tackett, Timothy. *Priest and Parish in Eighteenth-Century France*. Princeton, NJ: Princeton University Press, 1977.

Tackett, Timothy. *Religion, Revolution, and Regional Culture in Eighteenth-Century France: The Ecclesiastical Oath of 1791*. Princeton, NJ: Princeton University Press, 1986.

Tackett, Timothy. "Rumor and Revolution: The Case of the September Massacres." *French History and Civilization* 24 (2011): 54–64.

Taillefer, Michel. "Une loge maçonnique toulousaine à la veille de la Révolution: Les 'Coeurs réunis' (1774–1789)." *Annales du Midi: Revue archéologique, historique et philologique de la France méridionale* 87.122 (1975): 201–223.

Tallett, Frank. "Robespierre and Religion." In Colin Haydon and William Doyle (eds), *Robespierre*. Cambridge: Cambridge University Press, 2006. 92–108

Tavakoli-Targhi, Mohamad. *Refashioning Iran: Orientalism, Occidentalism and Historiography*. Houndmills, Basingstoke: Palgrave, 2001.

Taws, Richard. *The Politics of the Provisional: Art and Ephemera in Revolutionary France*. University Park: Penn State University Press, 2013.

Teissier, Octave. *La chambre de commerce de Marseille: Son origine—sa mission*. Marseille: Barlatier et Barthelet, 1892.

Thomas, Chantal. "Terror in Lyon." *SubStance* 27.2 (1998): 33–42.

Thompson, J. M. *Robespierre: From the Death of Louis XVI to the Death of Robespierre*. New York: H. Fertig, 1968.

Thomson, Ann. *Barbary and Enlightenment: European Attitudes towards the Maghreb in the 18th Century*. Leiden: Brill, 1987.

Thornton, John. *Africa and Africans in the Making of the Atlantic World, 1400–1800*. Cambridge: Cambridge University Press, 1992.

Tissier, André. *Les spectacles à Paris pendant la révolution: Répertoire analytique, chronologique et bibliographique*. Geneva: Librairie Droz, 1992.

Tocqueville, Alexis de. *The Old Regime and the French Revolution*. Trans. Stuart Gilbert. New York: Doubleday, 1955.

Tolam, John V. "European Accounts of Muhammad's Life." In Jonathan E. Brockopp (ed), *The Cambridge Companion to Muhammad*. Cambridge: Cambridge University Press, 2010. 226–250.

Tozzi, Christopher J. *Nationalizing France's Army: Foreign, Black, and Jewish Troops in the French Military, 1715–1831*. Charlottesville: University of Virginia Press, 2016.

Trouillot, Michel-Rolph. *Silencing the Past: Power and the Production of History*. Boston: Beacon Press, 1995.

Uzunçarşılı, İsmail Hakkı. "Selim III'ün Veliaht Iken Fransa Kralı Lüi XVI ile Muhabereleri." *Belleten* 2.5–6 (1938): 191–246.

Valensi, Lucette. *Ces étrangers familiers: Musulmans en Europe, XVIe–XVIIIe siècles*. Paris: Payot, 2012.

Valensi, Lucette. *On the Eve of Colonialism: North Africa before the French Conquest, 1790–1830*. New York: Africana, 1977.

Valin, Claudy. *Lequinio: La loi et le salut publique*. Rennes: Presses Universitaires de Rennes, 2014.

Van Kley, Dale. "The *Ancien Régime*, Catholic Europe, and the Revolution's Religious Schism." In Peter McPhee (ed), *A Companion to the French Revolution*. Oxford: Wiley-Blackwell, 2012, 123–144.

Van Kley, Dale K. *The Religious Origins of the French Revolution: From Calvin to the Civil Constitution, 1560–1791*. New Haven, CT: Yale University Press, 1996.

Velicu, Adrian. *Civic Catechisms and Reason in the French Revolution*. London: Ashgate, 2010.

Vergé-Franceschi, Michel. *Napoléon, une enfance corse*. Paris: Larousse, 2009.

Verjus, Anne. *Le bon mari: Une histoire politique des hommes et des femmes, 1780–1804*. Paris: Fayard, 2010.

Verskin, Alan. *Islamic Law and the Crisis of the Reconquista: The Debate on the Status of Muslim Communities in Christendom*. Leiden: Brill, 2015.

Vivien, A. F. A. *Études administratives*. Paris: Guillaumin, 1845.

Vovelle, Michel. *Piété baroque et déchristianisation en Provence au XVIIIe siècle*. Paris: Pion, 1973.

Vovelle, Michel. *Religion et révolution: La déchristianisation de l'an II*. Paris: Hachette, 1976.

Vovelle, Michel. *1793, la révolution contre l'église: De la raison à l'être suprême*. Brussels: Complexes, 1988.

Wahnich, Sophie. "L'étranger, paradoxe de l'universel: Analyse du discours politique révolutionnaire sur l'étranger de la Fédération à Thermidor." Doctoral thesis, Université de Paris 1, 1994. 3v.

Wahnich, Sophie. "Hospitalité." In *Dictionnaire des usages socio-politiques (1770–1815): Notions pratiques*. Paris: ENS Éditions, 1999. 31–47.

Wahnich, Sophie. *L'impossible citoyen: L'étranger dans le discours de la Révolution française*. Paris: Albin Michel, 1997.

Wahnich, Sophie. *In Defence of the Terror: Liberty or Death in the French Revolution*. Trans. David Fernbach. London: Verso, 2012.

Wahnich, Sophie. "La notion d'étranger, paradoxe de l'universel dans le discours révolutionnaire (1789–1794)." In *Langages de la Révolution (1770–1815): Actes du 4ème Colloque international de lexicologie politique*. Paris: ENS Éditions, 1995. 503–512.

Wahnich, Sophie. "Les représentations de l'universalité dans les Archives Parlementaires: Les fêtes de la fédération mises en scènes; Représenter et annoncer l'universalité du genre humain." *Quaderno* 2 (1989): 159–171.

Walton, Charles. "La liberté de la presse selon les cahiers de doléances de 1789." *Revue d'histoire moderne et contemporaine* 53.1 (2006): 63–87.

Wanquet, Claude. "Un Jacobin esclavagiste, Benoît Gouly." *Annales historiques de la Révolution française* 293–294 (1993): 445–468.

Wanquet, Claude, and Benoît Jullien (eds). *Révolution française et Océan Indien: Prémices, paroxysmes, héritages et déviances*. Paris: L'Harmattan, 1996.

Watbled, Ernest. "Pachas, Pachas-Deys." *Revue africaine* 17 (1873): 438–443.

Weaver, Jace. *The Red Atlantic: American Indigenes and the Making of the Modern World, 1000–1927*. Chapel Hill: University of North Carolina Press, 2014.

Weber, Eugen. *Peasants into Frenchmen: The Modernization of Rural France, 1870–1914*. Stanford: Stanford University Press, 1976.

Weiss, Gillian. *Captives and Corsairs: France and Slavery in the Early Modern Mediterranean*. Stanford: Stanford University Press, 2011.

Whiteman, Jeremy J. *Reform, Revolution and French Global Policy, 1787–1791*. Aldershot: Ashgate, 2003.

Windler, Christian. *La diplomatie comme experience de l'autre: Consuls français au Maghreb (1700–1840)*. Geneva: Droz, 2002.

Woell, Edward J. *Small-Town Martyrs and Murderers: Religious Revolution and Counterrevolution in Western France, 1774–1914*. Milwaukee: Marquette University Press, 2006.

Yacono, Xavier. "Les débuts de la franc-maçonnerie à Alger (1830–1852)." *Revue africaine* 103 (1959): 55–88.

Yacono, Xavier. "La franc-maçonnerie française et les algériens musulmans (1787–1962)." *Anales de Historia Contemporánea* 6 (1987): 103–125.

Yacono, Xavier. *Un siècle de franc-maçonnerie algérienne, 1785–1884*. Paris: Maisonneuve et Larose, 1969.

Yalçinkaya, Mehmet Alaaddin. "Mahmud Raif Efendi as the Chief Secretary of Yusug Agah Efendi, the First Permanent Ottoman-Turkish Ambassador to London (1793–1797)." *OTAM* 5 (1994): 385–434.

Yardeni, Miriam. *Huguenots et juifs*. Paris: Honoré Champion, 2008.

Yaycioglu, Ali. *Partners of the Empire: The Crisis of the Ottoman Order in the Age of Revolutions*. Palo Alto: Stanford University Press, 2016.

Yazdani, Kaveh. *India, Modernity and the Great Divergence: Mysore and Gujarat, 17th to 19th c.* Leiden: Brill, 2017.

Yeşil, Fatih. "Looking at the French Revolution through Ottoman Eyes: Ebubekir Ratib Efendi's Observations." *Bulletin of the School of Oriental and African Studies* 70.2 (2007): 283–304.

Yeşil, Fatih. "The Transformation of the Ottoman Diplomatic Mind: The Emergence of Licensed Espionage." *Wiener Zeitschrift für die Kunde des Morgenlandes* 101 (2011): 467–479.

Yıldız, Aysel. *Crisis and Rebellion in the Ottoman Empire: The Downfall of a Sultan in the Age of Revolution*. London: I.B.Tauris, 2017.

Youssef, Ahmed. *Bonaparte et Mahomet: Le conquérant conquis*. Monaco: Rocher, 2003.

Zelkina, Anna. *In Quest for God and Freedom: The Sufi Response to the Russian Advance in the North Caucasus.* New York: NYU Press, 2000.

Zizek, Joseph. "Revolutionary Gifts: Sacrifice and the Challenge of Community during the French Revolution." *Journal of Modern History* 88.2 (2016): 306–341.

Zorlu, Tuncay. *Innovation and Empire in Turkey: Sultan Selim III and the Modernisation of the Ottoman Navy.* London: I.B. Tauris, 2011.

Zysberg, André. *Les Galériens du roi: Vies et destins de 60,000 forçats sur les galères de France, 1680–1748.* Paris: Seuil, 1987.

Index